LONDON'S METROPOLITAN RAILWAY

Alan A. Jackson

DAVID & CHARLES
Newton Abbot   London   North Pomfret (Vt)

'The Metropolitan is really a trunk line in miniature' – Lord Aberconway, chairman, to the company's annual meeting, 20 February 1930.

British Library Cataloguing in Publication Data

Jackson, Alan A.
  London's metropolitan railway
  1. Metropolitan Railway – History
  I. Title
  385'.09421   HE3020.M/

  ISBN 0-7153-8839-8

Typeset by Typesetters (Birmingham) Ltd
Smethwick, West Midlands
and printed in Great Britain
by Redwood Burn Limited, Trowbridge, Wilts
for David & Charles Publishers plc
Brunel House   Newton Abbot   Devon

Published in the United States of America
by David & Charles Inc
North Pomfret   Vermont 05053   USA

CONTENTS

Contents

LIST OF ILLUSTRATIONS

PLATES

LINE ILLUSTRATIONS IN TEXT

MAPS IN TEXT

PREFACE

Unique in several respects, the Metropolitan was a splendidly independent little railway which, seeing itself as something a cut above the District Railway and the deep level tube lines, fought hard to be regarded as a 'main line' company when during the late 1920s and early 1930s schemes for a coordinated London transport authority were being evolved. As with most other small railway companies, the direction and fate of the Metropolitan was much influenced by personalities; it had its share of lions, along with the occasional cat and mouse. In recent years it has come to be regarded with affection, thanks in part to the late Sir John Betjeman, who knew it well.

Nostalgia for its trains and its 'Metro-land' has been seen to run quite thickly but the Metropolitan has so far lacked the full history it surely merits. A firm basis for this existed in the form of a veritable surfeit of original written records; indeed there is so much that it took me eight years of spare time merely to read, note and collate it before this book was started. This vast store, 876 files of general managers' correspondence, chairmen's correspondence and other papers, 13 fat bound volumes of board minutes, board and committee reports, notices, posters and miscellaneous documents, owes its survival to a bout of bureaucratic indigestion. Some years ago, George Gallop, one of the very few Metropolitan men to become an officer of the London Passenger Transport Board, told me the story. In 1933–4, he and one or two colleagues in the former Metropolitan Railway secretary's office at Baker Street were left with time on their hands whilst the new Board decided what to do with them. They used this break to sort out and arrange the contents of many cupboards full of papers going right back to the 1860s. Some fairly light weeding was done, but the bulk survived, classified and tied neatly into titled folders. This great mass of paper was then consigned to the basements of the LPTB headquarters at 55 Broadway, Westminster, where it was occasionally consulted. After the war, it went to the newly-established British Transport Historical Records Office at Porchester Road, Paddington, where some of its secrets were first revealed to me in the early 1960s when I was preparing *Semi-Detached London*. Finally, thanks to an enlightened decision at 55 Broadway when British Transport

Historical Records was broken up, these papers found a caring home in central London at the Middlesex (later Greater London) Record Office. But for that action, it is doubtful whether this book would ever have been written.

Although this great archive formed a sound foundation for this book, its material often required interpretation and placing in proper context. This necessitated examination of many contemporary and secondary sources, not least among the latter the scholarly and thorough official history of London Transport prepared by T. C. Barker and Michael Robbins.

I was much heartened when Michael Robbins readily agreed to look through my early drafts. He not only made valuable comments and suggestions, but was also kind enough to draw my attention to several original papers and some unpublished works which added to my knowledge and assisted interpretation. I am also indebted to Ken Benest, a leading authority on matters Metropolitan, especially on the engineering side, for making many useful contributions on reading my drafts and genially guiding me back on to the right track from time to time. He has also amplified my somewhat brief references to signalling by contributing an appendix on this subject. Once again I pay tribute to H. V. Borley, doyen of London railway chronology, for casting a critical eye over my typescripts, ever alert for inaccuracies of fact and date. George Dow responded helpfully when I approached him with a tentative assessment of Watkin's motives. For help in a search for representative and hopefully not too familiar illustrations (the latter now very much at a premium) thanks are due to Bob Greenaway of the London Underground Railway Society (who also made his personal collection available to me) and to my friend of many years, John Price.

At the Greater London Record Office, Mr Samways and his colleagues were always patient and courteous, despite the strain of moving the whole of their records first from Dartmouth Street, Westminster (where my research began) to The County Hall and then to Clerkenwell. (How appropriate, incidentally, that the Metropolitan's archives should now be housed almost above its very first section of line).

Others who eased my task at particular points included W. A. Morris, archivist at the Institution of Civil Engineers, James Bettley, at the Royal Institute of British Architects, Betty Masters, Deputy Keeper of the Records, Corporation of London, and Peter Walne, County Archivist, Hertford. All maintain the high standards we have come to expect from the bodies they serve.

Perhaps I should emphasise that this book is intended to be a history of all aspects of the Metropolitan until the disappearance of the original company in 1933; rolling stock and other engineering matters are I hope given due, but not excessive, attention. There remains scope for further work on them by greater experts than myself and for some treatment of the post-1933 period which goes beyond my brief remarks at the end of chapter 15. Whilst the Brill line is given what I trust is adequate mention proportionate to its importance, I have very much had in mind that (incredibly) it has been the subject of no less than four books and booklets in recent years. My mention of the Great Northern & City Railway concentrates largely on its absorption into the Metropolitan; here again there is adequate published work and, I believe, something even more substantial in preparation.

There are few now living able to recall clearly the Metropolitan in its prime, but the Railway's strong ethos, its pioneer engineering and its variety of equipment make it attractive in retrospect and I have tried to convey this. Its promoters, engineers and managers certainly contributed a major asset to London's railway infrastructure which remains to serve the city and its suburbs today and I hope this book will be enjoyed by all who take an interest in the modern history of London and its hinterland.

ALAN A. JACKSON
Dorking

ABBREVIATIONS

A&BR	Aylesbury & Buckingham Railway
BTH	British Thomson-Houston
C&SLR	City & South London Railway
District	Metropolitan District Railway
ELR	East London Railway
GCR	Great Central Railway
GER	Great Eastern Railway
GN&CR	Great Northern & City Railway
GNR	Great Northern Railway
GWR	Great Western Railway
H&CR	Hammersmith & City Railway
H&UR	Harrow & Uxbridge Railway
HMSO	His/Her Majesty's Stationery Office
L&YR	Lancashire & Yorkshire Railway
LBSCR	London, Brighton & South Coast Railway
LCC	London County Council
LCDR	London, Chatham & Dover Railway
LER	London Electric Railway
LGOC	London General Omnibus Company
LMSR	London Midland & Scottish Railway
LNER	London & North Eastern Railway
LNWR	London & North Western Railway
LPTB	London Passenger Transport Board
LRCC	London Road Car Company
LSWR	London & South Western Railway
LTSR	London, Tilbury & Southend Railway
m	millions
MBW	Metropolitan Board of Works
MDET	Metropolitan District Electric Traction Company
MDR	Metropolitan District Railway
MRCE	Metropolitan Railway Country Estates Ltd.
MSLR	Manchester, Sheffield & Lincolnshire Railway
NLR	North London Railway
O&AT	Oxford & Aylesbury Tramroad
SER	South Eastern Railway
SR	Southern Railway
UDC	Urban District Council
WLR	West London Railway

MONEY

All money figures are given at the contemporary price levels and can therefore only be used for comparisons in the period concerned. Conversion to current values can of course be made by using suitable indices. Decimal equivalents of the old British currency are (disregarding inflation):

1d=½p
6d=2½p
1s(shilling)=12d=5p
20s=£1

DISTANCE

As the Metropolitan Railway was constructed to miles and chains these measures are normally used in this book.

1 chain=22 yards=20.12 metres
1 furlong=220 yards=201.17 metres
80 chains=1 mile=1.6093 km

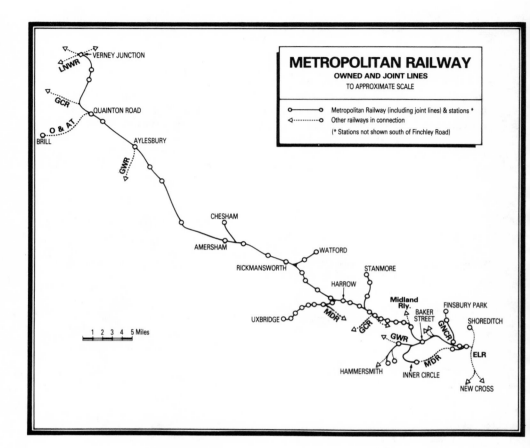

METROPOLITAN RAILWAY
OWNED AND JOINT LINES
TO APPROXIMATE SCALE

○——○ Metropolitan Railway (including joint lines) & stations *
◁·······◁ Other railways in connection
(* Stations not shown south of Finchley Road)

VERNEY JUNCTION
LNWR
GCR
QUAINTON ROAD
O & AT
BRILL
AYLESBURY
GWR
CHESHAM
AMERSHAM
WATFORD
RICKMANSWORTH
STANMORE
HARROW
Midland Rly.
FINSBURY PARK
UXBRIDGE
MDR
BAKER STREET
GCR
SHOREDITCH
GWR
GNCR
ELR
HAMMERSMITH
MDR
INNER CIRCLE
NEW CROSS

1 2 3 4 5 Miles

1

BEGINNINGS

Those who first sought to make underground railways in London in the middle of the 19th century were primarily hoping to relieve heavily congested inner streets of local traffic, but considered that if such railways could attract longer-distance business into the heart of the City this would be financially advantageous. Even before the first lines were built, this dual function was becoming entrenched in the thinking of promoters. Once the railways were made, it was inevitable, given the common track and loading gauge, that both tasks were to be attempted. This process was to continue, with increasing damage to effective operation, as more and more main line suburban and freight traffic was imposed on lines and stations also carrying local movements. In the light of this dichotomy of role, it is interesting that the Metropolitan Railway was to develop into a quasi-main line company on its own account, with an urban underground system as an appendage at its inner end. Initially this was far from anyone's mind.

The timing of the arrival of underground railways in Victorian London was largely determined by one particular aspect of feasibility. This was not so much the problem – which may seem the most obvious one to us today – of operating tunnel lines with steam locomotives, but the sheer cost of property compensation involved in penetrating the narrow, wayward streets of the historic centre when using untested methods of tunnel construction. At this period, unless some agreement could be reached regarding shoring-up walls and reconstruction of affected parts of foundations, a railway company was obliged in law to purchase the whole of any property it wished to pass under, irrespective of how little of it was over the tunnel. Robert Stephenson and others had in the 1830s and 1840s considered carrying conventional railways right into the heart of London in shallow tunnels but the promoters had always been deterred by the compensation factor. Thus the practicability of shallow underground railways in the central area was closely related to the existence over substantial portions of the chosen route of suitably wide roads under which they might be built with the minimum of property acquisition and disturbance, or alternatively, to the likelihood of such roads appearing in the course of urban improvements.

A SCHEME EMERGES

In 1838, eight years after completing the first part of Farringdon Street (between what is now Ludgate Circus and Holborn Viaduct), the City Corporation had obtained powers to extend this new street northwards to Clerkenwell Green, through a close web of mean streets around the partly open sewer that had been the River Fleet. A Clerkenwell Improvement Commission was formed in 1840 to undertake the rebuilding of the whole area. Little progress was made owing to difficulty in financing the work, but when the first schemes for bringing trunk railways into the City came forward in the 1830s it was foreseen by some that economic and social benefits could arise if such railway projects could be combined with urban improvements.

A prime mover, if not the originator, of this concept was Charles Pearson[1], a lawyer with visionary and progressive ideas. His proposal was that the urban poor might be removed to healthy accommodation at the edge of the built-up area if they had access to City workplaces through the provision of cheap travel over new railway facilities which were in themselves part of central area improvements. In 1850, at a time of financial optimism, the Great Northern Railway had arrived in London, stimulating Pearson into making a concrete proposal. Assisted by John Hargrave Stevens Jr[2], an architect and civil engineer, Pearson produced plans in June 1851 for a 100ft wide road, with railway beneath, from Farringdon Street to the GNR at King's Cross. His arched railway tunnel was to be wide enough to accommodate eight parallel tracks, two of 7ft 0¼in gauge for the Great Western Railway and the rest of the standard 4ft 8½in gauge. It was suggested that this tunnel could carry the traffic of the main lines (presumably the GWR, the GNR and possibly the London & North Western) to a large terminal complex each side of Farringdon Street at its southern end. Here there would be some 20 acres of facilities for long distance and local passenger traffic, for freight traffic, and for the servicing of locomotives. At King's Cross it was suggested the new line might rise to join the GNR as far as a terminus at Copenhagen Fields, where connection could be made to what was to become the North London Railway. Undeterred by a virtually complete lack of interest and support from either the main line companies or the City Corporation, Pearson, with Stevens, Acton Smee Ayrton (another lawyer) and others deposited a City Terminus Railway Bill for the 1852–3 session in which they sought approval for a £600,000 scheme for a railway and associated street improvements. To reduce the initial cost they cut back the terminus to the north side of what is now Holborn Viaduct (Holborn Bridge), leaving the facilities on the south side for later.

14

But others were also now on the scene, men with a greater degree of pragmatism and with experience in launching railway enterprises. Their bill for the same session proposed a Bayswater, Paddington & Holborn Bridge Railway to run underground from St James's Church, Paddington (Sussex Gardens) to King's Cross, where it would join the City Terminus to Holborn Bridge. These promoters had noted the commercial success of London's first local railways, the Blackwall, the Greenwich and the East & West India Docks & Birmingham Junction[3], as well as that of the road omnibuses catering for City commuters from the newly-developed high-class residential areas north of Hyde Park. Above all, they had seized on the potential of the New Road[4] as a comparatively inexpensive route for a 2¼ mile underground railway. Behind this £300,000 scheme were William Malins MP, a wealthy businessman of Montagu Square, Marylebone, the principal promoter, who was to become the company's first chairman, William Burchell[5], a Westminster lawyer experienced in railway promotion, and the railway contractors Samuel Morton Peto, John Jay, Thomas Brassey, and Edward Ladd Betts.

At the first meeting of the enterprise on 10 January 1853, attended by Malins, Burchell and five others, J. H. Stevens (none other than Pearson's collaborator) was appointed surveyor. From the minutes of this meeting, it is apparent that John Fowler[6] had already agreed to act as the scheme's engineer. The £22,500 parliamentary deposit was found by Heywood, Kennard & Co in return for appointment as the company's bankers and a directorship.

Writing in *Herapath's Railway Journal* on 3 September 1853, Malins saw the project as but the first in a series of underground lines providing an answer to the growing street congestion in central London. His vision was thus different from that of Pearson, closer to the concept of a system of 'underground omnibuses', a term later used by Sir Edward Watkin to describe the Metropolitan and Metropolitan District Railways.

Some cunning and skill were deployed in easing the Malins Bill through Parliament. By bringing the western terminus back to the east side of Edgware Road and stressing that the transfer of much of the traffic burden from the streets would bring benefits to ratepayers in reduced maintenance, local authority opposition was dissolved. No engineering evidence was brought forward against the scheme and the 2¼ mile line was incorporated as the North Metropolitan Railway by an act of 15 August 1853. John Fowler was formally appointed engineer the following November with J. H. Stevens as architect and assistant engineer.

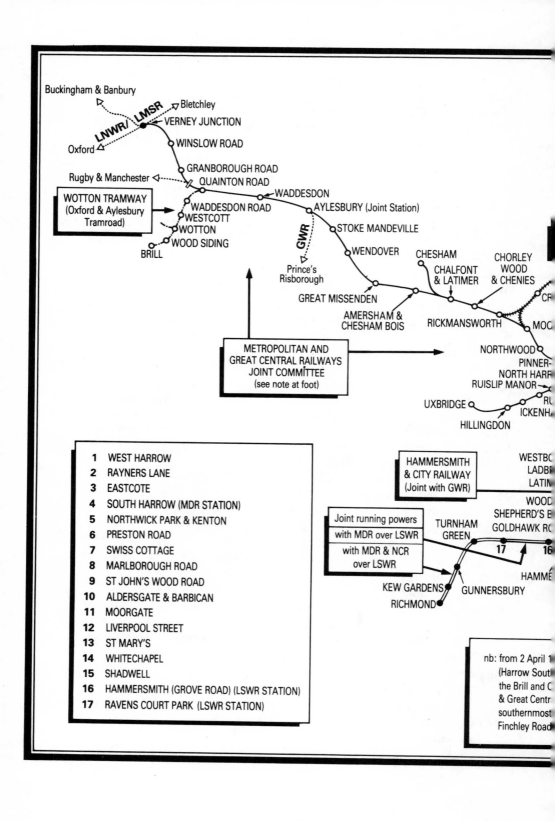

Buckingham & Banbury

Bletchley

LNWR/LMSR

VERNEY JUNCTION

Oxford

WINSLOW ROAD

GRANBOROUGH ROAD

Rugby & Manchester

QUAINTON ROAD

WADDESDON

WOTTON TRAMWAY
(Oxford & Aylesbury
Tramroad)

WADDESDON ROAD

AYLESBURY (Joint Station)

WESTCOTT

WOTTON

STOKE MANDEVILLE

WOOD SIDING

GWR

BRILL

WENDOVER

CHESHAM

CHORLEY
WOOD
& CHENIES

Prince's
Risborough

CHALFONT
& LATIMER

CR

GREAT MISSENDEN

AMERSHAM &
CHESHAM BOIS

RICKMANSWORTH

MOC

METROPOLITAN AND
GREAT CENTRAL RAILWAYS
JOINT COMMITTEE
(see note at foot)

NORTHWOOD

PINNER-
NORTH HARR
RUISLIP MANOR

UXBRIDGE

RU
ICKENH

HILLINGDON

HAMMERSMITH
& CITY RAILWAY
(Joint with GWR)

WESTBC
LADBR
LATIN

Joint running powers

WOOD
SHEPHERD'S B
GOLDHAWK RC

with MDR over LSWR

TURNHAM
GREEN

with MDR & NCR
over LSWR

17

16

KEW GARDENS

GUNNERSBURY

HAMME

RICHMOND

1	WEST HARROW
2	RAYNERS LANE
3	EASTCOTE
4	SOUTH HARROW (MDR STATION)
5	NORTHWICK PARK & KENTON
6	PRESTON ROAD
7	SWISS COTTAGE
8	MARLBOROUGH ROAD
9	ST JOHN'S WOOD ROAD
10	ALDERSGATE & BARBICAN
11	MOORGATE
12	LIVERPOOL STREET
13	ST MARY'S
14	WHITECHAPEL
15	SHADWELL
16	HAMMERSMITH (GROVE ROAD) (LSWR STATION)
17	RAVENS COURT PARK (LSWR STATION)

nb: from 2 April 1
(Harrow South
the Brill and C
& Great Centr
southernmost
Finchley Road

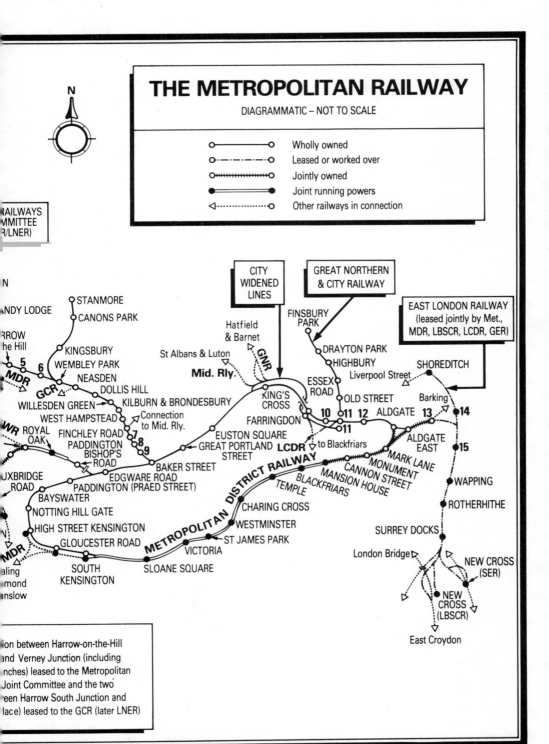

THE METROPOLITAN RAILWAY

DIAGRAMMATIC – NOT TO SCALE

o———o	Wholly owned
o–·–·–·–o	Leased or worked over
o++++++++o	Jointly owned
●———●	Joint running powers
◁·······o	Other railways in connection

RAILWAYS
MMITTEE
R/LNER)

N

CITY
WIDENED
LINES

GREAT NORTHERN
& CITY RAILWAY

EAST LONDON RAILWAY
(leased jointly by Met.,
MDR, LBSCR, LCDR, GER)

NDY LODGE
STANMORE
CANONS PARK

Hatfield
& Barnet

FINSBURY
PARK

RROW
he Hill

KINGSBURY

St Albans & Luton

DRAYTON PARK

SHOREDITCH

5
6
WEMBLEY PARK
NEASDEN

GNR

HIGHBURY

MDR
GCR
DOLLIS HILL
KILBURN & BRONDESBURY

Mid. Rly.

Liverpool Street

WILLESDEN GREEN

KING'S
CROSS

ESSEX
ROAD

OLD STREET

Barking

WEST HAMPSTEAD

Connection
to Mid. Rly.

FARRINGDON

10   11 12

ALDGATE   13   14

WR
ROYAL
OAK
FINCHLEY ROAD
PADDINGTON
BISHOP'S
ROAD

7
8
9

EUSTON SQUARE
GREAT PORTLAND
STREET

LCDR   to Blackfriars

11

ALDGATE
EAST

15

UXBRIDGE
ROAD

BAYSWATER

EDGWARE ROAD
PADDINGTON (PRAED STREET)

BAKER STREET

MONUMENT
MARK LANE
CANNON STREET
MANSION HOUSE

WAPPING

NOTTING HILL GATE

TEMPLE

BLACKFRIARS

ROTHERHITHE

MDR
aling
mond
nslow

HIGH STREET KENSINGTON
GLOUCESTER ROAD

SOUTH
KENSINGTON

CHARING CROSS
WESTMINSTER
ST JAMES PARK
VICTORIA
SLOANE SQUARE

METROPOLITAN DISTRICT RAILWAY

SURREY DOCKS

London Bridge

NEW CROSS
(SER)

NEW
CROSS
(LBSCR)

East Croydon

ion between Harrow-on-the-Hill
and Verney Junction (including
nches) leased to the Metropolitan
Joint Committee and the two
een Harrow South Junction and
lace) leased to the GCR (later LNER)

Pearson's scheme was less fortunate. It met opposition on the grounds that it contravened the recommendation of the Royal Commission on Metropolitan Termini of 1846 that no main line railway should be brought any further into London than the edge of the principal built-up area at that date (ie in this sector, the New Road). More important, as there was still not the slightest glimmer of support from the main line companies, the City authorities suspended progress on the bill. They also appeared to resent the implied threat to their monopoly control over street improvements.

Whilst having little interest in the costly main line terminal Pearson had envisaged, the Malins party clearly needed access to the City for their 'omnibus' traffic. They therefore set about absorbing the City Terminus scheme, adapting it to meet their own requirements. No time was lost in appointing the City Terminus promoter A. S. Ayrton to the North Metropolitan board – he became a director on 31 August 1853 and deputy chairman a few weeks later. Anxious to improve the access to its somewhat remote terminus at Paddington, the GWR had also begun to take an active interest, securing places on the board for two of its directors. The amended proposal which emerged from all this discarded the large terminal at Farringdon Street, starting instead at the General Post Office, St Martin's-le-Grand, following the original City Terminus alignment to King's Cross, then over the North Metropolitan to Edgware Road, whence it ran to a terminus in Praed Street opposite Paddington station, having shortly before thrown off a broad gauge spur to join the GWR. Junctions were also proposed to the GNR at King's Cross, and (standard gauge only) to the LNWR at Euston[7]. Although running powers were refused to the GWR it was agreed the North Metropolitan would haul GWR carriages over the full length of its line in return for the GWR taking £185,000 in North Metropolitan shares, £53,000 of which represented the cost of the junction at South Wharf Street, Paddington. The capital for the 4¼ mile line, which was to be laid in mixed broad and standard gauge, was set at £1m.

This time round, stronger opposition was faced, calling for all Malins' abundant diplomatic skill. Supported by Rowland Hill (who had suggested the line should run into the basement of the General Post Office for ease of mail handling), Malins made much of the benefits to the Post Office as well as to mankind in general. When doubts were cast on the technical feasibility of the scheme, Fowler came to the fore. Backed by the GWR's engineer I. K. Brunel, he explained that in view of the brevity of the journeys there would be no difficulty in operating with fireless steam locomotives, which would not pollute the atmosphere of the tunnels. Although engineers produced by the opposition poured some well-based scorn over this suggestion, Parliament was convinced of the general practicability of the proposals. With another change of name, the scheme was sanctioned as the Metropolitan Railway, the act of 7 August 1854 repealing the earlier one.

THE LOST YEARS

Some years of difficulty for the promoters now followed. With the Government borrowing large sums for the prosecution of its Crimean War against Russia, it was not a propitious time to raise commercial capital, especially for such a novel scheme. Investors must have viewed with some scepticism the confident assertions of the prospectus, reproduced in *Bradshaw's Shareholders' Guide*, that 'the traffic is to be worked without the introduction of fire, or annoyance by steam' and that 'the line is to be divided into short sections and no train allowed to start from any station until the departure of the preceding train from the next station, so that no collision is possible'. Finally, and not least, relationships with the GWR, and all they meant as backing for the scheme, were allowed to deteriorate.

After coming into conflict with the GWR in his separate capacity as chairman of the Railway Reform Group, Malins departed in February 1856. The manner of his going was undignified; he had bought two houses for the Company and had resigned in a pique when his application for repayment was met with a request that the money be applied to the liquidation of unpaid calls due on his Metropolitan shares. Ayrton took his place temporarily until the arrival in July of John Lewis Ricardo MP, chairman of the North Staffordshire Railway. Ricardo's Electric Telegraph Company had made an arrangement in December 1853 to use the Metropolitan's tunnels for its wires, promising financial support in return for monopoly rights. He also offered limited guarantees on the railway's capital. But after an unsuccessful attempt to raise hard cash from the railway's shareholders in the summer and autumn of 1856 he withdrew from the scene in February 1857.

Meanwhile, in 1855–6 the City Corporation had opened its new street from Holborn Hill to Clerkenwell Green (now Farringdon Road), had cleared the land either side and had completed the move of the Smithfield Cattle Market to Copenhagen Fields, north of King's Cross. An opportunity thus arose to acquire open land in the Fleet Valley for the railway at a reasonable price before new developments

19

pushed up values. Pearson, whose enthusiasm for seeing the Metropolitan built was considerable, despite the alterations made to his scheme, suggested to the Company in March 1857 that it should threaten to wind itself up unless some financial backing was forthcoming from the City Corporation. At the shareholders' meeting of 28 August 1857 a winding-up bill was duly authorised for the 1857–8 session unless the directors could in the meantime make arrangements with other parties for the construction of the railway. Realistically enough, given the state of the money market late in 1857 and the failure to get any more financial support from the GWR, or any at all from the GNR, an abandonment bill was prepared. Whilst endeavours to make financial arrangements with the main line companies continued, an unsuccessful shares sales campaign was mounted in the spring of 1858.

LAUNCHED AT LAST

Then, quite suddenly, things began to take a turn for the better. With a revival of optimism in the money market, two energetic imports appeared on the board. William Arthur Wilkinson, member of the Stock Exchange and former chairman of the London & Croydon Railway, became a director in August 1857 and chairman from the following April. He was joined in May 1858 by John Parson, another lawyer experienced in railway matters. A close associate of William Burchell and former partner in his law firm, Parson had a large holding in Metropolitan shares. He had enjoyed a lucrative and somewhat shady career as legal adviser to the Oxford, Worcester & Wolverhampton Railway, virtually controlling its affairs, until 1856. In February 1860 he was made deputy chairman of the Metropolitan, becoming chairman in May 1865, continuing until the crisis of 1872 (chapter 5). As we shall see, his management of Metropolitan affairs was then to be severely criticised.

At the half-yearly meeting on 26 April 1858, following an arrangement with the contractor John Jay, who had held shares from the start, it was resolved to drop the abandonment bill. The GWR directors had dissented, only to be over-ruled. Although doubts about going ahead persisted in some quarters, there was now some iron in the board. From 3 August 1858, Pearson attended board meetings, virtually making the going, assuring the directors of his intention to devote his energies to securing the construction of the line. His pressure on the City Corporation was constant, culminating in a large public meeting on 1 December 1858, chaired by the Lord Mayor. As a contingency measure, another abandonment bill was prepared for the 1858–9 session but in March 1859 the City Corporation at last agreed to subscribe, offering £200,000 so soon as the remainder of the capital was properly subscribed, as well as allowing the Metropolitan favourable terms for land purchase in the Fleet Valley. In return, at Pearson's suggestion, the board discarded the St Martin's-le-Grand terminus in favour of a site at the corner of Victoria Street (now Farringdon Road) and Charles (now Cowcross) Street. To reduce cost, the western end was to be confined to the junction with the GWR, omitting the terminus in Praed Street and a deviation was to be made at Clerkenwell to avoid the expense of purchasing the Coldbath Fields Prison[8]. These changes reduced the capital of the line (now 3 miles 59 chains) to £850,000.

A grateful board passed a vote of thanks to Pearson on 20 April 1859, mentioning 'the high sense they entertain of the zeal and ability with which he has associated the interests of the Public; of the Corporation; and of this Company' – a nice order of precedence. With the backing of the GWR and the City Corporation and a much improved financial climate generally, sufficient capital could now be raised to assure a start on construction. The Company's act of 8 August 1859 duly authorised the altered terminus in the City and the other route changes, with the reduction in capital.

Following an open competition, contracts were awarded in December 1859; the difficult section between the west side of Euston Square and the City went to John Jay, builder of the London end of the GNR, King's Cross station and hotel; and the remainder to Smith & Knight after R. Brotherhood had withdrawn. John Parson was made managing director in charge of construction. In January 1860 Fowler was authorised to order a prototype broad gauge locomotive 'on the new principle' for working the line without atmospheric pollution. Offices were established in the house at 17 Duke Street, Westminster, where Brunel had died in 1859. Formal notice was given on 13 March 1860 for the contractors to start the works and in the following August the City Corporation took up its £200,000 holding[9], appointing three directors to the board. It was all happening, at last.

CONSTRUCTION AND OPENING

In engineering the new railway, Fowler was ably supported by
Thomas Marr Johnson[1], who, as resident engineer, handled most of
the detail and all the supervision. On the City side of King's Cross, the
work of making deep cuttings and a tunnel through rubble and clay,
crossing the Fleet Ditch sewer three times, proved more troublesome,
and hence more costly, than expected. An act of 11 July 1861 authorised an additional £300,000 capital and borrowing to £100,000, but
continued public scepticism about the project made it necessary to
attach a preferential dividend of five per cent before this money could
be raised. Construction problems, together with the delays and
difficulties over motive power and signalling arrangements were to
wreck the original intention of having the line completed in time to
profit from the International Exhibition of 1862.

As construction advanced, the directors became enmeshed in discussions on the future use of their line: with the City Corporation on
arrangements for bringing freight trains into the basement of the new
markets which they proposed to erect at Smithfield just beyond the
Farringdon Street terminus; and with the GNR regarding the method
and terms of working of that company's traffic. The act of 11 July
1861 authorised an eastern curve from the GNR at King's Cross as
well as the rail link to the Smithfield markets. A third potential user,
appearing in November 1859, was the London, Chatham & Dover
Railway, which was planning a terminus at Ludgate Hill with a
connection to the Metropolitan at Farringdon Street. This company
wanted access both to the GNR and Smithfield, but given the very
limited capacity it could offer, the Metropolitan gave the newcomer no
great encouragement. As these negotiations with the City and other
railway companies were not only time-consuming but called for the
experience of a professional railwayman, the board advertised in
March 1862 for an 'operating superintendent' to advise it in its
negotiations with other companies and in the arrangement of trains
and similar matters. Myles Fenton[2] was the chosen applicant,
appointed from 1 July 1862 at £500 a year with a bonus of £100 for
each one per cent increase in dividend paid above five per cent. In
October 1863 he was confirmed as general manager at £800 a year with

a three per cent bonus on any excess of dividend above five per cent.

Byelaws drawn up by Burchells in November 1862 placed a total ban on 'smoking tobacco in trains or elsewhere on the Company's premises on penalty of a £2 fine, the offenders to be forcibly removed should they not desist.' This was no prophetic foresight of the health dangers of the weed, rather a desire not to add unnecessarily to the pollution below. It is doubtful whether any thought was given to the fire risk. Given the several hostages to fortune associated with the design of the railway (tunnels, steam traction, and wooden, gaslit carriages) lighted tobacco was a minor item. Only by luck did the Metropolitan escape a major fire in its first 40 years. A byelaw also forbade riding on engines, tenders, or roofs and steps of trains, whilst a £2 fine was reserved for anyone found on the railway intoxicated, using obscene or abusive language, committing a nuisance, or interfering with the comfort of passengers. Dogs were to have tickets and be put in charge of guards.

But we must return to the construction of the line, which was not continuing without incident. Just west of King's Cross a landslip occurred on 24 May 1861, to be followed a year later, on 18 June 1862, by a much more serious occurrence: the Fleet Ditch was ruptured near Farringdon Street, 21 days after the first trial run over the full length of the line. This brought down newly-built retaining walls, the unsavoury emissions flooding the works up to 10ft deep as far west as King's Cross. Remedial work was commendably prompt, allowing shareholders and other guests to traverse the line from one end to the other on 31 August. Two weeks later, on 14 September 1862, Charles Pearson died, having seen his cherished scheme almost completed. A grateful board recorded 'their high sense of the very valuable services so long and so cheerfully rendered by him to this Company without fee or reward.' With the latter in mind, they later obtained the shareholders' consent to award his widow a £250 annuity. This was no more than just. Over the years, he had spent around £8,000 from his own pocket advocating his railway proposal.

TUNNELS AND STATIONS

Where the route passed along streets, the usual method of construction was to close the road to all but pedestrian traffic a few hundred yards at a time, before sinking shafts from which huge trenches were excavated. These cuttings were then shored up with large timbers which gradually gave place to retaining walls of brick, 11ft high and three courses thick, resting only on 4ft wide footings for much of the route. Fowler's omission of an invert was to prove a weakness which had to be corrected at some points in later years. Between the walls, which were of course wide enough apart to take two 7ft 0¼in gauge tracks, a roof was formed from a six-ring elliptical brick arch of 28ft 6in span, 16ft above rail level at its crown. Where depth was insufficient to allow this form of construction, the side walls were constructed in brick and concrete in 8ft bays of piers and recesses supporting a roof of cast iron girders 1ft 6in to 2ft 6in deep and spaced at 6–8ft intervals.

Between Paddington and King's Cross most of the route was under the roadway apart from a lengthy opening to the sky east of Edgware Road station. At King's Cross, the line emerged into open cutting which continued to Farringdon Street, interrupted by the 728yd tunnel beneath Mount Pleasant, Clerkenwell. At an early stage a connection was established with the GWR at Bishop's Road, Paddington to enable spoil to be removed by rail, this arrangement to be supplemented later by trains through the tunnel connection to King's Cross, whence the material was taken for dumping on the east side of the line between Hornsey and Wood Green. Much of the excavation was made through the dust and debris of past ages, which in some places lay in a stratum up to 24ft deep. Human remains were encountered, payment being made to the London Necropolis Company for their removal and reburial at Brookwood, whither the bones of those who had never known railways travelled by train.

As was customary at this period, station design was left very much to the engineers[3]. It seems probable that the architectural adornment, in a degraded Italianate style, may have been the work of J. H. Stevens, who had been appointed architect for the original scheme, but the papers do not confirm this. In any case it was cheap and nasty. All the street frontages except Edgware Road and Farringdon Street were decorated with imitation stonework and mouldings of cement rendering, earning the sneers of *The Builder*. All except King's Cross, Farringdon Street and Bishop's Road had flat roofs, concealed by low ornamental walls around the edges. At Bishop's Road, Edgware Road, and Portland Road (now Great Portland Street) the single-storey building accommodating the entrance hall and booking office was placed across the line. King's Cross and Edgware Road, in open cuttings, had high elliptically-arched wrought iron and glass overall roofs without ties. Placed between arcaded retaining walls, these protected passengers from the elements as well as helping to disperse the smoke and steam, here liberally ejected after some restraint in the adjacent tunnels. Edgware Road was something of a misnomer as it

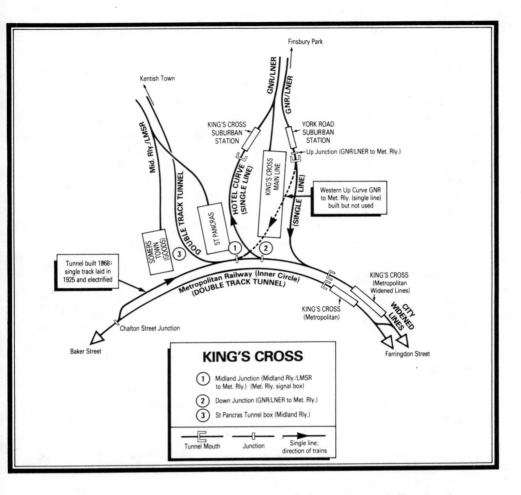

Finsbury Park

GNR/LNER

GNR/LNER

Kentish Town

Mid. Rly./LMSR

KING'S CROSS SUBURBAN STATION

YORK ROAD SUBURBAN STATION

Up Junction (GNR/LNER to Met. Rly.)

HOTEL CURVE (SINGLE LINE)

KING'S CROSS MAIN LINE

DOUBLE TRACK TUNNEL

(SINGLE LINE)

Western Up Curve GNR to Met. Rly. (single line) built but not used

ST PANCRAS

SOMERS TOWN (GOODS)

Tunnel built 1868; single track laid in 1925 and electrified

3

1

2

Metropolitan Railway (Inner Circle) (DOUBLE TRACK TUNNEL)

KING'S CROSS (Metropolitan Widened Lines)

KING'S CROSS (Metropolitan)

CITY WIDENED LINES

Chalton Street Junction

Baker Street

Farringdon Street

KING'S CROSS

1 Midland Junction (Midland Rly./LMSR to Met. Rly.) (Met. Rly. signal box)

2 Down Junction (GNR/LNER to Met. Rly.)

3 St Pancras Tunnel box (Midland Rly.)

Tunnel Mouth   Junction   Single line; direction of trains

was situated in Burne Street, to the east of the main road. Farringdon Street station was a temporary wooden structure with a ridged roof on the site of what was later to become the GNR goods depot as by the time construction was advanced to the point where station building started, it had been decided the line would be extended to Moorgate. Baker Street and Gower Street (now Euston Square) had no structures at street level apart from small pavilions each side of the road containing separate booking offices for the up and down lines. At these two stations the platforms had low curved roofs beneath the street broken by vaulted alcoves at the sides which were at first fully glazed.

In deference to its position on the Crown Estate, Portland Road (Great Portland Street), on its island site, was given additional splendour in the form of a pair of domed projections each side of the entrance. These may have been required by the Commissioners of

Works with whom siting and plans were discussed in March 1860. They lasted only nine years, when, after consultation with the Commissioners, they were removed, probably to avoid heavy maintenance costs. Largest of the seven stations was King's Cross, where the spacious train shed sheltered additional accommodation for the GNR. Across the western end, a gallery and bridge linked stairs from each platform to the booking offices. At street level there was little more than a façade along the side of the train shed, whose arched roof rose above the roadway. Entrances with small cobbled cab yards gave access each side, from Pentonville and Gray's Inn Roads. At Bishop's Road, where the site, together with the final 12 chains of track was GWR property, the station was designed and built by that company in its favoured French Renaissance style with ornamental iron trellis work along the roof.

When completed, the stations were brightly lit by coal gas lamps in very large glass globes suspended over the platforms. During 1864 gas lights were also placed along the tunnel walls. By the end of 1863 much of the wall space behind the platforms had been plastered with advertisements and bookstalls had appeared. Both these items were provided by James Willing, a former director of the London General Omnibus Company, who had agreed to pay the Metropolitan £1,150 annually for five years in return for the privilege. His firm was to retain these contracts until 1907 when a new and more favourable agreement was made with W. H. Smith & Son, under which the Metropolitan received 75 per cent of advertising receipts and 12½ per cent of bookstall takings. Willing also arranged subsequently to place advertisements on the Company's tickets and inside the carriages, as well as employing wall space between stations for his clients' posters, the latter a telling comment on the speed of the trains.

Another early feature of the stations were refreshment rooms, a welcome facility for the many who found that travelling on the Metropolitan was apt to dry the throat. These establishments, dispensing alcoholic and other drinks, sandwiches etc, were operated by Messrs Spiers & Pond, whose initial contracts, negotiated in 1864–5, provided for payment to the Metropolitan of a percentage of the gross takings, with a guaranteed minimum. Their association with the railway lasted even longer than that with Willing – they were still the catering contractors in 1933. After the completion of the inner London lines, they operated some 15 bars and restaurants on the Company's stations[4].

RESCUED BY THE GWR

In constructing the line, Fowler had successfully penetrated hitherto uncharted engineering territory, improvising calculations for which there were no precedents and getting them right. His tunnels and cuttings stood well, and with one or two minor problems here and there, would endure. But this triumph was marred by a conspicuous failure in another aspect of his discipline.

The question of suitable motive power for underground operation had been confidently dismissed as no problem. Parliament and subscribers had been told there would be a system of locomotion eliminating all nuisance of combustion products in the long tunnels. Assurances given by Fowler, backed by the respected I. K. Brunel, that this was feasible had proved convincing. Given the novelty of the proposition, there was doubtless much discussion between Fowler and Robert Stephenson & Co as to the options and solutions, yet there is no suggestion that anyone either saw this matter as a likely cause of delay or fully appreciated the magnitude of the task Fowler (who was not a locomotive specialist) had accepted amidst his many other cares. This says much for the infectious nature of Fowler's self-confidence. No information as to what was happening appears to have been given to the board for most of the 21 month gestation period between the order being given to Fowler to produce a sample engine and delivery of the prototype by Stephensons in October 1861. Their distress on learning that they faced a bill for £4,518, or almost twice the cost of conventional locomotives, for a machine which could not do the job for which it had been designed may be imagined.

This 32-ton, 2-4-0, with its 1,400 gallon water tender, was fitted with a high pressure boiler containing a chamber of fireclay bricks and had a small firebox. It was proposed that it should be stoked up furiously whilst traversing open sections of the line, bringing the firebricks to white heat so that these alone would maintain the required steam pressure in the tunnels whilst the fire was damped down and the blast completely shut off. To further reduce the emissions, steam was condensed through a cold water tank under the boiler.

During October and November 1861 trials were carried out on the GWR main line as well as in the Metropolitan tunnels, but although the desired cleanliness of tunnel operation seems to have been achieved, the locomotive was a total failure as regards running and pulling power[5]. A chastened Fowler appeared before the Metropolitan board early in November 1861 with the news that the GWR would work their trains for them. So successfully did he cover his traces that to this day locomotive historians have not succeeded in unearthing the full facts.

Heads of agreement with the GWR for working the new services were quickly settled and in December Daniel Gooch, the GWR locomotive superintendent and J. Gibson, its carriage man, were before the Metropolitan board with their plans for broad gauge locomotives and carriages. As for the hapless 2-4-0, apart from the payment of Stephensons' account, there is no further mention of it in the Metropolitan papers, although there is some photographic evidence to suggest that it reappeared on the newly-completed line in 1862 before being discarded for good.

For working the Metropolitan services Gooch designed a 38-ton 2-4-0 well tank with 16×24in outside cylinders and 6ft driving wheels for rapid acceleration. Rescuing something from Fowler's concept, he incorporated means of diverting exhaust steam into cold water tanks under the boiler. Although this reduced steam emission during tunnel running, there was nothing to prevent discharge of the unpleasant vapours from burning coke into the atmosphere of an underground railway built without proper provision for ventilation. A certain amount of doubt as to the state of the tunnels was evident in the complete absence of any protection for the crew, it being feared that the spectacle glasses of a weatherboard might become obscured, impeding the forward view. These locomotives started to arrive in June 1862, with 12 available at the end of the year (a total the board regarded as insufficient) when almost everything else was ready for opening the railway. Eventually there were 22, six from Vulcan Foundry (named after winged insects), six from Kitson of Leeds (with foreign monarchic titles); and ten from the GWR Swindon works (named after flowers)[6].

The 45 passenger coaches supplied by the GWR had eight rigid wheels and measured 42 feet over buffers, somewhat longer than most of the stock then operating on British railways. Six were rebuilt from existing vehicles, the remainder constructed new by Brown, Marshalls of Birmingham. First, Second and Third class compartments were lit by uncompressed coal gas carried in collapsible bags on the roofs, the first such installation of its kind for regular use in Britain.

Help with signalling also came from the GWR when problems were experienced with the double-arm mechanical system originally chosen. This took the form of telegraphic communication with disc block instruments for one, two or three wires devised by the GWR telegraph superintendent C. E. P. D. Spagnoletti[7] to work in combination with the manually-operated signals and points installed by Saxby & Farmer (see Appendix 8). Absolute block applied, with all points and signals interlocked, making the Metropolitan the first railway in Britain to be so worked throughout. This much-vaunted claim was not what it might seem. As opened, the line had only seven stations, each with its signal box, plus another box for the double junction at the Farringdon Street end of the Clerkenwell tunnel. With perhaps 30 levers each at most, the largest boxes, at Bishop's Road and Farringdon Street, were the only ones requiring interlocking; the intermediate stations, with not so much as an emergency crossover, did not require such refinements. Installation was thus a very simple task compared with fitting up many thousands of levers on a large system, such as the GWR. Following a series of minor accidents, the Board of Trade inspectors nagged for improvements in the signalling arrangements until an electric locking system designed by Spagnoletti was installed throughout the railway from 1885 onwards[8].

Iron running rails were laid, 62lb per yard, Vignoles section, with a ¹⁄₁₆in steel surface imposed by the Dodd case-hardening process. They were bolted to longitudinal sleepers with fishplates riveted in place. Once the traffic had started, the Dodd steeling rapidly broke down on curves, leaving the iron to fracture and split. By 1866 the whole length had been relaid on new transverse sleepers with Bessemer steel Vignole section rails at 86lb per yd, 11½in high, a 6⅜in flange offering maximum bearing surface. Conventional chaired bullhead track was to be adopted from 1873 onwards.

Before the line was opened, Fowler made two proposals, both of which were taken up. He urged an extension of 58 chains to Moorgate, for which the contractor John Kelk was offering loan of the parliamentary deposit. Sanctioned by the company's act of 6 August 1861, the extension was to terminate at Moorgate Street immediately north of Fore Street at a point referred to as Finsbury Circus. Capital for this was obtained by the issue of £500,000 five per cent shares early in 1863. With the first part of the line successfully operating there was a satisfactory response. No time was lost. Fowler was again the engineer and (naturally) Kelk undertook the contract, securing ten per cent profit on cost. Parson also did well, receiving a £3,000 supplement to his director's fees for 'supervision'. Widening works for the permanent layout at Farringdon Street, which were to serve in the interim to accommodate GNR trains, were begun by Kelk in the middle of 1863. From its opening, the station here, with its temporary buildings on the west side, had one extra track and a 'Windsor' platform to accommodate the GWR through suburban services. There was also a small carriage shed, a locomotive shed and a turntable. These facilities were partly subsidised by the GWR. After receiving his contract in November 1863 Kelk started work on the extension itself the following March.

Fowler's second suggestion, made in March 1862, was that arrangements should be made to feed the railway from bus services. In February 1863 Fenton concluded an agreement with the London General Omnibus Company but this proved short-lived as much of the LGOC service was withdrawn after a few months and other operators had to be persuaded to fill the gaps. At the beginning of 1866 Fenton obtained the directors' approval to organise the railway's own bus service between Portland Road station (now Great Portland Street) and Regent (now Oxford) Circus. This became the first of a series of feeder bus services worked by or on behalf of the Metropolitan, details of which are given in Appendix 5. It started on 6 August 1866, on which day a booking office offering tickets to Metropolitan Railway stations was opened at Regent Circus.

A SUCCESSFUL DÉBUT

Whilst hurried arrangements were being made regarding rolling stock, the engineering and station works were virtually complete. Although the rolling stock problem was crucial to the fixing of the opening date there were also other difficulties, not least the signalling system, already mentioned. The Board of Trade inspector was also not entirely happy about the carriages, having discovered that if the doors were opened in the tunnels they fouled the walls. Eventually, after working through the 24 hours, the Board of Trade declared itself generally content on 31 December 1862. Col Yolland carried out a final inspection on 3 January, which was followed by a daily rehearsal of the full public service from 4 to 8 January to train the staff. An opening ceremony was held on 9 January for which guests were carried in special trains to a 700-seat £540 banquet at Farringdon Street station.

Public service began on Saturday 10 January 1863, attracting almost 40,000 anxious to sample the novelty of an 18-minute, all-stations underground rail journey from Paddington to the City. Bennett relates[9] that such was the interest in the first few days that the GWR was obliged to bring in non-condensing locomotives and extra carriages to soak up the crowds, whilst the booking offices at some stations were several times temporarily closed to clear the packed platforms. This heavy usage and the use of unsuitable locomotives caused such an accumulation of foul air in the tunnels that several railwaymen at Gower Street (Euston Square) were overcome, one so seriously that he was admitted to University College Hospital.

Much scepticism had been voiced before the opening as to the public reaction. On 30 November 1861 *The Times* suggested that people were unlikely to give up a cheap open air ride by horse bus to the City in order 'to be driven amid palpable darkness through the foul subsoil of London'. Yet in its first six months the line attracted an average of 27,881 passengers daily including Sundays (not counting season ticket journeys). The total absence of any really serious or alarming incident[10] built up public confidence in the new facility. Indeed throughout the entire 42 years of manual signalling and steam locomotive operation no passenger was killed in a train accident or fire, although there were many minor collisions and derailments. Nor did the underground atmosphere appear to deter patronage, at least initially. Once the tumult of the first few days had passed, the new tunnels remained fairly fresh as the train service was still relatively infrequent and the engine crews conscientiously discharged the warmed condensing water, replacing it with cold at Farringdon Street at the end of each trip. This latter practice lapsed as train services intensified and the line was extended. It was not long, as we shall see, before 'ventilation' became a matter of concern, remaining an intractable problem until cured by electrification.

In January 1863 the board had asked the GWR to aim for a minimum service frequency of ten minutes between 8am and 8pm, in the meantime operating trains to the maximum length feasible without emitting 'steam and smoke'. It was suggested that any excess of passengers should be taken up by adding further trains. But the best that could be achieved from April 1863, following the arrival of more locomotives and carriages, was a basic frequency of 15 minutes, ten minutes at peak hours and 20 minutes from 6 to 8am and between 8pm and midnight. From 1 February to 31 March the GWR had injected seven additional trains at peak hours, these stopping only at Edgware Road (later also Baker Street) and reducing the end to end time by four to five minutes. Sunday trains were worked from the start, apart from the then customary 'Church Interval' which was supposed to allow the staff to attend morning services and continued until Sunday 3 October 1909. Fares were 6d, 4d or 3d according to class for the full journey, or 9d, 6d and 5d return.

It was the train service and terms of working that were soon causing friction with the GWR, culminating in the first of what was to be a long series of tiresome disputes. As we have seen, the Metropolitan sought a more intensive service for their local traffic, but the conservative GWR officers had resisted this, fearing financial loss and accidents. Indeed they had sought to alter the arrangements previously accepted. Their attitude caused the Metropolitan to look for alternatives, a move duly reported back by the GWR representatives on the Metropolitan board, generating more bad blood because the GWR regarded any increased usage of the Metropolitan as a threat and impediment to the City access it had obtained for its own services. Further ill feeling was produced when the Metropolitan began to question the legality of the GWR purchasing shares in its Moorgate extension.

From March 1863 the GWR withheld payments due under the working agreement, mention of this appearing as the first reference to the dispute in the Metropolitan minutes. When the junctions at King's Cross[11] were ready for use in July, the board decided to complete these by installing points, despite GWR objections. This brought the matter to a head and on 18 July the GWR issued an ultimatum putting the Metropolitan on notice that all GWR trains would be withdrawn after the last service on 30 September (a date subsequently brought forward to 10 August), unless the Metropolitan accepted new terms of working. Subsequently it became clear that the GWR would not be prepared to sell the locomotives and carriages to the Metropolitan after it had withdrawn.

Reinforced by the attitude of Parson, who had previous battle experience with the GWR, the Metropolitan board bravely stood its ground. It resolved to work the line itself, in the meantime seeking to avoid any break in service by obtaining help from the most obvious source – the GNR. That company, anxious to secure its access to the City, proved sympathetic, showing itself ready to lend the condensing locomotives it had started to build for its own services to Farringdon Street, whilst hastily lashing-up others to condense their exhaust steam after a fashion[12]. Carriages were secured from the GNR and the LNWR. Although these arrangements ensured continuity of operation from the morning of Tuesday 11 August 1863, it did not prove possible to operate more than a 15 minute service all day. There were also some derailments owing to misalignment of the hitherto unused 'middle rail' affording standard gauge. This deterioration in service caused traffic to drop by almost 200,000 in the second half of 1863 compared with the first, although the latter figure was of course

Plate 1 (left) Charles Pearson (1793–1862), father of the Metropolitan (source unknown)
Plate 2 (right) Sir John Fowler (1817–98), engineer to the Metropolitan from 1853 to 1873 (source unknown)

Plate 3 A GWR-operated broad gauge train leaving the Metropolitan at Praed Street junction for Bishop's Road, Paddington in 1863 (from a chromolithograph by Samuel J. Hodson)

Plate 4 Baker Street station as opened in 1863, looking to Edgware Road. Note the characteristic globe gaslights used for many years, the signal box at the west end of the Up platform and the Down starting signal in the arch of the tunnel headwall (*from a chromolithograph by Samuel J. Hodson*)

Plate 5 The first type of Metropolitan locomotive, as delivered; No 18, *Hercules*, at Hammersmith in the 1860s. Original Metropolitan carriages are also in evidence. Note the gas boxes on the roofs of the carriages and the white paint above the waist rail over both first and second class compartments (*F. Moore*)

distorted by the 'novelty' riding of the opening weeks.

To keep business secret from the GWR, a 'special committee' of the board was formed at the end of July 1863, thus avoiding full meetings with the GWR appointees present. Only two full board meetings were held between then and 13 January 1864, when it was resolved that as the GWR 'no longer subscribes to the extent of £175,000' (the shares had been sold) its right to appoint directors under the 1854 act had lapsed. New directors were then admitted to fill the vacancies.

By October 1863 fences had been mended to the extent of concluding a provisional agreement with the GWR which covered the continued use of Bishop's Road station, the absorption of GWR staff used on the Metropolitan, settlement of outstanding accounts, continued use of GWR tickets, and the operation of GWR trains from Windsor and other suburban stations to Farringdon Street from 1 October 1863. These through trains were suspended after 31 December 1863, resuming on 2 May after the new concord had been formally sealed. With one small interruption, mentioned later, GWR suburban services then worked continuously over the Metropolitan to the City until 16 September 1939, though not without occasional disputes[13].

The GNR was also now in on the act, its trains joining those of the GWR on 1 October 1863, journeying to and from Farringdon Street through the steeply-graded single line tunnels of the East and Hotel Curves at King's Cross (1 in 46 downhill, 1 in 48 ascending). The West Curve, towards Baker Street, never used for regular traffic, lost its track in 1865.

INDEPENDENT OPERATION

Early in 1863 Beyer Peacock was asked to provide 18 standard gauge tank locomotives at £2,600 each. Passenger carriages were ordered from the Ashbury Railway Carriage & Iron Co and 34 were delivered by 1 October 1863 at a total cost of £26,300[14]. Six more Third Class coaches were sought in January 1864 from the Oldbury Co.

Although they were to suffer troublesome axle and connecting rod failures, the powerful 42¼ ton condensing 4-4-0T were to prove a most successful tool for the job, so much so that the basic design was perpetuated until steam traction ceased 41 years later. Fowler laid down the specification, but it was Robert Harvey Burnett and others at Beyer Peacock who developed the detailed design from two types of 4-4-0T supplied to the Tudela & Bilbao Railway by Fairbairns and Beyer Peacock in 1861 and 1862. The result was a sales success as the basic design was adopted by several other railways, not least the Metropolitan's neighbour, the Metropolitan District Railway.

These locomotives had 17in×24in outside cylinders, 5ft 9in diameter coupled driving wheels and a coupled wheelbase of 8ft 10in. A crude weatherboard gave the enginemen a modicum of protection. Livery was olive green, changed to dark chocolate about 1885, enlivened by burnished copper chimney tops decorated with brass numerals at the front and a large steam dome with brass cover (later painted over). Prominent pipes each side carried the cylinder exhaust to the tops of the side water tanks. Together with 26 more, delivered in batches between June 1866 and February 1870, these engines were later to be classified 'A'. For a few years, the first 18 carried names of classical origin such as *Jupiter*, *Daphne* and *Hercules*. Another 22, slightly heavier, with an 8ft 1in wheelbase and minor alterations, were delivered in 1879–85, becoming class 'B'[15].

With frames shorter than the body and 39ft 6in long, the standard gauge carriages could be coupled fairly closely. They each had eight wheels, not on trucks but with some play available in the axle boxes to permit negotiation of the tighter curves. Internal dimensions were generous, so that it was possible for a six footer in a top hat to stand up in the centre of a compartment without embarrassment. Livery was varnished teak, painted white above the waist rail, the latter a feature subsequently restricted to First Class accommodation. First Class passengers enjoyed four-aside seats in well-padded blue cloth above a carpeted floor. Second Class was distinguished by a strip of American Cloth on the seats – the extra fare merely secured segregation from *hoi polloi*. Thirds had bare varnished planks. As with the GWR vehicles they replaced, which they resembled in some respects, they were lit by uncompressed coal gas carried in india-rubber bags within wooden boxes on the roof. These bags were weighted at the top, the weights operating an indicator at the side of the box as the level dropped. Inside door handles were not fitted to Metropolitan stock until the mid-1880s, although the process of conversion had started in 1877 after they had been adopted on the MDR[16].

At the end of July 1863 Fowler was instructed to arrange with Kelk for the erection of locomotive and carriage shops at Chapel Street, east of Edgware Road station, for which some additional land was acquired. Kelk was paid £1,500 for the work, which was completed in early 1865.

Before the last of its stock was returned, the GNR provided the Metropolitan with its second accident. Locomotive no 138 had begun to move out the 9.05 am from Bishop's Road to Farringdon Street on 9

May 1864 when its corroded boiler exploded, projecting the steam dome into a flight which ended 200yd away. Other fragments fell through the roof of the main line station. Although the enginemen miraculously escaped with light injuries, a passenger in an adjoining train was seriously hurt, as were a Metropolitan office boy and a brakeman. When the GNR refused to pay the Metropolitan's costs, the board tactfully decided to abandon the claim 'in consideration of the services rendered by the Great Northern Company at a period of great pressure', not a happy choice of words in the circumstances. At the same meeting (14 December 1864) it was resolved that best thanks be conveyed to the GNR locomotive superintendent, Archibald Sturrock 'for his great energy and attention in providing engine power for working the traffic of this line at a period of great emergency'. With the message went £100 for distribution amongst the staff engaged on these engines as Sturrock thought fit. Perhaps they would have got more if the locomotives had been in better order and the Metropolitan had not been obliged to find accident compensation for the injured.

The Beyer Peacock locomotives were delivered between 20 June and 30 August 1864, the carriages around the end of September 1863, the last of the GNR stock returning home in October 1864. From the early autumn of 1864 the Metropolitan was at last able to offer its desired ten minute service with strengthening at morning and evening peak hours.

Burnett was enticed from Beyer Peacock by an offer of £300 a year to become from 1 May 1864 the Metropolitan's 'resident engineer and locomotive superintendent', a somewhat formidable post embracing responsibility for the repair and maintenance of locomotives and carriages, permanent way and structures, as well as supervision of the staff involved. The Metropolitan was of course now employing a full staff on trains and stations and the first uniforms were ordered in May 1864.

Proposals to exploit the railway for freight as well as passengers came forward at an early stage. A 'warehouse and exhibition scheme' conceived by William Burchell Jr in 1864 emerged as the Metropolitan Railway Warehousing Company, registered in August 1865 with John Parson and Burchell among the promoters and a generally intimate connection with the railway company. This new enterprise proposed to build and operate a large goods warehouse on land cleared by the City Corporation west of the line and immediately north of Farringdon Street station, served by a double track branch linked to sidings in its basement. Negotiations were begun with the City Corporation and a manager was appointed, but no work was started as the scheme failed to attract investors, causing the company to be dissolved in 1872. Many years were to pass before the Metropolitan possessed its own City goods depot, although as we shall see, it was meanwhile to host the depots of other railways and offer the GWR a lease of its freehold sidings under the City's Central Markets at Smithfield.

With service frequency now matched to traffic demand and rolling stock efficiently meeting the operating requirements, passenger loadings resumed steady growth, almost reaching 7.5m in the first half of 1865. Ordinary stockholders received five per cent in 1863, 5½ in the first half of 1864, and subsequently seven per cent, although the latter rate, to quote the 1866 and 1867 editions of *Bradshaw's Shareholders' Manual*, was 'aided by subsidies from the contractors'. Wilkinson and Parson consistently held out the promise of a rising flow of good dividends, forcing up the price of the stock (it reached 145½ in 1865) and relying on future prosperity. It was, as we shall see, a house of cards, a precarious game in which the level of dividend was kept up at all costs, by finding the money from somewhere, with no regard to sound accounting or financial rectitude.

HAMMERSMITH & CITY

Contributing to the growth in traffic receipts was a new line feeding in business from the west. This was the Hammersmith & City Railway, launched in 1860 with support, but no financial backing, from both the GWR and the Metropolitan[17]. Its act of 22 July 1861 had authorised a double track branch of mixed broad and standard gauge from the GWR at Green Lane Junction, about a mile west of Paddington, to Hammersmith. From what is now Westbourne Park, the 2 mile 35 chain line ran first south west then south just beyond what was then the western edge of built-up London, much of it on a 20ft high brick viaduct to reduce land costs, terminating in line with what is now Glenthorne Road, just north of the Broadway. Simply-built intermediate stations were provided at Notting Hill (now Ladbroke Grove) and at Shepherd's Bush, south of the present station. As extension to Richmond was proposed, the terminal buildings were also unpretentious.

One of the main promoters, John Fowler, had no difficulty in securing the job of engineer. It was confidently expected that the tide of London's house building would soon flow up to and across the new line and with Hammersmith (population almost 25,000) receiving its first proper railway communication to the City, a healthy commuter traffic was correctly foreseen. As the GWR wanted direct access from Paddington to the West London Railway, thence to the railways south of the river, powers were included in the act for the requisite 39 chain curve, from Latimer Road Junction to Uxbridge Road Junction. A contract was placed with F. Rummens, who accepted £150,000 of H&CR shares in payment.

At Fowler's suggestion, the Metropolitan chairman (Wilkinson) and deputy chairman (Parson) joined the H&CR board in March 1862. Parson, made chairman, was soon up to some of his old tricks, using his knowledge of H&CR affairs to buy up land through which the railway was to pass. He and a fellow conspirator named Blake then proceeded to demand a highly inflated price for the plots the company wanted. This episode earned him dismissal from the H&CR board in 1864 but despite the scandal, he somehow managed to retain his position on the Metropolitan.

When the H&CR was opened on Monday 13 June 1864, a half-hourly GWR broad gauge service ran between Hammersmith and Farringdon Street. This was supplemented from 1 July by a GWR half-hourly service from Kensington (Addison Road) (now Kensington (Olympia)) which was joined up with and split off from the Hammersmith trains at Notting Hill[18].

Towards the end of 1864, the Metropolitan and GWR reached a new accord covering station arrangements at Smithfield, Farringdon and Moorgate; the terms of use of the Metropolitan by the GWR; and the leasing and working of the H&CR by both companies. As a result, from 1 April 1865, Metropolitan standard gauge trains were worked to and from Hammersmith, the GWR broad gauge workings continuing between Kensington and the City. In May 1865 the Metropolitan ordered 20 carriages from the Oldbury Company for its H&CR services.

Powers to lease the H&CR in conjunction with the GWR were obtained in the Metropolitan's act of 19 June 1865 and from 1 June 1866 the line was operated by a joint management committee. The leasing did not last long. A GWR (Various Powers) Act of 15 July 1867 sanctioned the joint vesting of the undertaking in the two companies from 1 July that year.

From what has been said, it will be obvious that the GWR and Metropolitan were for the time being working together in harmony. An important agreement was concluded on 11 August 1868. This came into operation from the previous 1 July, covering a whole clutch of topics: the removal of the broad gauge on the H&CR and the Metropolitan; the right of the GWR to run up to 15 standard gauge trains a day over the Metropolitan from 1 March 1869 (not more than ten to be freight trains); the nature of the accommodation to be provided for the GWR at Moorgate; through bookings; and the stopping of GWR trains at all Metropolitan stations to pick up the latter's local passengers without charge to that company. Following this agreement, GWR broad gauge trains, which had been extended to Aldersgate Street (now Barbican) on 1 March 1866 and to Moorgate Street on 1 July that year, were withdrawn after close of traffic on Sunday 14 March 1869. Broad gauge rail was then removed from the H&CR and the Metropolitan.

It had been agreed in 1864 that as the additional trains from the H&CR would cause the GWR operating problems between Westbourne Park and Paddington, the latter would provide two additional tracks on the north side for the H&CR services. These came into use on 30 October 1871. Following very strong objections from the Board of Trade, the flat crossing over the GWR main lines at Westbourne Park was replaced by a fly-under from 12 May 1878.

More station accommodation was soon required on the H&CR. Westbourne Park, a wooden structure at Green Lane Junction, was opened on 1 February 1866, at first serving only the H&CR, but rebuilt for both H&CR and GWR from 1 November 1871. Latimer Road, 34 chains from Notting Hill, at the junction with the spur to the West London line, followed on 16 December 1868. At the other end of the spur, near Norland Road, beyond the junction with the West London, a station called Uxbridge Road, to LNWR design, was opened by the West London Railway on 1 November 1869[19]. Finally, with the additional tracks on the north side of the GWR, Royal Oak came into use on the same day (30 October 1871). When the London & South Western Railway constructed their Kensington to Richmond line, the works disturbed the H&CR terminus at Hammersmith, causing it to be rebuilt a few hundred feet further south, with standard gauge tracks only. With an entrance from The Grove, this new station came into service from 1 December 1868.

In pursuing the H&CR, we have somewhat run ahead and must return in the next chapters to the important extensions and improvements to the Metropolitan completed in the second half of the 1860s.

3

THE ST JOHN'S WOOD SIDELINE

A small undertaking promoted independently in 1863 and designed by John Fowler to act as a second feeder to the Metropolitan was to play a crucial role in the latter's development. This, the Metropolitan & Saint John's Wood Railway, was authorised by an act of 29 July 1864 to build a 2¼ mile line, mostly underground, from the Metropolitan at Baker Street to a point adjacent to the LNWR (Hampstead Junction Railway) at its Finchley Road station. Capital was £300,000, with borrowing powers for a further £100,000. Another act dated 26 May 1865 sanctioned a branch from just north of Swiss Cottage, climbing up to Hampstead village, where it would terminate at the northern end of Flask Walk. This act authorised a further £200,000 capital, to which the Metropolitan could subscribe £100,000[1]. John Fowler and his partner T. Marr Johnson (who lived in the district) were the principal promoters. Others interested included Donald Nicoll, seeking to improve and develop his property at West End Lane, Hampstead, and one of the first directors[2].

ANOTHER STATION AT BAKER STREET

After a contract was let to Lucas Bros & Aird & Son in 1865, works progressed satisfactorily until December 1866 when they were checked by lack of capital. Relations with the Metropolitan, with which the 1864 act allowed agreements to be made, were soon close: there were two Metropolitan directors on the original board (one, William Austin, was the first chairman); and the two companies shared offices and secretary. Negotiations were begun in April 1864, concluding in an agreement of 30 December 1865 which provided for the line to be built as single track, from an 'exchange station' at Baker Street, terminating at either Swiss Cottage or Finchley Road (Hampstead Junction Railway). The Metropolitan was to maintain and work the line for 50 per cent of the receipts. With bitter hindsight, the Metropolitan required (but did not in the event entirely get) adequate ventilation arrangements.

Financial difficulties, already evident in the scaling-down of the original proposals[3], were exacerbated by the panic following the

41

Overend, Gurney bank failure of May 1866. To meet its continuing problems in this area, the new company secured a second agreement dated 23 May 1866 providing that the Metropolitan would give a rebate on gross earnings from through traffic to its stations which would be returnable with four per cent interest as soon as the St John's Wood was able to pay six per cent dividend in any half year[4]. Supported by this and by the Metropolitan's decision of November 1866 to subscribe £100,000 at par of St John's Wood five per cent Preference stock, the company was able to place enough of its remaining Preference stock to pay for a single track of 1 mile 76.16 chains.

This little railway climbed 97ft from Baker Street to its terminus 156 yards beyond Swiss Cottage station. At Baker Street it made a double line junction with the Metropolitan at the east end of that company's station, aligned for through running to and from the City. This 7 chain connection had been requested by the St John's Wood company in 1866, the Metropolitan obtaining powers to build it in its act of 17 June 1867, agreeing to pay half the cost. It did of course give the St John's Wood the advantage of a somewhat awkward access to the Metropolitan's engine and carriage depots at Edgware Road, saving the cost of providing new facilities. From the junction, the two tracks proceeded northwest through the side platforms (at six chains) of a station which was to become known as Baker Street East. Beyond, they entered the tunnel, in which, after a short distance, they became single and the tunnel a single bore. At 56 chains from Baker Street East was St John's Wood Road station, in open cutting, with double track and two side platforms almost 300ft long. There followed another tunnel to an almost identical station called Marlborough Road, 47 chains further on, sited at the junction of Queen's Grove and Finchley Road. At the end of another tunnel, the line entered the double-track side-platform station named Swiss Cottage, 38 chains from Marlborough Road and partly underground. At street level, all three stations had rather plain single-storey buildings of stock bricks with tall arched windows[5].

The district traversed was thinly populated, consisting mainly of detached and semi-detached villas in large gardens. Little or no new house construction was in progress or planned, and at its northern extremity the railway reached the outer edge of built-up London. Hopes of traffic development seem to have rested on the unachieved links to the LNWR and to Hampstead village.

PILOTMEN AND EXPERIMENTS

Public service started on 13 April 1868, the passengers travelling with tickets headed 'Metropolitan Railway', despite the line's separate status. As the proposed Hampstead branch was to have stretches of 1 in 27 and as there was also a climb at 1 in 44 to get over the Regent's Canal, Burnett had designed condensing locomotives more powerful than the Beyer Peacocks. These five 0-6-0T, (34 to 38) with their 4ft diameter wheels, were supplied by the Worcester Engine Co at £2,556 each. They had what were for the period very large (20×24in) inside cylinders, a working pressure of 140lb per sq in and a grate area of 22½ sq ft, providing ample power, even when condensing, to haul the normal load of three or six 14-ton coaches up to Hampstead.

In practice the Beyer-Peacock tanks were found to work the trains to Swiss Cottage without difficulty, so by November 1868 the Metropolitan was trying to exchange the 0-6-0T for some the Midland Railway had built to the Beyer Peacock design. This failed, but in 1873–5 four of the locomotives were sold to the Taff Vale Railway and one to the Sirhowy Railway. In their new South Wales home they performed well on heavy coal trains.

At first there was a 20-minute service each way between Swiss Cottage and the Metropolitan's new City terminus at Moorgate Street, supplemented for three months in the summer of 1868 by a poorly-patronised local service between Baker Street and Swiss Cottage. Disappointed with its receipts, the St John's Wood board pressed hard for a 10-minute service between Swiss Cottage and Moorgate but the Metropolitan refused, believing the congestion it would cause on its line would delay other services. So much difficulty had in fact occurred at Baker Street Junction, including two minor accidents, that the Metropolitan soon refused to continue through working, offering instead a ten-minute shuttle service on the St John's Wood line. This change was made on 8 March 1869 after a footbridge had been built at the east end of the Metropolitan platforms to afford access to and from Baker Street East. The link from the Down (west-bound) Metropolitan line was subsequently removed and the single line junction with the Up line was then normally covered by a draw-bridge resting across the ends of the two Baker Street East platforms.

Single line working to and from Swiss Cottage was controlled by the conventional train staff and ticket system combined with the block telegraph, using train staffs and tickets of disparate shapes and colours for the three inter-station sections. About 1874 in an attempt to increase the speed of working, pilotmen were introduced to act as human train staffs, normally travelling on the locomotives and moving

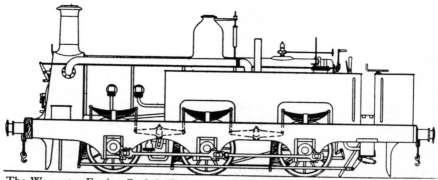

The Worcester Engine Co 0-6-0T designed in 1868 for the St John's Wood Railway and the proposed Hampstead branch (courtesy *The Railway Magazine*)

with astonishing speed and dexterity from one footplate to another at St John's Wood Road, which became the normal crossing place. The first man wore a red shoulder belt and worked on the southern section, the second, with blue shoulder belt, protecting the line between St John's Wood Road and Swiss Cottage[6]. Following this change, the second track and signal box at Marlborough Road went out of use.

At each station there were up and down distant and starting signals placed centrally over the arch of the tunnels. Facing points to and from the single lines were interlocked with the distant signals, but if these were inadvertently put back to danger before a train came to a stand, the facing points unlocked. This led to two minor accidents.

With its isolation, its steep gradients and its tunnels comparable to those on the Metropolitan, the St John's Wood offered an ideal test bed for new equipment such as the Wilkin & Clark chain carriage brake, the Heberlein brake, the Smith simple vacuum brake, Silber's petroleum carriage lamps and Julius Pintsch's high-pressure oil gas carriage lighting. An adapted version of the Wilkin & Clark chain brake was generally adopted by the Metropolitan from 1869[7] only to be replaced by Smith's non-automatic vacuum brake on all 44 loco-motives and 180 carriages about 1876. As the Metropolitan was the first company to adopt the Smith brake for all its stock, fitting was undertaken at a cut price (£3,335). During 1875–6 all the St John's Wood trains were converted from coal gas lighting to the more economical Pintsch system. Modification of the entire Metropolitan fleet of 180 carriages followed from 1877.

INTO THE ARMS OF THE METROPOLITAN

Predictably the financial results of the new line were abysmal[8]. In desperation, from 1869 the independent element on the board, led by the contractor John Aird Jr (whose firm had taken up much of the original share capital in return for building the line) pressed the Metropolitan to provide more frequent trains and restore the through service to the City. They also turned for advice to James Staats Forbes[9], paying him a generous £1,000. It was unlikely that Forbes' new relationship with the Metropolitan District Railway would bring him to take an impartial attitude to Metropolitan Railway interests and so it proved. By following his suggestions, the St John's Wood and the Metropolitan were involved in heavy parliamentary costs in 1871–3 as they sought and obtained powers to make extensions to Willesden and junctions with both the LNWR and the Midland Railway as a means of making the line more viable. This activity much upset the Metropolitan, which interpreted it as a move to raise the take-over price. Some work was started in 1872 on an extension towards Finchley Road, Midland Railway, Lucas Bros completing a single line tunnel which was to become a playground for local boys after the works had been abandoned.

Requests for increases in the train service were always resisted by the Metropolitan on the grounds that they would prove unremunerative. In 1870 the Metropolitan's general manager pointed out that in the middle of the day, the trains were already running almost empty, adding that he saw no great inconvenience in the obligatory change at Baker Street, where a City or West End train would arrive in two to four minutes.

Through the 1870s the Metropolitan waited for an opportunity to buy out the independent shareholders on the most favourable terms, meanwhile increasingly looking upon the undertaking as its own, purchasing more ordinary shares and debentures[10], guaranteeing 2¾ per cent dividends on the five per cent Preference stock (from 1 January 1879) and offering capital for double tracking and extension, something we shall examine in Chapter 6. With the Metropolitan's purchase of the £200,000 Lucas & Aird shares at half their nominal value in 1874, Aird and other independent directors resigned and charges for management and direction and other expenses of separate organisation ceased. Papers and business were transferred to the Metropolitan's care. From this time three of the four directors were Metropolitan appointees.

After much haggling, agreement on terms was eventually reached and the little company was fully absorbed on 1 April 1882. By then, as we shall see, with a new captain at the helm, a fresh course was being plotted for the Metropolitan. But we must first return to what was happening in the centre of London around 1866.

4

A CIRCLE UNJOINED

John Kelk's contract for the eastward extension to Moorgate Street
had proceeded without serious problems. Following a board decision
of November 1863, four tracks were to be provided. Two, on the
north side, were ready on 23 December 1865 together with the intermediate station at Aldersgate Street (now Barbican). This had an
impressive iron and glass arched-rib roof 308ft long, with an elliptical
span of 80ft covering the four tracks and three platforms. Many years
later it inspired Sir John Betjeman into verse[1]. At Farringdon Street,
the permanent through station, with its double span overall roof,
mainly glazed and supported on shallow bow-string girders, was as yet
unfinished, as were the terminal platforms for other companies'
services at Moorgate Street.

A CONNECTION TO THE SOUTHERN LINES

One of these users was the LCDR, which had crossed the Thames into
the City, with a station near the foot of Ludgate Hill, in December
1864. From there, the company was authorised to proceed underneath
Snow Hill, descending at 1 in 39 to meet a Metropolitan extension of
10 chains from Earl Street Junction, Farringdon, at a point known as
West Street Junction, the latter line sanctioned by the Metropolitan
Railway Act of 25 July 1864. This, the first and only conventional
railway link across the heart of London, was quickly built, most of it
across land already cleared for the City's new markets. It was opened
on 1 January 1866.

Under the Metropolitan and LCDR acts of 1864 the latter had
running powers as far as the proposed junction with the Midland
Railway at St Pancras, and LCDR trains (some with through carriages
to and from Dover and Ramsgate) began to run over the Metropolitan
to King's Cross, GNR, whilst most of the LCDR's local trains were
extended to Farringdon Street. The latter was designated an interchange station between the Metropolitan and the LCDR, which paid a
proportion of the interest on its cost, together with part of the working
expenses and maintenance bill. Mileage payments and freight tolls
were also required from the LCDR.

Some GNR suburban trains started to run through to Ludgate Hill station over the Metropolitan on 3 January 1866, GNR freight trains to south London following on 20 February. From 1 August 1866 GNR and LCDR trains worked between Herne Hill and New Barnet, some of the GNR trains going on to Hatfield[2]. The Midland Railway's use of the connection will be mentioned later. Strangely, the Metropolitan never used it for its own trains; although a service between Hammersmith and Herne Hill was approved by the Metropolitan board in August 1865, with additional locomotives and carriages to be ordered, this proposal was not implemented.

Not satisfied with the arrangements made, the LCDR persuaded the Metropolitan to obtain powers (Metropolitan Railway Act, 13 July 1868) for a 14 chain curve from Snow Hill Junction to Smithfield Junction, to afford the LCDR access to the new Smithfield Market and Moorgate Street. LCDR use of the new facility was governed by an agreement of July 1870 which required it to pay the Metropolitan for the use of the two passenger stations and mileage receipts, leaving it free to fix its own fares. The Metropolitan inserted a provision that the LCDR should run 80 passenger trains each way every weekday (six an hour) over the curve into Moorgate, but although the service (Victoria-Moorgate) started on 1 September 1871, the full quota was not reached until 1 January 1872. Totally unrealistic in relation to the business offering, it was allowed to decline steadily from 1875 so that by 1880 there were 70 each way, by 1907, 59 and by 1913, only 48. With the opening of the curve, LCDR trains ceased to terminate at Farringdon Street.

The second pair of tracks between Farringdon Street and Moorgate came into use on 1 March 1866 as far as Aldersgate Street (now Barbican), reaching Moorgate on 1 July. They carried GWR broad gauge trains to and from Kensington (Addison Road)[3]. With the completion of the new works, the original Farringdon Street station closed after traffic on 28 February 1866.

THE CITY WIDENED LINES

This four-track section between Farringdon and Moorgate was part of a larger scheme made necessary by the Metropolitan's acceptance, in the hope of useful financial gain, of passenger and freight services from no less than four main line companies: the GWR, the GNR, the LCDR and the Midland Railway. With the first two in view, doubling between King's Cross and Farringdon Street had been decided upon early in 1863. The works, authorised by the Metropolitan Railway Act

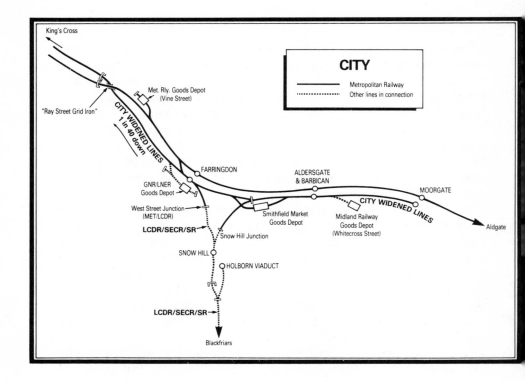

of 25 July 1864, were undertaken by John Kelk. Following the
drawings of John Fowler, he constructed a double track which began
with new connections at King's Cross then proceeded along the north
side of the original lines to a second Clerkenwell Tunnel, 733 yards
long. This descended at 1 in 500 and then 1 in 100, debouching under
the 1863 tracks, which were carried high above on a dramatic skew
bridge to become known as the Ray Street Gridiron. From this point,
the new double track climbed at 1 in 40 to reach the level of the
existing line on the west side of Farringdon Street station. This
burrow, which was to be the cause of several minor collisions and
loose-coupled freight train breakaways and was also vulnerable to
flooding, was required to bring trains to the Junction with the LCDR,
to the proposed GNR goods depot on the west side of Farringdon
Street station, and to the Smithfield Market sidings[4].

Discussions with the Midland Railway, then building its London
Extension, had started in November 1866, culminating in an
agreement of 2 September 1867 which gave running powers into
Moorgate Street and to West Street Junction, Snow Hill. The Metropolitan was to receive a mileage proportion of the gross receipts from
passenger traffic at a minimum of £7,000 a year as well as tolls on

freight workings. Subject to the interests of the Metropolitan and to the relative importance of its traffic to that of other companies using the lines, the Midland was free to fix the number and times of its trains. Station charges were payable. This agreement was modified on 3 and 9 September 1874 to set new tolls and rent and to give the Midland running powers to its new freight depot, built on land leased from the Metropolitan at Whitecross Street on the south side of the line between Moorgate and Aldersgate stations and controlled from a new 10-lever cabin called Barbican. Whitecross Street depot received traffic from 1 January 1878.

Midland trains left the new main line into the high level St Pancras station at St Paul's Road Junction (just south of Camden Road) whence they descended at 1 in 58 in a double line tunnel to join the Metropolitan at Midland Junction, beneath the point where Pancras Road runs into Euston Road. Taking advantage of the surface clearance for the construction of the Midland terminus, the Metropolitan acquired a new double line tunnel from here to a point 260 yards west, parallel to the 1863 tunnel. Built by the Midland, under the Metropolitan Railway (Additional Powers) Act, 1866, this was intended as the start of quadrupling towards Praed Street Junction, Paddington, but no more work was ever done and the tunnel remained unused until March 1926 (see Chapter 13).

With its main line into London completed, but St Pancras as yet unfinished, the Midland began a Bedford to Moorgate Street service on 13 July 1868. Over the next two years, additional workings followed: from stations on the Tottenham & Hampstead Junction line to Moorgate Street and Victoria; and from Midland suburban stations to the LCDR. From 1 July 1875 Midland suburban trains ran between Hendon or South Tottenham and Victoria whilst some LCDR trains ran between Victoria and Hendon.

An agreement very similar to that with the Midland was signed with the GNR on 25 May 1869 and it was that company's freight trains which made first use of the 'Widened Lines' or 'City Widened Lines' between St Pancras/King's Cross and Farringdon Street on 27 January 1868. A limited GNR passenger service ran to Farringdon Street from 17 February and from 1 March the Widened Lines carried a joint GNR/LCDR service between Edgware and Ludgate Hill (extended to Loughborough Junction on 1 June) and between New Barnet and Victoria. All GNR suburban trains over the Widened Lines were diverted to Moorgate Street from 1 June 1869, with the joint GNR/LCDR service continuing to operate to and from Victoria.

At Moorgate Street the Midland, GNR and LCDR each maintained their own station staff and separate booking offices until the whole operation was taken over by the Metropolitan on 1 July 1909. There were also separate Midland and GNR ticket offices at King's Cross (Metropolitan) until 1910, when common sense at last prevailed. Like other inner suburban services, the cross-London facility via Farringdon Street and Ludgate Hill proved vulnerable to tube and electric tramway competition in the 1900s, the GNR/LCDR service succumbing in September 1907 and the Midland/LCDR in June 1908.

A further 'foreign' working appeared on the Metropolitan on 1 August 1872 following an agreement between the Metropolitan, the GWR and the Metropolitan District Railway (of which more in a moment). This was a half-hourly service, known as the 'Middle Circle', running between Moorgate Street (extended to Bishopsgate 12 July 1875 and to Aldgate on 4 December 1876) and Mansion House via Westbourne Park, Kensington (Addison Road) and Earls Court[5]. It supplemented the GWR suburban trains using the Metropolitan which were mentioned in Chapter 2.

Running of GWR trains over the Metropolitan led to various disputes, the GWR's strength of grievance eventually causing it to challenge in the High Court of Justice the Metropolitan's contention that the statutory right of the GWR to insist on as many trains as it wished being taken over the Metropolitan by the latter's locomotives was limited to the line authorised in the Metropolitan Railway Act, 1854 (Paddington to Farringdon Street) in which act the GWR's power of access resided. As judgement given for the Metropolitan was upheld on appeal in 1882, this quarrel did nothing for the GWR but incur substantial legal costs.

INNER CIRCLE FRUSTRATED

Following the initial success of the Metropolitan, London railway proposals proliferated like wasps in autumn. So congested was the 1863–4 session with these bills that parliament appointed select committees to extract some order out of chaos: in 1863, a Select Committee of the Lords on Metropolitan Communication, to report generally; and in 1864, a Joint Select Committee to report on the individual schemes. The Lords Committee produced a recommendation for an 'Inner Circuit' railway connecting the existing and proposed main line termini, to be achieved by extending the Metropolitan round to Tower Hill via Aldgate and, in the west, to South Kensington, the two ends to be linked by 'a line on the north side of the Thames'. This concept of an inner ring railway had been offered to their Lordships by Fowler, who in the autumn of 1863 had launched a scheme which, with some modifications, would meet their recommendation. Fowler's scheme was therefore approved by the Joint Select Committee, which had thrown out many of the other bills[6]. To bring about the desired outcome, the legislation was arranged in three bills, all of which were given a smooth passage, receiving royal assent on 29 July 1864. They were:

(a) *The Metropolitan Railway (Notting Hill & Brompton Extension)* extending the Metropolitan from Paddington to South Kensington;

(b) *The Metropolitan Railway (Tower Hill Extension)* extending the Metropolitan from Moorgate Street to Trinity Square, Tower Hill; and

(c) *The Metropolitan District Railway*, a line linking (a) to (b) and serving the existing and proposed main line termini at Victoria, Charing Cross and Cannon Street.

Line (b) was authorised only as far as the crossing of the London & Blackwall Railway, at Vine Street, Minories. To maximise traffic on the MDR, powers were also included in (c) for branches to the West London Extension Railway at West Brompton (running parallel with (a) between South Kensington and Cromwell Road) and another, east to north, joining the WLER just south of Kensington (Addison Road) (now Olympia) station. Hopes that these two connections would attract services from the LBSCR and the LSWR on to the MDR were frustrated and apart from a temporary link in 1866–8 for spoil removal, no junction was ever made at West Brompton. However, the LNWR and GWR were persuaded to use the northern connection, the latter by the 'Middle Circle' service already mentioned. An LNWR 'Outer Circle', Broad Street-Willesden Junction-Kensington (Addison Road)-South Kensington-Mansion House was to start operation on 1 February 1872.

In 1864–5 the completion of the proposed and supposedly desirable 'inner circuit' railway seemed feasible enough. It was realised that raising the capital for the whole length between Paddington and Moorgate would be too much for the Metropolitan to tackle on its own, hence the separate promotion of the southern connecting link by an independent undertaking. It may well be (though no evidence has been found) that the Metropolitan itself suggested this gambit to Fowler, confident that the two companies would have to amalgamate within a short time. For this scheme, Fowler secured the valuable backing of a powerful consortium of eminent railway contractors: Peto & Betts; John Kelk; and Waring Brothers[7]. Support of the ordinary share-buying public was fully expected, following the success of the Metropolitan.

At the end of 1865 a joint committee of the Metropolitan and the fledgling MDR was set up, producing an agreement, signed in August of the following year, in which the Metropolitan undertook to work and maintain the MDR lines, effectively operating the Inner Circle under unified management. Even earlier (December 1863) the Metropolitan had agreed to appoint directors to the MDR board and in due course its chairman and three other directors took their places. It was assumed by all concerned that a merger of the two companies would come about, certainly no later than the completion of the Inner Circle. Terms for such a union were indeed discussed at the very first official meeting of the MDR board on 11 July 1864.

Yet it did not happen. Not only were the financial problems and dismal results of the MDR to render it a most unattractive asset; there was an early quarrel between the two undertakings which set them on to diverging paths, with the MDR starting to work its own trains. This latter decision, which put the seal on an enduring separation, owed much to the combative influence of James Staats Forbes, who had been imported into MDR affairs, quickly becoming its chairman.

But at first all was sweetness and light. John Kelk wrote to the Metropolitan board in January 1864 reporting that 'Sir Morton Peto, Mr Brassey and Mr Waring are united with me in the prosecution of the Metropolitan District Railway', adding cunningly that it would be 'convenient and desirable for all parties' if the Metropolitan's eastern and western extensions towards the MDR were to be built by the same consortium of contractors as this would avoid 'competition for labour and materials and other complications' all of which were likely to increase costs. As bait he offered assistance with and underwriting of the substantial parliamentary deposits which the Metropolitan faced for the extension bills. This bribe was accepted, subject to the Metropolitan retaining full control of the legislation. Fowler was also cosy, assured of the engineering fees for all three schemes, in the design of which he was again to be assisted by Thomas Marr Johnson.

Passing as it did through the then fashionable residential areas of Bayswater, Notting Hill and Kensington, the Metropolitan's western extension proved burdensome in compensation payments for property demolition and damage. A curious facet of this was the erection at 23/24 Leinster Gardens of false elevations for a five-storey house to conceal the railway where it passed under the road and preserve the continuity of the terrace. Stipulations in the act required the stations to be of suitably ornamental character, restricted to passenger and parcels traffic.

Adequate ventilation was a lesson now well-learned. To maximise dispersal of the products of combustion, almost all the line was in open cutting over its length of 3 miles 2 chains, with the major interruption of the unavoidable 421 yard tunnel through Campden Hill. There was a perceptible climb up from the banks of the Thames; from Gloucester Road to Notting Hill Gate there were two stretches at 1 in 70 and between Westminster Bridge MDR where the tunnel rails were 13ft below the Thames high water mark and Edgware Road station the total rise was 116ft.

Stations were provided at Praed Street (now Paddington), Bayswater, Notting Hill Gate[8], Kensington (now High Street Kensington), Gloucester Road 'for Brompton', and South Kensington. These showed their most pleasing prospect at rail level where elegant wrought-iron arch-rib roofs spanned the gap between the high arcaded side or retaining walls. At each end the arch of the roofs was closed by screens with glazing bars forming a pretty fan design. At street level the buildings were of the general pattern already seen on the original line and on the Metropolitan & St John's Wood, suggesting the same unknown and uninspired architectural hand. All were single-storey except that at Gloucester Road where there was a central second storey with five bays. Julian Leathart has aptly described the dignified and sober elevations as a 'spiritless adaptation of vaguely Italian Renaissance origins', noting that a little more expense and ornamentation was lavished on the snob areas of Bayswater and Kensington. It was not many years before hoardings and signs in dizzy confusion obscured whatever impact their architect might have hoped to offer.

No waiting rooms were provided at these or the original stations at platform level. A small shareholder, a civil servant commuting between Notting Hill Gate and Westminster, pointed out the need for this facility in January 1880, adding 'I can assure you that the draughts during the winter months are enough to kill a bronze rhinoceros' (civil servants are never vulgar). Our bureaucrat admitted there were buffets, but said he was not always willing 'to lay out sixpence or so' merely to seek shelter; although he never had to wait more than 10 minutes, this he felt was long enough to catch 'influenza or severe catarrh infections'. As no notice was taken of his suggestion, complaints on this score continued until small and cheap platform shelters were installed at seven Inner Circle stations in 1890–1.

Public services between Edgware Road and Gloucester Road stations began on 1 October 1868, to be extended to South Kensington[9] on 24 December. On that day, special efforts having been made to rescue something from the Christmas traffic, the first part of the MDR was also opened. Work on the MDR had started early in 1865, the intention being to carry it as far east as the proposed site of Cannon Street SER station, but as we shall see in a moment, this was not achieved. The first section available was the 2 miles 27 chains from South Kensington to Westminster Bridge (now West-minster) via the intermediate stations at Sloane Square, Victoria and St James's Park. By the summer of 1869, the connecting lines from South Kensington (west end of station) and High Street Kensington to West Brompton and northwards to Kensington (Addison Road) were all completed but at first were used only by a shuttle service between West Brompton and Gloucester Road which started on 12 April 1869[10].

To work the additional lines opened in 1868 (ie the sections just described and the St John's Wood Railway) the Metropolitan ordered 50 additional 8-wheeled carriages of the original pattern from Ashbury's (ten Firsts, ten Seconds, 20 Thirds and ten composites). In anticipation of the working of the MDR all the way to Cannon Street another 38 vehicles were obtained in 1869–70 from the Railway Carriage Co. The first of these comprised a pair of short 4-wheelers, each 20ft long, semi-permanently connected with a combined central buffer and coupling. As these were found satisfactory and as a pair were lighter than the long 8-wheelers, a further 24 were ordered. The balance of 12 were 8-wheelers, similar to the earlier ones.

AN INDEPENDENT NEIGHBOUR

Between Westminster Bridge and Blackfriars the MDR was planned to run below the new Victoria Embankment on which work had started in the summer of 1865, but the effects of the Overend, Gurney bank failure had serious repercussions for Peto & Betts, one of the MDR contractors, causing problems with the financing of the works. It was then decided to postpone completion of the Embankment section until potential investors in the MDR could see the results of opening the line as far as Westminster Bridge. There were also to be long arguments with the Metropolitan Board of Works about the compensation payments for the shared route along the river bank. As a result of all this instead of the railway construction being fully integrated with the building of the Embankment, it proceeded only slowly and fitfully and in some places new fill placed behind the Embankment wall had to be dug out again to make the railway tunnel. As MDR Ordinary Shares proved virtually unsaleable at this time of financial panic, parliament eventually came to the rescue by sanction-ing the issue of the capital for the Westminster Bridge to Cannon

Street section in the form of five per cent Preference Stock.

The 1 mile 28 chains under the Embankment was opened on 30 May 1870 with stations at Charing Cross (now Embankment), Temple and Blackfriars. Two months later, the service over the new section was augmented by extending the West Brompton to Gloucester Road trains over the full length, making regular use for the first time of the MDR tracks between Gloucester Road and South Kensington.

Just as the Metropolitan had with the GWR, the MDR began to find fault with its operator, the Metropolitan. Under the 1866 agreement, the Metropolitan paid the MDR 55 per cent of the gross receipts, including a proportion for through traffic. In the summer of 1870 the MDR pressed for a more frequent service in the belief that this would boost the disappointing revenue, but the Metropolitan used the terms of the agreement to make a surcharge, causing the net average payment to the MDR to fall to around 38 per cent.

This dispute had erupted around the middle of 1869, driving the MDR to seek independent advice. Its choice of counsellor fell upon James Staats Forbes, general manager of the LCDR, whose hand can be discerned in the notice served by the MDR on 3 January 1870 that it wished to terminate the 1866 agreement with the Metropolitan after the necessary 18 months interval. Early in October 1870, following the resignation of the Metropolitan representatives on the MDR board, Forbes became an MDR director and shortly afterwards, managing director. He continued as general manager of the LCDR, whose board not unreasonably reduced his salary and insisted on having first call on his services. However, in 1871 his ability and charm won him a place on the LCDR board, from which position it was easier for him to accept the post of chairman and managing director of the MDR in November 1872 whilst still remaining chief officer and a director of the LCDR.

There were several attempts by the Metropolitan to patch up the argument with the MDR with a view to concluding a new agreement on the basis of the 1864 legislation. In characteristic form, Forbes blew hot and cold over this, pretending even as late as May 1871 that he could see the possibility of a satisfactory fusion between the two companies. But he had already determined upon independence and had prepared for it.

Under Forbes, the MDR was pushed a further 34 chains into the City. As its 1871–2 bill for a terminus at Cheapside/Poultry had been thrown out, it had to compromise with a Mansion House station some way west of that point, at the junction of Great Trinity Lane and Garlick Hill (Cannon Street station when eventually built was to be considerably nearer Mansion House than the station of that name). This extension was opened on 3 July 1871, from which day, on the expiration of the notice, the MDR began to use its own locomotives and trains, operating from a new depot at Lillie Bridge, West Kensington.

Mansion House station was laid out for terminal working, with three platform roads and two platforms, each with tracks either side. There were spurs for locomotive coaling stages and water cranes. Part of the finance for these works had come from the LNWR in return for powers to operate six trains an hour between Mansion House and Broad Street via Kensington (Addison Road) and Willesden Junction. This 'Outer Circle' service was to start on 1 February 1872.

With the opening of Mansion House station, the two MDR platforms alongside the Metropolitan's at Kensington High Street were brought into use and a so-called 'Inner Circle' service was begun between Mansion House, South Kensington, Edgware Road and Moorgate Street. Operation was equally shared between the two companies, which duly prolonged it to Bishopsgate (now Liverpool Street) and then to Aldgate when these extensions were opened by the Metropolitan. Normally these trains used the Metropolitan tracks between South Kensington and Kensington High Street, of which more in a moment. Between Mansion House and Moorgate the 'Inner Circle' offered a ten minute service, but with the West Brompton-Mansion House trains there was a five minute interval all day between the latter and Gloucester Road. From 1872 the 'Middle' and 'Outer' circle workings added another four trains an hour to this stretch, whilst on the Edgware Road to Moorgate section the presence of Middle Circle, GWR suburban and Hammersmith & City trains provided a similarly intense frequency.

A further cause of friction between the two companies had arisen in March 1870 when the Metropolitan board had heard of the MDR's intention to build a new curve without statutory authority on its own land near Cromwell Road across the top of the 'V' formed by the lines running from High Street and from Gloucester Road to the West London Extension Railway and West Brompton. As it had success-fully opposed the inclusion of such a line in the 1864 legislation, the Metropolitan was understandably irked, resolving to retaliate by opposing the MDR bill for the 1869–70 session. Undeterred, the MDR pressed ahead, no doubt under Forbes' direct instructions, secretly connecting up the new link during the night of 5 July 1870. Fenton told the Metropolitan board next day that he had had the junction severed shortly after it had been made, receiving a writ for his pains. For the MDR the importance of this 'Cromwell Curve' (after the neighbouring Cromwell Road) was that it effectively completed a double track MDR line all the way from Kensington High Street to South Kensington alongside the Metropolitan. Gradually the situation was clarified. The respective boundaries of the two companies in this frontier area were resolved by Sir John Fowler, whose arbitration award of 27 July 1871 was set out in the schedule of the Metropolitan Railway Act of 21 July 1873. The lines between South Kensington and High Street Kensington became known as the 'Western Joint Lines' under a 21-year agreement signed by the two companies on 29 June 1871 and confirmed by the Metropolitan Railway Act of 27 June 1872. This provided for the working of the Joint Lines and stations on common account with division of the excess of receipts over expenditure, Metropolitan 66 per cent, MDR 34 per cent. These proportions were revised in 1878 to 50:50 in recognition of the additional traffic contributed by the MDR's subsequent western extensions. The Cromwell Curve was then used sporadically by MDR trains and by Inner Circle trains without undue friction, although remaining an irritant for the Metropolitan. On the expiry of the 1871 agreement in 1892 the MDR began to contend that it could run its 50 per cent quota of Inner Circle trains over the Cromwell Curve instead of using the parallel Metropolitan Circle tracks, thus diverting traffic from the Metropolitan between South Kensington and High Street. Various attempts were made by the MDR to reopen the 1871 agreement which meanwhile remained in force by mutual consent. Eventually the case of the Cromwell Curve was argued before Mr Justice Wright of the King's Bench Division, whose 1903 decision was in favour of the Metropolitan.

Two more details regarding the Western Lines remain to be noted. Under the spur of the 1871 International Exhibition, which the two companies had agreed to serve with jointly-subsidised buses to and from South Kensington station, the latter was finally completed, with two platforms for each company, on 19 July 1871. In the as yet undeveloped market gardens between Gloucester Road and West Brompton stations, the MDR opened a small wooden station called Earls Court on 30 October the same year.

Despite the extensions and the undoubted management skills of Forbes, the MDR proved to be a sickly child. As we have seen, its financing was affected by the 1866 panic and it had been unable to raise sufficient capital from ordinary shares for even a truncated version of the original proposal. At Mansion House, its capital really had run out, with no prospect of making a further line to meet the

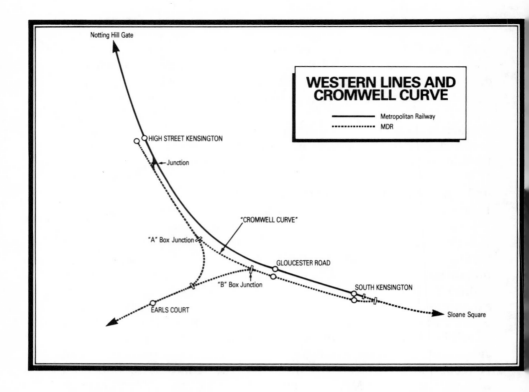

Notting Hill Gate

WESTERN LINES AND CROMWELL CURVE

——— Metropolitan Railway
··········· MDR

HIGH STREET KENSINGTON

Junction

"CROMWELL CURVE"

"A" Box Junction

GLOUCESTER ROAD

"B" Box Junction

SOUTH KENSINGTON

EARLS COURT

Sloane Square

Metropolitan in the east, or even to get to Cannon Street as once intended (although some work was done there). Its heavy commitment of Preference Stock was to prove a millstone round its neck. Traffic returns were consistently disappointing, passenger journeys rising only from around 21 million a year at the beginning of the 1870s to 30 million in 1877. In contrast, the Metropolitan's carryings over the same period increased from 43 million to over 56 million. Until 1878 the ordinary shareholders of the MDR received no dividend at all, then only a quarter per cent for the year. For 1879 they got one per cent, in 1880 1⅛th, in 1881 and 1882 ⅜th, and after that, again, nothing.

Apart from those occasions when it breaks significantly into Metropolitan affairs, we must now leave the history of the MDR, except to say that its parlous state, combined with the consistently abrasive interface between it and the Metropolitan were now to produce a long delay in completing the 'Inner Circuit' which parliament had deemed so important[11]. As we shall see in the next chapter, the Metropolitan was entering a crisis which would bring to its governance a man who would not only guide it virtually single-handed for 22 years, but would shape its character for much longer than that. Like Forbes, this new captain was a strong-minded autocrat, and the two men, who also conflicted as chairmen of the rival SER and LCDR, and were motivated by unhealthy mutual suspicion and hostility, were to become dominant influences on events. From this time until the end of the 19th century, the two underground railway companies were to waste much time and energy in futile fencing and squabbling; the Metropolitan suggesting and entertaining proposals for amalgamation yet never prepared to act unless it could get the MDR at a bargain price which Forbes always refused; the MDR, for its part, always fiercely defensive of its independence, mustering confidence in a separate prosperous future from the flow of bogus optimism emanating from Forbes.

The many disputes (which make arid reading today) brought nothing but employment for clerks and lawyers, the latter in particular always willing to encourage them for the profits they offered. In retrospect, the continuing separation of the two companies seems not only to have made little sense but not to have been in the best interests of the Metropolitan. Some, it is true, saw this at the time, and the Metropolitan board was more than once urged to secure the MDR without further ado. But the personalities of the two chairmen always prevailed; neither's heart was in a union. The longer the status quo persisted, the stronger became resistance to change as each company developed its distinctive traffics from new lines feeding into the incomplete Circle.

Symbolic of the waste arising from the inability to move into what should have been a single operation was the surplus of rolling stock left on the Metropolitan's hands after the two undertakings had drifted apart. When the GER needed more motive power for its new suburban services, the Metropolitan was able to lend it six locomotives for four months ending on 27 November 1872. For a long period the surplus carriages were stored in sidings at Moorgate Street, Smithfield and Farringdon Street. No new coaches were purchased by the Metropolitan from 1870 until 1879, when additions were needed for the extension to Harrow and a share in the working of the East London Railway.

5

ENTER WATKIN

About 57 per cent of the Metropolitan's issued capital, which had reached £6.15m by 1867, had been contributed by ordinary shareholders who had been kept sweet (and share prices forced up) by payment of highly inflated dividends. Taking into account the surplus of revenue over expenditure, the seven per cent paid between the second half of 1864 and the second half of 1867 was quite unjustified. At the end of the latter period the holders of the Extension shares received their first fixed dividend of six per cent. Dissatisfaction was expressed by Extension shareholder Frederick William Bloxham early in 1868 in a court action in which he alleged that cash received for Extension shares was not properly applied. He sought injunctions to restrain the payment of dividends on the ordinary shares. Judgement went against the company, the court finding that expenses of directors, auditors etc had been charged to capital account and that interest had been paid out of capital in defiance of both the Companies Act and special acts. Following this, the value of the ordinary stock fell to an all-time low of £101½.

With press speculation as to what was happening and dividends still being paid from capital, the board was again under pressure in the second half of 1868 when a substantial element among the shareholders began to express anxiety (unlike the rest, who were content to take the money and ask no questions). In fulfilment of an undertaking given after the Bloxham action, statutory powers had been obtained to convert the Extension stock into ordinary stock, and, more remarkably, to pay dividends out of contractors' payments to the company. When the dividend for the second half of 1868 could only be maintained at seven per cent by throwing into the distribution balance a dubious payment of £42,600 by the contractor John Kelk, this manoeuvre was challenged in the courts early in 1869 by shareholder Enoch R. G. Salisbury. An order was made restraining the company from including this 'sham payment' in its revenue account, causing the board to reduce the dividend to 4½ per cent. Salisbury then brought a further action after circulating some very damaging statements about the financial management exercised by the board.

As the amounts written off to capital and payments made by contractors constituted at least ⅔ of the total available for distribution
as dividend, strict financial probity would have indicated dividends as
low as 1½ or two per cent from the unassisted earnings. In desperation, the board cast about for another device to enable it to maintain
the promised high levels of dividend. It had the surplus lands valued,
then persuaded the accountants Turquand Young to suggest that the
Metropolitan should charge its unremunerative surplus lands with
interest (ie crediting revenue and debiting capital) whilst such lands
were retained with a view to gradual and advantageous sale. Back
came Salisbury in November 1869 with another action to challenge
this move. Vice Chancellor James described the new arrangement as
illegal and 'fictitious income', whilst the final judgement of the Court
of Chancery in 1870 was that the board was 'using the conjectural
income of a conjectural value as a plain and palpable device for
violating an act of parliament'. Found guilty of a breach of trust, the
Metropolitan directors were ordered to compensate the company's
funds from their own pockets[1].

By January 1870 several influential shareholders were campaigning
for a reconstitution of the now thoroughly discredited board. In
response two newcomers (James Caird and Graham Menzies) were
admitted 'to give additional confidence to the shareholders and the
public at large', but this did nothing to arrest the sharp collapse in the
market value of the shares or to boost the dividend on ordinary shares,
down to 2¾ per cent by the second half of 1871. At the half-yearly
meeting of 14 February 1872, when Parson spoke amidst continuous
uproar, there was near-rebellion. Excuses about the competition
generated by the MDR extension to Mansion House were brushed
aside and the board was obliged to concede that two more of its
number should depart, in favour of new blood nominated by the
shareholders. Chosen were Henry David Pochin and Benjamin
Whitworth, two representatives of the substantial Manchester investing interest, both Liberals and industrialists.

Amidst this general crisis, in May 1872, Peacock, the store keeper,
absconded, leaving a deficiency in his cash account. Responsibility for
mismanagement of the stores accounts and lack of oversight of sales of
old materials fell upon the unfortunate resident engineer, Burnett, as
Peacock's immediate line manager. He found himself summarily
dismissed with three months' salary in advance, the directors remaining unmoved by his three written appeals for reinstatement. In his
place came Joseph Tomlinson, a former locomotive superintendent of

the Taff Vale Railway, appointed from 30 November 1872 at a salary rising in two years to £800, a sum evidently higher than that he could command as an independent consulting marine and civil engineer after leaving the Taff Vale in 1869.

By the summer of 1872 the reign of the old regime was drawing to a close as the remaining representatives on the board were driven into a corner. In a move probably organised by Pochin, the 'large share-holders' attended the board meeting of 31 July, bringing with them a new shareholder, Sir Edward William Watkin[2]. Introduced by Pochin, Watkin, another Manchester man, was of impressive presence and ability, 52 years old, with an established capacity for hard work and experience both as railway manager and chairman of two large companies, the Manchester, Sheffield & Lincolnshire Railway (MSLR), and the SER. With a show of reluctance, Watkin agreed to take over the Metropolitan chairmanship and at the next meeting (7 August) the wily and suave John Parson was voted out to make way for the newcomer. In October the last of the old brigade were ejected by three more Manchester men, Andrew Cassels, John R. Lingard and Joseph Shuttleworth. In that month Watkin took the chair for the first time, bringing in John Bell from the MSLR at £500 a year to oust John Henchman as secretary. Henchman lost his other job, as secretary to the trustees of the surplus lands, at the end of the year. Burchell, who has been thoroughly enmeshed in Metropolitan affairs from the start, could not be so easily dislodged, though some saw him as the villain of the piece:

> I hope the Directors will appoint a Solicitor to conduct our law business at a fixed salary and leave Messrs Burchells; our late Chairman, Secretary, and several other officers connected with the Line, were mere creatures of our Solicitor and amongst them, they have nearly ruined what might have been a sound, good property.

The writer, a clergyman-shareholder, was no doubt incensed to find Burchell retained, though his firm was compelled to accept a fixed annual fee (initially £3,000) for all legal and conveyancing business from 1 October 1872, the latter to be conducted from the railway's offices.

Notwithstanding the 'confused and entangled state of its affairs' and the various offences against capitalist morality, the old board of directors had presided over the birth and early years of a valuable London railway facility. Nor did the events just described have any effect on the day to day working of the railway, or on its passengers. But quite apart from the internal reorganisation in the long term interests of the shareholders, they did form an important watershed because the crisis brought into the affairs of the Metropolitan a man who was to change the whole direction of the railway's development.

Combative, secretive and empirical in his approach, Watkin was a man used to getting his own way and running his own show. Within a very short time he had consolidated his position on the board[3] and henceforward for more than two decades all major initiatives would originate from him. As his personal papers have not survived and the Metropolitan's records put little flesh on the decisions he made, it is not always easy at this distance to discern his motives and policies. Nevertheless two things clearly stand out in his governance of the Metropolitan between 1872 and 1894: his determination not to let his rival Forbes on the MDR get the better of him in any sense (and damn the public good); and his ambition to see the Metropolitan used as a link between Lancashire, the Midlands, London and the south-east, to serve his MSLR and SER interests.

In 1872, the simplest way of achieving this connection would have required the cooperation of the GNR, which carried the MSLR London traffic under a 50-year agreement signed in 1857. Even before he had been made chairman of the Metropolitan, Watkin was approaching the GNR as 'allies' of the MSLR, suggesting what he described as a 'wise and prudent arrangement in their interest' – joint management of 'my new charge' by the GNR and SER. Although Oakley and the GNR board did not bite[4], this initiative of July 1872 serves not only to show that Watkin had by that time already made up his mind to take the Metropolitan in hand, but from the start was determined to use it for his wider designs.

For the time being this new Hercules had to put aside such ideas to attend to the Augean stables of Parson & Co. A Committee of Investigation was promptly appointed, whilst Edwin Waterhouse of the public accountants Price, Hoyland & Waterhouse was deputed to examine the books. Reporting on 5 October 1872, the Committee stated that about half the capital expenditure had been absorbed in property purchases and compensations, all the transactions passing through the hands of Burchells, whose accounts had not been examined or agreed by the Metropolitan since the railway came into being. Rent books kept by them did not form an accurate register of the company's property. The railway's accounts were found to be very carelessly kept, with apparent inaccuracies and omissions (later Waterhouse was to discover a total discrepancy of almost £202,000 in the capital expenditure account) and large numbers of payments were unhelpfully classified as 'various'. It might be added that the minute books of the Parson regime were not well-ordered either; they survive to frustrate today's historian by frequently not following through on important matters which they record with breathtaking brevity, or by furnishing little or no detail on significant decisions and events, so that the pattern can only be pieced together from other sources. Although the minutes improved noticeably in the Watkin era, this was not always sustained.

The Committee's report also noted that the contracts for the eastern and western extensions had been given to contractors at terms to be settled by the engineer after the contractors had advanced the required parliamentary deposits. It was suggested that the contract prices were unduly inflated and could have been materially reduced 'under a more judicious administration'. There was criticism of the Parson board for unnecessarily extensive property purchases in the belief that the company might reap profit from holding such surplus lands, but the Committee observed that some properties for the eastern extension, bought in 1865, had remained unproductive for seven years during which work on the line had not been started.

Much of the blame for all this was placed on Parson, the former chairman, whose actions had never been questioned by the other directors. His policy of engendering hopes of high dividends (he had promised as much as 10 per cent at one point) had for some time unduly inflated the value of the shares in the market. He had also approved an agreement with the LCDR which was considered highly disadvantageous to the Metropolitan.

From now onwards the books were to be properly kept on a system devised by Waterhouse, with all the transactions and liabilities duly recorded and apportioned to capital or revenue, for audit by professional accountants. Watkin was to be paid £2,000 a year from a total of £3,600 allocated to the new board of seven directors, none of whom, the Committee recommended, should be associated with the Parson regime. Finally, it was thought that the Bishopsgate extension should proceed as it would be remunerative, but further extension to Aldgate was more doubtful, requiring consideration by the new board.

In the first months of his tenure, Watkin generously expended his bad temper, tart tongue and well-developed gut reaction on what he considered the fearsome bloodsucking Metropolitan Railway shareholders had experienced from lawyers and contractors. Deciding that Fowler had been much overpaid and was still overcharging for his services as engineer, he quarrelled with him and ensured the company never used him again. Fowler remained engineer to the MDR, earning the following homily from Watkin on 3 October 1872:

> . . . if you and I are to cooperate in the completion of the Circle, you must deal with the Company in a far more considerate spirit than that which the papers before me would testify to . . . no Engineer in the world was so highly paid . . . you have set an example of charge which seems to me to have largely aided in the demoralisation of the professional men of all sorts who have lived upon the suffering shareholders for the past ten years . . . the whole thing with any notion of what is fair *pains my mind*.

Many convicted criminals have had a more gentle address from the Bench.

The entry of the men from Manchester was marked by a sharp rise in the Metropolitan's stock as well as the declaration of the lowest dividend so far – a mere one per cent, for the first half of 1872. Shareholders were given a complex explanation for this: heavy compensation for accidents (none of them serious, but at this time lawyers actively touted for business amongst passengers involved in quite minor incidents); meeting arrears for unpaid professional services (see above . . .); MDR competition; the failure of the 1871 International Exhibition; and higher prices for labour and materials. But within five years the ordinary share dividends were up to five per cent, a level maintained for several years. It should be realised that all the results mentioned so far reflected a combination of railway and property revenues. It was not until June 1887 that these two categories were sorted out.

The Committee of Investigation had no fault to find with the physical condition of the railway, stations and rolling stock, and Fenton, the general manager, emerged with escutcheon unblemished. Between 1863 and 1872 passenger journeys and revenue had grown steadily, bringing receipts per mile to £720 16s, a higher level than any other railway company. In August 1867 Fenton was given a vote of thanks at the half yearly meeting for

> the prudence, skill and vigilance with which he has conducted the traffic arrangements of the Metropolitan Railway and has succeeded in carrying 69,700,000 passengers upon the line in a period of 4½ years without a single accident resulting from any neglect on his part or that of the staff under his command.

This last phrase was carefully composed. On 19 December 1866 there had been the first fatal accident on the Metropolitan, although it arose from causes outside its control. Shortly before 1 pm, as a cross girder for the new Smithfield Market was being lowered into position by employees of the Thames Ironworks Company, it fell across a passing

Kensington train, killing three passengers and injuring the guard[5]. A moveable shield was subsequently erected by the contractor to protect the railway from any further damage.

Watkin's expansionist inclinations were soon evident. He favoured a City & West End Railway scheme for a line from South Kensington to the Metropolitan at Farringdon Street via Piccadilly and Holborn, aimed to take advantage, over part of the route, of the construction of new streets proposed by the Metropolitan Board of Works (MBW) (Shaftesbury Avenue, Theobald's Road and Clerkenwell Road). A bill was deposited for the 1872–3 session which sought to attract investment by the trunk line companies by offering them running powers, but as none was interested the proposal was withdrawn[6].

THROUGH CORPSES AND BULLOCKS' HORNS TO ALDGATE

When the Parson board had decided in August 1869 not to build any further east than Bishopsgate, the MBW had opposed this, causing parliament to substitute an extension of time for completion. Anxious to expand his new kingdom, Watkin secured the shareholders' consent in 1874 to the raising of another £250,000 (authorised in the 1872 act). His eyes were as much on a connection to the East London Railway, with its access to lines south of the river, as on completion of the Circle[7].

But the first task was to get the trains to Bishopsgate (now Liverpool Street), where the GER was busy completing its new terminus. Edward Wilson, an independent engineer, who had designed the new GER facilities, was engaged by the Metropolitan in January 1873 to superintend and execute the Bishopsgate extension. Six months later he was appointed consulting engineer to the company with a retainer of £315 a year, but he was to live only till 1877, when his place was taken by Charles Liddell, whose experience at that time commanded a fee of only £100.

(*opposite*) *Plate 6* Aldergate Street (now Barbican) station exterior in 1866. The arch of the train shed can be seen at the extreme left (*Illustrated London News, 10 February 1866*)

Plate 7 Looking south from Farringdon Street station in 1866. Lines to the LCDR at West Street junction and Snow Hill on right, City Widened Lines in centre, Metropolitan 'main line' on left. Note the double arm signals. The line towards Snow Hill and Blackfriars is correctly depicted in an open cutting with timber baulks supporting a structure to protect the railway from falling masonry during construction of the Smithfield Market (*Illustrated London News, 27 January 1866*)

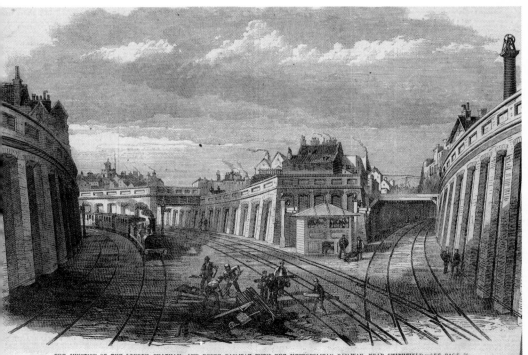

THE JUNCTION OF THE LONDON, CHATHAM, AND DOVER RAILWAY WITH THE METROPOLITAN RAILWAY, NEAR SMITHFIELD.—SEE PAGE 86.

Plate 8 Praed Street station (now Paddington) looking to Edgware Road in 1868 just before opening. Note the starting signal and cabin on the Up platform at left (*photographer unknown*)

Plate 9 Bayswater station exterior in 1868 just before opening (*photographer unknown*)

At the beginning of 1873 the Bishopsgate contract was given to Messrs Kelk & Lucas[8] on the understanding that if the board decided to go on to Aldgate they would be awarded that as well. Construction was begun in earnest in June 1873, more or less from scratch as there had been little activity after the Parson board's decision to make a start in August 1868. It had been hoped to persuade the GER to run trains into Moorgate, paying towards a second pair of tracks, but they did not respond, consenting only to a double line junction for interchange of traffic at Liverpool Street in an agreement dated 9 April 1872 scheduled to the Metropolitan Railway Act of 27 June 1872 (Watkin, as a GER director, had had his first contacts with the Metropolitan in the early negotiations about this). As no other trunk line showed any interest in running on to the GER via the Metropolitan, the board decided in May 1873 to build only two tracks but to arrange for the brickwork of the Finsbury Circus tunnel to have footings designed to reduce the cost of any future second tunnel alongside. Before running under Finsbury Circus, the new line passed through the site of the former refreshment rooms at Moorgate station.

Watkin had much experience of railway construction and contractors but little of the special difficulties of forcing a railway through a congested built-up area. This caused him to show marked impatience with what he saw as the painfully slow progress of the Bishopsgate works. On 3 November 1874 he sent a petulant missive to Charles Lucas:

> . . . the work seems only to dawdle on; and in looking at the preparation and appliances I see nothing that looks like *push*. I greatly regret this as it involves not only loss of interest but disappointment to the shareholders – who – God knows – have been disappointed enough already. May I ask for your personal interference.

Lucas calmly explained that there was difficulty in obtaining possession of the Liverpool Street site and in getting access to the Roman Catholic chapel of St Mary's which impinged on the east side of Finsbury Circus. After some deliberation, the board decided not to buy the school and presbytery of St Mary's but to underpin the foundations. This was to involve provision of a temporary iron church on the site of the Moorgate Street station cabstand, some costly and difficult work at the site, and subsequent repairs to the damage caused to decorations inside the church. Reporting to the board in July 1876, Wilson noted

> this has been a very troublesome job to the contractors as the vault was full of dead bodies and it was a difficult matter to keep the men at work.

Delay in getting on to the Liverpool Street site was followed by problems in obtaining delivery of the wrought iron roof girders for the station, causing the Metropolitan to open the connection to the GER first. This comprised a 3½ chain curve from the north side, close to west end of the future Metropolitan station, meeting a GER connection (authorised in that company's 1870 act), all in a double track tunnel which debouched at the head of what are now platforms 1 and 2 of the main line station. From October 1874 a single line through this tunnel had been in use to remove spoil, then on 1 February 1875 Hammersmith & City trains were extended through it to terminate at Liverpool Street, GER, the Metropolitan meeting the cost of staffing and lighting on the two platforms used. With the opening of the Metropolitan station, 'Bishopsgate (for the Bank)', in unfinished condition, on 12 July 1875, all Metropolitan and MDR trains formerly terminating at Moorgate Street ran into it and the GER connection was never again used for regular workings[9].

At Bishopsgate there were three platform roads, all signalled for arrival or departure, as well as a siding between the bay road and the southern retaining wall. There was also a locomotive siding, with engine pits, water cranes and coaling stages in the south west corner between the platform ends and the tunnel headwall. Offices and shops were completed in 1877 over the platforms to generate income from commercial letting. In collaboration with the SER, (Watkin pulling the strings) a feeder horse-bus service began on 3 January 1876 between Liverpool Street and Cannon Street via the Bank. Just over a quarter of a mile (26¾ chains) of new line had been added, together with the new station and the 3½ chain curve to the GER for £541,489, of which only £138, 973 was construction cost.

At this time the Metropolitan's administrative staff were housed at a number of small sites, mainly in the area of Paddington station[10]. Watkin sensibly suggested they should be brought together and having failed to persuade the GER to find space in its new Liverpool Street building, he sought to get his fellow directors to agree to a new headquarters on Metropolitan land at Liverpool Street station – 'one roof, the master's eye, the concentration of business, economy of staff, all point to removing to Liverpool Street.' But this proved to be one of the very rare occasions when his will did not prevail, principally because some of the directors found it inconvenient to attend board meetings at Liverpool Street, though at least one was held there, in August 1876.

Another Watkin proposal that came to nothing was the Metropolitan Grand Hotel over Moorgate Street station, which was rebuilt for the extension. An 80-bedroom hotel was designed by the architect W. I. Green in 1873–4 but although steps were taken to form a separate company to launch it, neither Metropolitan shareholders nor other investors showed much inclination to contribute and nothing was done.

Pushed by Watkin, the board consented to going on as far as the north side of Aldgate High Street. Finding the Kelk & Lucas estimate too high, Watkin brought in Francis Brady, the SER's engineer, to check it, then engaged him in July 1875 to supervise and execute the works 'without prejudice' to Wilson's position as consulting engineer. As the SER had found it an economy when building its extension east from Greenwich, Brady recommended the use of cement concrete instead of bricks for retaining walls. With his advice, the contractors were persuaded to reduce their estimate and work started on 1 March 1876. There were two incidents of note. A thick stratum of bullocks' horns was encountered at one point, 20ft below the surface, a ready sale being found for the several hundred cartloads removed. On 6 September 1876 there was a serious accident at Devonshire Street when an unequally-loaded arch collapsed, killing four men. Apart from the underpinning of the St Katharine's Dock Company's tea warehouses and some other buildings, there were no other difficulties.

Double track was laid with the Metropolitan's now standard 86lb per yd bullhead steel rails, in 24ft lengths resting on 39lb cast iron chairs keyed outside the rails with oak keys. Red fir transverse sleepers rested on gravel ballast one foot deep. The steepest gradient was 1 in 268. There were no less than five separate tunnels, all built in brickwork, the longest 195 yd. At Aldgate the rails were 28ft below street level but elsewhere average depth was 17ft. 'Large and very pretty with shops, waiting and refreshment rooms, lavatories and all conveniences', the terminus on the north side of Aldgate High Street had two platforms, each with a line either side, but that on the easternmost side (no 1 road) was not available to passenger trains pending possession of Bull Yard to complete the works. Half the platform length was sheltered by an overall roof resting on the side walls. As the start of the first tunnel was about 200ft from the booking office, this was thought by *The Engineer* to be 'one of the best ventilated stations on the Metropolitan.' At the approach to the station, on the west side, was a 40-lever signal box with five spare levers, its equipment and construction by Saxby & Farmer.

From 18 November 1876 a shuttle service was worked to and from Bishopsgate[11] but all Metropolitan and MDR trains worked through to Aldgate from 4 December. The station was completed with the opening of no 1 road on 11 September 1877. As part of the new works, the Metropolitan was obliged to rebuild the Three Nuns hotel in Aldgate High Street, whose tenant was engaged to run the station refreshment room. This new building, with its clock tower designed by Tarring & Wilkinson was completed in 1878.

Very soon after the opening of the station there were strong complaints about the effects of discharging hot water from locomotive condensing tanks into the sewers at Aldgate. Some 218,000 gallons of water at 200°F were entering the drains every 24 hours, at a rate of 10,000 gallons an hour between 8 am and 9 pm. This caused steam to rise through the road grilles to frighten the horses, but far worse, it belched up through the untrapped water closets of neighbouring properties, bringing with it 'offensive effluvia which are injurious to health'. This stench made it virtually impossible for the sewer men to carry out normal maintenance. Legal action was initiated against the railway by the Commissioners of Sewers but eventually the problem was satisfactorily resolved at the Metropolitan's expense by constructing a special sewer to carry the hot water directly to the Thames. Not including this extra item, the total outlay on the 28.27 chains extension was £343,500, of which £253,500 was for property.

NO MERGER WITH THE DISTRICT

Some influential shareholders had begun to worry about the board's seeming lack of interest in what they saw as a logical merger with the MDR likely to bring savings and general benefits. A. G. Kitching, who coveted but did not get a seat on the board for many years, formed a committee in the summer of 1874 to press for such an amalgamation. Watkin told him that it would only benefit the MDR, and brought all his influence to secure defeat of Kitching's motion by a large majority at the half-yearly meeting on 31 July. Despite this, Watkin did approach Forbes with Kitching's proposal, embellishing it with the comment:

> At present the position of antagonism of the two companies can only lead to the depletion of each; for neither body of shareholders will, I take it, sit down and leave what they deem to be aggression, unrequited. A union would lead to a single policy, protective of the entire interest, and to some economy, in which all the shareholders would participate.

After asking whether Forbes was ready to favour such an outcome, he went on to say that he was willing to retire if Forbes were to be chosen by an amalgamated board as its chairman, saying:

I joined the Metropolitan from no personal consideration, in the hope of retrieving its fortunes, so far as past mistakes rendered it possible . . . I did hope, also, to see the two companies united, and the Circle completed by their joint efforts and without the waste and effort of an intermediate party of professional men and contractors. In these two objects, I have, I admit, so far failed.

(The 'aggression' referred to was the MDR's extension to Hammersmith, of which more in a moment.) Forbes' reply was regarded by Watkin as unhelpful. By February 1875 even Kitching had concluded that Forbes' professions in favour of amalgamation were 'utterly insincere' and 'nothing is further from his intentions than allowing it to come to pass'. As for Forbes, he told the MDR half yearly meeting in the same month 'we are all agreed about amalgamation, but we cannot agree about the price'. At later meetings, he explained his reasons for rejecting Watkin's suggestions of arbitration on the price by references to Watkin as a 'very clever man', capable of swinging round any arbitrator. Surprisingly this specious reasoning went without question.

The MDR extension from Earls Court to Hammersmith Broadway of 9 September 1874 was a boost to that company's low morale and of course in direct competition with the Metropolitan and GWR Hammersmith & City service. By making use of the LSWR's Kensington to Richmond line, this Hammersmith link was later to form the springboard for MDR extensions to Richmond, Ealing, Hounslow and, eventually, Harrow, drawing in commuter traffic from an extensive area of west London and Middlesex over the MDR to the City to create a slight upturn in the company's fortunes and make it a more difficult fruit for the Metropolitan to pick off. A further irritation was a revision of MDR fares concurrent with its opening to Hammersmith, forcing the Metropolitan to reduce some of its rates.

In response to the 'Hammersmith Aggression', the Metropolitan started an hourly service between Aldgate and Richmond on 1 October 1877, working via the Hammersmith & City line and its 1870 connection to the LSWR Kensington-Richmond line, a link hitherto used only for three months in 1870 by a GWR Bishop's Road-Richmond service[12]. On the H&CR proper, traffic continued to grow at a satisfactory rate, bringing in an annual surplus for the joint operating companies. The GWR Middle Circle service (Chapter 4) provided a half-hourly service between Latimer Road and Westbourne Park from 1 August 1872 in addition to the Hammersmith-City trains, whilst in rush hours, two extra trains an hour were introduced in 1889 between Kensington (Addison Road) and Aldgate to relieve congestion between Hammersmith and the City. From 1 January 1894 the GWR and the Metropolitan each provided half the trains between Hammersmith and Aldgate, together giving a basic ten-minute service.

Disputes with the GWR regarding the use of Bishop's Road station, division of the H&CR receipts and other matters relating to the joint operation accumulated over the years. Eventually they were resolved by a lengthy arbitration award from Lord Herschell dated 3 August 1897. But that was not the end of squabbling between the two companies.

As the 1870s progressed, Watkin's attitude towards a merger with the MDR cooled considerably. When asked about the possibility by a fellow MP in 1876 he replied:

> This line is doing well – and has nothing to gain – tho' the public may have, by a union. Personally I have exhausted all proposals which seem to me reasonable and they have been refused – therefore I have nothing more to say at present, at least, unless some practicable proposal comes from the other side.

It is interesting to see public benefit so summarily dismissed in this cold war between the two railway barons. Nor did the public yet have the Inner Circle that parliament had deemed in its best interest. As will be seen in Chapter 7, some important steps had already been taken towards it, but they were made in a manner which only served to harden the postures of the two companies.

6

THE DRIVE NORTH-WEST, OR MAIN LINE MANOEUVRES

BREAKING THROUGH

Watkin's accession to power and influence in Metropolitan affairs in the summer of 1872 was to change the whole character of the railway. Hitherto, the means by which this change was achieved, the St John's Wood line, had been considered solely as a feeder to the 'main line' with no suggestion that it should be extended beyond the original destinations proposed: Hampstead village, and connections to the LNWR and Midland at West Hampstead. But to Watkin it quickly became 'our only conduit pipe to the north'[1] and the 22 years of his chairmanship were to be much occupied with ways of 'breaking through the circle of railways to the north', which, as he put it, prevented the Metropolitan 'from getting out into the country and shaking hands with any new or old neighbours who wanted to get their traffic through to London'[2].

This broadly expressed objective was a priority for Watkin, who preferred it to mere development of suburban outlets, as practised by the MDR from the mid-1870s. Such a policy would in any case have been attended by some risk, as in its surburban territory, actual and potential, the Metropolitan was uncomfortably close to powerful neighbours: the LNWR, the Midland, and to some extent, the GNR[3].

Watkin of course also wielded power on the boards of the MSLR and the SER and although not openly expressed for some years, his true long term intention was to join up these two railways to provide through communication between the Mersey and the Channel. In this the Metropolitan could play an important role. We have already noted the significance of his abortive approach to the GNR in the summer of 1872 with the suggestion that that company and the SER should jointly take over the Metropolitan. This was followed by a private revelation of his thoughts to W. P. Price, chairman of the Midland Railway:

> . . . undoubtedly my policy will be, if other arrangements are not made between the Great Northern, the Midland and the Sheffield, and some of them are not one, and I live so long, to connect the new Sheffield line with the Metropolitan and extend it thro' London to a junction with the South Eastern[4].

But if the Metropolitan were to be so used, it would need to be brought out into the gap between the GWR and LNWR trunk lines as they approached London. Watkin no doubt saw the idea of extension of the Metropolitan into this gap as a convenient deception, certainly a good deal easier than overcoming the opposition of the older main line companies to a new trunk line squeezing between them to get at the heart of London.

Having failed to achieve amalgamation between the MSLR and the GNR or the Midland, or to get the Lancashire & Yorkshire Railway interested in sharing a new main line to London, by the end of the 1880s Watkin was trying to persuade his fellow directors on the MSLR board to go it alone as far as the Metropolitan's outer end. The first mention of such a prospect in the surviving Metropolitan papers is in a letter from the engineer Charles Liddell to Watkin dated 6 July 1888 in which he refers to getting the Metropolitan and linked lines 'nearer to the MSLR'.

By popular legend, Watkin is alleged to have nursed an even grander ambition than the MSLR/SER link: through trains from Manchester to Paris and beyond via the MSLR, the Metropolitan, the ELR, the SER and the proposed Channel Tunnel, in all of whose boardrooms he exercised influence. But if this were true, it seems unlikely to have crystallised in his mind until the MSLR was at last set on its way to London in the early 1890s, by which time his energies were spent. There is certainly no hint of such a proposal in the very large quantity of Metropolitan Railway papers which have been preserved.

To find the origins of the Metropolitan's distinctly curious geography we have to go back to 23 September 1868, five months after the opening of the St John's Wood line. On that day, a company called the Aylesbury & Buckingham Railway started a service, worked by the GWR, over a 12¾ mile single line between Aylesbury, where it was to share a station with the GWR, and Verney Junction, on the Buckinghamshire Railway's Bletchley to Banbury line, which was worked and leased by the LNWR. These trains called intermediately at Quainton Road, Grandborough Road and Winslow Road. Even before they started to run, the Aylesbury & Buckingham had considered an extension towards London through the Missenden Valley[5]. Watkin would have known of this, and it sowed a seed which would germinate.

Very soon after his arrival on the Metropolitan board, Watkin formed the view that the only way of making anything of the St John's Wood Railway lay in its extension, or in junctions with the Midland

and the LNWR to bring those companies' trains on to the Metropolitan. The latter prospect did not appeal to either of the trunk line companies, but in the early 1870s much of the land around Willesden Green, just outside the London building frontier, and other land between Willesden Green and the Finchley Road, came on to the market for house building. This offered an interesting possibility of traffic development, especially as the LNWR, whose territory it was, showed little or no enthusiasm for suburban business. We have seen how the Metropolitan was at this time working towards outright purchase of the St John's Wood line; in 1874 Watkin had identified its value as the means of getting the Metropolitan out towards the north and he deemed it worth a sacrifice to secure it, eliminating what he described as 'an *imperium in imperio*'. His feelings must have been mixed when, on Forbes' advice, the still independent St John's Wood board sought powers to extend through the new building district to Kingsbury (now Neasden), to double the existing line, and to make junctions with the Midland and the LNWR. Parliament authorised all this in the Metropolitan & Saint John's Wood Railway Act of 21 July 1873 and negotiations for the acquisition of land as far as the Edgware Road were begun in the first half of 1875.

Meanwhile Watkin had been parleying with the Duke of Buckingham and was able to report to his fellow Metropolitan directors on 10 September 1873 on a scheme to link the Kingsbury extension of the St John's Wood Railway with the proposed London & Aylesbury Railway, a scheme authorised in 1871, which was to run from Aylesbury to the LNWR-worked Watford to Rickmansworth line. It was settled with the Duke (who was something of a railway promoter) that the London & Aylesbury would apply in the 1873–4 session for powers to build from Rickmansworth to Harrow, whilst the St John's Wood would seek authority for a Kingsbury to Harrow extension to meet it. In the event the Kingsbury & Harrow bill, for a 4½ mile line from the river Brent to Harrow (a town poorly-served by an outlying LNWR main line station) was promoted jointly by the Metropolitan & St John's Wood Railway and the Metropolitan Railway. It received royal assent on 16 July 1874. The Rickmansworth and Harrow extension of the London & Aylesbury was also successful.

This only for a start. Watkin was now enmeshed in an even more ambitious concept, evolved in the previous year by the Duke and others. In June 1874 the Metropolitan board was told of the establishment of an association to complete a new and independent route to the north, making use of the St John's Wood, the Kingsbury & Harrow, the Aylesbury & Buckingham (with which they had already made agreement) and other existing and proposed lines. At the subsequent half-yearly meeting the no doubt astonished Metropolitan shareholders were regaled with vague hints of a 'breakthrough' to Northampton and Birmingham. This was hardly the Metropolitan Railway they knew and loved. And although it was a bubble soon burst to disappear without trace, the Buckinghamshire & Northamptonshire Railways Union bill thrown out by parliament in 1875 was a powerful portent. Its feet back on the ground, the Metropolitan decided to go on to Harrow anyway, despite the collapse of the London & Aylesbury. Watkin saw to that.

Although the extension to Kingsbury was formally promoted by the Metropolitan & St John's Wood Railway and that to Harrow jointly by that company and the Metropolitan, the latter was very much in the driving seat. It would be tedious indeed to recount in detail the complicated legal, statutory and financial relationships between the two companies, also it would be largely futile since they became irrelevant with the disappearance of the St John's Wood as a separate entity in 1882.

Watkin was again pursuing the idea of a railway between the Metropolitan and Aylesbury and beyond in 1875 when there was a bill before parliament for a line from Verney Junction to Towcester. To secure Metropolitan interests in the area, he and Myles Fenton, the Metropolitan general manager, got themselves on to the Aylesbury & Buckingham Railway board in March 1875 and Watkin briefly served as that company's chairman. In June a paper was prepared setting out the estimated cost of a railway from London to Verney Junction to form what was described as the first section of 'a new through route'. But for all Watkin's diplomacy, neither the Buckinghamshire landowners nor anyone else was at this time ready to find money for such a scheme.

SWISS COTTAGE TO WILLESDEN

Work now started on pushing the Metropolitan out of built-up London. As related in Chapter 3, the St John's Wood Railway had built 156 yards of its planned Hampstead extension beyond Swiss Cottage station. This single line tunnel was incorporated in the extension to Walm Lane, Willesden, begun by the contractor Joseph Firbank in 1878. Later that year Firbank was instructed to carry the works on to the river Brent, using the spoil from the Walm Lane contract to form an embankment. Signalling work, including the above-ground elements of the signal boxes, was given to Saxby &

Farmer, with Spagnoletti undertaking the telegraph installation. Apart from completion of the cut and cover tunnels between Swiss Cottage and the south end of Finchley Road station and a long brick viaduct between the LNWR crossing and Kilburn station, the construction was fairly straightforward railway-making in open country. Charles Liddell was the engineer for this line and all subsequent work out to Aylesbury.

Watkin tried to hurry Firbank as he wanted the line open in time for the Royal Agricultural Society's show at Kilburn in the summer of 1879, but long frosts in the winter of 1878–9 followed by very wet weather delayed the works, despite 24-hour activity on the viaduct. In an endeavour to reap something from the show traffic, a single line was opened on 30 June 1879 as far as West Hampstead with the stations and other works far from finished. One train was used, giving a ten-minute service between Swiss Cottage and West Hampstead, calling at a temporary platform at Finchley Road and carrying a somewhat superfluous pilotman. West End Lane was crossed by two other railways, the Midland and the LNWR's Hampstead Junction line, but the Metropolitan's West Hampstead station was the first of what were eventually three adjoining stations at this point.

The double track through to the station at Willesden Green, together with the almost-completed buildings and platforms at Finchley Road, West Hampstead and Kilburn & Brondesbury stations, came into public service on 24 November 1879. Street buildings were designed by A. McDermott in a heavy-handed *cottage-orné* style replete with mock timbering and massive chimneys. Finchley Road, somewhat larger than the others, had accommodation above the street entrance as well as a refreshment room. Platforms, at first given only minimal shelter from the elements, were brick-paved for only a part of their length. No provision was made for freight until 1894 (at Finchley Road and Neasden) and 1899 (at Willesden Green). By 1903 there were also sidings at West Hampstead. All these goods facilities were on the north side of the line.

Tracks were laid on a 30ft formation with 86lb bullhead rail in 24ft lengths resting on shingle and burnt clay ballast. When the contractor faced a shortage of ballast, Watkin, in his anxiety to get the line open had shingle expensively brought from the SER-owned beach at Dungeness.

Although some house-building had started on the Ecclesiastical Commissioners' Mapesbury Estate (immediately south of Kilburn station), on the British Land Company's Iverson Road Estate at West Hampstead, and on the United Land Company's Netherwood Estate (south of the line between West Hampstead and Kilburn), traffic was at first very thin. In an effort to beat up a little business on Sundays, cheap 6d return tickets were issued from City stations as far as West Hampstead from August 1879, the first of many Metropolitan 'country excursion' facilities.

In November 1879 the Metropolitan deposited a bill for a further extension of 7 miles 18 chains from Harrow to Rickmansworth via Pinner and Northwood, alleging that it was to meet a threatened MDR scheme for an Ealing-Harrow-Rickmansworth line. This bill became the Rickmansworth Extension Railway Act of 6 August 1880. In evidence before the parliamentary committee, firm intentions were expressed to press on towards Aylesbury and to carry freight traffic. The next session of parliament saw bills for a 21½ mile extension from Rickmansworth to a junction with the Aylesbury & Buckingham at Aylesbury and one for an LNWR line from Rickmansworth to Chesham. Watkin started discussions with the LNWR in which he suggested a joint line between Rickmansworth and Chesham, but this came to nothing. The Aylesbury and Rickmansworth Railway was authorised on 18 July 1881 but the LNWR scheme was rejected. Purchase of land for the Aylesbury line began at the end of 1881.

COAL AND QUEEN ANNE FOR HARROW

In March 1879 the Metropolitan board authorised a start on works between the River Brent and Harrow. Firbank was again the contractor with signalling and telegraphs by the trusted Saxby & Farmer and Spagnoletti. No difficulties were encountered apart from the now familiar problems of working through the heavy and sticky Middlesex clay, and from 2 August 1880 31 trains ran each way daily between Baker Street and Harrow-on-the-Hill.

In deference to historic Harrow, the main entrance to the new station was on the south side of the line. Here was a large cab yard which was left unpaved until the resultant evil odours brought complaints from passengers. Perhaps as a tribute to the status of the little town, a vaguely Queen Anne style was used for the long single-storey building with its imposing triangular pediment enclosing a large clock over the entrance. Entrance hall and waiting rooms were decorated with painted dados, coloured bricks and stained glass windows. McDermott was probably the architect, both here and at Neasden.

Harrow also boasted locomotive and carriage sheds and the company's first coal yard. The Harrow Gas Company was persuaded to transfer its coal traffic from the LNWR and after completion of the permanent connection between the two lines at Finchley Road on 1 October 1880 coal was brought in via the Midland Railway. An inaugural train on 13 October marked not only the opening of freight traffic on the Extension Line, but the first freight movement by the Metropolitan on its own account.

An intermediate station was built 1¼ miles beyond Willesden Green at the point where Neasden Lane crossed the line. Its building on the road overbridge, labelled KINGSBURY NEASDEN METROPOLITAN RAILWAY and adorned with the company's coat of arms, was in the same *cottage orné* style as its predecessors, a curious mixture of mock timbering, ornamental ironwork, hipped gables and wide chimneys. An attempt was made to build up traffic on 1 October 1880 when a bus service was started to and from The Red Lion at Harlesden, in LNWR territory, but the service was unsuccessful and short-lived (see Appendix 5). Another move to provide business at this isolated spot was the lease in December 1882 of a little over 16 acres of railway-owned land for 21 years at £100 a year to the Willesden professional cricketer W. L. Morley. He established a cricket field and recreation, athletics and cycling grounds which were joined to the station by paths made at Metropolitan expense in 1883, but the site had to be given up for the MSLR depot a few years later.

Ballast on the extension was burnt clay and gravel, the track in other respects to the same specifications as that to Willesden Green. A major engineering feature of the 5 miles 37½ chains of new line was a 66ft 2in span skew bridge over the LNWR main line. There were signal boxes at Neasden (20 levers, 11 spare) and Harrow (16 levers, 4 spare). Harrow was initially worked as a single track terminal, using the platform on the down or south side.

In his report, the Board of Trade Inspector pertinently observed 'the extension of the Metropolitan Railway to Harrow introduces an entirely different state of things. This new line, practically speaking, is not a Metropolitan Railway.' His concern was that tank locomotives were going to run bunker-first on the long stretches of 1 in 94 down between Harrow and what is now Preston Road with a clear run of some 4¼ miles between Harrow and Neasden. The Metropolitan protested strongly, averring the trains would not exceed 25 mph, and other railways were shown to be using tank locomotives on faster runs over longer distances without turning, but the Board of Trade insisted upon turntables being provided at Harrow and Baker Street East. Whilst a 30ft turntable was ordered for Harrow in September 1880 and the old gas works site at Baker Street East was cleared for a turntable, there is no evidence that one was ever provided at the London end.

Including stations, the cost of the 7 miles 51 chains between Swiss Cottage and Harrow was £271,966; when Firbank complained he had not had a sufficient profit margin and sought compensation his pleas were ignored. Houses for clerks-in-charge and inspectors at the Extension stations proved to be necessary owing to lack of suitable local accommodation and were provided in 1881 to Tomlinson's designs at £620 a pair.

A NEW DEPOT: AND THE BEGINNINGS OF METRO-LAND

Quite apart from fulfilling Watkin's grand strategic design, there were matters of more immediate moment for the Metropolitan in extending into the fields beyond the Finchley Road. Its original depot at Edgware Road, where workshops had been added in 1872-3, was much too cramped and inadequate for the needs of the expanding railway. Some rolling stock had to be stabled overnight and undergo its routine cleaning and maintenance at sidings east of Farringdon Street station, where sheds had been erected to hold 14 carriages. When land purchases were started for the Kingsbury extension in the summer of 1875 the board was told that it would be 'more economical and desirable' to buy large parcels of grassland totalling 377 acres either side of the line at Willesden Green and Kingsbury rather than purchase piecemeal under notice. This was accepted and negotiations began with the Ecclesiastical Commissioners and another owner.

One of the purchases provided an extensive area either side of the proposed line immediately east of the River Brent between what are now Neasden and Wembley Park stations. It was here that the board decided in 1880 to build new carriage shops immediately north of the alignment. That November a contract was awarded to John Garlick of Saltley Works, Birmingham, who used bricks made from the clay on the site. Two Cowans-Sheldon carriage traversers were ordered in 1881 for delivery in time for the opening of the depot early in 1882.

As there was no accommodation in this quite rural area for the employees coming out from London, 102 cottages of three grades 'with gardens and convenient back premises' serviced by ten shops with living space over were completed in 1882. The houses were in two streets unimaginatively designated 'A' and 'B' until 1903, when they became Quainton and Verney Streets whilst the shops faced Neasden Lane. These properties were intended to be remunerative, their rents fixed to return 6½ per cent on the cost of construction.

As the workmen soon began to make use of their new privilege tickets to shop in Willesden or Kilburn, only five of the Neasden shops found tenants and in 1889 the board authorised conversion of the remainder to dwellings. By 1903 there was an off-licence and beer shop (the only prosperous business); a grocery; a haberdashery and post office; a confectioner's and bread shop; and a coffee and eating house. A schoolroom and mission church appeared in two of the shop buildings in 1883 after the railway company had contributed cash. In 1885 when there were 200 children in the railway community requiring education, the Metropolitan gave a site to the Wesleyan Church for the erection of a permanent day school at the corner of Neasden Lane and 'A' street.

More accommodation was needed when the electric power station was built for the railway and four semi-detached houses and 40 cottages were completed in the new Aylesbury Street during 1904–6. Finally another 202 semi-detached cottages, designed by the company's architect, C. W. Clark, were added in 1924–7, some of them of reinforced concrete construction. All dwellings at Neasden were fitted with electric light in 1929.

The original housing and other provision just described was also required for the staff of the locomotive repairing shops, whose removal to the same site was approved by the board in October 1881. In the following month the contract for erecting the new shops was given to B. N. Smith of Birmingham. Equipment included a traverser capable of carrying locomotives weighing up to 50 tons and a shunting tank locomotive supplied by Smith in March 1883 for £200[6]. Tomlinson had pointed out that if the drawing office and stores department at Edgware Road were also transferred to Neasden the accommodation released would be sufficient to enable all locomotives to be stabled there under cover at night for cleaning and running repairs. (Until this time locomotives had to stand on the main line or in siding space which might be required for a crippled train.) This was agreed, and the new facilities at Neasden, designed by Tomlinson, were finished early in 1883. They included a shed for ten engines but no carriage accommodation under cover[7].

Following complaints from residents about the nuisance created by the manufacture of gas for carriage lighting at Baker Street, a new gas works was provided on the Neasden site when the works were being built. Similar protests about gas production at Hammersmith and Bishopsgate brought about the closure of these plants, all such activity being concentrated at Neasden from 1884. Some of the Bishopsgate equipment was of course fairly new and this was rebuilt at Neasden in 1888 to provide a standby capacity. One of the early tasks for the new Neasden workshops was to build in 1888 a gas truck to carry two spare gas holders for replenishing stock stored in London. This was the result of a misunderstanding; similar trucks had been built earlier by Ashbury, and later ones were also provided by that firm.

Little time was lost in organising the development of much of the remaining surplus land for housing. Building leases on the Willesden Park Estate were on sale from the end of 1881. During the following year many houses were built and occupied, bringing some traffic to the adjoining station (Willesden Green). This was the true beginning of what was later to become known as Metro-land; the manner in which the surplus lands business was handled will be elaborated in Chapter 9.

BAKER STREET TO BIRMINGHAM – OR OXFORD?

During 1881 Watkin was engaged in yet another set of negotiations regarding lines north of Aylesbury. Ashurst, Morris & Co, agents for the promoters of a trunk line from Birmingham, Worcester and Northampton designed to enter London via the Aylesbury & Buckingham and the Metropolitan to Baker Street East, cheekily sought to exploit the Metropolitan's newly-acquired surplus lands in the Willesden area for house building. The latter was firmly refused and when they saw the Metropolitan's terms for the rest of the deal they found them unacceptable. This little setback did not stop Watkin from beguiling shareholders at the July 1882 meeting with visions of the Metropolitan as an integral part of future railway connections between the north and south of England. Honest enough, as it was always at the back of his mind, even if there was no immediate prospect of it happening, and it did help to hoist the value of the shares. Physically the London end was now ready to receive any newcomer that might appear. Doubling of the St John's Wood line between Baker Street and Swiss Cottage had been completed on 10 July 1882, with a new Saxby & Farmer signal box at Baker Street controlling the additional tracks.

Expansion in a new direction was raised in 1882 when a bill was deposited for an 11 mile 8 chain line from Brill, terminus of a 6½ mile tramroad branching from the Aylesbury & Buckingham at Quainton Road[8], to St Clement's, Oxford. John Aird Jr, the railway contractor, drew Watkin's attention to this proposal, his efforts succeeding in getting the Metropolitan to pay for referencing and surveying the route[9]. Pochin, a Metropolitan director, was also involved in the preliminary negotiations for the goods and passenger station site at Oxford. An integral part of the scheme was the reconstruction of the

Brill Tramway as a full scale railway, and the new company sought running powers over the Aylesbury & Buckingham. The Oxford, Aylesbury & Metropolitan Junction Railway was duly authorised on 20 August 1883, but although it had the support of the Duke of Buckingham & Chandos, Baron Ferdinand de Rothschild and Sir Harry Verney, influential landowners at its eastern end, it failed to attract investors. Revived as a more lightly-built line, to cost £50,000, terminating at Magdalen Bridge, Oxford, it received fresh statutory authority in an act of 7 August 1888, but again financial backing was not forthcoming. This Oxford & Aylesbury Tramroad Company as it was now called did however maintain a formal existence, purchasing some rolling stock and taking over the lease and working of the Brill line from 15 October 1894. It also obtained an extension of time for completion to Oxford in a further act of 27 June 1892, which envisaged the use of electric traction. A final act of 17 August 1894 sanctioned some deviations on the route between Brill and Oxford. By the end of that year the O&AT had reconstructed the shaky track of the original Brill line, also rebuilding the stations at Waddesdon, Westcott, Wotton, Wood Siding and Brill. After the acquisition of some rolling stock, an improved passenger service was worked between Brill and Quainton Road from January 1895.

Meanwhile Watkin continued tirelessly to pursue any railway promotions which seemed likely to feed into the Metropolitan from points north of Aylesbury. He was given virtually *carte blanche* by the Metropolitan board in May 1883 to offer subscriptions towards any promising schemes. One such appeared in November 1884, seeking Metropolitan support for a line linking Verney Junction with the East & West Junction Railway (later the Stratford-upon-Avon & Midland Junction) at Towcester. This proposal became the Banbury, Northampton & Metropolitan Junction Railway bill, towards which the Metropolitan contributed £500 for expenses. It failed.

ON STEEL SLEEPERS TO RICKMANSWORTH

At this time (1885) the contractor William Maxwell was constructing the line from Harrow to Rickmansworth and services as far as Pinner (2 miles 13 chains) began on 25 May. The station was an unpretentious single storey building on the north side of the line close to the High Street, with no architectural features. Its designer, like those of the other intermediate stations between Harrow and Aylesbury, receives no mention in contemporary papers; the choice of an architect, if one was used at all, was left to the engineer Charles

Liddell. Like the passenger building, the goods yard was on the village side of the line.

At Harrow all trains continued to use the down platform as the other had no shelter and there was no footbridge until 1886. With the extension, the goods yard here was resited on the north side[10].

With Maxwell's progress beyond Pinner slowed down by personal financial difficulties his contract was terminated in July 1886, the Metropolitan taking over the completion of the line. There were also delays in getting on to Lord Ebury's land, as arguments continued about the price to be paid. Following a court action, his lordship's claim for £12,500 for 23 acres of agricultural land was reduced to £6,845. From March 1886 the Metropolitan began to use Ebury's ballast pits at Batchworth. Sidings here were to survive for the rest of the Metropolitan's existence and some years after that.

An hourly service to Rickmansworth began on 1 September 1887 supplemented by a daily coal train each way which was restricted to 12 wagons in wet weather, otherwise 16. Following successful trials starting in January 1884 at locations near King's Cross and Notting Hill Gate[11], about 3½ miles between Northwood and Rickmansworth were laid with steel sleepers, known to the navvies as 'pig troughs'.

At Rickmansworth, where all trains used the up platform pending further extension, there was a locomotive turntable (probably that formerly at Harrow), goods sidings and a goods shed[12]. The intermediate station at Northwood, 2½ miles beyond Pinner, had a three-road goods yard. Station buildings were rather plain single storey structures featuring generous and decorative canopies over the platforms. Pinner's signal cabin had 24 levers (2 spare), Northwood's 20 (plus 5 spare) and Rickmansworth's 14 (plus 11). As elsewhere on the Extension Line, starting and advance starting signals were electrically-controlled from the station in advance.

Although the *Financial News* thought the new addition likely to prove a flop and the initial traffic was indeed very light (Rickmansworth's population was only just over 1,800 and Northwood's considerably less) it is interesting to note that almost all the 53 building plots adjoining Northwood station found purchasers in the first sale of this kind in the district in September 1887. Commuter traffic at Rickmansworth could have been no more than a trickle at this time, yet the LNWR, which had worked a branch from Watford since 1862, was sufficiently aroused to improve its services. A 'new express' was operated from Watford at 8 am in connection with the 7.50 am departure from Rickmansworth, arriving at Euston at 8.27 and at Broad Street, after division at Willesden Junction, at 8.45. Two

LNWR trains each way at peak hours were also given through London coaches from the time the Metropolitan line opened.

In 1886 it was decided to build to Aylesbury, but to go only as far as Chesham in the first instance[13]. There had been some agitation from the Chesham townspeople who feared they might be fobbed off with a station on the Aylesbury line purporting to serve them. As this town of some 6,500 population had several thriving industries (woodware, boot and shoe making, brush making, straw plaiting, brewing and watercress growing) it promised useful freight traffic and this no doubt influenced the decision to build a line of 2 miles 39½ chains into the town itself, a line which would eventually form a branch from the main route. Watkin looked towards the LNWR at Tring and the extension (authorised by the Metropolitan Railway Act of 16 July 1885) was laid out to facilitate future extension in that direction. It was decided to construct a double track for the five miles beyond Rickmansworth, then a single one into Chesham, taking enough land for four on the through section and two on the branch. Firbank started work late in 1887.

With the appearance of new houses close to Willesden Green station (at first mostly on the Metropolitan land) and new housing developments advancing at Kilburn, at West Hampstead and between there and Swiss Cottage, traffic at the London end of the Extension Line was now producing steadily increasing receipts. Business grew sufficiently to justify an additional coach on peak hour trains after Marlborough Road platforms had been lengthened to 260ft early in 1887. By 1888 even rural Neasden had 150 season ticket holders, who were petitioning for the ten-minute Willesden Green-Baker Street East service to be extended to their station. All in all, the Extension Line was seen as something of a success, the half-yearly report for December 1889 noting that it was neutralising 'the serious depletion of traffic on the parent line caused by competition – at ruinous fares – between rival omnibus companies'. This competition particularly affected stations between King's Cross and Paddington and in an attempt to break it, the Metropolitan established omnibus services alongside those of the London General Omnibus Company and the London Road Car Company (see Appendix 5).

MORE MAIN LINE MANOEUVRES

Between the beginning of 1888 and the end of 1890 there was much activity in relation to Watkin's ambitions for the Metropolitan. At first he affected some hesitation about building beyond Chalfont Road (now Chalfont & Latimer and the point of divergence for Chesham), hoping and trying to induce others to meet the Metropolitan there. But in July 1888, Liddell, who was much occupied at this time in surveying possible northward routes from Verney Junction, recommended Watkin to support a scheme for a link between Chalfont Road and the East & West Junction Railway at Moreton Pinkney, using the Aylesbury & Buckingham as far as Quainton Road. This he said 'would bring you nearer to the MSLR by 45 miles at insignificant outlay', providing the Metropolitan with the shortest route between London and Aylesbury, Brackley, Stratford-upon-Avon, Worcester and Droitwich.

Watkin did not take much convincing. By August he had persuaded the Metropolitan board to sanction a start on the line to Aylesbury, raising the capital separately from the general undertaking[14]. It also agreed to negotiations towards taking over and working the Aylesbury & Buckingham. The requisite issue of £350,000 at four per cent, guaranteed by the Metropolitan Railway, was made in 1892.

To cover these moves, the Metropolitan deposited a bill for the 1888–9 session, when Parliament also had to consider a bill for a line from Moreton Pinkney to Aylesbury (the Worcester & Metropolitan Direct Railway) and another for a Towcester & Buckingham Railway. The Worcester & Metropolitan had been promoted by the Railways & General Company with strong support from the Metropolitan, and backing from Firbank, whilst the Towcester & Buckingham, to Watkin's chagrin, was supported by the main Buckinghamshire landowners, whom he had imagined to be on his side. This railway sought running powers over the LNWR between Buckingham and Verney Junction then over the Aylesbury & Buckingham. Also in this session there was an MSLR bill for a line from Beighton, near Sheffield to Annesley, Nottinghamshire, ostensibly to gain access to the Nottinghamshire & Derbyshire coalfield, but in truth its first thrust Londonwards. Watkin saw to it that Pollitt, the MSLR general manager, was closely involved in the Worcester & Metropolitan Direct negotiations as this line was a piece of the jigsaw puzzle he was now assembling in earnest. Then things went slightly wrong. After it had agreed to allow running powers to the Metropolitan, the Towcester & Buckingham was authorised by Parliament and the Watkin-backed Worcester & Metropolitan Direct was thrown out. However the Metropolitan's own bill was passed and the MSLR got its line to Annesley. To secure the withdrawal of GWR and A&BR opposition, the Metropolitan had been obliged to delete the clause giving it running powers to Verney Junction but negotiations continued with the A&BR with a result that rendered this only a temporary setback. On 13 November 1889 an agreement was signed which provided that the Metropolitan would purchase the bankrupt A&BR outright in 1891, using £100,000 of the three per cent Guaranteed Stock created specifically for this purpose.

This much settled, Watkin was now determined to push ahead relentlessly with the MSLR London extension, even though he failed to get the GNR cooperation he had sought and knew he faced powerful opposition. At least he could get the Metropolitan and the SER alongside him; in an agreement signed with the SER and the MSLR on 18 January 1890, the Metropolitan was promised contributions of £50,000 from each towards the cost of its Aylesbury extension, in return for running powers. Watkin's grand concept envisaged that once the MSLR had got its London powers, there would be an amalgamation of some sort with the Metropolitan and SER, the East London Railway providing the necessary physical link across the Thames. In the month this agreement was signed, Firbank was given the contract for the final northern extension of the Metropolitan.

At their February 1890 meeting, the Metropolitan shareholders learned of their company's new role: 'No board', Watkin proudly announced, 'ever brought their shareholders a more valuable present than we bring you today.' Suitably filled with awe, they approved the running powers for the MSLR between Quainton Road and London. On 10 June, the two general managers settled an MSLR bill for the 1890–1 session covering the construction of a 92¼ mile line surveyed earlier by Liddell between Annesley and Quainton Road via Nottingham, Leicester, Rugby and Brackley to a junction on to the A&BR at Quainton Road, with running powers inwards. A formal agreement between the two companies of 18 December 1890 referred to these running powers extending to Baker Street East, but Liddell had already pointed out the advisability of constructing a separate London terminus for the MSLR alongside Baker Street station, with its own approach tracks paralleling the St John's Wood line inwards from Finchley Road and this was soon accepted. The 1890 agreement also awarded the Metropolitan four per cent interest on all capital it expended on facilities for the newcomer until its London Extension was fully open for public traffic.

The Drive North-West, or Main Line Manoeuvres

METROPOLITAN AT CHESHAM

Whilst these exciting developments were occurring, Firbank had completed the 8 miles 16 chains from Rickmansworth to Chesham. Public service started on 8 July 1889, using a station nearer the centre of the town than originally planned, thanks to a gift of land organised by local interests. This 71 chain extension had been authorised by the Metropolitan Railway Act of 5 July 1889.

At Chesham there was a single side platform and the much-travelled turntable, the tracks running beyond to a goods yard carefully aligned for the proposed Tring extension. Two stations were provided intermediately, both with goods yards: Chorley Wood; and Chalfont Road (now Chalfont & Latimer), the latter with a bay road on the up side to accommodate a shuttle service over the 3 miles 56 chains of single track into Chesham. Permanent way construction followed the same pattern as that of the earlier extensions but steel sleepers were not perpetuated. Signal boxes were at Chesham (20 levers and five spare), Rickmansworth (20, 5), Chorley Wood (19, 6) and Chalfont Road (22, 8).

Much to Watkin's distress, opposition from the Midland and GNR and local interests in St John's Wood secured rejection of the MSLR London Extension bill. His not inconsiderable diplomatic skills now called into play for what was virtually the last time, he so arranged matters that a second and similar bill passed through parliament, obtaining royal assent on 18 March 1893. This included a connection between the approach tracks to the Marylebone passenger terminus and the Inner Circle between Edgware Road and Baker Street, over which the MSLR intended to carry freight to and from a new depot in the City. Construction of the MSLR approach tracks between Finchley Road (Canfield Place) and the new Marylebone terminus was started late in 1894.

AYLESBURY AT LAST

Although its line to Aylesbury was not yet ready, the Metropolitan took over the A&BR on 1 July 1891 under the powers given in its act of 25 July 1890 and the agreement mentioned earlier. For the time being the GWR continued to provide locomotives and stock for the sparse weekdays-only service to Verney Junction. At the latter, the Metropolitan purchased just over 22 acres from Sir Harry Verney for a modest £100 an acre 'to be independent of the LNWR'.

The 16 miles 21 chains double track line from Chalfont Road to Aylesbury was opened on 1 September 1892 with intermediate stations and goods yards at Amersham, Great Missenden, Wendover and Stoke Mandeville[15]. Land had been taken for four tracks. There were signal boxes at Chalfont Road (30 levers), Amersham (24), Great Missenden (24), Wendover (23), Stoke Mandeville (21) and Aylesbury (13). As elsewhere, starting signals were interlocked electrically by the signal box in advance, placing control of train starting with the signal-men, who were responsible for seeing they did not leave before the scheduled time.

Track on the extension consisted of 24ft bullhead steel rails at 86lb per yd on 39lb cast iron chairs with outside key clip fishplates. Creosoted timber sleepers 9ft×10in×5in, nine to a rail length, were laid for 11¼ miles and steel sleepers, 8ft 4in×8in top, 13in base, nine to a rail length, for five miles. Ballast was made up from hard chalk, broken flints and gravel. Apart from a 20 chain radius curve at Aylesbury, the minimum was 63 chains whilst the steepest gradient was 1 in 105.

With the Metropolitan and the GWR locked in arguments over the terms for use of the joint GWR/A&BR station at Aylesbury, and the necessary rearrangement of tracks there, the Metropolitan trains at first used a temporary wooden platform at Brook Street. They were admitted to the Joint station on 1 January 1894 but could not operate beyond as the Metropolitan possessed no locomotives light enough to run over the weak bridges on the A&BR. When the GWR was asked to continue the Verney Junction workings, it refused, alleging Metropolitan unfriendliness (one of the periodic rows between the two companies was pursuing its weary course). Arrangements were there-fore hurriedly made with the LNWR, which provided suitable loco-motives to work the Verney Junction trains from 2 April 1894. Two Metropolitan 2-4-0T, especially purchased for the task, were brought into use from 1 February 1895.

At the Aylesbury Joint station, the GWR erected a new signal box with 44 levers, sharing the cost with the Metropolitan. This box controlled the junction between the two companies' lines, the junction with the GWR Princes Risborough line and the main goods yard. The Metropolitan freight sidings on the London side of the junction, known as Aylesbury East, were then controlled from an enlarged 34-lever Metropolitan cabin of that name on the site of the temporary station. There were also Metropolitan sidings (Hartwell Sidings) on the down side of the A&BR north of the Joint station, as well as sharing of the main goods yard.

In the summer of 1890 Watkin fell ill, recovering sufficiently to resume, at the age of 71, his ceaseless regimen of work. This illness

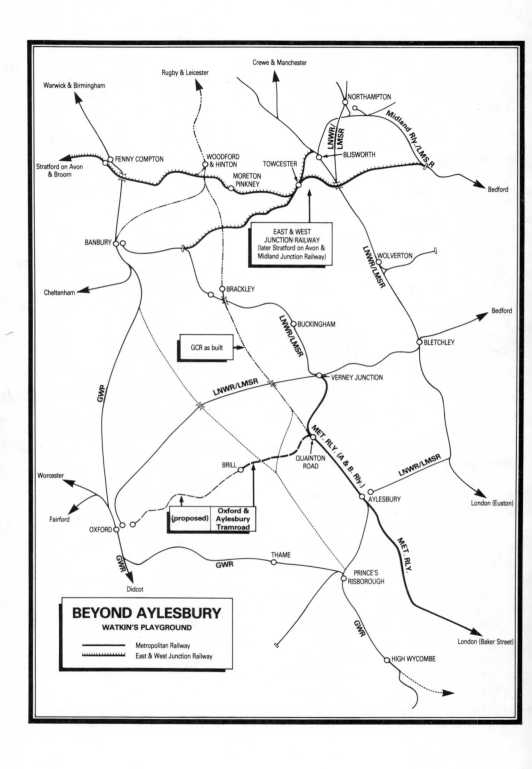

Warwick & Birmingham

Rugby & Leicester

Crewe & Manchester

NORTHAMPTON

Midland Rly./LMS.R

LNWR/ LMSR

FENNY COMPTON

WOODFORD & HINTON

TOWCESTER

BLISWORTH

Stratford on Avon & Broom

MORETON PINKNEY

Bedford

EAST & WEST JUNCTION RAILWAY (later Stratford on Avon & Midland Junction Railway)

BANBURY

WOLVERTON

LNWR/LMSR

Cheltenham

BRACKLEY

BUCKINGHAM

Bedford

GCR as built

BLETCHLEY

LNWR/LMSR

GWR

LNWR/LMSR

VERNEY JUNCTION

MET. RLY. (A & B. Rly.)

QUAINTON ROAD

LNWR/LMSR

Worcester

BRILL

London (Euston)

Fairford

(proposed)

Oxford & Aylesbury Tramroad

AYLESBURY

OXFORD

GWR

THAME

GWR

PRINCE'S RISBOROUGH

MET. RLY.

Didcot

BEYOND AYLESBURY

WATKIN'S PLAYGROUND

———— Metropolitan Railway
╥╥╥╥╥╥ East & West Junction Railway

GWR

London (Baker Street)

HIGH WYCOMBE

proved a harbinger. In the early part of 1894 his active participation in the affairs of the Metropolitan, the MSLR, the SER and the ELR was brought to a sudden end by a stroke. He was obliged to resign all his chairmanships in May, including that of the Metropolitan, which he had held for 22 years. He remained a director, too weak to take any active part in business, until his death on 13 April 1901.

VERNEY JUNCTION AND BRILL

In its agreement with the MSLR, the Metropolitan had undertaken to double the A&BR, rebuilding all its stations to main line standards. This was authorised by the Metropolitan Railway Act of 25 July 1890 and the contract was given to Firbank in November 1894. Engineering was in the hands of Edward Richards, partner of Liddell, who had died that August. All the bridges over roads and watercourses required reconstruction and no less than 22 level crossings were eliminated, leaving just two, at Winslow Road and Grandborough Road stations. Ballast was brought from the Chess valley alongside the Chesham branch for the new formation. During this work, which was completed through to Verney Junction on 1 January 1897[16], the normal train service was continued. Expenditure on the Quainton Road to Verney Junction section was not justified by existing or potential traffic, but the work was done to the same standards and the Metropolitan also contributed to a substantial rebuilding of the LNWR station at Verney Junction. Here its trains were accommodated at the southern face of the island platform on the south side. Three exchange sidings were built east of the station on the south side on the land bought from Sir Harry Verney. The only connection between the two companies' lines was a crossover at the Oxford end of the station, controlled, with the sidings, from a new Metropolitan signal box at the Aylesbury end. Metropolitan Yard Box, manned as required, was also provided at the east end of the new sidings.

As stipulated in the legislation, an additional station called Waddesdon Manor (Waddesdon from 1 October 1922) was erected at Lapstones between Aylesbury and Quainton Road, opening with the double line on 1 January 1897.

Electric telegraphs in the new signal boxes at each station, and at the junctions, were installed by Spagnoletti. In anticipation of the arrival of the MSLR from Rugby, the Metropolitan built Quainton Road Junction Box about ¼ mile north of Quainton Road station. All the stations between Aylesbury and Verney Junction were provided with freight facilities except Winslow Road, but at Sir Edmund

Verney's request, a seven-wagon siding was put in at the latter point in 1911. The appearance of the passenger buildings was broadly similar to those of the other stations beyond Rickmansworth; all were on the up side, except that at Waddesdon Manor. At Aylesbury, the layout was rearranged to give a double track right through the platforms, but the very antiquated station was otherwise left unaltered. Quainton Road, formerly a single platform to the north of the line on the Verney Junction side of the road crossing, was replaced by double platforms on the Aylesbury side, the down platform given an additional face for the Brill trains.

Hoping perhaps to profit from long waits between connections, a firm of brewers erected a public house near the isolated Verney Junction station. This was indeed a bleak and solitary spot for the terminus of the pioneer underground railway, 50½ miles from the nearest point on the Inner Circle. Thanks almost entirely to Watkin, the Metropolitan had got lost in the countryside of north Buckinghamshire[17].

But this was not the company's only venture into the quietest corners of that county. In its enthusiasm to establish itself in the area, it did not overlook the Brill Tramway. When R. A. Jones, the Brill manager, approached the Metropolitan in February 1899 to ascertain whether it would be interested in purchase, the response was positive. On 20 October, the fourth Earl Temple, who had inherited the freehold of this bankrupt and neglected asset from his uncle, the third Duke of Buckingham & Chandos, ten years earlier, accepted the proposal put by the Metropolitan. It was agreed the line would be taken over and worked from 1 December, pending an application in 1900 for parliamentary powers to purchase it. The Metropolitan undertook to maintain the track, stations, signals and rolling stock during the period of temporary working, paying a rental of £600 a year. All the rolling stock was bought by the railway company[18], some from Earl Temple, some from the Oxford & Aylesbury Tramroad. The latter company remained in existence to receive the rental payments.

Nothing more was heard of the extension to Oxford, but in 1901 H. F. Stephens, the well-known light railway advocate, vainly suggested an application should be made for a Light Railway Order. R. A. Jones, secretary and general manager since 1871, was retained in the latter capacity until his retirement in January 1903. Then the Metropolitan took over management of the line as part of its own administration.

In the event, no arrangements were made for the line to be

purchased by the Metropolitan. At first there was some difficulty over obtaining a small piece of land owned by a charity, but when this was resolved in 1911 (by which time the Great Central Railway was jointly involved with the Metropolitan) the Metropolitan appears to have been unable to persuade the GCR to find its share of the purchase money. Nor was it any more successful with the LNER after 1923. Thus, apart from the substitution of the Metropolitan & Great Central Joint Committee for the Metropolitan as lessee in 1906, the 'temporary' arrangements of 1899 subsisted until the end of the Metropolitan Railway in 1933.

Under the Metropolitan, the sleepy activity of the remote rural Brill branch continued much as before but Sunday trains were introduced on 5 April 1903. At first the newer Manning Wardle tank locos were used, then Metropolitan 'A' class 4-4-0T were imported to haul rigid Metropolitan Oldbury eight-wheelers of 1865–6 which had been rebodied around 1896. All the track was relaid with bullhead rail by the end of 1903 and all the platforms were rebuilt to 3ft height for 80–100ft to accommodate Metropolitan coaches. No other significant changes were made after this apart from the abandonment of the Sunday service after 25 April 1920.

LOCOMOTIVES AND ROLLING STOCK FOR THE EXTENSION LINE

To work its new lines, the Metropolitan acquired a variety of locomotives and rolling stock. At first the standard Beyer-Peacock outside cylinder 4-4-0T were used to haul close-coupled four-wheel coaches out to Harrow, Rickmansworth and even Chesham. Some of the locomotives were still in unrebuilt form, their crews suffering grievously from the complete absence of weather protection on the footplate, whilst passengers lacked any winter comfort beyond unreliable footwarmers. As this combination of locomotives and carriages was not designed for other than a leisurely trundle round the Inner Circle the trains offered an exciting ride on their new stamping ground, bringing complaints about oscillation so bad that the passengers often had difficulty in keeping their seats. In an endeavour to improve matters, four condensing 0-4-4T with inside cylinders were ordered in 1891. These were slightly modified versions of James Stirling's SER 'Q' class, built to the design of J. Hanbury by Neilson & Co of Glasgow for £2,200 each. Later designated 'C' class, they were numbered 67–70. For the first time on new Metropolitan locomotives, conventional roofed cabs were fitted. When working its inaugural public service from Baker Street East to Rickmansworth on 4 June

1891, the first of these locomotives disgraced itself. Defective sanding gear caused it to slip badly in the St John's Wood tunnel until it finally came to rest near Marlborough Road station, its crew staggering from the heavy accumulation of fumes. At this point, the train was hit in the rear by the following down service, but fortunately there were no serious injuries.

Early in 1895 these 0-4-4T were joined by two 33-ton Sharp Stewart 2-4-0T (later 'D' class) bought for £1,575 each for the Aylesbury to Verney Junction service. They resembled some engines built by the same firm for the Barry Railway a little earlier. Four more, fitted with condensing apparatus, and slightly heavier, followed a few months later.

Between 1896 and 1901 the first locomotives specifically designed for Metropolitan service since the Beyer Peacocks were delivered for work on the Extension Line. Designed by T. F. Clark, the locomotive superintendent, these seven 0-4-4T (subsequently 'E' class) were built at Neasden Works (three) and by Hawthorn Leslie (four), the latter priced at £3,392 each. They were to be followed by four Yorkshire Engine Co 0-6-2T ('F' class) purchased at £3,350 each in 1900 mainly for freight working on the Extension.

When the first four-wheeled carriages were obtained in 1870 from the Oldbury Carriage Co, these vehicles, close-coupled in centrally-buffered pairs 43ft 8in in length, were much used on the St John's Wood line and its first extensions. In 1894 five went to work the Aylesbury-Verney Junction service. Their First Class compartments seated four aside in well-upholstered, padded-armrest comfort, but the Thirds had only wooden benches and shoulder-high partitions between compartments. With their rigid 16ft wheelbase, they had some difficulty in keeping to the rails over poor track or on the tighter curves on the Inner Circle and the design was criticised by a Board of Trade Inspector after a derailment at New Cross (SER) on 15 February 1886. As a result, when more stock was needed in 1887, a new design of four-wheeler was evolved. Known as 'Jubilee' stock, these carriages were formed into three trains of nine 27ft 5in long teak-panelled mahogany close-coupled vehicles with two Second Class coaches and two Firsts in each set. They were designed and built by Craven Bros of Sheffield and delivered in 1887 (one train) and 1889 (two more). Pintsch's high-pressure gas lighting was fitted and for the first time white paint was no longer used to distinguish the upper panels of First Class accommodation. Radial buffing and drawing gear followed a design used on the New York Elevated Railway.

These trains were intended for and used on the Inner Circle but four more trains of eight carriages of similar type were obtained from Cravens in 1892, each set arranged to split into two sets of four, one for Aylesbury, one for Chesham, at Chalfont Road. Cravens' design was faulty, producing complaints from passengers of unpleasant motion at speed. This was remedied by lengthening the wheelbases from 14ft to 17ft 4in, altering the buffers and substituting heavier springs. This second batch of Jubilee stock probably had automatic vacuum brakes from the start, the first new stock to be so fitted. Despite protests that the simple vacuum brakes on its earlier stock were adequately efficient, the Metropolitan was finally required by Board of Trade Order dated 20 November 1890 under the Regulation of Railways Act, 1889, to fit automatic vacuum brakes to its 328 passenger coaches and 66 locomotives, a task completed by May 1893.

With longer journeys, the footwarmers heated up at Chesham and Aylesbury stations proved insufficient to keep passengers comfortable when they ventured on winter journeys into the perceptibly chillier climes of the northern outskirts of London. 'In the interests of increasing the traffic', the board agreed that W. S. Laycock's patent storage steam heating apparatus should be fitted to the 1892 Cravens' stock and six locomotives. Three years after this work was completed in 1894 the two Chesham shuttle trains were similarly equipped.

Bogie stock more suitable for the longer runs on the Extension line was finally obtained in 1898–1900. By the latter date, there were 54 of these 42ft 4¾in long carriages, built by the Ashbury Railway Carriage & Iron Co of Manchester. For all three passenger classes there were five-aside seats in each compartment. The initial order was for four six-coach trains at £7,150 each; five additional sets, some built at Neasden, followed in 1900. Besides steam heating and continuous vacuum brakes, these carriages were the first on the Metropolitan to be electrically-lit; using Stone's system, this provided two eight-candle power lamps in each compartment. All steam stock trains were electrically-lit by January 1917 and from 1922 onwards electric heaters belatedly supplied some warmth when running over electrified sections.

All the carriages mentioned were of the compartment type, with accommodation for all three passenger classes, fitted with a somewhat flattened version of the round-topped doors adopted in 1867 to minimise damage when doors were opened in the London tunnel sections. But for some, even the heavily-padded Firsts were not good enough. When Wendover station was opened in 1892, Alfred (later Lord) Rothschild of Halton House transferred his patronage from the LNWR to the Metropolitan. To make certain of retaining this

97

custom, worth some £600 exclusive of goods and parcels for the house and estate, and also to provide accommodation for other special purposes, the board ordered two private saloons from Brown Marshalls & Co in 1896. At £660 each, these were 32ft long six-wheelers embodying a servants' compartment, lavatory and luggage compartment adjoining a main saloon furnished with two settees, a table and two armchairs. Pintsch's gas lighting and Laycock's steam heating were installed. These saloons were normally marshalled as a special train with two rebodied First Class carriages in each of which one compartment was adapted for the accommodation of a guard. By combining the two saloons into one 58ft long carriage, the Metropolitan produced what was virtually a new vehicle in 1905. This was fitted with four-wheel bogies and Stone's electric lighting and furnished with movable chairs and tables. In later years it formed a reserve Pullman vehicle also finding use on directors' and officers' inspections and other special occasions.

As we have already noted, the Metropolitan had entered the freight business on its own account with the opening to Harrow. Between 1891 and 1897 over 250 freight vehicles were obtained, ranging from conventional trucks and vans and brake vans to horse boxes, trucks for carrying horse-drawn vehicles, and milk vans. Six of the latter were provided in 1893–4 by modifying some of the four-wheeled First Class carriages of 1869, removing the seats and partitions and providing central double doors each side. As these proved light and lively in movement demanding a position in the centre of passenger trains, they were replaced in 1896–1903 by purpose-built and larger vans. Further substantial additions were made to the freight stock in 1900–4[19].

MODEST EXPANSION AT BAKER STREET AND FOLLY AT WEMBLEY PARK

As traffic on the Extension Line built up, there were many complaints from passengers using at busy times the hopelessly inadequate accommodation at Baker Street East, virtually unaltered since the opening of the little St John's Wood line. A modest rebuilding was started in March 1891 and during the following year the old overall roof was taken down to allow enlargement of the existing two-track, side-platform layout to three tracks and four platform faces. Umbrella-type canopies were erected over most of the length of the two new platforms. The single track connecting the 'Extension Line' with the 'Main Line', in use only for empty stock working, light engines and engineers' trains, was given a platform face either side,

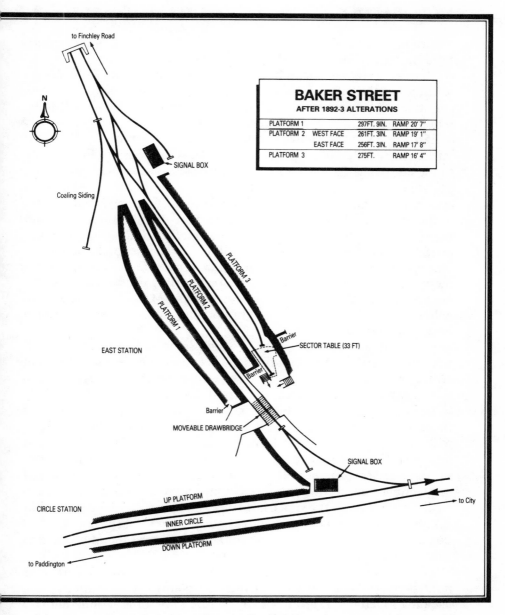

to Finchley Road

N

BAKER STREET

AFTER 1892-3 ALTERATIONS

PLATFORM 1		297FT. 9IN.	RAMP 20' 7"
PLATFORM 2	WEST FACE	261FT. 3IN.	RAMP 19' 1"
	EAST FACE	256FT. 3IN.	RAMP 17' 8"
PLATFORM 3		275FT.	RAMP 16' 4"

SIGNAL BOX

Coaling Siding

PLATFORM 3

PLATFORM 2

PLATFORM 1

EAST STATION

Barrier

SECTOR TABLE (33 FT)

Barrier

Barrier

MOVEABLE DRAWBRIDGE

SIGNAL BOX

UP PLATFORM

CIRCLE STATION

INNER CIRCLE

to City

DOWN PLATFORM

to Paddington

with a new movable bridge across the inner end protected by closed
gates when the line was to be used. At the head of the other two platform lines was a 33ft locomotive sector table manufactured by the Isca
Foundry Co. On the west side of the site was a 70ft coaling stage with
a siding and a long building with waiting and refreshment rooms,
lavatories and accommodation for porters and inspectors.

Although the new platforms came into public use on 14 November 1892 the works were not fully completed until the following summer. As they were still obliged to battle their way in rush hours from one set of trains to the other between the two separate stations, passengers continued to complain. It was not long before Baker Street had to be rebuilt again.

Early in 1890 the railway company and its Surplus Lands Committee spent £32,500 in purchasing the 280 acre Wembley Park on the south side of the Extension Line between Neasden and Harrow, some 6¾ miles from Baker Street. The reason for this move was soon apparent. Watkin had been much impressed by the financial success of the 984ft Eiffel Tower erected for the Paris Exhibition of 1889 and subsequently retained as a permanent attraction. Late in the summer of 1889, after making use of Eiffel and Gladstone to obtain advice, he formed a resolve to give London a similar attraction. Rejecting several more commercially-viable sites nearer to the centre (because he believed the benefits would go as much to the MDR as to the Metropolitan) he decided his tower might find a suitable home in Wembley Park, then on the market.

A scheme was drawn up under which some 124 acres of the Park were to be converted to London's finest sports, leisure and exhibition centre with the tower as its ever-visible symbol. This, Watkin thought, would bring a great new traffic to the Extension Line likely to be supplemented later by commuter housing on the remainder of the land[20]. A separate Tower Company was formed on 14 August 1889 with £300,000 capital to develop this concept. After Eiffel had declined, Sir Benjamin Baker reluctantly accepted the post of consulting engineer. Many weird and wonderful designs were submitted in a competition, but when construction started early in 1892 it was to erect a four-legged, three-platform steel tower not unlike Eiffel's, but 1,159ft high. The work was entrusted to a subsidiary, the International Tower Construction Company (later renamed the Metropolitan Tower Construction Co) with a capital of £200,000.

To cater for the expected traffic, a new station, Wembley Park, was built between Neasden and Harrow. Its platforms came into public use on 14 October 1893[21]. Nearby, at the same time, a junction and signal box were provided for a long siding into the Park.

Alas, both investors and the public showed a disappointingly low level of interest in the project. Despite a huge injection of funds (£60,000) by the Metropolitan and its Surplus Lands Committee, construction of the tower, on the site of the present Wembley Stadium, ceased when it reached first platform level, a height of only 200ft. On

Plate 10 (left) Sir Edward Watkin (1819–1901), chairman of the Metropolitan from 1872 to 1894 (*source unknown*)
Plate 11 (right) Metropolitan Railway seal, being a simplified version of the company's first coat of arms

Plate 12 The final Metropolitan Railway coat of arms (*courtesy The Railway Club*)

Plate 13 Aldgate looking south to buffer stops as opened 1876. As customary, after faithfully sketching the fabric, the artist has added the passengers and trains later and the accuracy of the rolling stock is questionable (*Illustrated London News, 2 December 1876*)

Plate 14 C class 0–4–4T No 70 as delivered at Neasden, 1891 (*source unknown, courtesy London Underground Railway Society*)

Plate 15 D class 2–4–0T No 75 alongside the locomotive repair sh at Neasden soon after delivery in 1895. The wall-mounted signal protects the traverser at the west e of the loco shop (*photographer unknown, courtesy J.H. Price*)

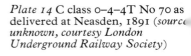

12 May 1894, the public were admitted to the Park to enjoy the large ornamental boating lake, the variety hall and the cycling and sports grounds. From May 1896 after lifts had been installed, they were allowed on to the first platform of the incomplete tower. But less than one fifth of those paying to enter the Park went on to the tower, which quickly acquired the label 'Watkin's Folly'. Written off as a failure, its foundations tilting in the treacherous Middlesex clay, it was dismantled in 1907.

Eight years after the purchase of Wembley Park, the Tower Company had acquired it on mortgage from the Metropolitan. In 1906 the mortgagors changed their name to the more appropriate Wembley Park Estate Company. The Park remained open for some years but from around 1908 the estate was developed for house building and other purposes which gradually overlaid the original scheme.

There will be more to tell in Chapter 10 of the arrangements made to accommodate the London extension of the MSLR, soon to be renamed the Great Central Railway, but sufficient has been said to indicate that as the end of the 19th century approached, the Metropolitan had evolved into two almost separate railways: the original urban underground lines, still referred to by directors and officials as 'the Main Line'; and the 50½ mile line deep into rural Buckinghamshire, which they called 'the Branch' or 'the Extension', now awaiting its new task of carrying trains from Manchester, Sheffield and other towns to the heart of London in addition to its developing suburban and extra-urban traffic. These two railways were tenuously linked by a single track at Baker Street which saw no revenue-earning services.

From this time onwards the Metropolitan was increasingly to regard itself as a minor main line railway company, and although this was never accepted wholeheartedly by the other companies, the undertaking was certainly a somewhat different animal from its neighbour, the MDR, with which it had to share an important section of its inner London services. It is to that side of the business we must now return.

7

A CIRCLE AT LAST

Whilst the prickly relationship between Forbes and Watkin could always be relied upon to produce scope for delay and argument over every kind of detail regarding the completion of the Inner Circle, it is also true that the financially weak MDR was in no position to raise on its own account sufficient capital to build its section from Mansion House to the Metropolitan at Trinity Square, Tower Hill. And, for his part, Watkin could see no direct interest for the Metropolitan in working with an independent MDR to complete this link. Indeed, with no sign of movement from the MDR, Watkin sought to discard the Metropolitan's powers south of Aldgate, only to arouse the successful opposition of the Metropolitan Board of Works. In an attempt to resolve the impasse, the MBW suggested in March 1873 that there should be a combined underground railway and road improvement scheme between High Street Aldgate and Mansion House. Watkin responded positively, withdrawing the Trinity Square abandonment clause in the Metropolitan bill for the 1872–73 session.

A 'MISERABLE CONFEDERATION'

But the MBW's attention was quickly attracted to an alternative, apparently independent, proposal. Principally initiated by George G. Newman, a City lawyer, who declared he had 'the interests of London at heart', and enjoying influential support in the City, this Metropolitan Inner Circle Completion Company proposed a 1 mile 4 chain line from Mansion House station to the Metropolitan at Aldgate, passing beneath a new street from the junction of King William Street and Eastcheap to Fenchurch Street, near Mincing Lane, thence beneath a widened Fenchurch Street. Connections were proposed with the Great Eastern Railway, the North London Railway and the East London Railway. As Newman had some influence in the decision-making of the MBW, his scheme had been endorsed by them by the end of January 1874 as offering not only the best features but the greatest public advantage. Watkin had arranged for the deposit of a Metropolitan bill on similar lines but parliament preferred the Newman proposals, which were given royal assent on 7 August 1874 after deletion of the GER, NLR and ELR connections. With serious street congestion arising from the attempts of the ever-growing traffic to and from the docks to pass through the medieval lanes which formed the City's main thoroughfares, the authorities were much interested in the valuable road improvements which the Newman scheme offered, so much so that the City's Commissioners of Sewers and the MBW made a firm promise of a combined capital contribution of £500,000.

Watkin bitterly opposed the Newman scheme, seeing its railway not only as a threat to his control of half the Circle, but to his plans to carry the Metropolitan east and south of the City. Rejecting an invitation from Newman to participate, he was furious when he found that the latter was being encouraged and supported by Forbes, who no doubt saw the scheme as the only hope of getting the District east of Mansion House. The MDR had found £1,000 for Newman's parliamentary expenses whilst another £12,000 had come from the City Solicitor.

In January 1874 Newman wrote to Watkin:

> I believe that substantially there is no difference in the views as expressed by both of you [Forbes and Watkin] though I find the unfortunate jealousy existing between the two companies as that to which several years ago Mr Parson alluded as an impediment to the completion of the Circle.

Such frankness did nothing to improve Watkin's attitude to the scheme and he was further incensed to discover in March 1876 that 'behind our backs' the MDR had entered into an agreement with Newman's Completion Company to work their line, guaranteeing a minimum toll annually. In a typical bad-tempered outburst, Watkin told Forbes that 'this liability of great gravity by the District' would stop for all time any fusion between the two companies.

But the MDR guarantee did nothing for Newman. As his scheme failed to attract any support from financially sound railway companies, notably the Metropolitan, it failed when it came into the money market in November 1877. Its only tangible asset was the firm promise of subsidies it had secured from the sewer and highway authorities. In the view of one of its promoters, this made the whole package worth no more than £50,000.

As noted earlier, Watkin had by 1874 formed the opinion that useful new traffic could be generated for the Metropolitan by a link to the East London Railway[1], enabling its trains to connect with those of the main line railways south of the Thames. Bills for such a connection were unsuccessfully launched in the sessions of 1874–75 and 1875–76. Watkin also sought to secure the Metropolitan's position by obtaining parliamentary powers on 12 July 1877 for a line under Aldgate High Street and started buying properties in the Minories at the end of that year. This last action, together with the realisation that the Newman scheme was getting nowhere whilst public pressure for completion of the Circle was likely to endure, forced the MDR's hand. Thus both Forbes and Watkin were amenable to an invitation from the contractor Charles Lucas that they should meet on the neutral ground of his office to discuss terms on which the two companies might combine to complete the Inner Circle. At this meeting, which took place in December 1877, it was agreed to proceed on the principles of complete control by the Metropolitan and the MDR and no other party; of protection of their shareholders against undue liability with a view to securing a minimum of four per cent on outlay; and of a revision of the route. Without delay Sir John Hawkshaw[2] was commissioned at joint cost to recommend the best route, Watkin expressing to him the hope 'to see your name associated with the completion of this great public work, and trust that no time may be lost, as it has been a dead horse so very long, and we should like to have it at least fairly put on its legs'. This somewhat curious imagery of a dead horse stood up on its legs was not so far from a fair description of the finished product, as we shall see.

When he reported on 18 January 1878, Sir John advised a 1 mile 15 chain line from Mansion House station, running beneath Cannon Street, Eastcheap, Great Tower Street, Trinity Square and Minories to Aldgate station. He proposed that the heavily-congested Eastcheap and Great Tower Street be widened to 60ft and that a new 60ft wide street should be built over the line between Mark Lane and Trinity Square[3]. The construction of Tower Bridge was foreseen, with the prediction that this would bring the new line traffic from the south side of the river. Meeting again in Lucas's office in March 1878, Watkin and Forbes agreed to the preparation of plans on the lines of the recommendations, to be deposited with a bill for the 1878–9 session.

Watkin's wish to run Metropolitan trains over the ELR was also woven into the new bill. At Liverpool Street, the Metropolitan had been frustrated in its attempts to get on to the ELR via the GER by the latter's understandable refusal to have Metropolitan trains crossing over its approach tracks to get to and from the ELR at Shoreditch. This objection had obligingly been put into writing by the GER, providing a piece of paper which Watkin could use should that company wish to oppose a Metropolitan/ELR connection south of Shoreditch. Watkin's conviction that an ELR connection would generate new traffic from south London appears to have been accepted by Forbes as equally valid for the MDR, thus securing his cooperation in construction of a line at joint expense eastwards from Aldgate to join the ELR.

After the Forbes-Watkin proposals had been approved by the City Corporation, parliament sanctioned them in the Metropolitan & District Railways (City Lines & Extensions) Act of 11 August 1879. This covered construction of a jointly-owned line from Aldgate to Mansion House via Tower Hill together with an eastern arm under Whitechapel Road to join the ELR at that company's Whitechapel station, also a north curve from Aldgate to Whitechapel[4]. Provision was made in the same act for the cesser of the Newman scheme powers, subject to compensation. Section 89 was of interest, demonstrating as it did parliament's concern to secure in perpetuity a continuous operation of services round the Circle by requiring each company to allow the other's trains on its portion of the Circle.

As substantial street improvement works had been included, there was no question of the two railway companies proceeding without a large contribution from the highway and sewer authorities. Thanks to Watkin's persistence and after lengthy negotiations with the Lord Mayor, by August 1881 there were promises of a combined £800,000 subsidy in place of the £500,000 offered to Newman's scheme. Watkin also fought tenaciously to screw down the compensation payable to Newman and his fellow promoters. Their claim was £100,000 with £26,000 costs, but Watkin forced this to an arbitration which awarded £50,000 net of costs in September 1879. In a letter to Burchell in which he told the lawyer to 'knock off every possible farthing' when taxing Newman's costs, Watkin expressed his view of the Newman enterprise:

> You know that the whole thing was a miserable confederation to make a 'pile' for half a dozen of Newman's set and to damage the Metropolitan, in the fancied, tho' not real, interests of Mr Forbes.

WATKIN GOES TO THE TOWER

Fearing that the MDR might be unable to raise the capital for their share of the Aldgate to Tower Hill section, for which the Metropolitan had already bought land under powers in their act of 12 July 1877, Watkin decided upon unilateral action. Using the property purchases as a lever, he secured parliamentary approval in an act of 3 June 1881 for construction by the Metropolitan alone as far as Tower Hill. The move was afforded some sort of respectability by persuading the Lord

Mayor to start the works on 5 September 1881[5]. Sir John Hawkshaw and the Metropolitan's Joseph Tomlinson Jr[6] acted as engineers and the contract was given to Thomas Andrew Walker[7] whose £78,000 bid included provision of a 300ft long terminal station extending 55ft across Trinity Square Gardens to a point opposite All Hallows Church. Known as The Tower of London, or simply The Tower, this station had a wooden street-level building placed over the line on the east side of Trinity Square, which, in an attempt to establish squatter's rights, was erected in the remarkable time of 60 hours. Some Metropolitan trains were extended to this station from Aldgate on 25 September 1882. Price Waterhouse & Co certified the final cost of the works and property for this 631yd extension as £512,949. An area bounded by Minories and Church Street (now St Clare St) was allocated by the Metropolitan for construction of 1,000 rooms which were to be let to working class families displaced by the works at an average rent of one shilling a week per room.

So impatient had Watkin now become at the MDR's total lack of activity that he offered to build the Trinity Square to Mansion House section, giving the District opportunity to become a financial partner at a later date. For its part, the MDR alleged that the Metropolitan would not have agreed to a piecemeal start by the MDR and challenged the Metropolitan's construction as far as Trinity Square without settling the station arrangements. In response the Metropolitan began to complain about the unpunctual working of trains between Mansion House and South Kensington, alleging this was caused by the inability of the terminal layout at Mansion House to cope with the increasing traffic from the MDR's western suburban extensions. A formal complaint about the inadequacy of Mansion House was lodged at the Board of Trade. All this was of course designed to prevent any attempt to saddle the Metropolitan with any part of the cost of building new terminal facilities for the MDR, either at Mansion House or any point east.

A LINK TO SOUTH LONDON

So charged was the atmosphere that for a while the MDR withdrew entirely from the Joint Committee, taking the question of station accommodation on the new lines to arbitration, meanwhile succeeding in stopping the Metropolitan's works at Trinity Square. The arbitration award supported the Metropolitan's contention that a small extension of the existing Aldgate station would suffice for the MDR terminal facilities and the Joint Committee resumed its activities in

December 1881. Peace restored, it was agreed to make a firm start with the remaining sections. After the engineers Sir John Hawkshaw and J. Wolfe Barry[8] had worked up detailed plans, the contract for the joint line from Mansion House to Tower Hill was given to T. A. Walker in the autumn of 1882.

By August 1884, Watkin, in his capacity as chairman of the ELR, had persuaded the London, Brighton & South Coast Railway, the SER, LCDR and MDR to join the Metropolitan in agreeing to a physical connection between the ELR and the Metropolitan and MDR, on completion of which all five companies would act jointly as lessees of the ELR, with equal rights, guaranteeing the ELR a minimum rental. Control of the ELR was to be vested in a Joint Committee who would work it 'as a line connecting the railways south of the Thames with the Metropolitan system'. The ambiguity of the last three words will be noted. In this agreement provision was made for the GER to join the other lessees, which it did in 1885. The £135,200 contract for building the line from Aldgate to the junction with the ELR was let in April 1883 to Walker, who also got the job of constructing the 63 chain north curve at Aldgate at a cost of £22,750.

Following arbitration by Hawkshaw, the lines east of Aldgate were to differ from the proposals of 1879. Instead of a junction with the ELR at Whitechapel station, it was decided that a separate terminal station should be built there at a higher level, for the MDR alone. The joint line would leave the Inner Circle just south of Aldgate, and shortly after a junction with the Metropolitan's Aldgate north curve, would enter a station called Aldgate East. This was to replace the enlarged Aldgate formerly proposed. At 30 chains beyond Aldgate East there would be a second station, St Mary's, and east of this, a junction, with one line running to the MDR Whitechapel terminus and the other a 22 chain curve east to meet the ELR line at Whitechapel Junction, 11 chains south of Whitechapel station[9]. This last line, known as the Whitechapel Junction Railway, was authorised by the ELR Act of 10 August 1882. That act also created the ELR Joint Committee, which leased the ELR from 1 October 1884. With the opening of the Whitechapel Junction line on 3 March 1884 the SER diverted its Addiscombe Road (now Addiscombe)-Liverpool Street trains into St Mary's.

Shortly after this, the new tunnels under Whitechapel Road were ready and as a temporary arrangement, the MDR and Metropolitan began to work local services on the ELR from 1 October 1884. To give trainmen the opportunity to familiarise themselves with the new services and also because some of the new stations were not fully complete, the Metropolitan passengers were obliged to alight at Bishopsgate (Liverpool Street) from this date, the trains then running empty to St Mary's, whence they conveyed passengers to New Cross (SER). The same arrangement applied in the reverse direction. Similarly, MDR trains ran empty between Mansion House and St Mary's from the same day, but these served the ELR fork to the LBSCR at New Cross. Although some LBSCR services continued to operate over the ELR, the SER workings were withdrawn with these changes. Carriage sheds and a locomotive depot were provided on ELR-owned land near New Cross SER station at a cost of £11,182 and leased to the Metropolitan by the ELR in 1884.

CIRCULAR CONGESTION

By the middle of September 1884 the remaining works were ready for traffic. An official ceremony in the presence of the Lord Mayor and City Corporation and representatives of the Metropolitan Board of Works was held on 17 September. Experimental working of a full Circle service from 1 to 5 October inclusive was attended with some chaos. From Monday 6 October public services round the Circle were begun with Metropolitan and MDR trains sharing the traffic. On the same day Metropolitan trains started an all-stations service between Hammersmith (H&CR) and New Cross (SER) via King's Cross, whilst MDR trains served stations between Hammersmith (MDR) and New Cross (LBSCR) via Charing Cross (now Embankment). From 10 November both companies operated trains over the ELR every 30 minutes.

The sections between Mansion House and Aldgate and between Minories Junction (south of Aldgate) and St Mary's Junction (with the ELR) became the joint property of the Metropolitan and the MDR, but in paying its share of the construction costs, the MDR refused any contribution to the disputed wooden station at Tower of London or to the dwellings for the displaced working classes. As the MDR also did not allow passengers to book to the Tower station, it was closed after traffic on 12 October 1884. In conformance with an arbitration by Hawkshaw, another station called Mark Lane had been built to the west, despite Metropolitan attempts to retain its 'temporary' station[10]. Two further stations were opened with the Circle Completion Lines, at Cannon Street and at Eastcheap (renamed Monument, 1 November 1884). All the new stations on the joint lines had normal side platforms and rather plain buildings at street level.

The completed Circle was 13 miles in length, of which 7 miles 69

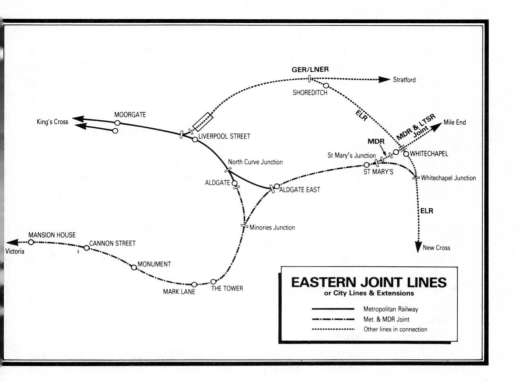

chains were Metropolitan property (South Kensington to Aldgate via King's Cross) and 4 miles 4 chains belonged to the MDR (South Kensington-Westminster-Mansion House). The remaining 1 mile 7 chains between Mansion House and Aldgate was jointly owned and, as already mentioned, the MDR had its own parallel tracks between South Kensington and High Street Kensington. It had been agreed that the two companies would provide a combined eight trains an hour, completing the round trip in 81–84 minutes. This totalled 280 trains daily (140 each way), to which were added another 684 to and from lines linked to the Circle. In practice this intensity proved impossible to maintain with steam traction and the existing signalling, causing the system to clog to a standstill at busy times of the day. One difficulty was that on 1 September 1884, in advance of the new services, the MDR had established an additional 23 trains daily each way between Hammersmith and Mansion House, a move which the Metropolitan at once cited as a cause of irregular working over the Circle. There is little doubt that it was a ploy by Forbes to render the agreed eight trains an hour each way round the Circle an impossibility, influenced as he was by the greater profitability of his suburban services. Bell, the Metropolitan general manager, reported to the

111

board that on the first day of full public service round the completed Circle, the MDR had 'lost' 85 trains and the Metropolitan 39. In his view the MDR's attempt to operate a service of 20 trains an hour each way between South Kensington and Mansion House was doomed as a physical impossibility.

The problem was put to arbitration by Henry Tennant, the NER general manager, who ruled that for an experimental period of three months, the two companies should endeavour to run eight trains an hour round the Circle on the basis of an 80-minute round trip timing, instead of the six an hour which had formed the old Mansion House-South Kensington-Aldgate 'horse shoe' service. This was started on 10 November 1884 but proved impossible to sustain with regularity. Further arbitration ensued, after which the round trip time was reduced to 70 minutes with only six trains an hour each way. This fixed ten-minute interval Circle service began on 7 April 1885. Thereafter no further changes were made during the steam era, although the Metropolitan tried hard to get the MDR to agree to a 60-minute all round timing.

Difficulties also arose over the necessity to withdraw locomotives for inspection and servicing, and over watering of the locomotives. By January 1886 watering and discharge of condensing water normally took place at Aldgate and South Kensington. Locomotives were withdrawn or put into service at South Kensington (Metropolitan Outer Rail trains), Aldgate (Metropolitan Inner Rail) and High Street Kensington (all MDR trains). In general crews of engines withdrawn from service replaced those of the following train ten minutes later. At Aldgate the replacement locomotive came off the previous Hammersmith service, terminating in the bay road[11]. Other measures to improve operation included the fitting of additional water tanks to Metropolitan locomotives, allowing a complete run of once or even twice round the Circle without a water stop. Larger water cranes of 2,000–3,000 gallon capacity were erected, reducing the watering time to the normal station stop period. Wear and tear of locomotive tyres increased noticeably with continuous Circle running, and to even out the wear, arrangements were made in 1885 for all engines to run in either direction, either chimney or bunker first.

Staff needs seem to have been overlooked initially. Guards were confined to their trains throughout their turn without relief until September 1885 when the addition of four guards enabled each Metropolitan guard to have three 20-minute breaks in his turn. No doubt this eliminated what may have been a puzzling factor in the delays.

At first, as with the former 'horse shoe' service, alternate Circle trains were worked by each company. Later the Metropolitan operated all trains on the Outer Rail and two on the Inner, the MDR taking up the balance, this proportion arranged to reflect the latter's smaller owned mileage. For the 'horse shoe' service, on 1 October 1883, the Metropolitan had introduced six-car trains in place of five, offering a total of 410 seats per train (90 First Class, 110 Second, 210 Third) instead of 340, and this formation was perpetuated on the new full Circle service.

To operate the new ELR and Circle services the Metropolitan acquired additional carriages as follows in 1884, all of them equipped with Pintsch's patent gas lighting:

8 First Class at £667 each from Craven Bros;
17 Second Class at £526 each from Brown, Marshalls & Co;
3 First Class/Second Class composite at £626 from Craven Bros;
16 Third Class at £436 each from Craven Bros;
16 Third Class at £400 each from Gloucester Wagon Co.

Predictably, the opening of the new joint lines increased the now established squabbling between the two underground railways. At an early stage the MDR challenged the Metropolitan's interpretation of the legislation regarding MDR payments of interest on the Joint Lines' capital and lost the argument. Further large sums were placed in lawyers' pockets following a generation of disputes over the MDR's right to fix fares unilaterally and book traffic between the new Joint Lines and the South Kensington exhibitions via Western Joint Lines stations, thus diverting traffic (some of it from the GER and LTSR) over the MDR section of the Circle. This round was won by the MDR, with the result that the Metropolitan withdrew some joint booking arrangements in protest, reducing fares over its part of the Circle. Litigation over this started in July 1886, not petering out until appeal procedure concluded in March 1888.

Yet, whilst all this was going on, for motives now impossible to discern, Watkin felt drawn to make a further attempt at reconciliation. Informal discussions he held with Forbes at the end of 1885 were, in his words, 'to put an end to all unpleasantness that existed and to fuse the interests of the two companies'. But Forbes would make no concessions and no positive response was forthcoming. Watkin learned from Currie, the MDR deputy chairman, shortly before Currie's death in 1886 that the reason for Forbes' lack of interest was that the MDR now saw itself as having an assured independent future, supported by what was expected to be lucrative traffic arising from connections with the LSWR. George Morphett, almost the only Metropolitan director occasionally prepared to question Watkin's policies and actions, expressed the hope that Watkin 'would never make so favourable a proposal to the District again'. Surviving papers are silent on the details of Watkin's suggestion.

GYRATION DISAPPOINTS

Contrary to the apparent high expectations of all concerned, the Circle Completion proved a financial disaster, producing much less new traffic than was necessary to service the £1.25m capital raised by each company at the agreed four per cent. Its opening coincided with a period when the street horse bus services were passing through a phase of development and competition[12] which attracted the public to the cheaper and more direct route they offered for many journeys. Nor was Watkin's optimism about a link with the railways south of the river justified. The ELR remained a lame duck, with LBSCR and SER passengers content to stay in comparatively fast trains to and from conveniently-situated central area stations rather than change at New Cross for a circuitous all-stations journey by Metropolitan or District.

Comfortably bolstered by its surplus lands income, the Metropolitan had been able to pay ordinary shareholders five per cent from the second half of 1877 to the second half of 1884, but after that, with the Circle completed and the ELR services in operation, expenditure rose steadily whilst gross receipts hardly increased at all. Dividends fell to four per cent, not recovering to the former level until the first half of 1887. The much more highly-geared MDR fared even worse.

In his evidence to the Royal Commission on London Traffic in March 1904, R. W. Perks MP, then chairman of the MDR, questioned the wisdom of Forbes and Watkin in completing the Circle and the extensions to join the ELR to their systems, referring to these works as 'one of the most unfortunate things the District Company ever went into and the cause of a great deal of our trouble'. He noted that after giving credit for the surplus properties and the subsidies by the sewer and highway authorities, the two companies had spent £937,564 a mile on these lines of 1884. Property compensation, often over-generous, together with the high cost of property acquired, had taken up two-thirds of the final outlay. The promoters had been 'totally mistaken' in their expectation of large traffic increases, which had led them into offering expensive street improvements only partly funded by the subsidies from the local authorities. In Perks' view the original concept of the Circle as a means of linking up the terminal railway stations and distributing their traffic within the centre of London had not been accomplished. He observed that 'the Circle is practically a deserted railway in both its eastern and western branches after 8 o'clock in the evening'. The six trains an hour round the Circle were to a large extent 'empty carriages for a number of hours of the day'[13].

Alfred Powell, general manager of the MDR, in an interview with *The Railway Magazine* in June 1899 cited the local traffic developed by the lines as 'comparatively trifling' adding that 'the previously existing Mansion House traffic has merely been projected over the additional City stations eastwards, with the result that the increase in working expenses has been little more than covered.'

Others, perhaps less familiar with the economic realities of private sector railway operation, suggested that instead of operating the Circle as an internal service for central London unimpeded by junctions with other lines the Metropolitan and MDR had striven to achieve exactly what the parliamentary committees of 1863 and 1864 had said should not be done: they had built junctions and used their respective sections of the Circle as termini for their suburban services, causing irregular working and delays and restricting the Circle service itself to a ten-minute frequency when more trains would have been desirable[14].

Nothing came of another Watkin expansionist move which would have put even more strain on to the steam-worked City Lines and Extensions. Towards the end of 1883 he agreed with H. D. Browne, chairman of the London, Tilbury & Southend Railway, that the latter should promote at joint cost with the Metropolitan, a £600,000 link between them, passing beneath the Mile End Road and rising to the surface near Gas Factory Junction, Bow. Although a bill was drafted for the 1883–84 session, it was subsequently withdrawn by the LTSR, apparently because that company had become aware of the potential problems in reaching the Metropolitan proper over lines wholly or jointly owned by the MDR between Whitechapel and Aldgate. Some years later the MDR was persuaded to share the cost of providing this link; the Metropolitan wisely rejected an invitation to join in.

Fenton did not remain general manager of the Metropolitan long enough to experience the hassle of creating some sort of order out of the completed Circle services. On 1 January 1880, after 17 years with the Metropolitan, he moved to the more extensive, but possibly more peaceful responsibilities of managing the SER, pocketing the grateful board's cheque for £1,000 and a gold watch. His place was taken by

John Bell, also rewarded with a gold timepiece in recognition of 'the attention he has devoted to the affairs of the Company during seven years of progress and improvement'. J. M. Eyles, Bell's former chief clerk, took his place as secretary at £400 a year, a figure which was to rise to £700 by 1883.

Watkin was also the recipient of largesse. 'Influential shareholders' suggested in January 1883 that he should receive the full £2,500 a year from the date of his appointment in 1872 'in consideration of the very valuable services he has rendered to the Company'. This was endorsed by a majority of the shareholders (26,321 to 2,276) at the following half-yearly meeting.

VENTILATION AND OTHER PROBLEMS

Believing that the railway could and would be operated by locomotives emitting little or no steam or smoke, Fowler had provided only a small number of openings when planning the first section of the Metropolitan. Over a distance of more than two miles between Edgware Road station yard and just west of King's Cross he placed the line in continuous tunnel. Despite their condensing gear, the ordinary steam locomotives used soon made this section a reservoir of the most unpleasant pollution, notably on the Down, or westbound road, where the engines were working against the grade. Fowler seems to have had a premonition of trouble; for a considerable length under Marylebone Road he built brick tubes above the haunches of the covered way with the intention that they could be used for a mechanical exhaust system should that prove both practical and necessary at some future date. These tubes were in fact later employed to blow fresh air into the tunnel with the aid of a fan installed at Edgware Road station.

Problems were also experienced on the St John's Wood line, where the steeply-graded exit tunnels from Baker Street to Swiss Cottage frequently became heavily-charged with fumes which gave rise to passenger complaints. As early as August 1864 Fenton produced a report 'on the atmosphere of the railway' in which he threw blame on the inferior grade of coke used by the GWR in their locomotives. That company agreed in September 1866 to burn the same quality of coke as the Metropolitan[1], but for many years after this, the fuels used on the GWR engines and the driving techniques of GWR men running over the Metropolitan remained the subject of complaint. The general problem of an unpleasant atmosphere persisted, especially in the 'long tunnel' between Edgware Road and King's Cross and after hearing in October 1865 of 'the very impure state of the atmosphere at some stations' the board asked Fowler to consider means of improving ventilation. His main recommendation was for a 'signal and ventilating station' open to the air at Chalton Street, about halfway between King's Cross and Gower Street (Euston Square) stations. The siting of this shaft, not completed until 1871, took into account the King's Cross to Praed Street quadrupling proposal mentioned in Chapter 4.

In the meantime the glazing of the apertures above the platforms at Baker Street, Portland Road (Great Portland Street) and Gower Street stations was removed and additional openings were also made at the western end of Portland Road station in 1868–70.

During 1869 the Metropolitan changed from coke to 'smokeless' Welsh coal, primarily to improve locomotive steaming capacity on the increasingly heavier trains[2]. This altered the smell and the nature of the atmosphere but did nothing to eliminate the problem. It may have been the proximity of the worst-affected section to University College, but whatever the reason, there was no shortage of suggestions and offers of assistance from the scientific community. Their efforts and proposals either proved of little value or were simply ignored. Then someone had quite a bright idea. At the Metropolitan's request in 1874, John Aird opened up a connection between the long tunnel and the Pneumatic Despatch Company's tube railway[3] at the point where the two crossed at Tottenham Court Road, near the summit level between Portland Road and Gower Street stations. The tube cars were drawn through the tunnel by means of a vacuum created by steam-driven exhauster fans at Holborn. As the driverless vehicles were thus moved towards Holborn from their other terminus at Euston, the tunnel behind them filled with air; a similar process was used in the reverse direction. The brilliant thought was that instead of sucking in the normal atmosphere behind the tube cars, the intake should consist of the Metropolitan's best bronchial mixture. Alas, this promising development was to be nipped in the bud when the Pneumatic Tube Railway went out of business on 31 October 1874.

With the pollution nuisance continuing unabated, two major steps were now taken. Between 1871 and 1872, openings were made in the crown of the long tunnel, venting through iron grilles at the centre of Euston and Marylebone Roads. Measuring 28ft by 2ft 6in, these 'blow holes' were located between Edgware Road and Baker Street (three); between Baker Street and Portland Road (three) and between Gower Street and King's Cross (five). Many can still be seen today. The author's father, who worked at the Railway Clearing House in Eversholt (then Seymour) Street, Euston, used to recall that these grilles afforded a lunchtime diversion for the younger clerks, whose custom was to keep them under close surveillance. The reason for this was that should any lady be unwise enough to stand over them whilst a train was passing below, the force of the blast would raise her skirts in a satisfyingly revealing fashion.

The second measure was suggested by Tomlinson, the Metropolitan's resident engineer. This was that a wooden partition should be erected for the full height of the tunnel to separate the Up and Down lines between Portland Road and Gower Street stations. Although this structure was completed in 1879, it had no perceptible effect on the pollution and was accordingly demolished when repairs became necessary about 1886.

When Watkin arrived at the Metropolitan, his initial response to the problem was to call in John Ramsbottom, the former locomotive engineer of the LNWR, to investigate the possibility of using ordinary non-condensing steam locomotives in combination with some system of mechanical ventilation. Reporting on 26 September 1872, Ramsbottom could find no case for making any change 'unless the traffic increases and the atmosphere in the tunnels gets worse, then mechanical ventilation will be the answer'. After this there was some piecemeal flirtation with mechanical ventilation: fans blowing in fresh air were installed at Edgware Road, Portland Road and also at Cannon Street. Costly to operate and productive of complaints as to their noise, they did not remain in use for very long. However exhaust fans at Eastcheap (Monument) and St Mary's stations, included in the new City Lines and Extensions opened in 1884, appear to have lasted until electrification.

As time passed, it was gradually realised that electrification was the only satisfactory answer, but that was still some years off and meanwhile the board determined to improve the state of the 'long tunnel' by making further openings to the surface. These good intentions only succeeded in arousing the opposition of the Metropolitan Board of Works and the other local authorities, who argued they would endanger public health, bring down property values (and therefore rate income) and create a nuisance for street traffic, frightening horses. As a condition of withdrawing its influential opposition to further openings, the MBW insisted in 1883 that there should be trials of a full system of mechanical ventilation. Sir Benjamin Baker[4] was commissioned to design the apparatus. He erected exhaust troughing along the top of the tunnel for a test installation attended with moderate success, but his system was rejected on grounds of high first cost and high maintenance expenditure. An alternative, designed by Christopher Anderson of Leeds, was tried out at Neasden in 1890–91, using a Metropolitan locomotive and iron plate trunking between the rails with box slides dragging along it, moved by the locomotive[5]. Benjamin Baker reported to the board that although the design was both good and workable it would heavily increase working and maintenance costs and was moreover very noisy. This too was therefore rejected.

The newly-formed London County Council was soon complaining about the atmosphere that the Metropolitan inflicted on its passengers and staff, and with LCC support, the district authorities began to insist that any further openings should be accompanied by expensive street widenings to modify the effect of their exhalations. This was of course resisted by the railway company as a form of blackmail and eventually the suggestion was made in the House of Lords that the Board of Trade should appoint a departmental committee of inquiry. This was asked in 1897 to report on:

> the best way of preserving a fairly pure atmosphere on a railway of very large traffic carried in short tunnels under important thoroughfares in the vicinity of good houses, without creating a nuisance in the streets.

Major F. A. Marindin RE CMG, the Government's Chief Inspecting Officer of Railways, was in the chair. Other members were Earl Russell, Sir Charles Scotter Bt (general manager of the LSWR), Sir Douglas Galton KCB and Dr John Scott Haldane, who made a major contribution.

It was learned that during the 19 daily traffic hours there were 528 passenger and 14 freight trains passing in both directions between Edgware Road and King's Cross. Each was hauled by a locomotive with an hourly appetite for 3cwt (152.4kg) of 'Powell Duffryn Welsh Smokeless Coal from the Aberdare Valley' and 350 gallons (1,591.087 litres) of water. At peak periods there were 19 trains an hour each way between Baker Street and King's Cross, at which time, every hour, 15cwt (762kg) of coal were burnt and 1,650 gallons (7,500.839 litres) of water evaporated, half of it condensed, the rest passing into the atmosphere as steam. On the platform at Gower Street (now Euston Square) measurements showed 89.4 parts of carbon dioxide per 10,000 volumes whilst in the tunnels there was up to two per cent of volatile sulphur. Dr Haldane sought out a pharmacist in Gower Street who had for many years dispensed his own 'Metropolitan Mixture' to ease the plight of persons emerging in distress from the nearby station[6]. This man described such customers as presenting all the symptons of irritation: coughing, shortness of breath and smarting of the eyes, exactly those produced by the worst London fogs. Haldane added that the atmosphere of the Metropolitan Railway was in effect 'concentrated fog'.

With evident enthusiasm, Metropolitan Railway representatives stressed to the committee the antiseptic qualities of the fumes, producing sickness records to demonstrate that there were no ill effects on the staff, who they declared were 'the healthiest railway staff

120

in the country'. Indeed, so beneficial was the atmosphere that the three stations in the long tunnel were used as 'sanitoria' for employees afflicted with bronchial and asthmatic troubles. John Bell unblushingly described how his own health had been restored. Diphtheria had left him with a very sensitive throat, making him a martyr to regular attacks of the quinsy over more than ten years. Since becoming general manager, which required more walking about the line than when he had been secretary, he had been without quinsy, a circumstance he (incorrectly) ascribed to the 'sulphurous acid gas' acting as a disinfectant. But he was forced to admit that the atmosphere in the tunnel was very unpleasant in warm weather and the passengers did not like it[7]. He added that the company wished to improve ventilation by making more openings.

The committee looked at the possibilities of fans, the provision of more openings and electric working, choosing the last as the preferable course. As an interim measure it was recommended that further openings should be authorised by parliament provided the Board of Trade was given power to order their closure in due course, a stipulation which would oblige the company to resort to artificial ventilation if the railway were not to be electrified. This was unreservedly accepted by the Metropolitan, which obtained parliamentary authority in its act of 2 August 1898 to make additional openings (including two on the St John's Wood line), subject to a Board of Trade veto after they had been made. But with electrification increasingly imminent, the powers were allowed to lapse in 1902.

SUBSIDENCE, CORROSION AND BOMBS

The tunnels provided other anxieties. Serious faults appeared in the Clerkenwell Tunnel, where in 1872 over 150yd the invert was seen to be forced up as much as 18 inches and to have fractured in several places. This was blamed on drainage changes following the completion of the second (Widened Lines) tunnel. After repairs had started, more cracks appeared and it was found that large quantities of water had accumulated behind the brickwork, swelling the surrounding clay, creating pressures the walls could not sustain. Repairs proved both lengthy and tedious, requiring attention to 256yd of invert and underpinning of the side walls in places. To reduce public apprehension, the work was done at night after traffic hours, and was not finished until 1873. Also during 1872, cracks were seen in the arch of the Gloucester Road tunnel after a large quantity of soil had been placed over it. This damage was repaired but needed further attention in 1873, when underpinning of the 4ft 10½in thick central pier between the Metropolitan and MDR tracks was also undertaken.

During 1876 vertical cracks were observed in the side walls 20yd west of Gower Street (Euston Square) station, a problem attacked by inserting an invert for 20ft, cutting out and rebuilding the side walls in the area for up to 10ft above the invert level. A 'somewhat serious defect' was reported in October 1885 on the north wall of the tunnel near Chalton Street signal box, Euston Road. Percolation of water into the tunnel foundations both from a leaky water main parallel to the railway and through cracks in the Vestry sewer, all aggravated by the weight of the Midland Railway goods depot (which had been built after the construction of the tunnel), had forced the wall inwards, cracking it in several places. As alarmist reports were appearing in the newspapers, inspection by the Board of Trade was invited. Major General Hutchinson found that a strong concrete invert was being built over a distance of 170yd between the two walls of the shored-up tunnel and professed himself satisfied as to public safety. Trains continued to run but the roadway above was not fully reopened until 22 April 1886.

Further trouble occurred in the Gloucester Road-South Kensington tunnel during a period when the MDR was responsible for its maintenance. In 1889 that company was obliged to carry out a substantial amount of underpinning, which was completed on 12 October. At Baker Street East in 1901, the tunnel wall on the east side subsided inwards. It was found that the soil was continuously waterlogged to a depth of four feet below the track ballast. Once again the remedy involved underpinning the tunnel walls and provision of an invert.

Apart from causing discomfort to humans, the products of combustion accelerated corrosion of the ironwork over the tracks. One example of this was at Smithfield Market, where in 1893 badly deteriorated wrought iron girders and other ironwork had to be replaced by masonry arches. Large-scale damage elsewhere in these sidings was then discovered, requiring extensive renewals from 1898 onwards, during which brick arching was substituted for girder work wherever feasible over the whole Market basement area of 625ft by 240ft, at the then substantial cost of £40,000. Towards the end of 1891 the wrought iron girders of the Ray Street 'gridiron' carrying the Metropolitan over the Widened Lines just north of Farringdon were found to be in a poor condition; renewal was not completed until 31 August 1893.

By no means all the unpleasantness occurring in the tunnels was related to engineering problems. During the 1880s and 1890s, Irish terrorists, then known as Fenians, were conducting a campaign in England, allegedly with American aid. They decided that explosion of bombs within the confined spaces of the Inner Circle would further their cause. Just before 8 pm on 30 October 1883 there was an explosion on the line 38yd east of Praed Street (Paddington) station which damaged a passing six-coach Up train, the force of the blast wrecking doors, panels and windows of the three Third Class vehicles at the rear, injuring 62 passengers, some of whom were described as 'in a lamentable condition with face and scalp wounds'. Much glass was broken at the station and in the signal box. Almost simultaneously, a similar explosion took place on the MDR between Charing Cross (now Embankment) and Westminster but fortunately no trains were passing at the time. On the evening of 2 January 1885 three trains suffered light damage from another Fenian bomb exploding 170yd west of Chalton Street signal box, King's Cross. Glass was broken, lights extinguished and the signal box damaged, but injuries were slight. A third Metropolitan bomb, its owners not traced, was placed under the seat of an 1868 Ashbury First Class coach, exploding at Aldersgate Street (now Barbican) on the evening of 26 April 1897. Debris from the severely damaged coach and station roof injured ten passengers on the island platform, one dying after admission to hospital, another succumbing to his injuries six months later. Fully repaired, the coach returned to give further service until electrification.

LOCOMOTIVE TROUBLES

Serious problems with the locomotives were first drawn to the attention of the board in 1873 after some tiresome interruptions of traffic and, in one case, an accident. Like others before him[8], Tomlinson considered the Beyer-Peacock tanks excessively heavy, attributing several failures of springs to a combination of this and poor track. The board ordered re-sleepering.

Another fault, increasingly apparent, was a weakness in the iron side rods which of course suffered the abnormal braking strains inseparable from working a railway of this type which intensified as traffic increased. Tomlinson began to strengthen the rods with iron.

An incident on 29 August 1873 not only illustrates the nature of this trouble but throws some light on the quite remarkable, if misguided, determination of the engine crews to keep the service going at all costs. Before departure of the 5.10 pm train from Mansion House, both outside coupling rods on the locomotive were found to be bent. The engine crew slackened the cotters back and the train left late. At Sloane Square one of the rods broke. Both rods were then removed by the footplatemen, after which a brave attempt was made by the driver to get his charge as far as the repair shops at Edgware Road. Slight rain on the rails caused some slipping after departure from Gloucester Road station and this was followed by a series of stops and starts on the rising grade in the tunnel. The driver then proposed to set back to the siding at Gloucester Road station, but before he could arrange this, his train was hit in the rear by the 5.20 pm Mansion House to Moorgate, which had mistakenly been given the 'line clear' by the Kensington High Street signalman whilst the 5.10 pm was still stationary in the tunnel.

This mishap was interesting for other reasons as it was said to be the first of its kind on the Metropolitan despite the daily telegraphing from signal box to signal box of around 1,000 trains. The Board of Trade inspector made the fairly obvious point that the force of the collision would have been modified had the trains been fitted with continuous brakes. He suggested that such mistakes by signalmen would be less likely to occur if each train were given a working number. Fenton, the general manager of the Metropolitan, could not accept this, alleging it was not always possible to run trains in the order shown in the working timetable, particularly as the GWR Windsor to Moorgate trains were susceptible to delay on the GWR line, causing them to present themselves to the Metropolitan signalmen out of order. Furthermore, he pointed out that at some boxes the men were physically unable to see the trains passing. And as for continuous brakes, the Metropolitan had so far been unable to find a satisfactory system; but the 46-ton locomotives had a powerful brake and each train carried both a guard and a brakesman, who worked the brakes on two of the five carriages, each of which weighed 16–18 tons loaded.

Another accident associated with this locomotive defect occurred on 16 December 1884 when the engine of the 5.30 am from Hammersmith bent its side rod on stopping at King's Cross. The offending part was removed, but in the blocking back that the delay caused, there was a slight collision at Devonshire Street signal box as a result of a signalman's error. After this incident, Tomlinson was required to provide a list of locomotive failures in the last six months of 1884. This revealed six side rods breaking or bending in service, ten broken springs, three burst tubes and three derailments on the MDR's awkward and sharply curved layout at Mansion House. Facing mounting displeasure from the board at what was regarded as an unduly high incidence of locomotive and rolling stock breakdowns, Tomlinson resigned as resident engineer in April 1885. He was replaced on 1 July by J. J. Hanbury of the Midland Railway locomotive department, who was made resident engineer and locomotive superintendent at £600 a year, rising in three years to £800. To mark the occasion, another locomotive broke its side rod on 24 October.

Hanbury told the board that all the coupling rod failures were on the 'B' Class engines and set about replacing these with rods of heavier section. Difficulties continued, no doubt associated with the unremitting strain, day in, day out, of working such an intensive, frequently stopping service. With 34 engine and 16 carriage failures in a single month (December 1890), Hanbury was also in disfavour with the board. From 1 December 1891 he was relieved of responsibility for permanent way and works to allow him to concentrate on locomotive and rolling stock matters. The other work was given to W. H. Gates, known at the time as 'clerk of works', although when he died in harness on 1 June 1903 he was referred to as 'resident engineer', despite a continuing separation of the locomotive and rolling stock responsibilities. Hanbury, who seems never to have enjoyed very happy relationships on the Metropolitan, either with his masters or the staff under his control, found the change did not improve matters and resigned on 31 October 1893. T. S. Raney, foreman of the carriage depot, was then put in charge of the locomotive running department on a temporary basis, but when the chairman and his son visited Neasden Works in 1895 they concluded that the rolling stock and locomotive work were altogether too much for the erstwhile foreman. During his absence on leave, T. F. Clark, the locomotive shops foreman, had been in charge, with the result that 'the epidemic of engine failures' had ceased. Clark was accordingly made locomotive superintendent on 1 January 1896 at £250 a year, Raney returning to his carriages and wagons until he retired on 30 June 1903.

Whilst Clark's abilities may have had some impact on the locomotive problems, it is interesting to note that during the early part of his term of office significant modifications were being made to the engines. The difficulties formerly experienced were largely overcome by redesigning the connecting rods and by fitting Gibson & Lilley link motion. After a three-year trial on no 29 in 1889–92 during the Hanbury regime, the latter device was found to decrease fuel consumption, save time on starting from stations and to provide a uniform motion which reduced wear and tear. By the end of 1896 all locomotives had been fitted with it. Trials with oil burning, using

Holden's apparatus fitted to no 62 in 1898, were less successful. Whilst the then somewhat conservative *Railway Magazine* thought this might offer a cheaper alternative to electrification, the Metropolitan engineers considered the smoke emission level unacceptable with fuels of suitable price.

WORKMEN'S TRAINS AND THE PASSENGER DUTY REVOLT

The Metropolitan was the first railway company in London to offer cheap fares to workmen. Reflecting the ideas of Charles Pearson, one of its originators, it operated from May 1864 two early morning trains at 2d for the full journey, with the facility of returning by any train after midday. It was not until the act of 6 August 1861, authorising the Moorgate extension (opened on 23 December 1865) that parliament required such a facility; similar provisions were inserted in later acts authorising new lines. Shortly after the opening of Metropolitan service to Hammersmith in April 1865 workmen's trains, at 4d return, were provided daily (except Sundays) between there and the City, bringing the daily total to three over the line.

Government Passenger Duty[9] was an imposition very much resented by Sir Edward Watkin so far as the Metropolitan was concerned. Seeking relief, he made several approaches to W. E. Gladstone, the Chancellor of the Exchequer (who was an MDR shareholder), for once acting in concert with Forbes, who considered it equally unjust upon the MDR. Later the London Trades Council were bullied into the fray by threats that no improvements could be made to the provision of workmen's trains (they were seeking some) until the government had made concessions on Passenger Duty. Watkin's first sally was attended with some success. In his usual blustering tone, he told Gladstone:

> Any institution like ours, which carries 50 million passengers at an average of 2½d per head, the bulk belonging to the poor and hard-labor class, is, I presume to think, not a fit subject for excessive taxation.

The Inland Revenue agreed to forego its outstanding claims for the Duty payable before 1 July 1872, but it did insist that before any exemption could be claimed, *all* Third Class passengers on any given train must be carried at not more than one penny a mile to *all* stations served by the train. The two underground railway companies accepted this stipulation, recovering the small extra cost by an increase in the price of season tickets from 1 July 1873.

The crux of Watkin's case was that the Duty charged was heavier proportionately than the payments extracted from the tramway and bus operators, yet the Metropolitan and MDR were, in his view, nothing more than 'underground omnibus services', with almost all their traffic arising from passenger travel. He described them as essentially 'lines of the working people', stressing the contribution they made to local rates, also proportionately higher than the payments made by the major bus company (the LGOC). He also bemoaned the Inland Revenue's rigid interpretation of the rules regarding exemption.

In 1873 the Metropolitan experimented by allowing a limited number of 'exempted rate' tickets to be used on every train all day, whilst continuing to pay duty on all tickets charged at higher than a 1d a mile rate. From 1 May, passengers holding such tickets were accommodated in a 'Parliamentary Compartment' set aside on each train, although they were allowed access to any Third Class compartment of MDR and GWR trains using the Metropolitan[10]. This measure, operated with growing laxity and confusion, increased the number of cheap fare, duty-exempted passenger journeys from 14,000 to over 300,000 a year, and, after modifications in 1878, to over six million a year. In 1876, much put out, the Inland Revenue suspended their approval of the Metropolitan's cheap train arrangements, Finally the Metropolitan removed all restrictions on use of their trains by penny-a-mile passengers, bringing the total to 20 million a year within the 70 million carried[11].

Shareholders were asked to do what they could to agitate for the removal of the duty, which was said to be equivalent in the five years to 1876 to a tax of 2s 2d (10.8 per cent) on each £ of dividend paid to all Metropolitan shareholders. It was emphasised that unlike most other railway companies, the Metropolitan could not afford to pass the tax on to its passengers. The campaign led to the appointment of a Commons select committee, which studied the situation in 1876, producing a recommendation for repeal of the duty.

Although urged to implement this measure by the Metropolitan, the government stood its ground, but the pressure continued, not only from the Metropolitan and the MDR, and eventually a useful concession was obtained in the Cheap Trains Act, 1883. This reduced the duty from the standard five per cent to two per cent on fares exceeding 1d a mile between stations in urban areas, as defined by the Board of Trade. As a result, the Metropolitan lost three-fifths of its previous liability. But having withheld payments for earlier years which the Inland Revenue considered were due, the company was taken to court in 1881. The verdict for the Crown obliged the Metropolitan to pay arrears back to 1878, amounting to the then very substantial sum of

£50,000. Financed by a special issue of four per cent terminable debentures, this commitment was not finally discharged until July 1885.

It had been decided that from 1 April 1882 the special category of 'parliamentary' fare should be abolished, as all Third Class fares from that date would be at the rate of one penny a mile, or less. Following the resolution of the disputes over the duty, the number of workmen's trains available at even lower rates was increased. By the end of 1883 the Metropolitan was operating 12 six-car trains at fares of 2d, 4d and 6d return, according to distance, every day except Sundays[12]. In response to local pressure, the Railway Commissioners required the company to run two more workmen's trains from Neasden to Baker Street East at a return fare of 4d. These were started on 1 June 1892, when the scale of workmen's fares on the system became 2d return for five miles or less, 4d return for five to ten miles, and 6d return for 10–15 miles.

SPECIAL ACCOMMODATION AND PASSENGER COMMUNICATION

Before the Metropolitan had been in operation for very long it became apparent that the complete ban on smoking imposed by the 1862 byelaws was resented by a significant number of passengers, who were adding the smell of the burning weed to the other flavours of the railway. Responding to complaints by non-smokers, the Board of Trade approached the company in March 1869 and November 1870 about its laxity in enforcing the byelaw. Urged to take action by the board, Fenton succeeded in obtaining several prosecutions, which for a time reduced the number of offences.

Meanwhile, in 1868, parliament bowed to the smoking lobby, requiring, in section 20 of that year's Regulation of Railways Act, that all railway companies should provide smoking compartments on all but the shortest journeys. Alone among the companies, the Metropolitan was exempted from this provision, but as its services were enmeshed with those of the Metropolitan the MDR also continued to ban smoking. However, when extending its line to Hammersmith in September 1874, the District felt obliged to conform to the statute. There was then little alternative for the Metropolitan but to follow suit and smoking carriages were provided on all its trains from 1 September 1874, simultaneously with the MDR change.

Another type of separation proved transitory. In October 1874 some public agitation arose for 'Ladies Only' carriages, in which, if the minutes are to be believed, 'gentlemen travelling with ladies' were to

128

be allowed. An experiment was approved for First and Second Class Ladies (there were no *ladies* to be seen in the Third Class, only *women*). It was soon found that the ladies preferred to travel with other passengers, producing complaints that the lightly-used reserved compartments were causing overcrowding elsewhere on the trains. The facility was accordingly withdrawn in 1875, not to be reintroduced until 7 November 1931.

Ladies, and others, could be forgiven for travelling more nervously on the Metropolitan than on other lines as communication cords or other passenger emergency stop devices were absent from its carriages for many years. On 9 August 1910 a male passenger was shot at in a train between Baker Street and Swiss Cottage. Fortunately the victim recovered, not having been seriously wounded, and the culprit was apprehended by a vigilant staff. Following this incident, the Board of Trade was concerned to discover that there was no passenger communication device on the train involved, in defiance of a recommendation made by its departmental committee of 1898 that all passenger trains should be so fitted. Around this time the Metropolitan still had 149 steam stock coaches lacking this feature and further expenditure was resisted on the grounds that trains ran no more than 20 miles between stops. As such a distance would not be covered in less than half an hour or so, this left plenty of scope for all sorts of unpleasantness, and, surprisingly, it was not until 1932 that all Metropolitan passenger stock was fitted.

NO STATION FOR CLERKENWELL

A problem which was to worry the Metropolitan at intervals over the years was whether a station should be provided in the gap of almost a mile between King's Cross and Farringdon Street, where the line passed through the populous and mainly working class district of Clerkenwell. The possibility of building a station here was first considered in 1866 and again three years later, but as the line was 60ft below the surface at this point, a circumstance which would add substantially to the cost of access, ventilation and lighting, the scheme was rejected. At Watkin's request, a further study was made in 1873 but this revealed that the increased working costs set against the estimated net extra receipts would produce only £3,000 net income a year. Given this Watkin did not consider the large capital outlay justified.

Pressure from the local authority and others continued and when R. H. Selbie became general manager he investigated the matter, declaring himself satisfied that a station would prove remunerative because there was no competition from tube railways at this point and little or none from electric tramways. He noted that the Mount Pleasant postal sorting office which had opened in 1900 employed around a thousand men, a large proportion of them likely to use the station. Parliamentary authority for a station adjoining the Post Office depot was obtained in the company's act of 1911, but in the following October a start was postponed, on Selbie's advice. He now concluded it 'too costly to contemplate at the present time' (gross revenue had started to decline). Always optimistic, the company kept the parliamentary powers alive until 31 October 1932 when they were finally allowed to lapse on the grounds that 'this heavily-stressed portion of the Inner Circle' could not accommodate an additional station.

A MIXED BLESSING: THE CITY WIDENED LINES IN USE

Passing beneath Clerkenwell were the City Widened Lines, another source of Metropolitan headaches, since for many years they were used exclusively by other companies, who often complained and were generally ungrateful for a facility for which the Metropolitan thought itself inadequately rewarded.

Watkin was much upset by a statement in the GNR half-yearly report for the second half of 1873 on the inconvenience of working GNR freight and passenger traffic over the Metropolitan owing to the crowded state of the line. Ever-abrasive, he threw back the charge, blaming the GNR for not presenting its trains on time to the Metropolitan and for doing nothing about the woefully inadequate Down Local station arrangements at King's Cross. Soon after his appointment as general manager at the beginning of 1880, John Bell, no doubt conscious of his master's view, but also in character, was adopting a staunchly aggressive stance with all the users of the Widened Lines, castigating them for unpunctuality and other sins. In February 1881 he was complaining of frequent special trains of one carriage and a saloon run at very short notice for the convenience of private individuals and families and for which the operating company retained the whole of the special 'per mile' charge, only crediting the Metropolitan with its proportion of the ordinary fares. In his mischievous way, but with a grain of justification, Forbes accused Bell of rendering himself obnoxious to all managers of companies using the Widened Lines, stinging Bell into issuing a printed apologia which he circulated to each Metropolitan director.

In this document of October 1883, it was suggested the cause of

130

unpunctuality on the Widened Lines lay in the timetables drawn up by the user companies, which were so varied from time to time to suit the companies' selfish convenience that trains were scheduled at intervals which made it quite impossible for them to work clear of each other. On its own line, the GNR allowed three to four minutes between each train but attempted to despatch over the Metropolitan towards the City trains timed to leave King's Cross at 7.29, 7.31, 7.34 and 7.38 am. In the reverse direction, trains from the City were supposed to leave King's Cross at 3.15, 3.16 and 3.18 pm in addition to a main line train which often left unpunctually and had been liable to cause a total block of up to 11 minutes on these Down trains. There were similar nonsenses in the Midland Railway timetable. Bell also commented on the manner in which both the GNR and the Midland inserted bogus freight trains in their timetables; hardly if ever run, these existed only to restrict the other company's competitiveness.

After two years 'of incessant worry, with complaints of delays, the investigation occupying two inspectors almost whole time', Bell claimed he had secured some modifications to the timetables which had reduced delays by about 50 per cent. He had brought the problem of short notice special trains under control by requiring due notice to be given, including some indication of the revenue to the Metropolitan. Even so the GNR superintendent of the line had proved difficult: 'I have experienced the utmost discourtesy from Mr Cockshott'. There had also been foot-dragging by the LCDR in settling its accounts with the Metropolitan, requiring intervention by the Railway Clearing House. And although the LCDR ran only 65 trains a day, some were regularly cancelled. However after he had persuaded the Metropolitan board to take action, a revised LCDR timetable with 70 trains a day had been introduced, with no cancellations now occurring, except after accidents.

Bell's paper noted that although the LCDR traffic with the Metropolitan's City stations had declined since 1871, there had been a progressive increase since 1880 in the business brought on to the Metropolitan by both the GNR and the Midland, the former in particular showing in 1882 a 43 per cent increase over the 1879 level.

Much ill feeling has been caused by the arrangement reached in January 1875 between the GNR and the North London Railway which allowed the latter's trains to run to and from Broad Street station, City over GNR suburban routes. This the Metropolitan saw as diverting traffic which would otherwise have used its Widened Lines. The three companies had however agreed at that time that GNR season ticket holders to and from Moorgate or Broad Street might return by either the Metropolitan or the NLR route, the receipts to be divided according to the number of trains run by each company.

This sore was long to heal. In March 1885, using the pretext of alleged GNR support for a new railway along the Regent's Canal, Watkin fired off a letter to Lord Colville, the GNR chairman, about the 'needless competition' this new line would cause and how 'very hard' it had been on the Metropolitan when the GNR and NLR made their arrangement in 1875. Watkin averred that the Metropolitan was obtaining rather less than a 2¼ per cent return on its outlay on the City Widened Lines. To all this the GNR replied that at the times when they were most needed the Metropolitan was unable to accommodate more than six trains an hour and as its suburban traffic was growing rapidly, the GNR had to find all the routes it could. Further, it was a fact that the GNR were paying more to the Metropolitan for running over the Widened Lines than had been the case before the NLR connection had been made. In this argument it seems likely that the GNR came closer to the truth than the Metropolitan. With 15 trains an hour in one direction through the City Widened Lines at peak times for all users, this section was being worked very close to the limit of its capacity, given its physical disadvantages, manual signalling, steam traction and the restricted terminal facilities at Moorgate.

Following more provocative comment at a GNR half yearly meeting the argument flared up again in 1890. It was said that the Metropolitan was 'almost choked' at peak hours, there being no question of increasing its capacity. This contention was at once challenged by Bell, who cited GNR refusal to contribute towards increasing the length of platforms at Widened Lines stations or to adopt Metropolitan suggestions for adding extra trains. Nevertheless it was still the case that with 29 GNR and Midland trains between King's Cross and Farringdon from 8.28 to 10 am and 42 between 5.01 and 7.11 pm in the opposite direction, the GNR had near enough reached the lip of the cup. Nor were longer trains the answer; at King's Cross the awkwardness of the curves and gradients limited the locomotive power that could be used for the 10–11 coach trains.

For his part, Watkin did what he could to maximise traffic over the Widened Lines. He seems to have played a major role in securing a connection between the LCDR and the SER at Blackfriars Junction, just south of the Thames, completed on 1 June 1878. On that date, a GNR passenger service was started to and from Woolwich Arsenal, six trains each way daily, via the Widened Lines and Snow Hill. The SER had no running powers over the Metropolitan, but from 1 August

1880 it ran this service to and from Enfield or Muswell Hill on behalf of the GNR. With the arrival of much-improved facilities across central London, loadings on these trains fell drastically, causing them to be withdrawn after traffic on 30 April 1907.

Life on the Widened Lines in the 19th century was not without its excitements, especially for the men in the isolated underground Granville signal box, halfway between Farringdon and King's Cross. Working loose-coupled freight trains down under the original Metropolitan tracks, then quickly up again, was conducive to break-aways, which often left the severed rear section and brake van to be hit by a following train in the smoke-shrouded gloom of the tunnel.

SORTING OUT AND DEVELOPING SURPLUS LANDS

'The Company has a very considerable estate and large and almost unlimited powers of dealing with it.' This remark by the Metropolitan's chairman in a 1902 report on organisation neatly summarises a circumstance, unique amongst British railway undertakings, which the company enjoyed for almost the whole of its existence.

When preparing for the construction of its central area lines and north western suburban extensions, the Metropolitan acquired large amounts of land not needed for railway purposes. Landowners, hoping to discourage railway building, or at any rate to profit from it, refused to sell small parcels of land for the line, insisting that the company take a great deal more adjoining property. Most expected to re-purchase at a bargain price in due course when the railway had increased the development value. Determined to make their railways, armed with the necessary capital and 'under the impression that they would be able to hold and develop at a profit'[1], the Metropolitan board had bought it all. Unlike the MDR, which had disposed of its unwanted properties soon after opening its lines, the Metropolitan had kept its surplus lands in a tight grip.

Such behaviour was however contrary to the will of parliament as expressed in sections 127–8 of the Land Clauses Consolidation Act, 1845, which directed railway companies to sell off all land not required for the purposes of the railway's special acts within a maximum of ten years from the expiration of time limited by the special acts for the completion of the works[2]. But by dint of inserting special provisions in its own acts, which passed through inert parliaments, the Metropolitan gradually manoeuvred itself into a very special and privileged position in this area. Firstly, it was enabled, by section 14 of its act of 30 June 1862 to grant building leases of superfluous lands within the ten year limit of the 1845 Consolidation Act. Then a power to purchase and hold (with the consent of the owners) any property not required for the construction of the railway was given by section 20 of the Metropolitan Railway Act of 13 July 1868. Most important of all, and no doubt at Watkin's personal initiative,

Plate 16 Amersham looking to London, about 1905 (*commercial postcard, courtesy London Underground Railway Society*)

Plate 17 The first type of electric train on trial run with Metropolitan Railway directors, probably in March 1904 at Rayners Lane (*photographer unknown*)

Plate 18 Westinghouse electric loco No 1 as delivered, Neasden, 1905; the shoe gear arrangements were soon to be altered (*Metropolitan Vickers*)

Plate 19 Evening scene at Ickenham Halte, looking to Uxbridge early summer 1906. The train is composed of the second batch of 1905 Westinghouse stock (*S.W.A. Newton/Leicestershire Museums, Art Galleries & Records Service*)

the Metropolitan secured a blanket provision which cut across the stipulation in the 1845 Act. This was enshrined in section 19 of the company's act of 21 July 1873, which allowed the Metropolitan to retain any superfluous lands *whenever acquired, including those acquired in the future*. To do this, it merely had to 'believe' such lands 'may hereafter be necessary' for the widening of the railway, or for stations, or sidings. In the expansionist atmosphere of 1870 onwards, such a qualification presented no problems of conscience. To establish the position beyond peradventure, the 1873 provision, together with power to grant leases, was repeated in several later acts covering acquisition of lands. Further statutory embellishment of the railway's property powers will be mentioned later.

Fairly quickly then, the Metropolitan became a land or estate company as well as a railway company, though for a long period no attempt was made to distinguish the two operations, the income from both sources being muddled together in the company's accounts to produce unrealistic dividends for what were ostensibly the ordinary shares of a railway company. The longer the situation was allowed to drift, the more difficult it became to consider selling off the super-fluous properties en bloc if the company was to secure a proper return.

One solution, the sale of the properties to a specially-formed limited liability company, had in fact been approved by the board at the end of 1869 but when the attempt was made, it had to be abandoned as an insufficient number of the issued shares in the new company were paid up. After this, the question of sale was never raised again. Instead, a committee of directors, known as the Land Committee, was formed in 1870 to manage the superfluous properties and approve further purchases. This committee published half-yearly reports, issued simultaneously with those for the railway undertaking. In the early 1870s the net income from the 700 or so tenants of surplus properties was around £36,000 a year. Administration was in the hands of a secretary, two rent collectors, two clerks and a surveyor, at a total cost of £2,085 a year. After becoming chairman, Sir Edward Watkin made some economies which reduced the staff to five and the annual cost to £1,220.

Steps were taken, in the Metropolitan Railway Act of 30 June 1874, to begin to consolidate the company's powers regarding these surplus lands, hitherto held by trustees. They were now vested in the company and the act also required the maintenance of separate accounts as well as allowing the company to convey surplus lands and apply the proceeds arising from their sale.

With the projection of the railway beyond Swiss Cottage a substantial addition was made to the surplus estate. At Willesden and Kingsbury, the Metropolitan found itself buying some 400 acres from the Ecclesiastical Commissioners and two other parties (Prout and Finch), the whole being valued in 1876 at £127,500. Following development of the employees' cottage estate at Neasden (Chapter 6) and the residential Willesden Park Estate, to be mentioned in a moment, the income and number of tenants rose sharply, until by 1885 there were 930 tenants and gross receipts of £66,000, almost a quarter of the total net balance available for dividend on the railway's ordinary stock.

Watkin was uncomfortable about the situation he found after his arrival at the Metropolitan. Despite the special legislative provisions, he felt the company remained vulnerable whilst there was no proper separation of the two sides of the business. In March 1886 he warned his fellow directors:

> The directors at large are little aware of the many struggles with the authorities in Parliament to prevent clauses compelling realization before ripeness, long ago. That struggle will recommence if the compromise be now ignored. It is an anomaly, more than once pointed out in Parliament and elsewhere, that a small railway company should have more than one third of its railway dividend on Ordinary Stock made up out of the proceeds of property not needed for the railway or any probable extensions of the lines and stations and anyone who takes the trouble to look around must be aware that the railway companies will not for long be allowed to be great surplus estate owners.

He sought an end to the muddle in the finances and accounts and wanted 'to prevent exaggerated notions of the profits of underground lines and therefore to prevent competition based upon too high dividends'. Clarification of the matter would, in Watkin's view, improve the selling value and steadiness of the stock as well as facilitate possible future amalgamations (presumably with the MDR)[3].

The 'compromise' referred to by Watkin had been drawn up with the able assistance of R. W. Perks[4]. They had concluded that a division of the ordinary stock (allowing shareholders to keep their two portions, or to sell either, or to buy either) was the only practicable and desirable answer, providing means of treating the surplus lands revenues separately, using them to service dedicated stock. They suggested that the surplus estate could be realistically valued at £2,640,915.

To permit the change to be made and thus sanctify the Metropolitan's unique situation for all time, a bill was drafted and successfully piloted through parliament as the Metropolitan Railway Act of 16 July 1885. Watkin's scheme was not unanimously embraced by the board. Morphett submitted a long memorandum summarising his misgivings. Pochin could see no advantage for the railway company, believing that the lands shares would quickly evolve into a separate and distinct interest apart from the railway as if they had never existed in united form; conflicts and complications between the two interests were foreseen which would be 'more than equal to the creation of another District Railway with which the future Metropolitan directors would have to battle'. That Pochin's fears proved groundless was due to the skilful management of the situation over the years whereby the railway board ensured that policy and administration of the surplus lands sector was always firmly under their exclusive control. In any case both Morphett and Pochin were soon to overcome their qualms, accepting positions in the new Surplus Lands administration.

When they were put to the shareholders at special meetings on 27 July and 23 November 1886, the Perks-Watkin proposals secured 75 per cent endorsement, as required by the act. With final parliamentary blessing obtained by scheduling the scheme to the company's act of 19 July 1887 it became effective from the beginning of that month. The ordinary stock of the railway was split into two portions, with £1 of the new £2.64m surplus lands capital issued for every £2 of Consolidated Metropolitan Railway Ordinary Stock held at 30 June 1887. All the surplus property remained very firmly vested in the railway company and was to continue as security for the debentures and mortgage bonds of the railway company existing at the time the scheme started, whilst also remaining available for service of the then existing preference stock of the railway company if required. The management of the surplus estate was placed under a Surplus Lands Committee, whose members received a total of £250 a year, two appointed by the holders of the Surplus Lands Stock and three nominated by the railway board. Separate accounts were to be maintained for the surplus estate showing income from rents etc and proceeds of sales (which the Committee had the power to undertake, together with new purchases, both in the name of the railway company). The income was to be applied to the payment of the dividends on the Surplus Lands Stock each half year. The railway company could and did make loans to the Surplus Lands Committee both for further purchases and payment of dividends.

It will be seen that the new Surplus Lands Committee was in every respect as much an undertaking of the railway company as the rest of the Metropolitan's businesses and that the Surplus Lands Stock holders were stockholders of the railway company, with stock served by a particular class of assets of the railway company, not by the railway business as such. As a further refinement, powers were obtained in the Metropolitan Railway Act of 5 July 1889 which allowed the railway company to buy any land it needed for railway purposes from the Surplus Lands Committee at a fair price. Then, in the Metropolitan Railway Act of 2 August 1898, the Surplus Lands Committee was permitted to improve and develop and lay out for building with a view to sale or lease any of its lands, including those acquired 'hereafter'. The same act also allowed the Committee to purchase and hold leasehold lands, erect houses and buildings and carry out structural alterations and improvements. Finally, the railway company itself was enabled, by a provision in its act of 20 July 1906, to build on or over stations and lines for letting and sale. We shall return to this aspect of the business in Chapter 12.

Following separation of the surplus lands, the dividend payable on Metropolitan Railway ordinary stock fell from five per cent in the first half of 1887 to 2¾ in each of the following three half years, fluctuating between 2¼ and 3¾ over the following 15 years. Surplus Lands Stock returned 2½ per cent each half year from 1887 to 1894, increasing marginally thereafter. Both sets of returns were satisfactory for safe 'trustee' investments at this time of low inflation.

EXPLOITATION OF SUBURBAN LAND: 1880–1914

Even before the financial reconstruction of 1887 the railway company had embarked on what was to be a long period of developing its suburban land for residential purposes. This beginning was made at Willesden Green, on the Willesden Park Estate, purchased from the Ecclesiastical Commissioners and situated immediately west of the station, south of the line. Plans were discussed early in 1879 before the opening of the railway that November from West Hampstead to Willesden Green. An independent solicitor was appointed to grant leases and influence the introduction of builders. Roads and sewers were laid out and trees planted, all at the railway's expense, in 1880–1, and the first building leases for semi-detached villas on this 12-acre site were granted in October of the latter year. In its report for the second half of 1881 the Land Committee noted: '. . . there is little doubt that the estate will be a residential property providing a considerable income and aiding in the development of traffic'. With the first houses coming into occupation in 1882–3, further building leases were granted, including some on additional land in Walm Lane, which had been purchased by the railway company to complete the estate. There was also some activity at Harrow. In 1888 the new Surplus Lands Committee put to auction building plots in Pinner Road and College Road, achieving a reasonable amount of success.

The second section of the Willesden Park Estate, further west, between Villiers Road and the railway, was laid out in the 1890s. About 350 houses had been erected by the middle of 1899 when the Willesden Council asked the Metropolitan to open a station between Willesden Green and Neasden to serve what was rapidly becoming a new suburb. Agitation for a station resumed in 1904, by which time there were built or building some 3,000 houses in the immediate neighbourhood and there was a population of about 10,000 south of the railway between Willesden Green and Neasden. But the board still hesitated. After building operations had begun north of the railway and a new motorbus service was taking some commuters from the area direct to London via Cricklewood, the Metropolitan's general manager told his board that the railway was losing traffic, persuading it to sanction a start on the new station, for which other developers had promised assistance. Named Dollis Hill & Gladstone Park, the 350ft long, 21ft wide island platform between the Metropolitan tracks was opened on 1 October 1909. An 8ft wide subway containing the ticket office linked the platform to both sides of the line but the down side entrance in Chapter Road did not open until 20 December. Patronage was good. Using the first five months' figures and making allowance for traffic abstracted from Neasden and Willesden Green, the general manager calculated that there was an approximate 50 per cent return on the £4,033 cost.

Some of the houses on the Willesden Green development were not well-built and with the opening of the GCR lines were subjected to a marked increase in vibration to add to their other problems. Tenants left them empty, but the occupation rate improved after repairs had been made at Metropolitan expense in 1903–04.

Development of two more estates was well advanced before 1914. At Cecil Park, south of the line at Pinner, some houses had been occupied by 1901 when the Surplus Lands Committee asked the board if residents might be given reduced season ticket rates. This was refused, but advertisements for the estate were allowed on the company's stations free of charge. Some of the Cecil Park houses were quite large semi-detached types with three storeys, three reception rooms and up to six bedrooms. These were leased at up to £70 a year to families a little higher in the social strata than those at Willesden Park, where the average rental was only £50. Further building leases

141

at Cecil Park were granted in 1911–12 and in the former year the adjacent Stanley Villas (named after the Surplus Land Committee's surveyor, Stanley Eyles) were also available. About 1913 an additional entrance was made on the Down side at Pinner station for the convenience of the Cecil Park residents. On the opposite side of the line, some preparatory work was done on the Committee's Grange Estate, but most of the houses here were not completed until 1920–28.

Following the failure of the Tower Company to pay its mortgage interest and the refusal of the Middlesex County Council to renew the horse racing licence, the Metropolitan board decided in 1905 that the best future for Wembley Park was to develop it 'as a building estate in the interests of the railway company'. The Tower Company then became the Wembley Park Estate Co Ltd, control continuing by filling the board with Metropolitan directors. From 1906 the renamed undertaking was making agreements with builders and selling off individual plots at £650–£750 an acre. Part of the area was let to a golf club at £600 a year. Within two years, houses appeared in Wembley Park Drive, Oakington Avenue and other roads, the railway company making loans at 4 per cent from its Reserve Fund to finance 'builders of good standing'. Money was also available from the same source in 1913 to assist the Estate Company to build on its own account. Here also the type of house was aimed at families just a little higher in the social scale than those at Willesden. By the end of 1914 there were 106 houses at Wembley Park and although the Estate Company had not paid any dividend, its activities had increased receipts at the station from £3,807 in 1906 to £6,150 in 1914. As an encouragement, from the beginning of 1915 the railway company undertook to pay the Estate Company a percentage on any increase in station receipts over the 1906 figure.

On the eve of the First World War, an enterprising new general manager was to produce a suggestion for a bold new initiative regarding the exploitation of the Metropolitan's territory. This would not only accelerate lineside building developments under the railway's control but also act as a catalyst for others. It will be considered in Chapter 14.

Whilst some energy was shown with regard to development of surplus lands in the suburban area, surprisingly little was done to make the most of the valuable inner area properties owned by the Metropolitan. This may have been deliberate, as such action could have provoked criticism in parliament of what many felt was an incongruous position for a railway company, perhaps leading to an upsetting of the whole apple cart. Early in 1900 it was reported that several plots of extremely valuable land between Aldgate and Mansion House had long been left unproductive; efforts by outsiders to find tenants had been discouraged, apparently on the express instructions of the directors[5]. Two years later, R. W. Perks, then chairman of the MDR, referred to this, citing the existence of two properties with a total value of £160,000 in Mark Lane and the Minories which had been left unlet for 18 years. He added, 'greater enterprise might be displayed in the letting of this land and I felt it my duty to press this very strongly upon our partners, the Metropolitan Railway'[6].

ACCOMMODATING THE GREAT CENTRAL

In Chapter 6 we left the Metropolitan with a double track completed through Aylesbury to Verney Junction, with arrangements concluded for the new main line of the MSLR (later the Great Central) to meet this at Quainton Road, some six miles south of Verney. From here it would use the Metropolitan as a means of entering London. Much was to happen before this last aim was achieved.

Shortly before the construction of the MSLR London Extension had begun, John Bell, the Metropolitan's general manager, took Watkin's place as chairman, whilst retaining his managerial responsibilities. Bell's propensity to upset other railway managements in defence of what he saw as the Metropolitan's interests has already been noted in his attitude toward the users of the City Widened Lines. This abrasive tendency was now to come into prominence as Bell found himself dealing with William Pollitt, the MSLR general manager. Many years earlier when the two men had jostled for promotion as fellow clerks on the MSLR, a jealous rivalry had formed between them, sending down deep roots as each sought to score points and establish superiority over the other.

Almost at once Bell assumed a strongly independent attitude with the MSLR, cutting the close bonds formed by Watkin. Relations very quickly became difficult, remaining so for some years. By the beginning of 1896, the situation had so deteriorated that Watkin's son, Alfred Mellor, thought he should give up his seat on the Metropolitan board 'under the present position of affairs between the two companies'. This was politely refused, but he did resign three years later, stating that he preferred to retain the connection he had with the Great Central and the MSLR which dated back to 1864.

An early bone of contention was the inclusion in the 1895 MSLR bill, after inadequate discussion with the Metropolitan, of powers to make a double track parallel to the Metropolitan between Wembley Park and Canfield Place, near Finchley Road station. This was intended in place of the modest widening in the 1893 act which would have been on the north side of the Metropolitan between West Hampstead and Finchley Road stations and was designed to facilitate connection to the LNWR and thus to the docks. Bell had fiercely but unsuccessfully resisted this as damaging to Metropolitan interests. Pollitt had now concluded that a widening as far out as Wembley Park was essential because the traffic of both railways, especially with the intended development of Wembley Park and Tower, could not be accommodated on the existing double track west of Finchley Road. He told Bell on 7 January 1895 '. . . we are dealing with the neck of the bottle and must have full control of the traffic on this piece'. As Bell contended that if such quadrupling were to be made, it should be built and controlled by the Metropolitan, he advised his fellow directors to oppose the MSLR bill. At the last minute, the MSLR gave way, agreeing the Metropolitan should construct the additional lines, subject to the MSLR having exclusive use of them and relinquishing the running powers over the parallel Metropolitan tracks given in the 1890 agreement. To protect access to the Wembley Park goods yard and Wembley Tower siding, the Metropolitan insisted upon powers to cross the new lines to reach any Metropolitan land south of it not purchased by the MSLR. These arrangements were sanctioned by the MSLR act of 6 July 1895.

Whilst all this was going on, Bell also succeeded in persuading the MSLR to buy some 150 acres of Surplus Lands Committee property at Neasden for use as its London locomotive depot, workshops and coal yard. This was in place of South Forty Farm north of Wembley Park, the MSLR's first choice. The sale was completed in September 1896[1].

As it was necessary to rebuild overbridges between Wembley Park and Harrow to accommodate MSLR locomotives, the Metropolitan decided it might as well combine this work with an extension of the quadrupling to Harrow, a further 2¼ miles. It was expected that such a widening would be justified by traffic increases within a few years, and there were economies to be had in doing both jobs at the same time. Learning of this, the MSLR requested running powers over the second pair of tracks as far as Harrow. These were granted, but the Metropolitan preferred not to allocate this extension of the widening for the newcomer's exclusive use – just another example of Bell's intransigence. Powers for the additional works were included in the Metropolitan's act of 7 August 1896. Sir John Wolfe Barry was appointed engineer for the whole length from Harrow to Finchley Road.

Construction of the MSLR's own line between Canfield Place and the London terminus at Marylebone was begun by Firbank in November 1894. A temporary junction was agreed with the Metropolitan for the removal of spoil and conveyance of construction materials inwards. This double line connection, which was just south of St John's Wood Road station, by the canal, carried up to 18 spoil trains daily at the height of the work. Under an agreement which had been made by the Metropolitan & Saint John's Wood Railway in 1873, certain property owners had to be compensated with lump sum payments (met by the MSLR) before heavy freight could be carried over this section of the Metropolitan. A second connection for spoil removal was made at Broadhurst Gardens, just east of West Hampstead station and a third at Neasden.

Many more minor works were required to accommodate the demands of the newcomer. These included new intermediate signal boxes at Mantles Wood (on a gantry, between Amersham and Great Missenden), at Dutchlands (between Great Missenden and Wendover) and Harrow Yard, or North box; all were opened in 1900. Temporary signal boxes for the widening works were erected at Canfield Place, Mapesbury (Willesden), Brent North and South Junctions and Preston Road. The first of these remained in use until automatic signalling was installed in 1911, whilst the second, though installed and equipped, never came into operation. At the north end of the widening, a permanent box, Harrow South Junction, was built and Harrow Station box was reconstructed in 1901. Existing signal boxes at Finchley Road, Kilburn, and Pinner were lengthened to accommodate additional levers. Many Metropolitan signals had to be raised or repositioned to improve sighting for express running; the most urgent cases had all been dealt with by February 1899. New instructions for working the block system combined with the Spagnoletti electric interlocking, together with new bell codes, came into operation at 6 am on Tuesday 28 February 1899. Metropolitan type block instruments and interlocking were fitted into the GCR 'fringe' boxes at Calvert and Canfield Place.

To ensure that GCR locomotives and rolling stock could pass without risk it was necessary to lower the track under certain bridges by two to three inches (in one case by six inches). When this work was completed, the Metropolitan Extension line was able to accommodate the rolling stock of all other major railway companies except the LBSCR and the North Staffordshire Railway, although GWR and Midland stock would require careful running past the bridges[2].

A long list of new works, mostly justified by the arrival of the GCR, but also in part to cope with the Metropolitan's own traffic growth,

was authorised by the board in October 1897. These included enlarge-
ment and improvement of freight facilities at West Hampstead,
Willesden Green, Harrow, Northwood, Chesham, Wendover, Stoke
Mandeville and Quainton Road. Not all were carried out immediately.
At 11 stations between Finchley Road and Aylesbury the siding points
had to be locked from the main line.

Permanent way required a great deal of attention. A divisional
superintendent, appointed early in 1900 to look after the tracks
between Swiss Cottage and Verney Junction, very soon asked for extra
gangs as he found so many of the existing men spent much of their
time fog signalling. Between Finchley Road and Rickmansworth some
of the track had to be completely relaid, whilst elsewhere long
stretches needed new sleepers and chairs, some also requiring
reballasting. This work, completed by 1901, included replacement of
steel sleepers on 8½ miles of double line between Northwood and
Rickmansworth and between Amersham and Great Missenden, the
removed material finding further use on siding extensions.

Another tranche of expenditure in 1899–1901 included more freight
facilities and the installation of a number of refuge sidings accommodating trains of up to 50 wagons[3]. Even this was not enough. In 1902
works were necessary at Rickmansworth, where contracts for gravel
and sand movement had been lost because the traffic could not be
accommodated; there was also inadequate provision for the GCR
freight trains, which often had to be split to get into the existing
siding. Two new sidings were provided, 1¼ miles on the London side
of Rickmansworth, between Croxley Hall Farm bridge and the canal,
on the Up side. The existing intermediate signal box at Watford Road
(the former Rickmansworth Yard box, moved there in 1899) was
resited almost half a mile north towards Rickmansworth to control the
new sidings whilst continuing its former function. This new work cost
£1,600 but it guaranteed additional sand and gravel traffic worth a
minimum of £4,000 a year.

Other Extension Line works carried out in this period were mainly
required to meet the growth in the Metropolitan's own traffic, but
may be conveniently mentioned here (works relating to electrification
will be dealt with in Chapter 11). These included extension of the
freight sidings and facilities at West Hampstead (1903–04), an
additional siding at Neasden (1903) and an additional goods shed and
goods office at Willesden Green (1903). At Willesden Green passenger
station, where traffic growth associated with housing development had
been considerable, all the unpaved sections of the platforms were
covered with York stone or tar in 1902 whilst in the following year

platform roofing was extended and an additional entrance provided. A widening here on the north side, completed in 1904, was at first used as sidings but from 4 January 1906 a new bay road and junction were available for passenger trains terminating or starting. At Harrow, the rough wooden shed on the Up platform was the subject of much complaint by passengers. It was pointed out to the board by the general manager that this station enjoyed a 'superior traffic', which included 'a large number of the aristocracy' paying frequent visits to the School. With their comfort and the First Class income in mind, the shingle platform was paved and new waiting rooms provided in 1904–05. In 1904, between Harrow South Junction and Preston Road, an intermediate box called Kenton was built near Kenton Road bridge to break up this long section.

The continuing growth of freight and special traffics including gravel and ballast from Rickmansworth required more rolling stock. In 1904, 18 low-sided (ten of them secondhand) and 20 high-sided wagons and six box vans were obtained, together with three more horse boxes (making a total of ten) to cope with the peak demand in the hunting season.

Having settled the matter of the widening to his satisfaction, Bell continued to make life difficult for Pollitt so far as other Metropolitan facilities were concerned. A provision in its 1893 act allowed the MSLR to build a double line connection with the Metropolitan at Marylebone, starting at a point on the west side of the approaches to the new terminus between Lorne Gardens and Alpha Road and joining the Inner Circle, facing the City, between what are now Balcombe and Great Central Streets[4]. This was intended to carry both passenger and freight traffic and possible sites for a MSLR freight depot at Farringdon or Smithfield were investigated in 1896. Bell then expressed concern about adding to the congestion between Edgware Road and the City, making difficulties about the number and timing of trains over this proposed connection. His suggested terms were unrealistically onerous. Before long, the MSLR, no longer subject to Watkin's empire-building policies, and very short of capital, had decided to abandon the idea of constructing this link; so far as freight was concerned, it could make an equally satisfactory transfer to the southern lines via the GWR at Banbury and Reading. When told of this at the end of 1896, Bell protested, but got short shrift from Pollitt.

Other disputes arose over a proposed £8,300 locomotive depot at

Aylesbury to house banking engines for the three stretches of 1 in 117 south of that station (which never did get built); over telegraph lines; coal depots; and signalling bell codes. (The Metropolitan's signalling practices were quite rightly regarded as somewhat outdated.)

Friction between the two companies reached the law courts shortly after the GCR tried to run trains for the first time south of Quainton Road. As a purely temporary arrangement, Bell had agreed that a maximum of four Up coal trains could be worked over the Metropolitan into London from 25 July 1898. Contractors and Metropolitan staff were hustled into having everything ready by that date, an exercise which involved much night work. Bell had made it clear that this temporary arrangement did not constitute a full public opening of the GCR new line, so that company would still be liable to pay four per cent interest on the cost of all Metropolitan expenditure on GCR account under the terms of the 1890 agreement.

A junction was put in just north of Quainton Road station by Metropolitan staff and the records of the two companies show that the first coal trains ran over it to London (Neasden) on 26 July 1898. However, the GCR was not content with this, claiming a right to run coal trains off the Metropolitan at Aylesbury on to the GWR as well as into London via Harrow. This was bound to irritate the Metropolitan as it drained off what it saw as its rightful traffic under the 1890 agreement. The GCR decided to organise a test, issuing a notice that the first of such trains via Quainton Road, Aylesbury and Princes Risborough would be run in the early hours of Saturday, 30 July 1898. Bell decided upon personal supervision of the battle. Forsaking his bed, he stationed himself in the Metropolitan box at Quainton Road Junction, instructing the signalman to refuse the test train when it appeared at 3 am. Frustrated GCR officials were obliged to organise its return to Woodford & Hinton yards.

Two days before this incident, the GCR had issued a writ to prevent the Metropolitan from hindering operation of these coal trains. On this issue, Bell won the day. The courts upheld the Metropolitan's contention that the trains were operating by temporary licence only, as specifically agreed by the Metropolitan, and as the running powers of the 1890 agreement were not operative until the line was fully open to all forms of public traffic, the GCR interest payments must continue. As a result, no GCR trains were permitted on to the GWR via Aylesbury until 20 March 1899, suitable terms having then been agreed.

Marylebone station was ceremonially opened on 9 March 1899 with special passenger trains worked via Quainton Road and the Metropolitan line, but the Metropolitan continued to receive its pound of flesh a little longer as public passenger traffic over the GCR to London did not begin until 15 March and full freight facilities were not available until 27 April.

These dates were linked to the completion of the Metropolitan's quadrupling works, which Henry Lovatt had started between Finchley Road and Wembley on 28 April 1896 and J. Strachan between Wembley and Harrow on 8 November 1897. The heaviest tasks were the erection of a 32-arch brick viaduct at Kilburn and the widening of the clay cutting between Willesden Green and Neasden. At West Hampstead, the Metropolitan tracks were slewed either side of the Up platform, which became an island with a new signal box at its south end. The old Down platform here was removed to make room for the two new tracks and a new group of sidings was placed between the Metropolitan running lines at the country end of the station. Rebuilding of the station itself was not fully completed until early in 1899 but the realigned tracks and new signal box were in use from 13 June 1897.

When the first of the GCR sidings at Neasden were ready at the end of 1896 trains had to be backed into them and reversed out through a junction called Brent South, but from 7 September 1898 there was direct access off the widened lines from the Harrow direction via Brent Junction North, controlled by a new signal box.

Owing to the pressure of orders on the steel manufacturers, girder work for the bridges was delayed. It was therefore decided to make a temporary connection between the original and the new tracks at Preston Road, opening the latter south east of this point from 9 March 1899 and enabling the GCR to start its passenger services in and out of Marylebone. Although the remainder of the widened lines as far as Harrow were put into use on 16 September 1900 they were initially shared by the Metropolitan and the GCR whilst repairs were made to the bridge carrying the original Metropolitan tracks over the LNWR. It was not until 31 March 1901 that all four lines were available between Harrow and Finchley Road, when the GCR at last had exclusive use of the two new roads on the south side.

A space 9ft 6in wide had been left between the original and the widened lines, whilst there was a 7ft 6in gap between the new lines and parallel sidings. Rails were 86lb per yd bullhead in 30ft lengths.

In several places the sides of embankments and cuttings through the unstable clay had to be supported with retaining walls of cement concrete. A wall near Kilburn station gave trouble for some time owing to the great pressure of the clay behind it. In 1903 the offending soil was removed and the viaduct extended for 165yd. In his report on the widening, the Board of Trade inspector commented adversely on the 'now little used' siding into Wembley Park, which crossed the new lines on the level. This siding did in fact see occasional use carrying coal and building materials into the Park and the dismantled parts of the Tower were moved out over it in 1906. It was finally removed in the summer of 1909 but the connection across the GCR tracks remained to provide access to the as yet little-used Metropolitan goods yard.

THE GREAT CENTRAL FINDS A NEW WAY IN

With the departure of Sir Edward Watkin from the policy-making of both the GCR and the Metropolitan, the former's doubts about the suitability of its Metropolitan entry to London began to surface. And the sustained posture of prickly superiority adopted by Bell served only to increase the GCR's dissatisfaction.

From an operating point of view there could be no enthusiasm about working express trains between Quainton Road and Finchley Road. Coming off the beautifully-engineered new main line with its ruling gradient of 1 in 176 and easy curves, GCR drivers had to cope with the sinuous switchback which constituted the Metropolitan's Extension Line. Quainton Road junction was perfectly aligned for the Metropolitan's leisurely amblings to Verney Junction but GCR expresses were treated to a tight reverse curve. At Aylesbury, the severe reverse curves through the station area represented a major hazard, all too soon to be underlined by tragedy. South of Aylesbury, the GCR drivers had to tackle a long climb at 1 in 117 through Stoke Mandeville and Wendover to the summit at Dutchlands. Then followed a six mile descent at 1 in 105 offering them little joy as another treacherous curve lay ahead at Rickmansworth station. For the rest, it was a series of undulations with stretches of 1 in 90 and 1 in 95 against Up trains.

As early as 1897 the GCR and GWR had reached an understanding over a connection between their lines from Culworth Junction (near Woodford & Hinton) to Banbury. In return, the GWR got the GCR to drop some hostile moves. At this time the GWR was planning a direct line from Acton to High Wycombe and beyond to deflect competitive proposals and shorten their route to Birmingham. As this line would be roughly parallel to the GCR and Metropolitan at a distance of some five to six miles to the south west, the GCR sought to use it as an alternative route into London. The GWR was receptive and a joint committee of the two companies was set up to build and operate a section of the new line between Northolt and Ashendon (near Brill). From each point it was proposed the GCR would build its own connecting line; at the northern end to Grendon Underwood Junction, just north of Quainton Road; and at the London end, from Northolt across to Neasden on the Metropolitan. At the cost of only 4 miles 39 chains of additional running, this afforded a much more easily-graded, better-engineered route for the GCR in and out of London, avoiding all Metropolitan tracks apart from the new widened lines between Neasden and Finchley Road.

When towards the end of 1897 the full impact of these proposals reached the Metropolitan they were judged 'incompatible with both the spirit and terms of the agreements made between the GCR and the Metropolitan'. Protest was vehement but in vain. Parliament was unmoved, granting powers for the Neasden–Northolt line on 12 August 1898 and for the remainder a year later. The Metropolitan's opposition did however secure a right to claim compensation for its expenditure between Finchley Road and Quainton Road to the extent this was not required for its own traffic should the GCR traffic be removed.

NEW MEN TO PICK UP THE PIECES

Perhaps only Watkin could have prevented the GCR and GWR from jumping into bed together; indeed had he remained in power, the love affair would never have started. But he had gone from the chair, his energies spent, his grip loosened, before any suggestion of such a possibility arose. As it was, the new alliance came as a major blow to the Metropolitan during the period of strained relations with the GCR engendered by the personality clash between Bell and Pollitt. It would however be wrong to argue, as some have done, that Bell's attitude was entirely responsible for pushing the GCR into the arms of the GWR.

As the new century dawned, the old protagonists were about to depart from the stage, leaving others to mend the fences and, so far as the new men on the Metropolitan were concerned, to rescue what advantage they could from their inheritance. Early in 1901 Bell's health deteriorated, obliging him to give up the managerial duties he had undertaken for 21 years. He remained chairman until the end of the year, when he was awarded £1,500 a year for life as a retiring allowance. After relinquishing his directorship in February 1902 he lived on until 12 February 1911. His place as chairman was taken by Col John James Mellor, Lancashire cotton magnate and former MP, Metropolitan director since 1887, deputy chairman since 1895 and brother-in-law of Watkin. An enthusiast for electric traction (he told the January 1903 shareholders' meeting it would bring back 'the best days of the old Metropolitan'), he held the office only until 1904. Then, at 73, he gave way to Sir Charles B. B. McLaren Bt[5] who, as Lord Aberconway from 1911, was to remain chairman for the whole of the rest of the Metroplitan's existence as a separate company.

The new general manager was Abraham Charles Ellis[6], the company's solicitor. Appointed from 1 November 1901, his salary of £2,000 included £500 for supervising and directing the solicitor's department in which he was to be aided by C. de Winton Kitcat, designated assistant solicitor at £500. A. B. Garside, an 'old soldier' chief clerk in the general manager's office, was given the new post of assistant general manager at £750, rising to £1,000 in 1904, in a further move to assist Ellis with his dual responsibility. These new men, chairmen and general manager, not only restored some order to the relationships with the GCR, but also, as we shall see in the next chapter, achieved a new harmony with the MDR, aided as all were by the departure of the contentious Forbes.

As for the GCR, we must briefly note Pollitt's retirement in May 1902 and his replacement by the genial and competent Sam Fay, who enjoyed a cordial acquaintance with Ellis. These personality changes, effected in a few short months, were to have a powerful influence on the affairs of the two companies.

One of Ellis's early duties was to receive and accompany King Edward VII on what appears to have been the first journey of a British monarch on the Metropolitan[7]. Staying at Penn as a guest of Lord Howe, the King desired to travel privately on 16 January 1902. Ellis arranged a special train, taking 'all precautions as regards the permanent way' as well as 'altering the train service to allow a clear road'. Royal unpunctuality caused a six minute delay in departure from Baker Street East, whence the train left at 6.16 pm, running the 24 miles to Amersham in 36 minutes, the King well packed around with Metropolitan top brass capable of coping with any conceivable contingency.

In October 1902 the GCR invited the Metropolitan to submit its claim for compensation under the GWR & GCR Act of 1899 mentioned above, but some time was to elapse before this was ready to be discussed. Meanwhile, towards the end of 1903, Ellis and Fay agreed that season ticket holders between London and principal stations Harrow to Aylesbury inclusive should be free to use either company's trains.

Discussion of the Metropolitan claim began at the end of 1903 between directors. It was agreed that Lord Robertson should act as arbitrator. The objective of the Metropolitan was one of damage limitation – to ensure that a reasonable amount of GCR traffic remained on its line between Quainton Road and Neasden once the GWR & GCR Joint Line and its connections were opened. With the new route via Northolt and Ashendon well under construction, the GCR was talking from a position of considerable strength, but the Metropolitan could (and did) threaten to interfere with the opening of the new lines at the London end. Eventually a deal was hammered out between Fay and Ellis on terms which were the best the Metropolitan could have expected in the circumstances, promising as they did an assured revenue in the future. Heads of agreement were signed by both chairmen on 20 October 1904 and ratified by the Metropolitan and Great Central Railways Act of 4 August 1905. The new arrangements, to come into operation on 2 April 1906, the day the new GCR and GWR & GCR Joint Line opened to public traffic, are summarised here:

(a) The widened Metropolitan lines between Canfield Place and Harrow South Junction to be leased to the GCR for 999 years at £20,000 a year from 1 March 1906; the Metropolitan to have running powers over these lines between Harrow South Junction and Neasden.
(b) The Metropolitan Extension Line between Harrow South Junction and Verney Junction, including the Chesham branch to be leased to a new Metropolitan & GCR Joint Committee at £44,000 a year for 999 years, each company to take turns for periods of five years, beginning with the Metropolitan, to manage the line. Each company to use its own rolling stock for its services over the Joint Line. The Joint Committee to assume the obligations of the Metropolitan Railway with regard to the Brill Tramway[8].
(c) Willesden Green station to be enlarged at joint cost (Metropolitan land to be used without charge) to form an exchange station between Metropolitan and GCR services[9].
(d) The GCR not to convey local traffic to and from any point between Marylebone and Harrow South Junction.
(e) The Metropolitan to retain the through crossing to the south side of the line at Wembley Park.

(f) The GCR to guarantee a minimum traffic over the Joint Line of £45,000 a year gross.

(g) Each company to be allowed 33⅓ per cent of the mileage receipts of its own trains for running expenses: the Joint Committee to pay all maintenance and other charges.

(h) If in any year the Metropolitan mileage proportion of passenger traffic receipts between Baker Street and Harrow South Junction relating to journeys between the Inner Circle stations and stations north of Harrow should fall below the estimated receipts for 1904 by reason of diversion of such traffic via Marylebone, the GCR to pay the Metropolitan 66⅔ per cent of the mileage proportion accruing to the railway between Marylebone and Harrow South Junction in respect of such diverted traffic up to the amount of such ascertained receipts. Should this traffic exceed the 1904 figures, the balance after deducting running expenses at 33⅓ for each company should be divided half yearly ⅗ths to the Metropolitan, ⅖ths to the GCR, and then in equal proportions. GCR 1904 carryings to and from Marylebone to be excluded from these calculations.

(i) Fares and rates Marylebone to Harrow and points north not to be less than those from Baker Street.

(j) Subsequent capital requirements for the Joint Line to be dealt with by the Joint Committee and contributed equally by each company.

In 1907 the two companies agreed a provision related to (h) regarding diversion of traffic to and from the Joint Line stations (including Aylesbury) by passenger trains working to Marylebone via Aylesbury and High Wycombe.

Following the settlement the GCR, using comfortable modern stock, with which the Metropolitan's contrasted most unfavourably, started suburban services between Marylebone, Aylesbury and Chesham, the first of these trains running on 1 March 1906.

The falling-off in Metropolitan revenues after the diversion of GCR traffic via Northolt, coming as it did on top of deep level tube competition in central London and higher capital charges after Metropolitan electrification, was openly admitted by the chairman at the half yearly meetings as a factor in the poor results. In the half year ended 30 June 1906 the net income of the company totalled only £219,216 against £254,847 in the same half of 1905. In the last half year of 1906 net income was £204,837 against £245,231 in the comparable period of 1905. Freight and parcels receipts in particular fell with a bump as a result of the new situation. Shareholders saw a decline in dividends reflecting all this: 3 per cent in 1904 became 2⅜ in 1905, 1 in 1906 and only ½ per cent in 1907 and 1908, some of these levels only attained by dipping into the reserve fund.

There was one event to ruffle the new harmony with the GCR, an occurrence which must have strengthened the latter's resolve that it had done the right thing in going for the alternative route. In June 1904 the Metropolitan's superintendent of the line reported to Ellis that some GCR trains were running over Metropolitan tracks at what he considered to be excessively high speeds, a matter on which he had complained to his opposite number on the GCR. He cited the 5.15 am Marylebone to Sheffield, allowed 49 minutes between Canfield Place and Quainton Road Junction but which had on occasions covered this stretch in only 45 minutes, involving speeds of up to 75 mph on the downhill stretch between Wendover and Aylesbury. Another train, the 11.25 am Manchester to Marylebone, booked at an average 54 mph over the Metropolitan, had in practice averaged 56 mph. On some days this train had been presented at Quainton Road Junction up to nine minutes late, revealing that its average speed on the GCR was no more than that on the much more difficult stretch from there to London with its three speed checks at Quainton Road Junction, Aylesbury and Rickmansworth. The GCR chose to ignore the implicit warning. On 23 December 1904, the 2.45 am from Marylebone to Manchester, carrying mainly newspapers and parcels, derailed at 3.38 am to become a total wreck as it passed over the 9-chain radius curve between the Metropolitan and the GWR south of Aylesbury station. There were no members of the public on the train, but the fireman, and a driver and fireman travelling as passengers were killed, the driver of the train dying from his injuries the following day. The 10.20 pm ex Manchester, also without passengers other than an off-duty driver and fireman, collided with the wreckage, but there were no further casualties. The Metropolitan signal box records showed that the driver of the Down train had covered the 2½ miles from Stoke Mandeville to Aylesbury, mostly at 1 in 117 down, in two minutes flat, despite a dense fog – he had clearly lost his bearings.

Even after this disaster there were several instances of GCR trains taking the Aylesbury curve at excessive speed but by June 1905, after the GWR had reduced the permitted maximum from 15 to 10 mph, discipline improved. Rebuilding of Aylesbury station, long sought by the GCR, had been resisted by the GWR, but so far as the curve was concerned, the stable door was firmly closed during the summer of 1908. The main line through the station was slewed a few yards to the east and the Metropolitan junction moved slightly nearer London, virtually straightening out the offending curve[10]. The station itself, under the joint ownership of the GWR, the Metropolitan and the GCR[11], did not get its much-needed reconstruction until 1925–6, when the layout was again altered.

156

11
ELECTRIFICATION

SOMETHING BETTER THAN CHOKING

Such were the disadvantages of operating an intensive service under-ground with steam traction it had always been apparent that should some practical alternative appear, the Metropolitan would welcome it. It is fair to say that the company was always receptive to a promising innovation in any field, especially during the Watkin regime[1], and as early as 1865 the board had considered a suggestion for experiments with a compressed air locomotive. Nothing more was heard of this after a brief mention in a minute of 15 November – more detailed examination by the engineer was apparently disappointing. As the century advanced, it became clear that electricity was going to be the answer, but it was not until the 1890s that traction motors capable of meeting the rigorous demands of operating conditions on the Inner Circle became available.

Meanwhile, the Metropolitan was one of the first British railways to employ electricity for lighting. An experiment using carbon arcs was conducted in 1879 by the Electric Light, Generator & Power Co at Aldersgate Street station. This was found dependable, giving an improved level of illumination against gas, if a little more costly. From 10 October 1881 the same firm provided electric light at Moorgate Street, Aldersgate Street and Farringdon Street stations. An experi-mental tunnel lighting system by the Swan Electric Lighting Co was installed over 100 yards between Aldgate and Trinity Square, but after operation in September and October 1882 this was deemed not worthy of adoption. The following year saw Notting Hill Gate, King's Cross, Gower Street (Euston Square), Edgware Road and Aldgate stations fitted up with a Gaulard-Gibbs single circuit main electric lighting system, and in 1895 electric carbon arcs made night working easier at Finchley Road goods yard. A similar installation followed at Harrow yard.

It is intriguing to learn that Frank Julian Sprague[2], one of the great pioneers of electric rail traction, was inspired to dwell on the possi-bilities of electricity as a motive power after seeing operating conditions on the Inner Circle in 1882[3]. By 1887 Sprague had perfected his work sufficiently to embark, at the age of 29, on a contract for installing an electric tramway system in the hilly streets of Richmond, Virginia. Although not the first electric tramway in the USA, Richmond was an outstanding success, proving conclusively that this type of electric rail traction was fully practical and reliable. Within two years, there were hundreds of electric tramcars operating in American cities and towns, nearly all of them on systems based on the principles established by Sprague. The electric tramway era had truly begun, Europe quickly following the North American lead. But moving a small tramcar weighing around 15 tons was rather a different proposition from providing motors and equipment of sufficient power and durability to operate 125-ton trains every few minutes round the Inner Circle, day in, day out, with a very high measure of reliability. From 1887 a series of proposals began to arrive at the Metropolitan's offices regarding electrification of the railway, but when Bell visited North America in 1889 he returned with the information that whilst some railway developments were being pursued, the main thrust of electric traction progress was confined to street tramways.

Though as yet unproven for working intensive traffic of the sort handled on the Inner Circle, electric motors and equipment for heavy railway use were starting to become available around the middle of the 1890s. Meantime Sprague had turned his ingenuity to electric lift systems, where his work provided him with the germ of an idea for multiple-unit rail traction. When his opinion was sought on the electrification of the South Side Elevated Railway in Chicago, he suggested this principle be adopted. It involved fitting several of the cars in a train with motors and control equipment, all of which were linked by a master control line running through the train. By this means there was complete flexibility in operation in that trains could be run to any length within the current-carrying capacity of the master controller and trains could be split up into shorter lengths, each separately controlled by its own master controller. Successfully demonstrated in Chicago in 1897, multiple-unit traction with direct current electric motors was soon adopted by the Brooklyn Elevated Railway of New York and at Boston. Its invention by Sprague made electric traction an ideal means of working urban and suburban railway systems.

In London the possibilities of electric traction were first demonstrated on a major scale by the City & South London deep level tube railway, which was operated by small locomotives having two 50hp motors using traction current at 450V dc taken up from conductor rails. Watkin, Bell and two Metropolitan directors were given a ride on this line from King William Street, City to Elephant & Castle on 13 March 1890. A Metropolitan minute recording this notes with shattering perceptivity 'it was evident that electricity as a motive power is steadily advancing'. But the C&SLR was also important in showing that the advent of electrically-powered trains and lifts had made it possible to exploit the deep tube tunnelling techniques developed earlier in the century by Sir Marc Isambard Brunel, Peter William Barlow and James Henry Greathead as a means of avoiding the penal property compensation costs and environmental disturbance associated with shallow tunnel construction in urban areas. The operational success of the C&SLR after its opening to the public on 18 December 1890 led to the promotion of many similar deep level tube railway schemes, some of them offering serious potential threats to the inner London business of the Metropolitan and the MDR.

Meanwhile, in the late 1880s, some British engineers had gone down the blind alley of battery electric railway traction. In October 1887 the Electric Traction Co of Malden Works, Prince of Wales Road, Kentish Town, offered the Metropolitan an experiment with two battery locomotives which, it was promised, would equal in power and efficiency the Beyer-Peacock tanks, the trial to be conducted at the Traction Company's expense at Neasden or nearby. An agreement was concluded but the Traction Co made constant excuses, pleading problems with design development. Finally they admitted they were defeated. No order was ever given to Beyer-Peacock, the intended manufacturers of the prototypes. When the Traction Co then stated that the direct current system was a practical alternative, the Edgware Road to South Kensington section was placed at their disposal for a demonstration at their expense, but although plans were submitted at the beginning of March 1889, the company finally withdrew after the Metropolitan had refused to pay an installation cost of £9,820.

Michael Radcliffe-Ward, described in the Metropolitan minutes as 'inventor of the electric omnibus', approached the board in February 1889 with an offer to provide a direct current train at his own expense, together with the necessary equipment and generating plant, the installation to be between Neasden and Harrow. After a draft agreement had been prepared, the matter was closed when Ward refused to allow the Metropolitan to be the arbiter of success. There then followed some fruitless negotiations with H. Smith regarding an experimental six-car electric train.

As we have seen in Chapter 8, the two underground railway companies were under increasing pressure at this time to remedy the pollution in their tunnels, notably the infamous Metropolitan 'long tunnel' between Edgware Road and King's Cross. When the news of the proposals just mentioned reached the press a typical reaction was 'It is sincerely hoped that the trial will be satisfactory, for under the present system, half an hour in the "sewer" is enough to choke anyone'[4]. But whilst the tunnel pollution problem was in itself a powerful incentive, pushing the two companies towards electrification, an even stronger motivation was about to appear.

One of the deep level tube schemes following in the wake of the City & South London was the Central London Railway, which proposed a route below the great traffic axis running through the heart of London from Shepherd's Bush in the west to the hub of the City at the Bank of England. Construction of this line began in 1896 after the legislation had been fiercely fought in parliament by the Metropolitan and the MDR. Soon to be fed by electric tramways from Hammersmith and the western suburbs, the Central London was opened to the public on 30 July 1900, offering a ride of any length at a 2d flat rate fare. Metropolitan and MDR receipts plunged, the two companies together losing over four million passengers between the second half of 1899 and the second half of 1900. By 30 June 1901, the Metropolitan had assessed the damage as equivalent to almost 1½ per cent on its ordinary stock each year. In response to the depredations of the new-comer, many Hammersmith & City and Circle fares were cut from 1 July 1902. Further reductions were made in Metropolitan fares from 1 June 1903, from 11 January 1904 and from 1 December 1905.

No prophet had been needed to predict this disaster for the two old companies. With travelling conditions on the Inner Circle and other underground lines little changed from those of 1863 (indeed, in the opinion of many, even less attractive), modernisation was overdue. When a regular passenger wrote at the end of 1897 that things were so bad that once the new tube railways were open they would draw off a large number of Metropolitan passengers, 'unless you turn over an entirely new leaf', it was little more than a statement of the obvious. In his letter to the chairman, Mr Heathfield noted 'a decently clean carriage owned by your Company is the exception rather than the rule', adding that the carpets in the First Class were practically never clean, the linings of the compartments were 'extremely filthy' and the woodwork was 'thickly coated with dirt'; there was only one light, generally with a bad supply of gas, making it virtually impossible to read. On his daily journey, at Baker Street in the morning, Heathfield found that all the First Class seats were occupied and it was not unusual for the compartments to contain ten seated passengers with up to six more treading on their toes.

Even as Heathfield wrote, things were on the move. The Metropolitan received powers to use electric traction on all parts of its system in its act of 2 August 1898, which also sanctioned erection of a generating plant near Edgware Road station. And in response to an initiative by Forbes in May that year, the two companies arranged to carry out a trial of electric working on both tracks between High Street Kensington and Earls Court. Each was to contribute half of the estimated maximum cost of £20,000 (but the final figure proved to be £27,350). Sir John Wolfe-Barry and (Sir) William Preece, engineer-in-chief and electrician to the Post Office, agreed to act as consultants and to provide supervision. Thomas Parker, whose Wolverhampton firm had equipped the Liverpool Overhead Railway as Britain's first urban open air electric railway in 1893, accepted the job of laying down the plant and completing the trials within the agreed cost limit. But, after some backdoor manoeuvres by the Metropolitan, Parker withdrew in October 1898 and the work was given to A. Siemens Bros & Co Ltd.

Anxious to have an independent assessment, unencumbered by a possibly double-dealing Forbes, the Metropolitan wanted Parker to carry out a quite separate trial for it alone. He was invited to do this on 10 November 1898 at a cost of £7,000 (an estimate also exceeded; the final figure was £10,963). The long siding into Wembley Park was equipped with dc conductor rails and successful trials with two specially-built motor coaches were carried out there in 1900[5]. Such was the Metropolitan's satisfaction with Parker that he was appointed 'engineer for electric traction' in September 1900 at a fee of one half per cent of the company's outlay on any system adopted. Two years later he was to be found supervising the construction of the Metropolitan's Neasden power station, for which he managed to get his son Edward appointed clerk of works. When the Metropolitan secured the services of a full time electrical engineer in 1904, Parker continued as part time consultant.

For the joint experiment on the Inner Circle, a train of six bogie cars weighing 185 tons and seating 312 passengers was provided in October 1899 by Brown, Marshalls & Co at a cost of £5,560. This had a motor car at each end, the trailing one idle in motion. Both motor cars had four 110hp Siemens motors with armatures wound directly on the axles. To provide room for the electrical equipment, they had higher floors and larger wheels than the intermediate trailers and in contrast to the conventional compartments of the trailers, had a guard's compartment and passenger accommodation served by a central gangway. Westinghouse air brakes and electric light were fitted[6]. Motive power was provided by a temporary generating plant housed in a corrugated iron building 250yd west from Earls Court station, at Warwick Road[7]. Its two Babcock & Wilcox water tube boilers worked at 160lb per sq inch and two direct-coupled Belliss-Siemens 300–380hp generators provided 500–550V dc to the 75lb mild steel conductor rails, one outside each running rail and both three inches above those rails. This so-called 'four-rail' arrangement, with insulated conductor rail return, also adopted by Parker at Wembley Park, was used to avoid the possibility of what were seen as dangerous leakages to earth causing magnetic disturbances and other nuisances. It also offered some economy and was to become standard on the Metropolitan and the London underground, although subsequently the negative return conductor was always placed midway between the running rails[8]. No alterations were made to the signalling.

After trials between traffic hours at night and during the Sunday 'Church Interval', beginning on the night of 7/8 November 1899, the electric train went into successful public service on 21 May 1900 for one week at a special fare of one shilling, then later at ordinary fares. The train was withdrawn after traffic on 6 November 1900. It was intended to electrify only the Inner Circle and the section chosen embodied every difficulty likely to be encountered on that service. Performances on the 1 in 62 up into High Street Kensington station and the short stretch of 1 in 43 up in to Earls Court station were regarded as particularly good for a train 20 tons heavier than a loaded steam train and its locomotive. Speeds were found to be generally higher than with steam, with of course no loss of time for watering and re-fuelling. Forbes concluded that the experiment established 'beyond doubt' that electrification of the Circle was possible[9]. Yet it was hardly state of the art. When the editor of *The Railway Magazine* travelled on the train he raised the question of Sprague's multiple-unit system, only to find that none of the engineers in charge had ever heard of it.[10]

Nor was it the system that Preece and Parker judged the best to adopt. On 3 August 1900 the joint committee of the two companies on electrical traction sent out invitations to nine firms to submit proposals and estimates for electrifying the Inner Circle, and when these came in, the one that most impressed the two experts was that from the Hungarian firm of Ganz. After a visit to Budapest in February 1901 when they inspected the experimental installation on Buda Island, Preece and Parker returned full of enthusiasm for what they described as 'a decided step in advance over every other system in use in the United Kingdom or in America'. They declared it not only the most efficient on offer, but the cheapest to build and work. Ganz had proposed a traction current of three phase ac at 3,000V, using two overhead wires and the running rails. The economic advantages were that new motor cars only were needed, the rest of the trains could be made up from existing steam stock; and there were to be only five unmanned substations. Both railway boards accepted the advice of the experts and on 22 March 1901 Ganz was told that both companies viewed the proposals with favour, subject to the sanction of the Board of Trade. Therein lay a difficulty. When A. P. Trotter, the Board of Trade's electrical engineering adviser, worried about the novel and untried Hungarian system, required a test installation on part of the Inner Circle before he could consider it, neither company could stomach spending more money on trials.

Money was indeed the stumbling block to further progress, above all for the near-bankrupt MDR, which in the last half of 1900 had earned only £18,239 over its fixed charges. In decline even before the opening of the Central London, its traffic was now draining away alarmingly. There was no question of it being able to raise sufficient capital for the electrification, on which, in Forbes' words, 'the Railway's salvation depends'[11]. One way out of the impasse might have been amalgamation with the still relatively healthy Metropolitan but Forbes, true to form, had already backed away from this course. In November 1898, Alfred Willis, general manager of the SER, acting as intermediary, had suggested the Metropolitan might provide a guaranteed three per cent for the MDR five per cent preference shareholders, the ordinary shareholders to get a graduated dividend, rising from 1¼ to three per cent after 13 years. Forbes wanted his ordinary shareholders to have at least ½ per cent, rising to three after only five years, but this the Metropolitan refused, also rejecting a slightly less favourable compromise, although recognising fully 'the importance – both in the public interest and in that of the two companies – of a working union between the two undertakings with a view to ultimate fusion'. The Metropolitan's next suggestion was that it should work and manage the MDR as part of its own system for an agreed period, giving the MDR credit for the economies arising from a single management and keeping separate accounts. In this way an assessment could be made of the true revenue of the MDR from which equitable terms for a merger could be settled. Such drastic fairness not appealing to Forbes, the discussions terminated at the end of 1898. Forbes may already have had an inkling of a new option which would have justified his behaviour in the negotiations with the Metropolitan. Another solution to the dilemma of the MDR was about to emerge. A saviour was riding in from the west, a direction in which the MDR had always placed its hopes.

This *deus ex machina* was the USA financier Charles Tyson Yerkes[12], who came openly on to the London railway scene in 1900 when he bought the unbuilt but authorised Charing Cross, Euston & Hampstead deep level tube railway. He had been introduced to the potentialities of London by R. W. Perks, a character we have already encountered. By 1898 Perks had accumulated the largest individual holding of MDR stock, including £100,000 in ordinary shares, and with others, was well on the way to securing a controlling interest. His aim was to see the railway modernised and making money, but he and his friends needed a means of raising the necessary capital. Perks seems to have succeeded in attracting Yerkes' interest in the possibilities of electrifying the MDR as early as 1898[13], but Yerkes was also anxious to acquire the rights in new lines and to work towards attaining a monopoly position in London public transport.

A syndicate organised early in 1901 by the American, backed by £1m of US capital, formed a Metropolitan District Electric Traction Company to electrify the MDR and by the early summer of that year, the Metropolitan's Inner Circle partner was in new and dynamic hands. Forbes, the Metropolitan's doughty old antagonist, gave up the chair to Perks in September.

Up to this point both companies had appeared ready to accept the advice of their professional advisers, Preece and Parker, that the Ganz system was the right solution for the Inner Circle, but it now quickly became clear that the District's new American masters, familiar as they were with the success in their own country of low voltage dc conductor rail lines, would have nothing to do with this new-fangled Hungarian alternative. Yerkes asserted that he would not put a dollar into it[14] and in its bill for the 1900–01 session, the MDR arbitrarily sought power to dictate to the Metropolitan which system must be used when trains were worked over lines owned by the MDR. In response to Metropolitan protests, the offending clause was altered at the committee stage of the bill to provide for resort to arbitration should the two companies otherwise be unable to agree as to the electrification system to be used on the Inner Circle.

Yerkes, who revealed in evidence to the parliamentary committee on the bill that he had had his eyes on the two London underground companies 'for some years', and that in America they thought the way these two railways were run was 'something of a disgrace', castigated both managements for their inaction:

Here were a lot of men, who called themselves businessmen, in charge of railroad property, sitting by and seeing the Central London Road being built. When the Central London really opened, and their trade began to fall away, they did not even move then, but sat and looked further, and have continued to do the same ever since[15].

Frank Sprague was also in Britain at this time, undertaking 'over six months' concentrated study of the problem of rapid transit in London'. His conclusions, published in *The Engineering Magazine*, in October 1901, contain some scathing comments on the Inner Circle, whose operation was dismissed by Sprague as 'a travesty on rapid transit'. Noting that its gradients and curves were 'not worth mentioning', its stations only half a mile apart, he observed that the average speed was a mere 11½ miles per hour, in an atmosphere 'foul from the use of steam and the accumulations in the tunnels'. In his view the station stops were 'double what is necessary', the delays made worse by the need to change engines. He advocated that after electrification, all services coming on to the Inner Circle from outside should be banished, a two minute interval service should be run, and passengers should transfer on foot to and from other lines at suitably built interchange stations.

USA I: HUNGARY O

'Half measures have never characterised Mr Yerkes' undertakings and he is not accustomed to hesitating at trifles' commented an admiring *Tramway & Railway World* in April 1901. It was therefore no surprise, at any rate to that journal, when on 11 July Yerkes sought to bring the Metropolitan into line. He offered its board two alternatives. The first was that his new Metropolitan District Electric Traction Company (MDET) would electrify the whole of the Inner Circle, the Eastern Joint Lines, Baker Street to Harrow *and* the Hammersmith & City, meeting half the cost of the last, but the whole of the rest, the Metropolitan paying in return ¾d for each passenger carried. Electric locomotives would be supplied by the MDET for hauling freight and GWR passenger trains over the Inner Circle (Yerkes and his professional advisers did not subscribe to the Sprague isolationist concept), the payments for these and for the electric power used for freight haulage to be mutually agreed. Alternatively, if this did not appeal, the MDET would be prepared to work the whole of the Metropolitan Railway on lease, guaranteeing a net annual revenue sufficient to pay all debentures and other fixed charges as well as guaranteed and preference stock interest and 3½ per cent for ordinary shareholders. Under this proposal, all the railways mentioned in the first alternative would be electrified at MDET expense (the H&CR at 50 per cent cost) with rolling stock and substations provided. The MDET would take all revenues, appointing one director to the Metropolitan board, which would be left in control of 'general and railway policy'. Although the 3½ per cent guarantee for the ordinary shares represented an improvement on what the shareholders had been getting since the opening of the Central London Railway, and although some shareholders, led by Albert G. Kitching (an erstwhile advocate of a merger) were in favour of accepting the Yerkes offer, it was firmly rejected by the board, which was still resolved to adopt the Ganz system and maintain independence. (Kitching, made a director, and given more information, subsequently agreed with the board's decision.) As things turned out, Metropolitan ordinary shareholders were not to get a dividend as high as 3½ per cent until 1922, but how the MDET and its successors would have managed to meet the promised guaranteed rate in the late 1900s and the 1910s is another matter.

Yerkes' opinion on the merits of Ganz was soon confirmed by his engineer (James R. Chapman), by Horace F. Parshall, engineer of the Central London, and by Philip Dawson, chief engineer of Robert Blackwell & Co, all of whom, on his behalf, inspected the working of the system on its first public railway application, the Valtellina Railway from Lecco to Sondria, in Italy. Although this line was not yet open to public traffic, it was virtually completed and tests were made before the engineers. Similar demonstrations were also given for Trotter and Yorke of the Board of Trade Railways Inspectorate. Then in September and October 1901, the Valtellina was examined by Metropolitan representatives: Thomas Parker and Ellis; the chairman, Col Mellor; and Sir Charles McLaren. All these last reported favourably, apart from some reservations about acceleration and the overhead gear.

When it became apparent that neither would move from its view on Ganz, the two companies agreed in September 1901 to resort to the arbitration provided for in the MDR Act of 9 August that year. A guaranteed £1,500 contribution by Ganz to the Metropolitan's tribunal costs ensured a good fight. Acting quickly, the Board of Trade appointed the Hon Alfred Lyttelton KC MP as chairman. After a preliminary gathering on 7 October, evidence was taken between 29 October and 15 November, from amongst others, O. T. Blathy, Ganz's manager, Colman von Kando, its engineer and under-manager, H. F. Parshall (for the MDR), Thomas Parker (for the Metropolitan), Yerkes, Perks, Col Bell, Col Probyn and Jabez Light.

It was soon established that there was much in the Ganz proposals for the Inner Circle that was quite untested in comparable operating conditions and to the satisfaction of the Yerkes' camp, the decision announced on 11 December found in favour of the low voltage dc conductor rail system. The report placed emphasis on the need for a service of 'precise and imperturbable regularity' on the Inner Circle, requiring lively starting, good acceleration, deceleration and braking, and maximum safety for public and staff. The Ganz system, with its high voltage overhead gear, was untried on any system at all comparable with the Inner Circle, and in the tribunal's view the Metropolitan was seeking against the will of the MDR to displace a 'well-tried and widely successful system and to make an experiment under perhaps the most expensive and complicated conditions which can be found in Europe'. There was one small crumb of consolation for the Metropolitan: the tribunal deplored the manner in which the MDR had conducted the negotiations on the system to be adopted as 'most embarrassing to the Metropolitan Company and fully justified that Company in clearing up the matter by arbitration'.

Given the state of electric traction development at the time, the decision was the only possible one, and it was duly accepted by the Metropolitan without further ado. At last the way was clear for the modernisation of the two railways. One more attempt at coordination was made by the Yerkes group; it offered to supply electricity to both companies, but this was rejected in January 1902 after the Metropolitan had considered the likely relative costs. In the following month an order was placed with British Westinghouse Electric and Manufacturing Company Ltd for three turbo-generators of the single-cylinder double-flow Westinghouse-Parsons reaction type, with a capacity of 3,500kW. Fourteen substation units of 750kW each (later amended to 800kW, with three 1,200kW units for Baker Street) were ordered at the same time. In its act of 31 July 1902, the Metropolitan took further powers on the use of electric traction, including powers for the electric working of the Hammersmith & City railway and authority to erect its own generating station adjacent to the Neasden locomotive and carriage works. The £43,700 building contract for the power station was signed with British Westinghouse on 11 September 1902[16]; its equipment was to include 14 Babcock & Wilcox water tube boilers and three groups of two duplex wooden cooling towers with water softening plant of 13,000 gallons an hour capacity. A fourth 3,500kW turbo generator was ordered in August 1904. Now reinforced by the impressive backing of the international banking house of Speyer and reorganised with £5m capital as The Underground Electric

Railways Company of London Ltd, with control of three new deep level tube schemes as well as the MDR, the Yerkes group went ahead with the construction of its own power station for all these at Lots Road, Chelsea.

The decision to site the Metropolitan plant at Neasden rather than Edgware Road had been taken in June 1901. Although involving extra cabling and higher equipment costs, Neasden was seen as preferable to Edgware Road, where the site was restricted, difficult and costly to clear, with limited space available for coal and water storage and potential environmental problems from steam, smoke emission and vibration. There would also be difficulty in slotting in coal and materials movements amongst the Inner Circle's intensive traffic. There was some anxiety about water supplies at Neasden where neither the canal feeder nor the river Brent could be used, but much to the board's relief, two artesian wells were successfully sunk there in 1902 (a third was to be added in 1919).

The area chosen was that formerly occupied by the coal gas works, closed as uneconomic in 1895. British Westinghouse started the building work on 5 January 1903, the materials coming in over new sidings provided by the Metropolitan. With its classical pediment and stubby castellated tower at one side, this very solid-looking structure was designed by Matthew Garbutt, appointed full time architect and surveyor to the Metropolitan, the Surplus Lands Committee and the Tower Co in April 1898 at a salary of £500.

Once the decision had been made to place the power station at Neasden it was logical to electrify the line to that point instead of confining the conversion to the Inner Circle and the Eastern Joint Lines, and in July 1902 after considering a report from Ellis, the board had agreed to this for passenger workings. It had been pointed out that a further advantage would be that facilities would be available for staff training without waiting for the electrification of the Circle. Then, whilst preparations for the latter were going on, the Metropolitan acquired a chunk of new territory west of the Extension Line, a development which was to bring the electric trains even further into the country than Neasden.

FROM HARROW TO UXBRIDGE

Metropolitan access to Uxbridge was first discussed with local interests in October 1877, but as there was no prospect of any local financial support and as some influential landowners appeared likely to oppose any bill in parliament, the board rejected the approach.

Four years later a bill was deposited, together with others for branches from Harrow to Stanmore and Edgware, but none was successful, or even endorsed by the Metropolitan shareholders. In 1882 however, a Beaconsfield, Uxbridge & Harrow Railway, proposing a junction with the Metropolitan at Harrow, was successful in parliament, although it subsequently failed to raise its capital. From around 1880 the MDR had also had its eyes on this ancient west Middlesex town, with Forbes involving it in a number of proposed schemes. Finally, in 1896, a nominally independent company, for which in Forbes' words, the MDR was 'standing godfather', promoted a bill to extend the Ealing & South Harrow Railway (another MDR-inspired scheme, authorised by an act of 25 August 1894) through Ruislip and Uxbridge to High Wycombe. This engendered strong support in Uxbridge, a town which had long considered itself unworthily-served by the GWR branch from West Drayton, and local tradesmen contributed to the parliamentary expenses[17]. In the same session, the GWR, seeking authorisation for its Acton to High Wycombe cut-off line, opposed the Uxbridge bill, securing deletion of the Uxbridge-High Wycombe portion and leaving a 6 miles 21 chains line to be sanctioned as the Harrow & Uxbridge Railway Act of 6 August 1897. Scheduled to this act was an agreement with the MDR to work the line from South Harrow to the terminus in Belmont Road, Uxbridge.

All attempts to raise capital proved unavailing, despite activity by Perks in Manchester and London. Although financially weak, the MDR was now firmly enmeshed in two other projects: the already-mentioned Ealing & South Harrow[18] and the Whitechapel & Bow Joint Railway. To be shared with the LTSR, the cost burden of the latter was particularly onerous as it was to be entirely underground for 2 miles 5 chains from its junction with the LTSR at Bromley-by-Bow to Whitechapel[19]. As the MDR intended to develop freight traffic, using the Whitechapel & Bow, such resources as there were had to be concentrated on it.

Seeing their much-desired competitor with the GWR slipping away from them, the Uxbridge interests paid court to the Metropolitan in October 1898. They received sufficient encouragement to promote a bill for a link to the Metropolitan at Harrow from their line at Rayners Lane, together with a curve at the latter to allow direct running from South Harrow to Harrow. An agreement was signed with the Metropolitan on 18 June 1899 under which the latter consented to manage and work the Harrow & Uxbridge, which would be built as a 'first class double line for passengers and goods', the Metropolitan to take all receipts, to control capital expenditure and to pay the Uxbridge three per cent interest on the total outlay from the day the line was opened to public traffic. Two members of the original H&UR board, Col Frederick Cox and Major William Terry, were retained but the five other seats were taken by Metropolitan directors at the end of 1899. At the committee stage of the bill Forbes expressed a desire to see the H&UR as a joint Metropolitan and MDR operation, but admitted his company could not raise half the capital. MDR interests were therefore covered by granting it running powers from South Harrow to Uxbridge, a maximum of three trains an hour and eight freight trains each way daily, at a minimum rental of £2,000 a year. Assurances were given to parliament that the section between Rayners Lane and South Harrow would be built despite the addition of a direct connection to the Metropolitan. All this was incorporated in the Harrow & Uxbridge Railway Act of 9 August 1899 together with powers for electrical working. Metropolitan papers of 1898 give some indication that later extension beyond Uxbridge had not been ruled out and sufficient land was bought to accommodate four tracks between Harrow and Uxbridge. The Metropolitan's new engineer, E. P. Seaton, was in charge of construction, with the 34-year old A. W. Pearson as his resident engineer. Deviations and alterations of levels, together with substitution of a viaduct for an embankment between South Harrow and Rayners Lane, were authorised by the Metropolitan Railway Act of 26 July 1901.

By August 1903 the Metropolitan had subscribed to the H&UR the full £200,000 authorised by the 1899 act for construction, on security of 3 per cent guaranteed shares, investing additionally £107,370 of its own funds. As this proved insufficient to complete the works, the Metropolitan paid the balance from its own resources, taking over the separate undertaking from 30 June 1905, a step authorised by the Metropolitan's act of that date.

Although the Ealing & South Harrow line was virtually completed in the early part of 1901, the Yerkes group decided not to open it for public traffic with steam traction and the mechanical signalling installed. Instead it was to be used initially as a test bed and training ground for the MDR electrification and resignalling *à l'Américain*. Work on the Harrow & Uxbridge line was not started until 9 September 1901, under the contractors Bott & Stennett, construction proving straightforward but progressing slowly[20]. A public service of short steam trains working to and from Harrow, with some peak hour journeys through to and from Baker Street began on 4 July 1904. No regular service was given between South Harrow and Rayners Lane until 1 March 1910, when after considerable hesitation, the MDR began to exercise its running powers to Uxbridge[21].

On Thursday 30 June 1904 the Metropolitan laid on a lavish opening ceremony for its new line to Uxbridge. A special train, hauled by 0-4-4T no 1, gaily decorated with flags and evergreens, its coal painted white, was worked from Baker Street to South Harrow and Uxbridge. Luncheon was then served in a marquee in Uxbridge station yard, where two of the new Metropolitan electric stock trailer cars were parked for inspection by the guests. It was evidently a very pleasant day, for a journey that would be unrecognisable to present residents of the area:

> . . . bathed in glorious sunshine and scented with new mown hay, the countryside was at its best. Here stretches of meadowland, with herds of sleek cattle grazing lazily, there the clink and rattle of grass-cutting machines. Plump partridges raised their startled heads and a pheasant, with its glorious plumage shining like burnished gold, ran for cover[22].

From Harrow Yard Junction, the new branch turned south west to Rayners Lane Junction, where the line from South Harrow came in after running across the then desolate Roxeth Marsh for 46 chains of its 1 mile 5.21 chains length on a viaduct of 71 34ft-span brick arches and three steel plate girder bridges. The curve from Harrow towards South Harrow at Rayners Lane had not been laid. At 2 miles 21 chains from Rayners Lane was Ruislip, the only intermediate station. About half a mile below what was still a remote village, this had two platforms of 325ft connected by an iron lattice footbridge. On the Up side, the main building, a plain single-storey structure in red brick with courses of black, dominated by a central transverse gable was probably designed by Matthew Garbutt. To the east, also on the Up side, was a small freight yard with facilities for coal and cattle and a dock at which road vehicles could be put on and off trains. There was no goods shed. At Uxbridge, three miles further, the terminus was built on a through plan to allow for possible extension, with two 473ft side platforms. Similar in style to that at Ruislip, the single-storey building on the Down or south side included a small refreshment room. Also on this side was a seven-acre goods yard with goods shed, its other facilities as at Ruislip. Just before entering the terminus, the line veered due west, faithfully following the original alignment towards High Wycombe surveyed by Arthur J. Barry and C. A. Brereton for the Harrow, Uxbridge & High Wycombe deposited plans of 1896.

Apart from the Roxeth Viaduct, a deep cutting at Uxbridge Common and another shallow one between Ruislip and Ickenham, the branch passed through fairly level heavy clay mostly put to grass for the forage of London's horse population. Its steepest gradient was a long section of 1 in 95 from just outside Rayners Lane Junction towards South Harrow. There were five level crossings of farm tracks and one of a public footpath, none of them protected. Signalling was by the Metropolitan's usual block system with Spagnoletti locking and semaphore arms, operated from boxes at Harrow Yard Junction (50 levers plus 14 spare), Rayners Lane (22+3), Ruislip Station (24+3) and Uxbridge Station (35+5).

In accordance with the powers given in the 1899 Harrow & Uxbridge Railway Act, the H&UR board (in effect the Metropolitan board) had resolved on 12 February 1903 that the line should be electrified at an estimated cost of £28,000. This mainly involved laying 100lb conductor rail and the construction of a substation at Glebe Lane (now Glebe Avenue), Ickenham, known at first as Ruislip sub-station. Shareholders had been told in January 1902 that the line would 'open up an undeveloped district' but the decision to build and electrify was one of undiluted expansionism on the Metropolitan's part, a sanguine gesture of faith in the potential of the area served, the electrification particularly so.

HOT AND COLD WITH THE DISTRICT RAILWAY

Having settled on the system of electrification, it was still of course important that the two companies should agree on technical and operational details for the electrical working of the Inner Circle. At a joint meeting for this purpose in October 1902 Perks made the surprising statement that he attached no importance to the Inner Circle service as such and would be averse to seeing it increased (it seems likely that the MDR had decided that more profitable routes should have priority). This meeting accepted recommendations made by Parker for the Metropolitan and by J. R. Chapman, the MDR's US engineer. These envisaged 100lb conductor rails and traction current at 600V dc from substations fed at 11,000V, 33⅓ cycles ac. Platforms were to remain at existing heights above rail so far as the Circle was concerned and there was to be standard spacing of collector shoes. The Metropolitan learned that the MDR proposed to instal new signalling which would be fully automatic except at junctions, allowing headways as close as 75 seconds.

Whilst this technical liaison was in progress, others were reaching the view that the sensible thing would be for the electrification to be handled by one management team. In December 1902 a large group of Metropolitan shareholders, led by Sir Frederick G. Banbury Bt and

Lord Avebury, proposed the formation of a joint committee under 'an independent chairman of high standing' to work and manage the Metropolitan and MDR as one system. They affirmed a belief that the interests of both companies lay in united working and were especially anxious that the electrification work should be done by one undertaking. It was proposed to issue a circular putting these views to all shareholders after obtaining the consent of both boards, requesting those proprietors who assented to deposit their shares with trustees. Although clearly alarmed and treating this revolt with some respect, the Metropolitan board stood its ground, offering only token concessions towards better and closer relationships with the MDR without going near any kind of unification, for electrification or otherwise. All that emerged from this flurry of activity was the establishment of a joint consultative committee, meeting from 23 April 1903 to consider all matters of mutual interest related to electrification. However, with the departure of both Bell and Forbes from the scene by the end of 1901, the relationship between the two companies did become smoother than it had been for many years. Contributing to this improved atmosphere was the solution in 1903 of the longstanding dispute over the MDR use of the Cromwell Curve for Circle traffic, which has been noted in Chapter 4.

One small ripple disturbed the calmer waters. For the 1902–03 session, the MDR deposited proposals for loops around the through lines in Mark Lane and the old Tower stations, the object being to allow MDR trains from the west and LTSR trains from the east to terminate at a new enlarged station at this point. No doubt seeing this as a partial explanation of Perks' comment on the unimportance of the Circle service, the Metropolitan displayed much concern about the congestion such an arrangement would impose on adjacent lines and junctions[23]. It opposed the bill without success but no work was ever started on this scheme, the powers being abandoned by the MDR in its act of 1908.

METROPOLITAN ELECTRIC

Two important decisions were made in July 1902 about the Metropolitan's electric rolling stock: the cars were to be of the open saloon, tramcar type, similar to those the MDR intended to use, their height from rail level and platforms to be uniform with those of the MDR; and Second Class was to be abolished on all electric trains in the hope that most users would opt to travel First (a reduction in First Class fares from 1 February 1905 was intended to encourage this)[24].

Delivered in 1904–05, the first electric cars comprised 20 39-ton bogie motor cars with all four axles motored at 150hp each, two sets of traction equipment per car; and 50 20-ton bogie trailer cars. Electrical equipment, including the electro-pneumatic control, came from British Westinghouse whilst the bodies and trucks were products of the Metropolitan Amalgamated Railway Carriage & Wagon Co into which the original contractors, Brown, Marshalls had been absorbed. Built at Birmingham and Manchester, these cars were formed into ten six-car trains (3rd Class motor car – 3rd trailer – 1st trailer – 1st trailer – 3rd trailer – 3rd motor). These trains, which seated 362, cost £9,200 ready for the road. As the original intention had been to operate seven-car trains, there were ten surplus trailers (the change of policy was no doubt prompted by the realisation that the cost of platform extensions would be prohibitive).

The end-door, gate-platform cars had green moquette upholstery in the First Class non-smoking sections, green leather in the First smoking accommodation and buffalo hide in the Third Class. All 70 cars had electric heaters at £37 per car. Trip cocks were fitted for working over the MDR's new automatically-signalled lines; placed on the right hand side of the leading end of each motor car, these cost £2.15s each. The Westinghouse quick-acting compressed air brakes on these trains were to be perpetuated on all but six subsequent Metropolitan electric cars[25]. No luggage racks or hat pegs were fitted, but the former were installed late in 1905 after many complaints had been received. Livery was varnished teak with white waist and cant rail panels.

In an effort to entice the privileged classes underground and relieve the dreariness of their journey (just as modern airlines attempt to soften the sheer awfulness of air travel with decorative hostesses, 'free' alcohol and other comforts), an additional £102.2s was spent on each First Class car to provide 'extra upholstery, increased carving, more expensive elaboration and interior finish, bevelled glass in end doors, additional wainscot oak and Kork (sic) matting'. (It was also no doubt hoped that these features would attract some of the former Second Class users.) Another interesting aspect of the new additions to the fleet was the coat of arms transfer on their sides, adopted in 1904 and also used for steam locomotives and stock. This comprised a shield quartered with the arms of the City of London, Middlesex, Buckinghamshire and Hertfordshire, with the company's name below. Above the shield was a clenched fist radiating lightning flashes (symbolising electrical energy) and the motto VIS VINCTA SERVIT (strength subdued serves). A lavish crimson and ermine mantling formed a backdrop. Except on the company's seal, which remained unaltered until 1933, this device supplanted an earlier one showing the company's title in gilt letters shaded red on a Cambridge blue background encircling the arms of the City with the motto WE WORK FOR ALL in gilt on the red cross, all this above a depiction of two brick tunnel portals with a steam locomotive emerging from one and the tail of a passenger train disappearing into the other.

Two further batches of electric stock were delivered in 1906 and 1907. The first, 18 trains, included eight motor cars and eight First Class trailers equipped with gates at the inner ends only, the balance being vestibuled. Windows were larger than those in the original deliveries but the electrical equipment was of the same pattern. The second batch, consisting of ten trains, included First Class driving trailers. Electrical equipment was by British Thomson-Houston, some cars having GE 69 200hp motors instead of 150hp. The First Class cars were red-carpeted throughout but divided into a smoking section upholstered in leather and one for non-smokers in 'a delicate green and cream'. These cars of 1906–07 had all-steel frames and a higher degree of fireproofing elsewhere.

With the delivery of the last mentioned stock some of the original First Class trailers were converted to First Class driving trailers, providing enough to enable trains to be broken down in slack periods to two three-car sets. Four car trains were also formed and used on the Inner Circle service. By the end of 1907 all the gate stock had been vestibuled[26].

Other substantial items of electrification expenditure included: 72 miles of high tension copper cabling; many thousands of hardwood and creosoted red pine sleepers and crossing timbers; 8,500 tons of conductor rail; copper bonds for 8,000 joints; 32,000 insulators; 316,000 wrought iron fang bolts; 153,500 track chairs; signal cabling; electric lighting for stations fed from the conductor rail; carriage sheds; all the associated construction and laying costs; and of course the power station and substations already mentioned. Minor works included platform lengthening at several stations including Swiss Cottage. Together with rolling stock, the full outlay was around £1.25m at 1902–05 prices. To finance this, £500,000 of 3½ per cent Consolidated Preference Stock was issued in March 1904 followed by a further £750,000 in November. The Metropolitan Railway Act of 30 June 1905 authorised the issue of £380,000 3½ per cent debenture stock in substitution for the share and loan capital of the Harrow & Uxbridge Railway and a further £800,000 general capital for electrification and other purposes. Under this authority a £250,000 issue of

3½ per cent 'A' debentures was launched in June 1906.

Traction current at 550–600V dc was distributed to the trains through positive Vignole section 100lb per yd conductor rails placed 1ft 2in outside the inner face of the outer running rails, with the negative or return conductor rail midway between the running rails. The positive conductor was three inches above and the negative 1½ inches above the running rail surfaces. Spring-loaded cast iron collecting shoes were suspended from transverse oak beams at the ends of the motored bogies of the cars. This spring loading was not to last long and the transverse beams were replaced at the same time with short shoe beams bolted to the axle boxes. Both original features of current collection on the cars were instrumental in the chaos which attended the first day of electric operation on the Inner Circle. On the Extension Line only, station platform heights were raised from 3ft 1½in to 3ft 3in. Another early change was in the position of the positive conductor rails at stations, which were moved to the six-foot way from 1909 onwards and provided with double guard rails, the work being done gradually as ordinary maintenance. This change was not made for humanitarian reasons; much to the chagrin of the operating department, metal objects had fallen from the platforms to form a short circuit between the conductor rail and the continuous running rails.

From 1 July 1903 Charles Jones M Inst CE, MIEE was appointed full time chief electrical engineer at a salary of £650. Redesignated locomotive and chief electrical engineer in 1912 with responsibility for steam locomotives and all electric rolling stock in the works and sheds, he held the post until 30 June 1924, after which he continued for a time as consultant. Supporting Jones from 1903 were James Fox Heath as assistant electrical engineer at £300 and Alfred Ingram as 'carriage and wagon superintendent and rolling stock constructor' at £400.

Ingram's domain was to be the new repairing shed and shop for the electrical rolling stock at Neasden, with its 12 600ft roads served by overhead cranes and 550ft pits in each road. This was erected in 1904–05 at a cost of £55,434 to the plans of E. P. Seaton. Some eight miles of new sidings, all electrified, were installed in Neasden yard. The steam locomotive roundhouse there, in poor repair, was demolished in 1908 to allow the sidings into the electric running shed to be straightened. Steam locomotives were then housed in part of the existing sheds at the west end of the yard, reached by a new bridge over the Brent and a connection to the Wembley Park long siding. From July 1912 all roads through the car sheds and the northern exit from the depot to the Up Relief line at Wembley Park were electrified. With electrification, Neasden's importance much increased; by the end of 1909 there were 883 staff employed there[27].

Following the death of Gates, Seaton had been appointed as the new resident engineer from 70 applicants. He had previously acted as independent consultant and his salary as a full time officer from 1 October 1903 was £800 a year. He was the first of the Metropolitan's salaried engineers to be made responsible for new works as well as maintenance. Shortly after his appointment he informed the board that its engineering office possessed not a single reliable plan of any station, siding, or any part of the line (no doubt they were all in the offices of the various independent consulting engineers used in the past, but what had happened to the many plans handed over by Sir John Fowler?). Seaton reorganised the engineer's office, saw that proper plans were provided and generally enhanced its efficiency and value.

Struggling as they were to keep up with the rapidly developing electrical engineering technology of the period, British Westinghouse provided much trouble and disappointment for the Metropolitan. Many of the contracts were late in fulfilment, but the greatest problem was the delay in delivery of the turbo-generators for the power station, the first of which was not installed and operational at Neasden until the middle of November 1904, a year after the contracted date. By that time all nine substations[28] were ready for operation.

When the first electric cars arrived in March 1904 some trial runs were made between Rayners Lane and South Harrow using power from the MDR temporary plant at Alperton; one of these trains carried journalists. Full trials for staff training and testing the equipment under operational conditions began between Neasden and Uxbridge towards the end of November 1904, using the output of the first Neasden generator just mentioned. From 23 November electric trains ran daily to a timetable but were not available to the public. At Harrow station, to facilitate electric working to and from Uxbridge, a short electrified siding was laid behind the Down platform and used for Down departures. On the night of 1 December 1904 the first electric train ventured up to Baker Street East without incident. A press lunch was organised at the Great Central Hotel, Marylebone on 13 December after which the guests were taken out to Uxbridge and back by electric train.

To quote the public notice, 'From Sunday, 1 January 1905 a service by electricity of new corridor car trains with two classes (First and Ordinary)' was 'introduced into the regular working between Baker

Street and intermediate stations to Harrow and Uxbridge'. This consisted of three trains working to steam timings. Although the Inner Circle gate stock was ludicrously unsuitable for the rural peace of the Uxbridge branch, there was of course nothing else available. Further trains were added gradually until on 20 March, with 20 trains in service, all workings between Baker Street East and Harrow were electric apart from through trains for the Extension Line stations beyond Harrow. On that day, after close of normal traffic, a satisfactory trial run was made with an electric train from Baker Street to South Kensington and back to Aldgate. We shall return in a moment to what followed when attempts were made to operate a public electric service on the Inner Circle.

All footplate staff under the age of 50 as well as the younger guards and under-guards were invited to retrain as motormen for the electric trains. Older men, aged 60–75, 108 in all, were pensioned-off as they were thought unlikely to acquire the new skills. Not all the retrained men drove electric trains regularly but leading guards on electric trains and the conductors who opened the two sets of gates at each pair of end platforms were required to know how to move a train in an emergency. The daily (ten hours) rate for motormen was fixed at 6s or 7s according to the former rate of pay and was less than the comparable wage on the Central London Railway. Much of the training took place on the newly-electrified 'long siding' at Neasden, extended to Wembley Park to provide access from that end from 6 February 1905.

To reduce the amount of smoke and steam in the tunnels from an early date some steam trains were reversed at Wembley Park, the passengers being required to change to and from electric trains between there and Baker Street East. It was proposed to use electric locomotives to haul the longer distance trains between Baker Street East and Harrow, the GWR suburban trains working over the Metropolitan tracks, and the freight trains to and from Smithfield, although the last never happened in practice. An order for ten 47-ton, 1,200hp locomotives was placed with British Westinghouse in October 1904 at a price of £2,923 each, the mechanical parts and two four-wheeled trucks to come from Metropolitan Amalgamated at Saltley Works. Several months late, these locomotives began to arrive from April 1905 but pending completion of layout changes at Harrow station, most steam to electric changeovers continued to be made at Wembley Park and from 1 November 1906 all changes were made there. All Metropolitan passenger trains between Baker Street East and Wembley Park were electrically worked from 1 January 1907. Between that date and 2 September 1907 the new electric locomotives took over from GWR steam engines the working of that company's suburban trains east of Bishop's Road station, Paddington. On the Extension Line, Harrow became the normal changeover point between steam and electric traction from 19 July 1908. After that date there were no steam workings south of Harrow apart from freight to Finchley Road sidings and light running to and from Neasden sheds.

Although its passenger trains were now in charge of Metropolitan electric locomotives in the tunnels of the Inner Circle, the GWR continued throughout the Metropolitan electric era to work its freight trains to and from Smithfield with its own steam locomotives. Under Lord Herschell's award of 1897 (Chapter 5) these Smithfield workings were not included within the limited total of GWR trains permitted to run over the Metropolitan under the 1868 agreement but arguments about the operation of GWR trains over the Metropolitan lasted until 1902. At the end of that year all outstanding disputes were reported as settled, placing the relationship between the two companies on 'a most friendly footing'. The GWR had agreed to pay additional tolls on its Smithfield freights from 1 January 1903 and extra freight workings were admitted, together with four more GWR passenger trains to and from Aldgate. From that date all GWR trains operated at reduced fares between GWR and Metropolitan stations and were obliged to call at all Metropolitan stations and carry that company's local traffic free of charge.

The new Metropolitan electric locomotives, with their central cabs and sloping equipment compartments either side, suffered from a major defect which suggested that no-one with practical railway operating experience had checked the design – the driver had inadequate vision from his operating position. This was remedied by duplicating the driving equipment at each end of the cabs. A second batch of ten 47-ton locomotives was ordered in August 1906 from British Thomson-Houston at a unit cost of £3,750. Delivered from July 1907 onwards, these had a flat-ended van-shaped body, with driving controls at each end. They were fitted with Sprague Thomson-Houston all-electric multiple-unit control, operating internally only. There was one GE 69 200hp motor on each of the four axles, providing sufficient power to haul a 120 ton train on the level at 35mph or a 250 ton freight train up a gradient of 1 in 44. As with the first batch, these locomotives were dual-fitted, with quick-acting Westinghouse air and vacuum brakes[29].

Whilst on the subject of locomotives, we can note that two GEC electric machines were purchased from the Central London Railway in 1905 to carry out experiments with Raworth regenerative control. The trials were not attended with success and these locomotives, never used in public traffic on the Metropolitan, were sold to George Cohen Sons & Co as scrap in 1915.

Conversion of surplus steam compartment stock for electric working began at Neasden in 1905. Two four coach trains of 'Bogie Stock' were assembled, each including a brake-ended vehicle equipped with controller and brake valve. A control cable and jumpers ran through the train but there were no traction motors. Large end windows fitted across the full width of the coaches gave the driver a good forward view. The intention was that this train should be worked by a 150hp saloon motor car from one of the Westinghouse-equipped batches attached to the distant end, or in emergency by steam locomotive to maintain a service in the event of a major power failure. However the train was found to be underpowered and was later re-equipped to work with one of the 200hp BTH motor cars. Other coaches of 1898–1900 were then converted to electric working, their brake vans given four GE 69 200hp motors, Sprague-Thomson Houston multiple unit control and associated BTH equipment. This stock went into service between Baker Street and Harrow, the first seven-car train (two motor cars and five trailers) with 120 First and 280 Third class seats appearing in July 1906. In all 26 cars were converted for electric operation between 1906 and 1908[30].

During the transition from steam to electric traction a sufficient quantity of steam stock was kept in working order in case of breakdowns, but once the new system was established, preparations were made to sell off the surplus. Some 3,000 catalogues were printed to advertise the locomotives and stock released. These were distributed at the end of 1905 at home and abroad, some even going as far as China, but sales of the locomotives proved very disappointing as there were few conventional railway tasks for which they were really suitable. By the end of 1908 six engines had beeen sold to the Cambrian Railways, one to the South Hetton Colliery at Seaham, one to the West Somerset Mineral Railway and two to Bradford Corporation for passenger working on their Nidd Valley Light Railway.

With the introduction of more electric stock, an excellent service was provided on the Extension Line. From 2 April 1907 stations between Baker Street East and Willesden Green had trains every five minutes, with additional workings at peak periods making a three to four minute interval. To maximise the capacity of the double track between Baker Street and Finchley Road and meet the parallel motor bus competition, this section's stations were served by virtually all trains in the off peak period. Passengers for stations Harrow and beyond could of course obtain a faster run by changing in and out of GCR trains at Harrow.

Apart from the conductor rails, cables and related power distribution equipment, alterations for electrification on the Metropolitan portion of the Inner Circle were few. To accommodate the six-car trains it was however necessary to lengthen to 315ft the platforms at Gower Street (now Euston Square) and Edgware Road (Down side only). Where these extensions penetrated the running tunnels, space limitation restricted platform width to two feet below the Board of Trade's minimum of six feet. Platforms at Aldersgate (now Barbican) were also lengthened in 1905, making it necessary to relocate the signal box. Some track changes were made. New crossover roads were agreed with the MDR for Cannon Street, Monument and Mark Lane, and facing leads were made into the bay roads at South Kensington and Bishopsgate (now Liverpool Street). For safety of the men working on the line but also to facilitate track repairs, the two companies agreed that the positive rail in the Circle tunnels should be located in the six foot way, 1ft 4in from the nearest rail, rather than against the tunnel wall. As a fire precaution, hardwood sleepers were laid over most of the Metropolitan part of the Circle when the track was rebuilt for electrification in 1904–05. Fireproofing of rolling stock to be used in the Circle tunnels was discussed with the Board of Trade, but that department did not insist on obligatory standards or on the complete protection it required for the deep-level tube lines.

It was agreed that the MDR should supply power both to the Eastern Joint Lines and to the Metropolitan at South Kensington. The price at which the two companies would sell dc traction current to each other was fixed in October 1903.

Timing of the start of electric working on the Circle was mainly related to the availability of electric power and it was not until 1 February 1905 that the Underground Company's plant at Lots Road, Chelsea was available, then only partially. After much hard work, Westinghouse engineers succeeded in getting the third turbo-generator at Neasden and two of the rotary transformers at Baker Street substation in service by the middle of March. Trial trips having been made by each on their own sections, the two companies decided to begin the public electric service round the Circle on 1 July 1905 on the Outer Rail only, replacing the whole of the steam service in that direction. On the same day MDR electrics would begin to work to and from Whitechapel and Ealing. The rails were duly cleaned.

Alas, all did not go well. Metropolitan electric working was started at 5.48 am from Aldgate, seven Circle trains getting round over the MDR lines, the last three with difficulty, arriving back very late. An eighth did get round, ignominiously hauled over part of the distance by a steam locomotive to return almost three hours late. As soon as the trouble started an electric shuttle service was organised between South Kensington, King's Cross and Aldgate and after the return of the last Metropolitan trains from the MDR section, this worked well enough for the rest of the day.

The problems arose from three causes. Firstly the MDR line at Hammersmith was flooded by a torrential downpour early in the morning and this was followed by a derailment at Mill Hill Park (now Acton Town) which further contributed to the chaos. But there was something more serious. According to the contemporary Metropolitan report 'the District road "gave out" at several places', notably between Victoria and Sloane Square and current was lost altogether for some time. The MDR took one look at its track and formally requested the Metropolitan not to send any more of its electric trains over it. The truth of the matter lay in the manner in which the collecting shoes had been fixed to the Metropolitan cars, causing them to slip off the MDR positive conductors on some of the sharper curves, overturning the rails or damaging the supports, although there was no similar trouble on the Metropolitan's own tracks. In retrospect it seems ludicrous that this important aspect of compatibility was overlooked or at any rate that no practical tests had been arranged to ensure that each company's stock could run without trouble right round the Circle.

After this unfortunate start, the Aldgate-King's Cross-South Kensington service was continued, initially only between 10 am and 5 pm but from 24 July 1905 all day, alongside a resumed steam service each way round the Circle. Swallowing their pride, the Metropolitan engineers agreed to discard the use of spring-loaded shoes and to fit the MDR type, changing the shoebeam arrangement as already described. Similar alterations were made to the Metropolitan electric locomotives, in slower time. A partial Inner Circle service was successfully worked on 13 September 1905 followed by a full service in both directions from 24 September, using the same number of trains (14) at the same timings as steam. It was found that the electrics covered the distance between stations much more quickly, recovering with ease any time lost when delayed by other services. At this stage there were seven Metropolitan trains working the Outer Rail and five MDR and two Metropolitan on the Inner Rail. From 5 November, with the exception of the GWR suburban trains and the LNWR Outer Circle workings between Earls Court and Mansion House, all passenger trains round the Inner Circle and over the Eastern Joint Lines were electrically operated. LNWR trains east of Earls Court were hauled by MDR electric locomotives from 6 December.

Immediately before or shortly after electrification both companies cleaned up and renovated their Circle Line stations. Fresh whitewash was seen everywhere, but traces of soot and grime remained for a long time. On its section between South Kensington and Mansion House the MDR switched in new automatic signalling on 15 January 1906, but the remainder on the MDR and Eastern Joint Lines was not operational until 1907. This work included installation of new power frames at Aldgate East and Minories Junction signal boxes.

Aldersgate (now Barbican) sidings were adapted for examination of electric stock in 1906, with electric lighting installed. At the same time sidings for electric stock at Gloucester Road, Edgware Road, Ray Street, Farringdon Street, Moorgate Street, Bishopsgate (Liverpool Street) and Neasden were equipped with inspection pits lit by electricity or gas.

With electrification completed, the Metropolitan was anxious to make commercial use of the single line connection between the two parts of its system at Baker Street. For the first time for 38 years, four Up trains were run through from the Extension Line to the City from 28 January 1907. Once again this operation proved troublesome, causing the trains to be withdrawn early in May. A new automatically-signalled single track connection was subsequently made between the Down (Inner Rail) Circle and no 1 platform at Baker Street East. This was used from 1 July 1909 by 12 peak hour semi-fast trains from Aylesbury, Chesham, Rickmansworth and Uxbridge to Aldgate, arriving there between 8.07 and 10.30 am with a similar return service in the evening leaving Aldgate between 4.08 and 7.30 pm. As we shall see in the next chapter, this arrangement had only a short life as a double line junction was put into use from November 1912.

Patronage of the electrified Inner Circle service was disappointing, causing the two companies to reduce train length to five cars from 18 March 1907. On the following 2 April the all-round timing was cut from 60 to 50 minutes, trains running every ten minutes with a supplementary South Kensington-Aldgate service every five minutes (this ran at four car length instead of five from 11 April). At the same time the Hammersmith-Aldgate journey time was reduced from 39 to 32 minutes with more trains added and the Kensington (Addison Road) to Aldgate run was cut from 37 to 32 minutes with four instead of two trains an hour provided. This new timetable gave between 25 and 27 trains an hour between Edgware Road and the City at peak periods, the maximum possible whilst the old-style Metropolitan signalling remained in use and only achieved by installing additional signals and reopening the intermediate boxes at Devonshire Street and Chalton Street.

The MDR continued to show little enthusiasm for the Circle service, suggesting eventually that the Metropolitan should take it over entirely. Some alteration was in any case necessary as the 2 April 1907 timetable had not proved very easy to work in practice. After concluding a new agreement with the MDR, the Metropolitan worked the whole of the Circle service from 4 November 1907, using four-car trains operating at ten minute intervals. The MDR supplied power without charge over its own portion of the Circle, paying the Metropolitan running expenses at 1.8d a mile. This arrangement continued until 1 October 1908 when the MDR took back one third of the workings and the frequency was improved to six minutes.

ELECTRICS TO HAMMERSMITH BUT NONE TO NEW CROSS

After the usual arguments and difficulties with the GWR, always averse to any change of substance, agreement was finally reached in the summer of 1902 that the Hammersmith & City service should be electrified on a joint cost basis with jointly-owned rolling stock, the GWR surrendering any right it had to operate steam passenger trains over the Metropolitan portion of the Inner Circle. The electrification was sanctioned by the Metropolitan Railway Act of 31 July 1902.

Somewhat unexpectedly, the GWR undertook the whole of the electrification work between Bishop's Road, Paddington and Hammersmith including construction and equipment of a 6,000kW power station. Designed by its architect P. E. Culverhouse, this building was located at Park Royal and was to supply traction current for the Bishop's Road to Hammersmith section as well as for lighting Paddington main line station. Substations were sited at Old Oak Common, Royal Oak and Shepherd's Bush. Conductor rails weighed 102.8lb per yd and were of inverted channel section resting on iron-capped porcelain insulators. Twenty multiple-unit trains similar in design and finish to the vestibuled Metropolitan saloons were supplied by Metropolitan Amalgamated. The motor cars had four BTH GE 76 150hp motors and the six-car train formation was divisible into three car rakes after the conversion of some of the trailers to driving trailers in 1908–09.

A car depot was built by the GWR on the east side of the line just north of Hammersmith station, sited, much to the Metropolitan's displeasure, on an expensive piece of new land. This depot accommodated all 20 trains and with its overhead conductors for internal movements, was fully equipped for overhauls and light repairs. It was agreed that the Metropolitan should maintain the new fleet and operate the running shed.

A partial electric service between Hammersmith and Aldgate began on 5 November 1906, with a shuttle service on the electrified spur between Latimer Road and Kensington (Addison Road) (now Kensington (Olympia)). On Monday 2 December 1906 at close of traffic the through steam service between Hammersmith and New Cross via the ELR was withdrawn, an electric service between Hammersmith and Whitechapel (MDR) starting the following day. At the latter station, for which the Metropolitan had to pay the MDR for use, passengers transferred to and from the ELR on foot. Only two electric trains were used on 3 December, the balance of the Hammersmith-Whitechapel service being provided by steam trains but the electric trains were augmented every two or three days until all steam working was displaced.

With passenger traffic on the ELR in decline, electrification would have been a logical step but the other lessees (the LBSCR, LCDR, SER and GER) had refused in January 1902 a Metropolitan/MDR proposal that all the lessees should jointly fund conversion. Following withdrawal of the MDR service after that company's electrification, from 1 August 1905 the LBSCR provided a steam service between Shoreditch ELR and New Cross LBSCR. When Metropolitan steam trains were taken off, the SER worked a service from 3 December 1906 between its station at New Cross and Whitechapel. At the same time, the LBSCR service was augmented. The spur line between St Mary's station and the junction with the ELR was then converted for use by the Metropolitan as an electrified layby and shunting neck.

From 3 December 1906 the Kensington (Addison Road) spur was served by four electric trains an hour running to and from Aldgate, one train an hour continuing to Whitechapel until October 1908. Edgware Road became the weekday terminus for these trains from 31 October 1910 when the weekday service was increased to five 3-car trains each hour.

The other service using the Hammersmith & City line, the steam trains jointly worked by the Metropolitan and the GWR between Aldgate and Richmond, had begun to suffer electric tramway competition at its western end and was withdrawn after traffic on 31

December 1906. In its place a GWR steam rail motor worked every half hour between Notting Hill & Ladbroke Grove (now Ladbroke Grove) and Richmond. With many passengers changing on to the electrified MDR at Turnham Green this too was withdrawn after close of traffic on 31 December 1910. Reluctant to lose its access to Richmond, the Metropolitan then proposed to operate an electric service to that town. Negotiations with the LSWR had reached an advanced stage by the middle of 1914. However, in 1913, the Underground Company had obtained powers for extension of the Piccadilly tube service over the LSWR to Richmond and Sir Albert Stanley (later Lord Ashfield) offered the Metropolitan compensation in return for not resuming its running powers over the LSWR to Richmond. This was accepted and in November 1914 the 15 chain connection between the Hammersmith & City and the LSWR at Hammersmith was severed at its north end before complete removal on 7 May 1916.

On the Hammersmith & City, the off peak service was increased from six to 12 trains an hour on 2 April 1907, with three car units in use at these times from the following 1 January. A useful new source of traffic arose with the construction of the White City for the Franco-British Exhibition of 1908. An £8,000 temporary wooden station was opened on 1 May between Shepherd's Bush and Ladbroke Grove, landowners and exhibition authorities providing a one third subsidy to be refunded by a rebate of 15 per cent of net receipts. This station, with its direct pedestrian access to the exhibition grounds, was named Wood Lane (Exhibition). Despite the opening of a new Central London Railway station almost opposite, it was a financial success[31].

Between 1907 and 1909 the decaying wooden edifice at Hammersmith was handsomely rebuilt in brick for £20,410 to the plans of the GWR architect P. E. Culverhouse and those of the GWR engineering department. A spacious new concourse was made by setting back the tracks and two new platforms were provided, each with a road either side, giving an additional terminal road. The new street elevation was dominated by a large clock upon a pediment and a full width iron and glass canopy. In front of this was a small cab yard. In 1912 further improvements were made by constructing a handsome curved free-standing booking office in the concourse, allowing the old booking office area in the frontage to be converted to revenue-earning shops. A new entrance was also provided in Hammersmith Broadway opposite the recently rebuilt MDR/Piccadilly line station and alongside the George Hotel.

Although the inner London electrification was now complete, steam trains were not entirely banished. There were the GWR freights to and from Smithfield, already mentioned, the City Widened Lines services, engineers' trains, and even the occasional steam-hauled excursion[32].

POST ELECTRIFICATION PROBLEMS AND UNPLEASANTNESSES

One apparently unforeseen consequence of electrification was the fierce punishment which the new rolling stock administered to track which had not been altered apart from re-sleepering and re-ballasting. A depressing report was placed before the board by Seaton in June 1906 in which he explained that the greater weight of the motors, the extra wheels, the higher speeds and the strain and friction associated with more lively acceleration and braking (in which the wheels skidded and locked) were causing much additional expenditure on the sharply-curved MDR and Eastern Joint Lines, where rails were being removed for renewal every five months compared with a two year life in steam days. On the Metropolitan section of the Inner Circle, renewals were becoming necessary after six months to two years eight months compared with three years nine months to five years. Sandberg silicon steel rails were being laid at the most vulnerable places whilst crossings were being replaced in manganese steel. Shortly after this report Seaton was obliged to retire through ill health. His place was taken from 1 September 1906 by an LBSCR district engineer, William Willox, who was given a starting salary of £950. Willox compiled accounts of the state of the track throughout the system in which he commented that since electrification, the cost of maintenance had increased 'to an almost alarming extent'. He proposed to cease using mild steel rails on all electrified sections. In the tunnels corrugation became a serious problem, as on many other electric lines. A brake van was fitted up in 1908 with carborundum blocks, a 500 V 10 amp petrol generator producing sufficient power to hold the solenoids to the rails as the van was towed over the affected tracks at night by a steam locomotive.

Further difficulties arose with the British Westinghouse contracts. In 1906 the firm was obliged to replace the turret controllers in the original stock which had been the source of constant failures. Rectangular automatic controllers with electro-pneumatic unit switches grouped together side by side were fitted instead whilst alterations were also made to rectify poor performance by the electric motors. Neasden power station was attended with much dissatisfaction and failure. In the boiler house the Roney mechanical stokers were blamed for excessive coal consumption and smoke emission, the latter bringing down upon the Metropolitan the terrible wrath of the Willesden Urban District Council. Wags commented that the smoke had been removed from the London tunnels only to plague Neasden. Some improvement was evident when the mechanical stokers were replaced with Babcock & Wilcox chain grate stokers. In compensation for all this, and also for the delivery and completion delays mentioned earlier, the unfortunate British Westinghouse was obliged to agree to financial adjustments ending in a net credit to the Metropolitan of £33,000, paid in 1906.

That was not the end of it. Other difficulties arose from the unsatisfactory working of the accumulators placed in the cars for operating the 14 V supply for operating the traction control gear. These were replaced by motor generators driven from the 600 V traction supply located in the luggage compartments together with a back-up set in case of failure. There were stoppages in the train service in May 1905 when Westinghouse engineers were obliged to take the first three generators to pieces at Neasden. Matters had settled down sufficiently by October that year to allow Jones and his staff to assume charge of operations at Neasden power station.

By arrangement with British Westinghouse, the Metropolitan had taken over all four 3,500 kW generators on the understanding that the firm would make a cash adjustment for uncompleted work and the additional operating costs arising because the machines did not meet the specified efficiency and steam consumption. A condition of this arrangement was that the firm would convert each of the original four machines to 5,000 kW output and provide a fifth with the same capacity. This entailed extension of the power house with six new boilers of similar design to the originals, a second chimney and two more duplex cooling towers, giving a total cooling capacity of 1.64m gallons an hour. But the fifth generator, of the Westinghouse-Rateau impulse type, was also delivered late and broke down several times after its installation in 1908. By 1912, at a net cost to the Metropolitan of £74,900, all the Neasden generators had been converted to the Westinghouse-Rateau impulse pattern with alternators wound to provide 5,000 kW output. This gave a total station output of 25,000 kW and a satisfactory solution to the problems experienced with the original installation. The Babcock & Wilcox chain grates were replaced by Bennis close-link grates in 1913, these allowing burning of the more economical coal slack instead of nuts.

Some more unforeseen expenditure arose when the Board of Trade insisted in 1905 on the rebuilding of wooden platforms to reduce the fire risk at Baker Street, Great Portland Street, Euston Square, St

John's Wood Road and Swiss Cottage. Another safety requirement was the doubling of the single guard timbers on the positive conductor rail in stations. In 1906 the offending platforms were rebuilt in concrete covered with expanded metal and artificial stone.

By far the most unwelcome news received by the board and management shortly after electrification was that of the company's first fatal train accident. This took place in thick fog on 26 October 1907 at West Hampstead station when a Down train ran into the one in front, stationary at the platform. Three people were killed and 11 seriously injured. It was reported to the board that the West Hampstead signalman, having received road clear from Kilburn, accepted the 7.37 am Baker Street to Willesden Green train, booking it as leaving the station at 7.46½. Believing the train had in fact left, but unable to see it, the starting signal having been prematurely restored to danger, he manipulated the interlocking to pull off the home signal, thus admitting to the station the following 7.41 am Baker Street to Neasden train. Called to the scene immediately, the Government Inspector found the signalling in order. The fearsome telescoping, in which the bodies of the rear motor car of the first train and the leading one of the second were completely wrecked and their underframe and trucks badly buckled, dramatically demonstrated the weakness of the form of body construction adopted, whilst the whole incident served to stimulate a more rapid introduction of automatic signalling.

NEW SIGNALLING

Unlike the MDR, which had completely renewed its signalling with an automatic system based on the latest US practice, the Metropolitan had rejected the idea of signalling modernisation, restricting its expenditure in this field to the installation of metallic returns for the interlocking current and a few Westinghouse mechanical train stops at selected home and starting signals. Otherwise things remained much as in steam days. Thomas Parker had told the board in July 1905 that before the capacity of the electrified railway could be developed to its maximum some form of fully automatic signalling would be inevitable.

Some notice was taken of this statement in that an experimental section of mechanical automatic signalling was authorised for both roads between Praed Street (Paddington) and Notting Hill Gate. Trials began on the Up road on 6 April 1907 and shortly afterwards both roads were worked with the system, which was eventually extended to South Kensington. But the Board of Trade was not prepared to agree to its installation east of Praed Street Junction as it provided no positive protection against breakaways of the loose-coupled GWR freight trains to and from Smithfield. Track circuiting was therefore installed on the remainder of the Metropolitan section of the Inner Circle until, much to the relief of the Board of Trade, the whole was covered, from 26 September 1909. This automatic signalling allowed further improvements to be made to the train services from 1 October 1909. The system was then carried on to the Extension Line, which was equipped as far out as Neasden by January 1911, except at Baker Street itself, pending the rebuilding of that station[33].

Between South Kensington and Praed Street there were no track circuits. Power for lowering a signal and keeping it in the 'off' position depended on a neutral relay, normally energised and holding the signal at clear. When a train worked a depression bar, the signal was put to danger by removal of current from the relay, and it could not be restored to clear until the same train had depressed the bar of the next signal ahead and also passed over a treadle about 40ft ahead of the bar. Signals were of the lower quadrant semaphore and banner types. Train stops worked by electric motors prevented most signals from being passed at danger.

On the remainder of the lines re-equipped, that is the rest of the Metropolitan Inner Circle and the five miles of local lines between Baker Street and Neasden, the McKenzie, Holland & Westinghouse system of all-electric automatic signalling was adopted, with dwarf colour lights in the tunnels and Circle Line open sections and upper quadrant semaphores beyond Finchley Road, all combined with dc track circuits and train stops. At Praed Street Junction, a power frame with illuminated track circuit diagram came into use on 26 July 1908. There was a similar power frame at the Aldgate boundary with the MDR installation, operating from 26 September 1909. From the latter date all signals between these two points via King's Cross were automatically-worked but mechanical frames were retained at a few points semi-automatically worked. A decision was then taken to standardise on all-electric automatic signalling and point operation, making the Metropolitan the first British railway company to adopt this system. At first dc track circuits were used but as these were found to cause occasional interference with signals, all new work from 1913 was in ac. Conversion of the dc track circuits began in 1929.

EMPTY FIELDS ON THE UXBRIDGE LINE

As might have been expected, given its rural nature, the traffic on the new Uxbridge branch was very thin, not even covering running costs. It was of course hoped that the district would now develop as a residential area and when the Ickenham Parish Council requested an inexpensive halt in March 1905 they got one quite quickly. At a cost of a mere £275, oil-lit wooden platforms of three-car length with sign-boards reading ICKENHAM HALTE[34] appeared on the south side of the bridge carrying Glebe Lane (now Glebe Avenue) over the line and were opened to public traffic on 25 September 1905. When it was reported in March 1906 that the public were endangering themselves by sheltering under the bridge in wet weather, standing beside the track to do so, £80 wooden shelters were authorised.

Two other requested halts, at Eastcote and Rayners Lane, both with shelters, and costing £325 and £408, were agreed in March 1906 after Ickenham had attracted some new traffic. They were opened on 26 May 1906, but for many years business was very slight. Situated in open country and serving only a few scattered cottages, two sewage farms and an isolation hospital, Rayners Lane's main function after March 1910 was to serve as an exchange platform with the MDR service. Eastcote generated some summer pleasure traffic and its platform was accordingly extended from three-car to six-car length in 1910.

It was soon realised that operation of full-length electric trains to Uxbridge was highly wasteful. Within a very short time the off-peak workings were covered by a three-car unit shuttling between Uxbridge and Harrow, the motor car propelling two trailers in one direction and hauling them in the other. This practice quickly aroused the dis-pleasure of the Board of Trade, causing a 4-4-0T locomotive and three rigid eight-wheeled carriages to be substituted around the end of March 1905. After discussions with the department, electric service was restored at off peak periods from 1 June using a motor car, trailer and driving trailer formation, said to cost about the same to operate as a short steam train. A lineside observer at this time would also have seen the Metropolitan's first Westinghouse electric locomotives under-going trials on the branch.

Financial returns continued to be extremely disappointing as the Uxbridge traffic alone was insufficient to sustain the branch. Receipts in 1905 were only £2,935, rising to £4,157 in the next four years[35]. In these circumstances, management pressures for economies were unrelenting. In August 1908 we find the superintendent of the line proposing two-car trains but as this entailed altering the cars especially for this one service, the suggestion was rejected. Another discarded idea was to operate a shuttle service of compartment coaches hauled by the two ex CLR locomotives which had been rebuilt for the Raworth regenerative control experiments. It was finally decided that from 3 December 1908 all trains on the line would be three-car length shuttling only to and from Harrow, where interchange had been made easier. This allowed the closure of the substation at Ickenham.

A newspaper report at the time the branch was opened had noted that 'The neighbouring landowners are said to be averse from alienating land for building, and the hope of establishing a big population along the line does not promise to be realised immediately'[36]. This proved to be a sound prognostication, despite the not inconsiderable interest generated in the pioneer town planning scheme of the Ruislip-Northwood UDC under the 1909 Housing & Town Planning Act, with its proposed 'garden city', to be laid out by Ruislip Manor Ltd, straddling the branch. By the time wartime restrictions stopped building around 1915, the new suburban development was limited to the first portion of the Ruislip Manor (Manor Farm) cottage estate north of the line east of Ruislip station and a few roads south of the branch at West Harrow. A fifth halt, called Ruislip Manor, was opened on 5 August 1912 as the first 14 houses were being erected in Manor Way[37]. At West Harrow a wooden halt was provided from 17 November 1913.

Apart from the through traffic to and from Uxbridge and the very light all the year round business generated by Ruislip village and the small settlements at Ickenham and Eastcote, the branch saw most activity in late spring, summer and early autumn when pleasure parties and individuals came out from London to enjoy the Middlesex countryside, refreshing themselves at the several tea gardens, cottage tea rooms and inns. Another two decades were to pass before the branch would produce sufficient traffic on a daily basis to justify the optimism that had led to its construction and electrification.

Taken as a whole, the Metropolitan recovered quite quickly from the effects of the Central London Railway competition, thanks to electrification and the fare reductions mentioned earlier. After falling from 96 million in 1899 to 87.8 million in 1901, the total number of passenger journeys rose to almost 90m in 1902, reaching 98.4m in 1906. Dividends on ordinary shares, which had dropped to 2¼ per cent in 1901, had reached three per cent in 1904. But this apparent recovery was short-lived. Competition from other new tube railways and then from the motor bus, combined with the burden of interest charges on the electrification capital and the diversion of GCR traffic via High Wycombe was soon to produce another and more severe depression. The number of passengers carried continued to rise but not enough, with fare reductions and loss of Second Class revenue, to make a sufficient contribution to a net revenue affected by the factors just mentioned. A new general manager was now to come on to the scene and would have some success in arresting this disturbing trend.

STRIVING FOR MORE REVENUE

NEW BROOMS

A man whose quiet but strong personality was to shape the company's policy over most of its final quarter of a century came to the Metropolitan as its secretary in July 1903, following the death of G. H. Whissell the previous November. Robert Hope Selbie[1] so greatly impressed the board that it sent him to the USA in 1905 to study electric railway operation and lifted his salary from an initial £600 to £800 in 1908. That year, alarmed at the decline in the company's fortunes since the heavy capital expenditure on electrification, the board appointed a committee of directors to enquire whether 'the officers of the Company and their arrangements are sufficiently up-to-date to promote to the full the Company's interests, and to report what changes, if any, are in their opinion necessary'. There is no record of the committee's findings, but it is significant that the ailing Ellis was persuaded to resign as general manager before working out the full period of notice, giving way, from 1 October 1908, to Selbie, at £1,025 a year. This was to prove a sound decision. Setting out to devise and pursue all likely means of building up revenue and traffic, the newcomer took a firm grip on the helm. He showed himself ready to promote with vigour further electrification and other capital developments whenever he saw the time as ripe. A somewhat shy, yet pompous man, he was to manage the railway in an autocratic manner, keeping himself apart from most other officers. Very much in control, as general manager he was almost always the sole source of new initiatives and policy changes, treating his senior officers very much as second fiddles. Relationships with junior officials and the uniformed staff were conducted on a paternalistic basis, modified in later years by attempts to achieve a measure of employee participation. Although he was invariably scrupulously fair with his staff, Selbie was highly intolerant of any suggestion of slackness[2].

Another victim of the 1908 shake-up was H.B. Palmer, 'liberated' from his position as superintendent of the line on 31 December. His place was taken by the energetic Willis H. Holt, who had spent his early career on the GWR, rising to assistant station master at Padding-

Trips to LONDON

(METROPOLITAN STATIONS).

PROGRAMME OF

EXCURSION AND—
WEEK-END TICKETS.

13th JULY and until further notice.

Baker Street Station, N.W.,   R. H. SELBIE,

July, 1914.   General Manager.

The cover of the Excursion Leaflet, July 1914, showing the logo adopted in that year ton in 1893 before moving in 1907 to become station superintendent at Perth (General). Holt was given the title of traffic superintendent, his duties embracing those of the former goods manager, William Henry Brown, who had been made secretary in Selbie's place. Brown, who had joined the audit department of the Metropolitan in 1872 at the tender age of 13, had subsequently organised the Company's first goods traffic arrangements whilst also acting as audit accountant.

Before his departure, Ellis had arranged closer cooperation with the Underground company, which was now experiencing similar problems of disappointing traffics, a challenge being addressed in imaginative and dynamic style by its new American general manager, Albert Stanley (later Lord Ashfield). At Stanley's suggestion, a single map was produced for all the London underground railways, including the Metropolitan. In December 1907 5,000 large posters and a million folder versions of this were printed. At the same time, it was agreed that the central London stations of the Metropolitan, the MDR and the tube railways should be distinguished externally by vertical signs bearing the logo UNDERGROUND, a device which also appeared on the maps and new posters. The generic map, with each line shown in distinctive colour, was also put on enamel plates placed in special frames and illuminated after dark, the Metropolitan ordering 100 of these in October 1908. But so strong was its independent spirit, Metropolitan cooperation with the Underground company in publicity proved to be short-lived. When the Underground introduced its bar and circle logo in 1913, the Metropolitan opted for a bar and *diamond*. This appeared on publicity in 1914 and as station nameboards from early 1915 in the form of 6ft 6in square enamelled plates with bold white letters on an Oxford blue bar set across a solid red diamond against a white ground. Green diamonds were used after 1923 on the East London Railway, possibly a delicate compliment to the Southern Railway, which had the major single interest in the ELR, becoming the sole freeholder in 1925.

NEW STATIONS

One of Selbie's early initiatives was to propose reconstruction of the street buildings of inner London stations, which he described as 'old in design and dingy in appearance; there is nothing distinctive about them and they offer no attraction to the passer-by'. He thought they compared 'very unfavourably' with the modern tube stations and the rebuilt MDR stations of the Underground company. Astutely, he indicated that valuable commercial letting space could be secured by judicious rebuilding, especially in those cases where an intermediate floor could be inserted between the street and track levels for the station offices. He proposed to make efforts to secure firm offers for commercial space before rebuilding started. To add to the prominence of street entrances he suggested large canopies bearing the company's title, illuminated at night.

Some stations had already been rebuilt or improved and work at Baker Street East, West Hampstead and Hammersmith has been mentioned in earlier chapters. To these a few others must now be added. Portland Road (Great Portland Street) was given a new exit stair case in 1877 and a new booking office in 1884. Baker Street (Circle) had acquired a new street level building at the east end, next to Madame Tussaud's, in 1888 and a platform level interchange between the two stations here, with its own booking office, was added at the end of 1898. At Farringdon Street, the booking office bridge had been reconstructed in 1899. Built at shared cost with the GNR, a subway between the Metropolitan and main line stations at King's Cross was opened on 20 June 1892 (the Metropolitan Railway Act of 25 July 1890 authorising this had also sanctioned a similar foot subway from Gower Street (Euston Square) to the LNWR terminus at Euston, but this was never built).

The old wooden buildings and supporting piling at Notting Hill & Ladbroke Grove (now Ladbroke Grove) required complete replacement in 1900–02, so badly had the original cheap and nasty work deteriorated. During 1894–96 Moorgate had undergone complete reconstruction. Its roof had been reported in 1893 as 'in a most ruinous condition', so much so that at the end of that year the City Commissioners of Sewers served a dangerous structure notice. In the following year J. T. Firbank removed the overall roof, replacing it with umbrella canopies on the platforms. The GWR cooperated by agreeing to run all its trains on to Aldgate from 1 July 1894, leaving the terminal space available for the reconstruction work. A new street level building incorporating refreshment rooms was designed by the architect George Campbell Sherrin to maximise commercial letting. Initially it was built only to first floor level but offices above were added in 1902–03. The Metropolitan portion of the rebuilt station was in use from 17 June 1896.

Deterioration of the original overall roofs also triggered reconstruction of the three western joint stations, in conjunction with the MDR. At all three, umbrella canopies were erected along the new platforms. At Gloucester Road, where work was completed in 1907, a second bridge was erected (in 1906) across the west end of the platforms to reduce the congestion caused by passengers transferring between the Metropolitan no 1 Down platform and the MDR no 4. The similar schemes for High Street Kensington and South Kensington were also finished in 1907. At the former, an impressive shopping arcade, decorated in *art nouveau* style and lit by a central dome, joined the booking hall to the street, providing direct entrances to the adjacent large department stores (Ponting's on the west, Derry & Toms' on the east). The latter firm leased a new 800 sq ft space built out over the railway. At South Kensington, a new arcade of shops was formed at street level above the railway across the west end of the station after the booking hall had been resited at intermediate level. George Sherrin was the architect for all three schemes.

Three of the eastern joint stations also received treatment. At Monument in 1909 a new frontage by George Sherrin was completed, incorporating commercial premises which partly used space formerly occupied by the booking office, now moved to half level. Mark Lane was rebuilt in 1911 to the designs of the MDR architect H. W. Ford, receiving a new booking hall, entrance and frontage. Cannon Street's entrance and street elevation were reconstructed to Ford's plans in 1910, the result providing a pleasanter, lighter interior.

On the portion of the Inner Circle wholly owned, the Metropolitan first attended to Edgware Road, where a 40ft wide frontage to Marylebone Road, with a 7ft wide passage and footbridge to the platforms, was opened on 1 March 1911. Built for £1,446, this was above the site of the former locomotive shops and south side engine shed. Designs were by Frank Sherrin, son of George. At rail level, important track alterations had been brought into use from 30 September 1910. These involved slewing the Down (westbound) main line from the eastern tunnel mouth to connect with the former Down Siding, which became part of the Down Main. A new Down Siding was laid between the Down Main and the engine sheds. The old Down Main west of the new connection became a middle siding with a facing connection from the Up Main and a trailing connection to the Down Main. This middle siding would take four cars, or five 'with care'. The old engine sidings were taken up and a new dock siding put in to take a six-car train, with a trailing connection to the Down Main on the east side of the Down platform ramp.

Some minor improvements, including a passenger luggage lift, had been made at Liverpool Street in 1897–8, but a substantial rebuilding was undertaken in 1911–12. The old glazed arch roof of 80ft span over the platforms was replaced by a steel and concrete floor providing an area of 17,000 sq ft, carrying a 100yd long, 18ft wide shopping arcade linking Old Broad Street to Liverpool Street, with a new booking office, circulating area and tea rooms across the west end. This work, for which Frank Sherrin was the architect, was opened on 11 March 1912. Lettings yielded a 15 per cent return on the £34,548 cost. Both entrances were given canopies. A Metropolitan Railway information bureau in one of the arcade shops dispensed guides, brochures and postcards from 31 March 1913. Traders taking space in the 27 shop premises provided almost all the office worker might need whilst hurrying on his daily round: a ham & tongue dealer; fancy goods and toys; confectioner; hatter; hosier; watchmaker & jeweller; bookseller; chemist; fishmonger; and a tobacconist. In the station itself, the third platform track on the south side was removed and the platform widened for part of its length to bring it up to the former siding, which became a bay road for terminating trains from the Extension Line, replacing Moorgate. These track changes were completed on 1 February 1910.

An important scheme was undertaken at King's Cross, where the high arch roof of 80ft span, with its 12 22ft-long bays, was in poor condition. Fortuitously, the London County Council, then electrifying its tramways, was anxious to make a bridge over the Metropolitan to link Gray's Inn and Caledonian Roads, thus avoiding 35ft and 40ft radius curves at King's Cross, much too cruel for its new electric cars. The final contribution extracted from the LCC met almost 66 per cent of the £51,884 expenditure on rebuilding this station. Engineer for the scheme was O. G. C. Drury, the architect Frank Sherrin.

During 1910 the old roof was taken down, to be replaced on the island platforms by 88ft of umbrella roofing and by 132ft of lean-to roof on the Down Circle platform. The entrance building, along the west side of the new tramway bridge, came into use at the end of 1911. Its 16ft wide opening, flanked by shops, led to station offices slightly below street level where there was a 60ft wide booking hall with wide steps to the platforms as well as a 20ft by 36ft parcels office with a 20cwt electric lift from rail level. Around the corner, to the east, in Pentonville Road, the City Widened Lines were given a separate street entrance and booking office, opened in 1912. To carry the tramway, a 130ft long, 60ft wide ferro-concrete skew bridge was constructed on the Coignet system. On the east side of this, strong girder work was erected to give 5,640 sq ft of space for commercial development up to eight stories high above the railway. Construction of the King's Cross Cinema on this foundation started in 1914 but work was brought to a halt by the exigencies of war. The first tramcar crossed the bridge at 4.30 am on 1 July 1912, although the whole of the work at King's

Cross was not completed until the end of 1913.

Both King's Cross and Liverpool Street were equipped for electric lighting throughout in 1911 and 1912 respectively, the power coming via the railway substations. Great Portland Street and Euston Square were similarly lit in 1913 and Moorgate in 1913–14.

After J. Lyons & Co had agreed to take a 28-year lease of a tearoom and shop, Praed Street (Paddington) was rebuilt in 1914–15 at a cost of £6,472. The entrance and canopy, flanked by six new shops, with further commercial letting space at first floor level, was in a faience frontage designed by C. W. Clark, the Metropolitan's first resident architect, of whom more later. No doubt speaking from bitter experience, Lyons asked the Metropolitan to keep the air space below the teashop floor to a minimum 'to avoid forming a harbour for rats, which generally abound in railway stations'. During the rebuilding electric light was fitted throughout the station and the Spiers & Pond buffet was redecorated and repanelled. The Metropolitan was sensitive about its facilities at Paddington at this time as the Bakerloo tube had opened a station there on 1 December 1913. It was arranged with the GWR that a small Metropolitan booking office should be built against the 1916 subway leading to the tube station from the new GWR arrival platforms on the east side in the hope of diverting some of the interchange business. This office was opened on 26 June 1916 together with a subway from the tube booking hall to the Metropolitan station.

NEW LIFE FOR THE HAMMERSMITH & CITY

Selbie was much exercised by the poor results on the Hammersmith & City since electrification, grumbling that the line and the train service 'had not been kept up-to-date' in the face of severe tube, electric tram and motor bus competition. Formerly a profitable operation, the H&CR had shown a continuous and growing deficit since 1901. Earnings per mile were only £18,000 against £34,000 on the Metropolitan itself (excluding the Uxbridge branch) and what Selbie described as 'even the poorest of the tubes', the Great Northern & City Railway, did better at £22,000. The H&CR percentage of working expenses to receipts was 77.64 compared to 49.07 on the Metropolitan. It was difficult for the Metropolitan to make changes. In a report to the board in 1915 Selbie recalled that:

> although from its situation it is essentially part of the Metropolitan system, the Great Western Company have always been very jealous of our undue interference with its working and have insisted upon their rights as

Plate 20 Pullman car *Mayflower* as delivered, 1910 (*Staffordshire County Record Office*)

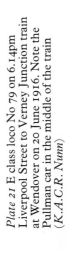

Plate 21 E class loco No 79 on 6.14pm Liverpool Street to Verney Junction train at Wendover on 20 June 1916. Note the Pullman car in the middle of the train (*K.A.C.R. Nunn*)

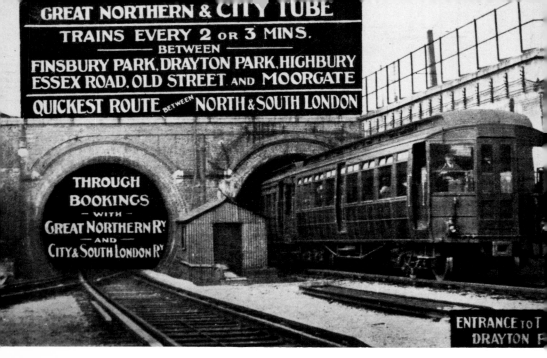

Plate 22 GN&CR publicity postcard of about 1913 showing Moorgate train emerging from the tube tunnel at the north end of Drayton Park station

Plate 23 British Thomson-Houston electric loco No 16 on the 1.50 pm Saturdays only Baker Street to Chesham train at Harrow in 1918 (*photographer unknown*)

partners in the general control of the line. This was by no means advantageous to the joint undertaking inasmuch as the methods adopted on a steam trunk line such as the Great Western were very different from those necessary on a suburban electric railway. Moreover, having regard to the relative sizes of the two systems, the Metropolitan was not infrequently placed by force of circumstances in the position of the 'little brother'.

In 1911–12 a chance arose to change things; and Selbie seized it. Discussions with the GWR, held under threat of some Metropolitan-inspired parliamentary unpleasantness for big brother[3], culminated in an agreement of 31 December 1912 under which the Metropolitan achieved 'practical control' of the H&CR train services and maintenance of its way and works from 1 January 1913. It was agreed that the Metropolitan should spend a minimum of £20,000 and a maximum of £100,000 on improvements to the line's infrastructure, the interest on such expenditure to be payable out of any increase in earnings over the 1910–13 average. The Metropolitan was given the power to fix local fares and through fares to its own stations and beyond, subject to GWR consent, which would not be unreasonably withheld.

The first batch of new works undertaken included the addition of canopies to the entrances to Westbourne Park and Ladbroke Grove stations and a new booking office on the Up side at the latter; a new booking office (mentioned earlier) and electric indicator at Hammersmith; and a new platform shelter at Latimer Road. But the most important change was the closure of the awkwardly-sited Shepherd's Bush station halfway between two main roads, and its replacement by two new stations, Shepherd's Bush, on the north side of the Uxbridge Road; and Goldhawk Road, on the south side of its namesake. Both were opened on 1 April 1914 and despite a depression in business caused by the outbreak of World War 1, Selbie could report to the board that in the year ended 31 March 1915, after taking into account the extra staff costs and other items, the net traffic increase over the previous year was 10.1 per cent, corresponding to a 23.1 per cent return on the expenditure. The approach roads to the first Shepherd's Bush station and the arches beneath the line were made to provide useful income by converting them to a retail market, opened on 29 June 1914.

STATIONS FOR NEW SUBURBS

New stations and halts to accommodate and encourage the growth of Metropolitan suburbia and opened in the 1900s and 1910s at Dollis Hill, Ruislip Manor and West Harrow have been mentioned in earlier chapters. By the end of 1908 a new station was also in place at Harrow. This had an island platform, making a total of four faces, connected by subway. The layout was completely resignalled. Associated track changes, completed in July 1908, involved provision of 750yd of new double line on the east side of the existing pair between Harrow South Junction and the north end of the station. Harrow South Junction signal box had a 32 lever frame (four spare) and Harrow Station box, given a new 70-lever frame (seven spare), was 250 yd from the north end of the widening. At Harrow North Junction, the 50 lever (19 spare) frame was relocked.

Two other new facilities were provided at this period, initially with other things than suburban development in mind, though both were to become important suburban stations soon after the end of World War 1. In 1909 the 18-hole Sandy Lodge golf course was laid out on the east side of the line halfway between Northwood and Rickmansworth. When the syndicate behind this enterprise requested a station for its golfers, the Metropolitan & GCR required a guaranteed minimum revenue of £350 a year. This given, they erected, at 15¼ miles from Baker Street, at a cost of £665, 350ft timber side platforms with oil lamps and simple shelters, connected by a footbridge. Named Sandy Lodge, this was opened for press visits on 9 April 1910, then on subsequent Sundays, and continuously, for public traffic, on 9 May. Receipts, at around £2,000 a year, were well in excess of the guarantee sum. From 1923 onwards, this halt served Moor Park, an up-market residential development, country club and golf course on the west side of the line which produced a modest but highly lucrative daily traffic. In connection with this development, the name was changed to Moor Park & Sandy Lodge from 18 October 1923. Two goods sidings, 400 and 416ft, on the Down side, were laid in September 1923 but did not come into continuous public use until June 1925. With the 1933 opening of the Merchant Taylors' School nearby expected to increase revenue by some £4,000 a year, some improvements to the crude passenger accommodation were authorised in 1932.

The second halt followed a decision to hold the clay pigeon shooting event of the July 1908 London Olympic Games in the 37-acre grounds of the Uxendon Shooting Club School. The Club petitioned the Metropolitan for a halt at the Preston Road bridge, between Wembley Park and Harrow. There had been some earlier agitation for a halt here and the petition was followed by another from the far from impressive total of 16 local residents who stated they were obliged to walk up to two miles to Wembley Park station. With the Club promising a £200 guarantee, the Metropolitan set about erecting two

260ft wooden platforms on the east side of the overbridge, each with a small shelter. A small booking office hut near the road entrance was to be opened as required. Altogether £600 was spent. Trains were stopped on request at Preston Road halt from 21 May 1908 and soon afterwards boards were erected reading STOP HERE FOR UXENDON SHOOTING SCHOOL AND CLUB. Some passengers, including the proprietor of the School and Club (the principal guarantor) were left on the platform when unregarding drivers omitted to stop for them and after several such incidents the booking clerk was instructed to go down on the platform when a train was expected and passengers had presented themselves, ready to wave a red flag. Between 1910 and 1912 some moderately spacious detached houses appeared along Preston Road north of the halt. By the early 1920s the facility was much used at weekends and on summer weekday evenings by visitors to the many sports grounds in the neighbourhood, incuding those of the Bank of England, Marshall & Snellgrove, and Selfridge's, as well as by patrons of the Harrow Golf Club.

A FLAGSHIP AT BAKER STREET

By far the most ambitious of all the station projects of the Edwardian period was the rebuilding of Baker Street as the company's principal station and headquarters. The works of 1892–3 at the East station had proved of little more than stop-gap value. There were only three running roads and three platform faces for the 1901 total of 281 trains entering and leaving this part of the station every day. A particular difficulty was that simultaneous use of nos 2 and 3 roads was prevented by the presence of the sector pit at the inner end. Moreover the new platforms were unduly narrow, the approaches constricted, and a double line junction with the Inner Circle was becoming a necessity which could not be long delayed.

For prestige reasons it was considered the company should have a terminal station with some main line pretensions to match its desired image, including a cab road between the platforms and the street. Proposals for a major reconstruction on these lines first came forward in 1899 but prolonged negotiations proved necessary: with the local authorities; with Lord Portman (the owner of the surrounding properties which the railway wished to take over and on which some of the leases were conveniently expiring); and with the new owners of the Baker Street & Waterloo tube scheme about their proposed station (on which some work had started but which the Metropolitan wanted

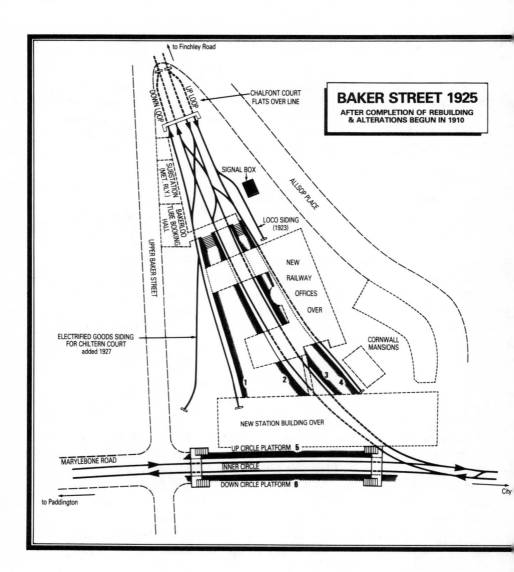

to Finchley Road

CHALFONT COURT
FLATS OVER LINE

SIGNAL BOX

ALLSOP PLACE

UP LOOP

DOWN LOOP

SUBSTATION
(MET. RLY.)

BAKERLOO
TUBE BOOKING
HALL

UPPER BAKER STREET

LOCO SIDING
(1923)

NEW

RAILWAY

OFFICES

OVER

ELECTRIFIED GOODS SIDING
FOR CHILTERN COURT
added 1927

CORNWALL
MANSIONS

1   2   3   4

NEW STATION BUILDING OVER

UP CIRCLE PLATFORM 5

MARYLEBONE ROAD

INNER CIRCLE

DOWN CIRCLE PLATFORM 6

City

to Paddington

moved to a site more suitable for the enlargement of its terminus). Powers for the acquisition of lands for the works were taken in the Metropolitan's act of 31 July 1902 and that autumn the board found itself in a position to buy in without too much difficulty the whole of the triangular site bounded by Upper Baker Street, Marylebone Road and Allsop Place. It was agreed this should be done, negotiations for purchase starting in May 1903. The decision to go ahead with the enlargement of the East station was confirmed in July 1905, despite the altered conditions prevailing after the agreement with the GCR. Sir John Wolfe Barry & Partners were commissioned, but their

elaborate plan, presented in April 1906, with its eight tracks, five platforms, cab road from the street and hotel was rejected as unnecessarily
extravagant and unsuited for the Metropolitan's traffic requirements.
In the light of the poor financial results of 1906–07 it was decided to
postpone the project.

Virtually all the properties in the triangle were in Metropolitan
hands by the end of 1908. Lord Portman was to receive £52,000 for
them, partly in cash, partly in Preference Stock. After a good deal of
dithering, during which plans were considered for a second pair of
tracks at a lower level, then abandoned as superfluous following the
proposed installation of automatic signalling, the board finally agreed
in January 1910 to press ahead with the rebuilding within a maximum
cost of £100,000. William Willox, the company's engineer, prepared
plans to meet three requirements: an opening out of the tunnel mouth
at the north end of the station to eliminate the sharp curves and constricted throat; a double line flat junction with the Inner Circle,
incorporating provision for a non-conflicting junction at some future
date; and an increase and improvement in the platform accommodation and station offices, to be obtained by moving most of the latter to
a new frontage on the Marylebone Road[4].

The first task was the rebuilding of 560ft of the St John's Wood
tunnel to make room for four tracks as far as a point 220yd north of
the platform ends. Perry & Co took down the 25ft span brick arch of
the tunnel, replacing it with a covered way of concrete walls and steel
girders with reinforced concrete between, this to support a block of
flats fronting Allsop Place and Upper Baker Street.

Provision was made in the Metropolitan Railway Act of 20 July
1906 that the elevations in or abutting upon Marylebone Road should
be of 'reasonably ornamental character' and subject to the approval of
the London County Council, who were also to sanction the arrangements for exit and egress. Responding enthusiastically, the Metropolitan prepared an impressive frontage of 400ft for the main road, to
be approached by a cab road raised three feet above the street which
would form a roof for the new station offices at intermediate level. The
first 200ft of this frontage block was erected by Henry Lovatt Ltd to
one storey height along the cab approach. It had a reinforced concrete
floor and its steel frame was filled with ornamental Portland stonework. Halfway between the cab road/entrance level and the platforms
were a booking hall 32ft by 16ft, a circulating area 77ft by 46ft, oak-
panelled refreshment rooms, cloak rooms, lost property office and
store, ladies' rooms, a parcels yard and other offices. This area was
reached by two 16ft wide staircases from the cab approach. Two sets

of 13ft wide stairs led down from the circulating area to the platforms. Above this partly completed frontage it was proposed to erect a large hotel.

At rail level, Lovatts built two island platforms 375ft long and 35ft wide serving four tracks, a double road in the centre passing through to the Circle, a single terminal road each side, these ending in Ransomes & Rapier hydraulic buffers capable of arresting a 180 ton train at six miles an hour. Since the opening of the Bakerloo tube railway on 10 March 1906, tube passengers from the Metropolitan had been obliged to cross by a footbridge (paid for by the tube company) from the north end of the East station platforms to the tube booking hall in Upper Baker Street. From 15 October 1914 this transfer was eased, by two escalators providing direct access to the tube platforms from a new circulating area and booking office reached by short staircases from the new Metropolitan platforms. The original lifts remained in use from the Upper Baker Street tube station but the Metropolitan ticket office there was closed, the two railways agreeing to sell each other's tickets. As it benefited from the heavy interchange traffic at Baker Street (almost three millions a year by 1911) and was anxious about diversion of business when the tube was extended northwestwards over the LNWR to Harrow and Watford, the Metropolitan met half the cost of the escalator improvement.

All-electric dc automatic signalling, with ac track circuits, was installed over the new layout between the Circle lines and the north end of the reconstructed station at a cost of £7,763. This was controlled from a new cabin on the east retaining wall replacing the former Junction and North boxes and fitted with an illuminated track circuit diagram extending from Edgware Road to Great Portland Street and St John's Wood Road. With its power frame of 18 levers for operating 24 signals and two indicators and 12 for working 20 points, plus six spares, the new cabin came into service on 4 January 1913. Shortly after this, the new manganese steel points and crossings for the station layout were installed. Electrically-worked McKenzie, Holland & Westinghouse illuminated train destination indicators, a large one in the main booking hall and satellites at the Upper Baker Street entrance and on the Extension Line platforms, were operated from the new box.

In conjunction with the new works, to permit the construction of a road circus at the confluence of Marylebone Road and Baker Street, the company demolished its 1863 Circle line street level booking offices at each side of the west end of the station. These were replaced by a subsurface booking hall over the Up Circle line with an entrance on the north side of Marylebone Road at the corner of Upper Baker Street. A ferro-concrete bridge was built to connect the two Circle platforms beneath the roadway at this end in 1911, but the works were not completed until 1913.

On 24 July 1912 there was a formal ceremony, during which Lord Aberconway laid the centre stone of the new Marylebone Road frontage in the wall of the cab approach[5]. He spoke of the new Baker Street forming

> the chief station of the Metropolitan Railway, the pioneer of underground traction, and instead of a collection of unsightly sheds which have so long disfigured this part of Marylebone, I trust you will shortly see a magnificent building.

He could not know that it would be 1929 before the project was finished.

Another aspect of the Baker Street scheme implemented a 1909 board decision to concentrate all the headquarters staff in one building. These new offices were designed by the company's recently appointed 'architectural assistant', Charles W. Clark[6]. His seven-storey building, shyly tucked away behind Allsop Place, had light faience elevations in neo-Grec style, its rear sitting over the East station platforms. Some 65,000 sq ft of accommodation were contained within a monolithic concrete frame, built on the Coignet system and erected by Lovatts. Embellishments on the frontage included a curious device of a crossed miniature telegraph pole and signal post and sets of small buffers adorned with coupling chains. The pleasure of the staff in occupying these fine new premises in January 1914 was mitigated by Selbie's decision to increase their office hours to 9am to 5pm on Mondays to Fridays instead of 9.30 to 5 (Saturdays remained unchanged at 9–12.30pm). Shareholders' meetings were held in the new building from February 1914. It also contained a suite for the general manager, with a private lift from the platform below.

Clark was also responsible for the architectural work at Chalfont Court, the eight-storey block of flats placed over the new covered way at the north end of the station and completed in March 1914. But his first task for the Metropolitan after his arrival in 1910 appears to have been to work up the elevations for the main Marylebone Road frontage and hotel which Frank Sherrin had originally drawn to show the London County Council in 1908. Agreement was reached in 1913 with Lyons' subsidiary, Strand Hotel Ltd, on the construction and leasing of the hotel above and each side of the new station, its interior design to be the responsibility of the architect F. J. Wills, who worked on several of Lyons' Corner Houses and hotels. Wills produced drawings for a building with 650 public bedrooms, each with its own bath and lavatory, on eight floors (seven on the Marylebone Road frontage) together with shops at street level. The contract was placed with James Carmichael, demolition starting on 22 March 1915. Clearance of the site was completed, excavation partly finished and some foundation work begun when all activity was brought to a halt by war conditions in 1917. The Carmichael contract was formally terminated two years later.

The double line junction with the Circle came into use on 4 November 1912, for a fortnight's trial working, after which a new timetable provided a much improved service between the Extension Line and the City. For this new facility and the through running to the newly-electrified East London Railway, additional high tension cables had to be installed between Neasden, Baker Street and Moorgate and a fourth 1,200 kW transformer added to the Baker Street substation; all this work was completed in 1913. Suitable equipment was placed in the substation at this time to enable the new buildings and platforms at Baker Street to be lit with power from Neasden. Moorgate Street substation had also received an additional 1,200 kW converter in December 1910 and Finchley Road the same in February 1912.

SALVATION IN OUTER SUBURBIA

It was soon apparent to Selbie that the excessive provision of new public transport facilities in central London would have a permanent effect in checking the Metropolitan's short-distance traffics, keeping the fares at uneconomically low levels. The one bright spot was the evident suburban growth being encouraged by the electric services, notably at Harrow, which by early 1909 was requiring three additional workings each way at peak periods together with longer trains.

By 1911 the motor bus had been developed into a commercially-successful vehicle which was doing great damage to Metropolitan in central London. After some rather fruitless discussions with Albert Stanley (Lord Ashfield) and the LGOC in the early part of 1911, Selbie brought his thinking to the board in October. He explained that the LGOC now had a motor bus 'out of which they make a good profit at low fares after allowing ample provision for depreciation' and had been and still were putting 20 such buses a week on the streets to replace horse buses and earlier uneconomic motor bus designs, or to create entirely new services. To add to the problem, the London County Council continued to extend their electric tramway system and were proposing lines along the Euston and Edgware Roads which would suck off Metropolitan traffic with fares so low no railway could compete. Selbie's analysis was that this present and prospective competition in central London obliged the Metropolitan to concentrate on the development of its longer-distance business. He had noted a tendency for businessmen to live further out of town, increasing the demand for houses 10–30 miles out, especially where the travelling facilities were good:

> there have been indications for some time past that the country served by this Company's Extension Lines to Aylesbury and Uxbridge is coming into favour and I see no reason why we should not in a short time very greatly extend our business on those lines, provided we put ourselves in a position to run a frequent and fast service of trains between the places they serve and the City.

Gross receipts from these districts, he observed, had already grown from £72,231 in 1908 to £88,318 in 1910.

There was however a difficulty. Whilst the new works at Baker Street were going to afford great relief, they would not in themselves permit any appreciable increase in the number of non-stop trains between the outer areas and London. At rush hours there were 24 trains into Baker Street East and an equal number out and although the automatic signalling would allow a small number of non-stop workings to be inserted amongst these, it was not enough. Selbie thus argued for a second pair of tracks for express working. These, he acknowledged, would be very costly to provide between Baker Street and Finchley Road but they were not immediately essential on that stretch[7]; the immediate requirement was a five mile widening between Finchley Road and the north end of Wembley Park station which would enable all trains to and from points beyond Harrow to run non-stop between Harrow and Baker Street alongside a frequent local service for the 11 stations out to Harrow. To reduce the inner bottleneck somewhat, it was already planned to open out the tunnel mouth at Baker Street and the same should now be done at the Finchley Road end. He explained that most of the land required for the widening was already in Metropolitan's possession and the only substantial new works would be a new viaduct against the existing one at Kilburn. This widening was agreed, powers being obtained in the company's act of 1912.

Developing his theme, Selbie also argued in 1911 that in conjunction with the GCR, the Metropolitan should build a two-mile electrified branch from Rickmansworth to Watford, whose inhabitants had been agitating for a link to the Metropolitan since the 1880s (possible routes had first been investigated as early as 1889). This project would of course involve extending the electrified track from Harrow to Rickmansworth but Selbie thought that would be 'necessary in any case shortly'. There seems to have been some suggestion that the Watford branch might eventually have gone on to St Albans, but although nothing more was heard of that, the threat of LNWR suburban electrification to Watford, supplemented by projection of Bakerloo tube trains over the new suburban lines beyond Willesden Junction, confirmed by an announcement late in 1911, convinced the Metropolitan board that parliamentary authority for a Metropolitan & GCR branch should be sought.

Selbie was involved in other moves to encourage outer suburban development. In 1910 he had reported to the board an arrangement made with a firm of estate agents to work in conjunction with the Metropolitan to publicise and develop property along the line between Neasden and Uxbridge and Aylesbury. Although nothing much seems to have come from this initiative, it did provide Selbie with the germ of a much more ambitious proposal he would soon be bringing to the board, one which we shall look at in Chapter 13.

BUTTERED TOAST ON THE CIRCLE

Selbie was quick to realise that the development of outer suburban traffic should as far as possible be directed towards encouraging First Class season ticket holders to live in Metropolitan territory, thus maximising revenue. This explains his positive approach to a proposal which came from Davison Dalziel (later Lord Dalziel of Wooler), chairman of the recently-anglicised Pullman Car Company, in October 1908. Dalziel suggested that four 'Parlor Cars' should be operated between Baker Street and Aylesbury and although Selbie thought that two might be enough to begin with, he saw the scheme as likely to generate the type of traffic he sought, as well as forming a valuable advertisement for the Metropolitan and its residential territory. It would also provide something to counter the superior outer suburban carriages of the GCR out of Marylebone. When one director had the temerity to express doubts in view of the very thin First Class traffic beyond Harrow, Selbie admitted that it was a non-paying quantity, but added that was 'all the more reason why we should take some steps to improve it'. He promised to arrange matters so that the only liability of the Metropolitan would be to haul about ten tons of additional weight on two trains daily. But it was not to work out quite like that.

The arrangement finally reached with the Pullman Company,

embodied in a ten year agreement of 1 April 1909, followed that company's normal practice. Pullman undertook to purchase two cars, to be built to Metropolitan specification; Pullman would provide the attendants, who, in Dalziel's words, would 'generally speaking, wait upon and provide for the comfort of the passengers travelling in them'; and the Pullman Company would be responsible for all internal decorations and maintenance of the interiors. Haulage by the Metropolitan would be free of charge, the railway also supplying lighting, heating and cooking services, maintaining the cars externally including running gear. Pullman would retain the income from the supplementary fares charged to the First Class passengers patronising the cars as well as the profits from the refreshments sold. Selbie made sure that if at any time the Metropolitan should transfer all operations north of Harrow to the GCR, the agreement would be terminated, as it would be, by either side, should the venture prove a failure. He also required Pullman to guarantee that it would not offer a similar arrangement to the GCR for its services between Harrow and Aylesbury.

The two 29-ton, wooden-bodied cars, built by Birmingham Carriage & Wagon to Inner Circle loading gauge[8], had interiors by W. S. Laycock Ltd of Sheffield. Externally, roofs were painted white, top panels cream ('broken white'), match boarding umber and parts below the solebars black. Lettered in gold in the usual Pullman style, they bore, for some unexplained reason, the names *Mayflower* and *Galatea* after two yachts defending and challenging the America's Cup of 1886. Following delivery by rail to Aylesbury in the early morning of 28 April 1910 a press run was arranged for 27 May from Liverpool Street to Aylesbury and back with lunch at Aylesbury's George Hotel. The next day's *Daily Telegraph* observed that 'Unsophisticated natives . . . gazed yesterday from their gardens and copses and pasturelands in open-mouthed astonishment at the sight of the "Galatea" and the "Mayflower" on the Metropolitan Railway'. Journalistic open mouths were otherwise engaged.

On 1 June 1910 the two cars entered public service, running singly in the middle of five trains daily to and from Amersham, Chesham, Aylesbury and Verney Junction. One was a theatre train, leaving Baker Street East at 11.35 pm, arriving Aylesbury 12.55 am, suppers served *en route*. On morning workings, breakfasts were available, followed by light luncheons at midday and teas in the afternoon. Between London and Rickmansworth the supplementary fare was 6d, beyond, 1s. There were no Sunday workings[9].

Passengers sat in 19 armchairs, mostly placed at glass-topped tables softly-lit by 'electric lamps of chased design', and equipped with finely-chased gilded ormolu bell pushes. Light switches and table number frames were also in gilded ormolu. Two main saloons, separated by a partition with clear glass upper panels, seated eight and seven passengers, but those requiring extra privacy and discretion had the option of a coupé compartment at one end of the car furnished with four chairs and a table. Next to this was a 'well-fitted' lavatory discharging on to the track. Whatever regulations may have said, this facility was seemingly available on the London tunnel sections of the journey, though no true First Class Pullman Lady or Gentleman would have dreamt of using it whilst the train was standing in a station. After a few years there were complaints that the attendants did not keep the lavatories clean and that they were poorly-ventilated (the air flow was subsequently improved). The eight-seat section had a buffet counter with a small pantry, gas stove and hot and cold water supply behind it. As electric lighting was extended to all its rolling stock, the Metropolitan found it inconvenient to continue supplying gas cylinders for the Pullman stoves, so from 1920 onwards cooking was precariously performed on Primus oil stoves in circumstances which would have produced heart tremors in today's safety officers.

Each car was 59ft 6¾in over buffers with 39ft 3in between the centres of the 7ft 6in wheelbase bogies. Entrance vestibules and partitions were panelled in mahogany and the floors here were rubber-tiled. Vacuum automatic brakes and Laycock's steam heating were fitted but once the cars passed on to the electrified section, passengers were left to shiver, which no doubt increased the consumption of the readily-available spirits. Electric radiators were belatedly installed in 1925.

Internally, apart from the entrance vestibules, the cars had distinctive decorative treatments. *Galatea* was in what was described as late 18th century style, its mural panels in fine fiddleback mahogany, the upper ones inlaid with satinwood on a fine quartered and veneered ground. The cored plaster ceilings had an ornamental band on the flat carrying suspended lights which supplemented the table lamps and wall brackets. Specially-woven green silk damask blinds, an ormolu baggage rack with finely-chased ornamentation and brass treillage panels, deep pile green carpet and green morocco upholstery completed the décor. *Mayflower* exhibited what were said to be 'Georgian influences', its panels of fine wainscot oak displaying in their upper parts 'enrichments of the Georgian period' on a ground of fine quartered and veneered oak. Carpet here was also deep pile, but crimson, whilst the chairs were covered in matching morocco. All other features were similar to the sister car.

There were soon some grumbles about the prices charged for the refreshments. Selbie suggested that whilst the occasional main line traveller might not object to them, they were apt to frighten off suburban passengers regularly given the opportunity of using the cars. But Dalziel did not give way. Towards the end of 1910 he asked for small boards to be hung beneath the train indicators at stations Liverpool Street to Baker Street inclusive to show when a Pullman car was included in a train. To cover occasions when either car was not available the Metropolitan obligingly adapted the Rothschild saloon as a relief Pullman.

Patronage of the cars was never very high. Even in the first week, when they were a novelty, the average daily number of passengers served was only 46. It was not long before the Metropolitan decided it was making a loss on the operation. A count made one day in October 1912 established only nine ordinary ticket holders entering the cars in addition to 33 season ticket passengers; corresponding figures for 8 May 1914 were four and 34. As the attendants received wages of only £7 a month, one hopes the tips were generous. In an endeavour to stem the loss, the cars were withdrawn from some midday trains in the last part of 1914, the supplement was reduced to 6d throughout from the following 1 January and some refreshment prices were cut at the same time[10]. These moves temporarily increased patronage but wartime difficulties soon forced up prices and the one shilling outer area supplement was reintroduced on 1 October 1919. With the passing of the years, reasonably-dressed Third Class passengers were never turned away provided they offered the supplementary fare, but the losses continued. The Pullmans owed their survival to their nebulous prestige and publicity value rather than accounting balances.

Repainted from 1923 in less striking but more practical all-over crimson lake livery, both cars outlasted the Metropolitan Railway, running under London Passenger Transport Board auspices until wartime conditions provided a welcome excuse for their withdrawal. They last worked on Saturday 7 October 1939, after which they were broken up at Hampton Court station, SR, to form portable dwellings.

FAST LINES TO WEMBLEY PARK

For the widening between Finchley Road and Wembley Park, O. G. C. Drury was appointed resident engineer and the contractors were Walter Scott & Middleton. Work started in February 1912, when clay was excavated between Willesden Green and Neasden, some of it to be burnt as ballast for the new tracks, the remainder to be dumped at Rayners Lane. By January 1913, *The Railway Magazine* was able to report 'Familiar embankments are gradually disappearing', meaning presumably cutting sides.

At Finchley Road, Perry & Co were the contractors for opening out the old tunnel mouth before girdering it over to accommodate the junction of the four new tracks with the double line to Baker Street. Manganese steel 95lb per yard switches and crossings were installed here at six times the cost of ordinary steel but offering ten times the life. From this point to the temporary Kilburn Junction (immediately east of the bridge over the LNWR Hampstead Junction line) the new lines were opened, in advance of schedule, on Sunday 30 November 1913[11]. These 'Through' tracks, on the north side of the old, were used by certain non-stop trains to Harrow from the following day.

The section from Willesden Green to Neasden, also on the north side, was opened from the morning of 5 January 1914. Beyond Neasden, as far as Wembley Park station, the widening was on the south side, the four running roads here becoming available from 11 January 1914. On the following 1 March an accelerated service began, using crossovers on and off the available sections of widening.

As it involved the heaviest constructional works, the remaining stretch from Kilburn Junction to the east side of Willesden Green station was not available until 31 May 1915. Even then the reconstructed entrance and booking hall at Kilburn station were not completed until 22 June 1916. This last section, with its lofty 35-arch brick viaduct of over one third of a mile included an impressive 600-ton, 221ft long hog-back lattice girder bridge over Kilburn High Road, which the Metropolitan crossed on the skew. This structure was embellished with a cast iron ornamental parapet rising to 7ft above the rails. The LNWR was crossed by an iron skew bridge with spans of 80ft and 97ft.

At Finchley Road the station now had a single island platform with shelters, placed between the 'Local' lines on the south side. This was connected to a new booking hall at street level which was ready in the late summer of 1914. Frank Sherrin provided handsome elevations for the rebuilt top station, which included shops and flats and had an entrance in Canfield Gardens as well as Finchley Road. On girdering over the four tracks, this structure was not completed (by Allan & Co) until June 1915.

No changes were made at West Hampstead, where there were again no platforms on the Through Lines. At Willesden Green new Up and Down Through Lines platforms were provided, the Down a conversion of the former bay road. Although the new layout here was in use from 17 December 1913, the shelters on the platforms and the covered footbridge were not finished until the following year. As there was at the time a big voltage drop between Neasden and Finchley Road substations, the new platforms were lit by gas. Suburban growth around Willesden Green station had now reached its peak, influencing freight as well as passenger arrangements. A milk dock was provided in 1915 near the goods shed, alongside the new Up Through Line.

Dollis Hill station was left untouched and no alterations were made at street level at either Willesden Green or Neasden. At the latter there was a new Up Through platform, the old Up platform becoming a 25ft wide island, with the Down Through Line on one side and the Up Local on the other. Both had a gravel surface, shelters, and partly-glazed concrete roofs extending 160ft from a new ferro-concrete footbridge at the London end. Completed by the end of 1914, the enlarged Neasden station was electrically lit from the carriage shed wiring. A signal box, formerly at Willesden Green, was erected at the country end of the island platform. After a ticket inspector had pointed out that employees were daily risking their lives at the level crossing at this end on their way to and from the depot and works, a subway was built in 1922.

At Wembley Park the old nos 1 and 2 terminal bays became Up and Down Local platforms whilst the north side of the central island platform formed the new Down Through and the northernmost platform, with a new shelter, served the Up Through Line. Electric lighting was installed, fed from the traction supply.

All the new lines had McKenzie Holland & Westinghouse upper quadrant automatic signalling with ac track circuits, using US equipment. The final cost of the widening, including land, works at stations and associated property developments, was £320,000. Taking into account the loss of some leased sites from the widening work, the net increase obtained in rental values was £2,600 a year.

The branch to Watford[12], authorised by the Metropolitan Railway Act of 7 August 1912 despite fierce LNWR opposition, had its commercial prospects very firmly nipped in the bud. Opposition from Watford Council on amenity grounds secured abandonment of the final 35.4 chains through Cassiobury Park to the proposed terminus close to the High Street. This short-sighted move left the Metropolitan and its GCR partner with a Watford station sited on the western edge of the town in an area not inappropriately known as The Wilderness. A Watford Joint Railway Committee was formed by the two companies in August 1912, but although some land was purchased, no start on construction was to be made for another ten years.

The years 1911 and 1912 proved to be exceptionally busy ones for Selbie, when crucial decisions were taken which would shape the future form of the Metropolitan. Whilst working up his outer suburban strategy, he found himself obliged to turn his attention to the company's interests in inner London. Late in June 1911 it was learned that from 1 July the Central London tube would adopt season ticket rates which were in many instances substantially lower than those on the competitive sections of the Metropolitan and the MDR. Despite the continuing existence of a loose form of coordination in the shape of a 'General Managers' Conference of the Underground Railways', the CLR had omitted to give the other companies any opportunity for discussion on this proposal. The two older undertakings were thus forced to reduce their rates between competitive points to the new CLR levels and to make corresponding reductions between other places affected. Selbie and Albert Stanley (managing director of the Underground Company since May 1910) marked their displeasure by withdrawing from the Conference, effectively killing it.

As competition from the LGOC buses and the Central London tube became increasingly tiresome, the Underground Group sought to bring both companies into its arms. Agreement on acquisition of the LGOC was announced in January 1912. At the same time, the weakest of the independent tube railways, the Great Northern & City (GN&CR) and the City & South London (C&SLR), under pressure from fierce competition by improved street transport, were increasingly amenable to suggestions of amalgamation with the larger groups. Both the Metropolitan and the Underground contemplated absorbing the GN&CR and the C&SLR; the Underground in particular had a very strong interest in the last, which it proposed to link up with its Charing Cross, Euston & Hampstead tube line to provide a through route from Hampstead and Highgate to the City.

Stanley eventually decided to leave the Metropolitan a free hand with the GN&CR, persuading Selbie to give up any idea of taking over the C&SLR in return for an undertaking which would protect Metropolitan interests if the C&SLR went into the Underground Group. He promised that the Underground would not in such circumstances extend the C&SLR west of Euston or extend the Bakerloo eastwards to join the C&SLR without Metropolitan consent; also, if after a connection had been made between the C&SLR and the Hampstead tube, total bookings and season ticket issues between West Hampstead, Finchley Road, Swiss Cottage, Marlborough Road and Euston Square, King's Cross, Moorgate Street and C&SLR stations south of Moorgate fell in any 12-month period below those of the last 12 months before such connection were made, the loss in receipts would be made good to the Metropolitan. Lastly it was accepted that the Underground Group would not oppose a physical connection between a Metropolitan-owned GN&CR and the Waterloo & City tube railway and the MDR would grant 'due and reasonable' facilities for a proposed Metropolitan electric service to Richmond via Turnham Green. An agreement covering all this was signed by Selbie and Stanley on 20 November 1912.

In this atmosphere of mutual empire building it was natural there should be some discussion of merging of interests by total amalgamation of the Metropolitan and the enlarged Underground group of companies. But once again the independent spirit prevailed, the Metropolitan rejecting the idea of complete amalgamation in favour of 'close and friendly co-operation' with the Underground, in mutual interest and towards the elimination of all unnecessary competition. A press notice was issued in November 1912 explaining that in reaching this conclusion the Metropolitan board were

> mainly influenced by the fact that their Company has large and expanding interests outside the immediate area of competition with the tube lines and the omnibuses for which no adequate compensation could be afforded in any scheme for a fusion with the Underground Company.

It was noted in the same statement that the Metropolitan was also involved in moving freight, whilst enjoying important and valuable working relationships with several trunk line railways in regard to both freight and passenger traffic. In this analysis we can detect the hand of Selbie, using arguments later to form the basis of the fierce resistance the Metropolitan would mount in the face of schemes envisaging its integration in a single new organisation of London public passenger transport.

The GN&CR was a deep level tube railway unique in that it had been built with 16ft diameter tunnels to take main line size rolling stock running between its City terminus at Moorgate and the GNR suburban stations north of Finsbury Park[13]. Its owners and management had consistently failed to reach agreement with the main line company regarding the through running which would enable it to fulfil its intended role, so it remained a mere 3½ mile link between the

City and the GNR station at Finsbury Park, where its platforms were beneath the GNR's, without any physical connection. As such its revenue had been seriously eroded after the electrification of the parallel London County Council tramways. It had carried only 12.82 million passengers in 1912 compared with an average of just under 16 million in its early years. Yet another round of negotiations with the GNR in 1909 had ended in stalemate, leaving the tube company in the bargain basement. The Metropolitan had pondered purchase for some years, establishing close contacts during the 1908–9 negotiations for improvement of the interchange arrangements at Moorgate. (A new subway and booking office authorised by the Metropolitan Railway Act of 26 July 1910 had been opened on 2 September 1912 between the Metropolitan platforms and the GN&CR and C&SLR stations.) Another and perhaps principal factor influencing the relationship was the large Metropolitan shareholding held by the railway contractors S. Pearson & Son Ltd, to whom the GN&CR was much in debt.

Selbie's public argument was that purchase of the GN&CR was an insurance policy to protect the Metropolitan's interest in the large traffic passing over the City Widened Lines from the GNR suburban stations. He suggested the continued independence of the GN&CR was a menace in that the Great Northern would always be tempted to take it over, then directing on to it the traffic using the City Widened Lines via King's Cross, which although worked by the GNR, was worth some £38,000 to the Metropolitan. To strengthen his case, Selbie postulated development of new traffic between stations on a Metropolitan-owned GN&CR and the eastern part of the Inner Circle and the East London Railway, also through workings over the GN&CR between the GNR and the Great Eastern Railway, South Eastern Railway, London, Brighton & South Coast and London & South Western, for which purpose there should be a physical connection between the GN&CR and the Inner Circle, at a point between Moorgate and Liverpool Street, and another between the GN&CR and the Waterloo & City, the latter to have its tunnels enlarged to 16ft diameter and carried up to meet the L&SWR lines outside Waterloo.

Convinced, the board authorised negotiations in October 1912. Agreement was quickly reached, in time for the Metropolitan to prepare a bill for the 1912–13 session in which provision was made for the GN&CR to be taken over as a going concern from 1 July 1913[14]. But all did not prove plain sailing. Whilst suitable steps had been taken to secure GNR consent, influential City property owners showed great anxiety over the proposed subterranean links, their opposition causing the bill to be shorn of all its railway works except a

506yd extension of the GN&CR from Moorgate to Lothbury. This was a revival of an earlier proposal which would bring the GN&CR close to the Waterloo & City and the Central London at the Bank, without junctions. The legislation was heavily qualified by requirements for the protection of a Bank of England hypersensitive to potential risk to its well-stuffed vaults. The resulting Metropolitan Railway Act of 13 August 1913 must have reinforced any tendency Selbie had towards superstition as well as bolstering his obstinacy; he saw to it that the powers for the Bank extension were kept alive until as late as 31 October 1932.

A second attempt to increase the value of the new acquisition was made in the 1913–14 session, in the form of a joint Metropolitan and GNR bill which sought to transfer the GN&CR to a joint committee of these two companies; to extend it to a junction with the Metropolitan near Aldgate; and to provide it with an exchange station *beneath* the Waterloo & City at the Bank, without any junction. The cost of the new works was to be equally shared by the two companies. Finally the GNR undertook to complete at its own expense the long-planned connections between the GN&CR and its suburban lines at Finsbury Park. Alas, this last proposal stung the North London Railway into angry opposition, that company seeing in it a direct threat to its long standing arrangements for working its trains over the GNR suburban lines via Canonbury Junction. Parliament inserted conditions for the protection of the North London Railway interests which were not acceptable to the promoters, who then withdrew the bill.

The Metropolitan now found itself left to make what it could of an isolated 3½ mile deep level tube railway, which it had started to operate on 1 September 1913[15]. There was some small compensation in that the physical assets were in good order and the line had been well-managed. Setting out to beat up as much business as he could, Selbie accelerated the service, improved peak hour frequencies and lengthened half the rush hour trains from four to five cars[16]. By the middle of 1914 he was able to report a small profit from increased patronage. Some economies were possible, notably the closure of the tiny power station at Poole Street, Hoxton, in October 1914, after which the line was supplied from Neasden through a new substation at Drayton Park equipped with three 800 kW three-phase rotary converters. Asserting its main-line aspirations, the Metropolitan introduced on 15 February 1915 the only First Class accommodation on London's deep level tube railways[17], thereby gaining some extra revenue from the GNR's First Class season ticket holders. Rebuilding of some of the 32 motor cars and 44 trailers which had been taken over was started in 1915[18]. In May 1929, five of the ten trains providing the basic service were lengthened from five to six cars, the remainder following on 6 October 1930.

At the 1912 meeting there was some harsh criticism from a section of shareholders about the GN&CR purchase, allegations being made that a run-down asset had been bought at an inflated price for the personal gain of some directors. In the negotiations it had been agreed that two GN&CR directors, The Earl of Lauderdale and Sir Clarendon G. Hyde, should join the Metropolitan board and the latter's arrival in the boardroom in November 1912, some time before the takeover, was thought suspiciously premature. There was some difficulty in getting his appointment confirmed in a 'state of uproar' at the February 1914 shareholders' meeting.

Whether or not one accepts the validity of the Selbie arguments, unlike the Underground Company which had been obliged to pay the CLR and C&SLR shareholders some £60,000 a year above the net earnings of the undertakings immediately after taking them over, the Metropolitan was not involved in a cash loss when it acquired the GN&CR. Initially, at any rate, a pleasing traffic growth was obtained, from 12.82 million passengers in 1912 to 20 million in 1920. But after the parliamentary defeats of 1913 and 1914 (which should perhaps have been foreseen, at any rate in part), it inevitably remained very much a stagnant backwater for the rest of the Metropolitan's existence.

ELECTRIFYING THE EAST LONDON RAILWAY

One of Selbie's over-optimistic proposals for the GN&CR had been to run trains through from the GNR to the East London Railway, which at the time of the GN&CR acquisition was at last undergoing electrification. In 1902 this line had carried 276 passenger trains every weekday (100 Metropolitan, 76 MDR, 64 LBSCR and 36 GER) as well as 32 freight trains worked by the GER. On Sundays the figures were 184 passenger and 14 freight. At that time, the total of passenger journeys was around seven million a year, of which almost 45 per cent were local to the East London. The loss on working, partly met by the Metropolitan, was about £20,000 a year. We have seen in Chapter 11 how the other lessee companies had refused in 1902 any cooperation with the Metropolitan and the MDR over electrifying the line, with the result that these two companies withdrew their services as soon as they had completed the electrification of their own lines, leaving the LBSCR, SER and GER to provide a slightly reduced level of steam passenger workings from 3 December 1906. Both the Metropolitan and the MDR, believing it would bring them more business, very much wanted to see the ELR electrified but had decided in 1904 that these hopes were not sufficient to justify their bearing the whole cost themselves.

When the managers of the lessee companies looked at the question of electrification again in 1908 they decided not to recommend any action on the grounds that it was unlikely to improve the existing poor financial position or produce the additional five million passengers a year required to remunerate what they calculated to be the estimated capital cost of £70,000. Traffic continued to decline and Lord Claud Hamilton, chairman of both the GER and the ELR Joint Committee, became convinced that only electrification could arrest disaster. A decision of 1911 to electrify followed largely from his personal efforts and Selbie's positive attitude to the question. When the general managers of the lessee companies met on 24 April that year, they had before them a tender from British Thomson-Houston which proposed to equip the section from platforms 14/15 at Liverpool Street to both New Cross stations for £100,944, this to include rolling stock on the 'four-rail' system. Before the meeting, Selbie had told a Metropolitan director, 'As you know, it would be very much to our advantage to get this line electrified, and I shall of course do all I can to convince the other companies that it is the proper course to take.' During the discussion he produced some figures of his own which pointed to a cheaper alternative than the BTH tender. Stanley was not present, but had expressed himself broadly in favour of Selbie's proposition. The outcome was that the six lessee companies agreed on 26 April to share the track equipment cost (Selbie's estimate was an optimistic £40,000) in proportion to their responsibility under the lease, the Metropolitan and the MDR to provide trains and power from existing resources, charging the Joint Committee only working expenses. Three months later, through the good offices of Lord Claud Hamilton, the GER agreed to find the capital, provided the lessee companies paid interest on it at four per cent a year in proportion to their liabilities under the lease. Parliamentary powers were obtained by the GER on 7 August 1912, sanctioning the electrification and the raising of £90,000 by the issue of four per cent debenture stock. Six months later, contracts were placed for the electrification equipment, automatic signalling and substation plant. The work proceeded under the supervision of the engineers of the Metropolitan, the MDR and the SER.

After further discussion, it was agreed that at least for the first five years, the Underground Group should supply power from Lots Road through its Whitechapel substation and a new substation at Deptford Road (now Surrey Docks) with the Metropolitan providing the whole train service, including the operating staff[19]. Allowing for the fact that some new cars were on order, the Metropolitan was able to find sufficient stock within its existing fleet. Seven First Class driving trailers of 1905–06 were converted to First/Third composites, three Third Class trailers were similarly converted, and 22 saloon type cars were fitted with middle doors for working over the ELR. The trick was partly achieved by reducing the two three-car shuttle trains on the Uxbridge branch to two-car length[20].

McKenzie & Holland ac automatic signalling, initially maintained by Metropolitan staff, came into operation over the running lines between Shoreditch and Canal Junction, New Cross on 30 March 1913. Running signals at Shoreditch, Whitechapel, Surrey Docks, Deptford Road Junction and Canal Junction were semi-automatic (ie controlled by signalmen or by track circuits) and signal boxes and ground frame were retained at these points, all except the first and the last with new frames. Under normal working the through signals at Surrey Docks station and Deptford Road Junction worked entirely automatically. Between Shoreditch box and Brick Lane (GER) ordinary block working applied. At Whitechapel the old Station and Junction boxes were replaced by a new cabin at the New Cross end of the Down platform. St Mary's Junction was worked from Whitechapel (MDR) and Whitechapel Junction (ELR) from the new ELR cabin at Whitechapel. Surrey Docks station box and Deptford Road ground frame were normally switched out. In the tunnels, lamp signals were installed but in the open air two-position lower quadrant semaphores were used, the latter with two red (or two yellow) circular spectacles and one green, ensuring that a green light only showed when the signal was fully off.

Electric services started on Monday 31 March 1913, four trains hourly of four car length operating each way on weekdays between South Kensington[21] and New Cross (working into and out of the LBSCR and SER stations alternately). There were also eight local two-car trains hourly each way between Shoreditch and New Cross (LBSCR and SER alternately). On Sundays this was reduced to four through and four local workings each hour. With the electrification, the water pumping plants at Rotherhithe and Surrey Docks were converted from steam to electric operation and the six ELR stations were renovated and lit from the traction supply. Platforms were raised to secure a uniform height of 3ft above the rails and with minor alterations, the old locomotive and carriage sheds near New Cross SER were converted to a car depot, accommodating all the stock for the ELR services. Two 30-passenger electric lifts, installed at Wapping station, where the rails were 55ft below the street, came into use on 4 October 1915.

Final net cost of the electrification was £82,815 of which £50,000 was raised by the GER capital issue and the rest from cash. There was a gratifying increase in passenger loadings, the number carried, excluding season ticket journeys, rising from 4.2 million in the last full year of steam to 6.2 million in 1914, 10.6 in 1918 and 14.7 in 1920. Despite this, the net loss to the Joint Committee continued to require support from the lessee companies. In the longer term it would be seen that electrification had merely checked the rate of decline.

<h2 style="text-align:center">ENHANCING THE TRAIN SERVICES</h2>

From 1909 onwards there was a steady improvement in the train services offered by the Metropolitan. Thanks to automatic signalling, it was possible in that year to inject four more trains an hour between the City and Edgware Road at rush hours, making a total of 36, as well as to improve the through services from the Extension Line. The timetable of 1 February 1910 provided a number of accelerations and additions including through trains from the Extension Line extended from Moorgate to the new bay at Liverpool Street. The following 6 November saw a six minute interval for trains between Hammersmith and the City with alternate trains missing some stations. From the same day, Kensington (Addison Road)-Edgware Road trains worked every 12 minutes instead of every 20 and Extension Line workings to and from Uxbridge, Chesham and Aylesbury were accelerated. Circle services on weekdays and Sundays were also improved from this date. Harrow benefited from March 1911 with 24 semi-fast trains each way per hour in the rush hours and nearly half the trains between 8am and 9pm working non-stop between Baker Street and Finchley Road, together with a few non-stops between Baker Street and Harrow. Stations between Baker Street and Finchley Road then got 12 trains each hour and those between Finchley Road and Willesden Green 18. In total, there were now 588 trains daily from Baker Street to Willesden Green, Harrow and Uxbridge compared with 567 in 1910. This last enhancement was made possible by the introduction of automatic signalling between Baker Street and Neasden, permitting headways as close as 50–80 seconds. The November 1912 improvements related to the opening of the double line junction at Baker Street have been mentioned earlier.

By the autumn of 1913, Edgware Road station was handling 559 Down (westbound) and 567 Up trains daily (including 17 Down and 18 Up GWR freights), about double the total movements through the station in 1901. Baker Street East also saw a considerable accretion in traffic: in 1901 it had 143 arrivals and 138 departures, mostly to and from Willesden Green, Neasden or Harrow, but by 1913 this had grown to 228 arrivals and 226 departures, with 67 Down and 70 Up through the new junction to the Inner Circle against none in 1901. Between 9 and 10 am there were 14 arrivals at this station in 1901; by 1913 this had increased to 22.

At rush hours, from 1 March 1914, some non-stop trains reached Harrow in 17 minutes from Baker Street, these proving so popular that train length had to be increased from six to seven cars. Overall, the increase in passenger train mileage between 1901 and 1913 amounted to 86 per cent. This was not achieved without additions to the original electric stock and the fleet of locomotive-hauled carriages.

NEW ROLLING STOCK

To facilitate operation of the improved Extension Line services of March 1911 two double-ended electric motor cars were built up by Metropolitan Amalgamated Carriage & Wagon from cars damaged in accidents. On one, the electrical equipment was by BTH, on the other, by British Westinghouse Electric & Manufacturing Co. These cars were designed to be used singly (for a Baker Street East-West Hampstead shuttle) or as part of a train. They had four 150 hp motors and Westinghouse quick-acting air brakes. Their teak bodies, 51ft 10in long, contained four Third Class compartments (36 seats) and two Firsts (16 seats) as well as drivers' and luggage compartments. Subsequently they appeared on the Uxbridge branch (until 1918), on the Edgware Road-Kensington (Addison Road) service and on the Watford-Rickmansworth shuttle.

As the operation of the increased services via the 1912 junction at Baker Street and the electric working of the ELR absorbed all the 'standby stock', more electric cars were ordered in January 1913. These new saloons, mostly to be used on the Inner Circle, were delivered later that year by Metropolitan Amalgamated. There were 23 Third motor cars, ten First driving trailers and ten Third ordinary trailers. Characterised by elliptical roofs studded with ventilators, their mostly steel bodies were 52ft 10in long. Motor cars had 38 seats, trailers 48, all rather uncomfortably upholstered in 'fine woven rattan'. All had hand-operated sliding doors, a single one at each end (except where there was a driving cab) and a double set in the middle. Motor cars had a small luggage compartment next to the driving cab. Thirteen of the motor cars had 200 hp British Westinghouse electrical equipments controlling the four type 86M motors which were also installed in the ten 1907 electric locomotives, displacing their BTH equipments and GE 69 200 hp motors. This second hand equipment and motors were then fitted to the remaining ten new 1913 motor cars. The 43 new cars were marshalled into six or three-car trains as required[22].

With these additions, there was sufficient electric stock by 1914 to allow each train one rest day in seven for examination. This perceptibly diminished the incidence of failures.

On the steam-hauled services beyond Harrow, the Metropolitan trains compared very unfavourably with the comfortable GCR suburban sets calling at the same stations. To meet this challenge, ten vestibuled First Class electric control trailers of 1905 (rendered redundant by the contraction of Inner Circle trains to four car length) were converted in 1910 to two five-car trains of elliptical-roofed compartment stock. This conversion, undertaken by Metropolitan Amalgamated at a total cost of £5,907, produced a total of 772 seats against the former 508. In the Thirds, three compartments were cut open by a central gangway with intermediate partitions rising only to the top of the quarter lights. Fittings included Pintsch's gas lighting, Laycock's steam heating and passenger communication cords.

These were followed by four entirely new five-car trains of similar pattern from the same firm in January 1912 for £33,200. As before, to induce quicker loading, the three middle compartments of the Thirds were linked by a central gangway. With their characteristic round-topped doors to each compartment, these trains of 1910–12 became known to the staff as 'Dreadnoughts', after the turbine-engined big-gun battleships then being introduced into the Royal Navy. With subsequent orders from the same firm up to 1923, the type finally totalled 92 cars.

MIXED RETURNS

The improvements and other measures described in this chapter were to have little initial impact on the railway's fortunes, which recovered only slowly in the years up to and including 1914. Passengers journeys (including an estimate for season ticket journeys), which had totalled 94.4 million in 1904, the last full year of steam traction, rose to 102.8 million in 1910, staying slightly below that level before mounting again, in the special conditions of wartime, from 1915 onwards. These figures concealed a substantial loss of short-distance traffic to buses, trams and tubes, especially noticed from 1911 onwards and to some extent countered by a growth in the longer-distance business from around 1912.

Street and tube competition, high interest charges on electrification capital, loss of Second Class revenue, diversion of GCR traffic via High Wycombe and fare reductions, all combined to cut net income and reduce ordinary stock dividends to just half a per cent in 1907, a year in which the accounts were later to be described by Selbie as 'the low water mark in the fortunes of the Company'[23]. Not until 1909 was one per cent achieved and for the next five years the ordinary dividend fluctuated between 1¼ and around two per cent as net revenue slowly improved.

Increasing trade union militancy secured pay increases whilst prices of materials and coal also increased, causing operating costs to steepen in common with those of the other British railway companies at this time. Selbie did however have some success in controlling working expenses, bringing down the ratio of gross working expenses to gross traffic receipts from 55.6 per cent in 1907 to 47.9 in 1913, the latter comparing with 59.24 on the LBSCR. One of the factors contributing to this followed skilful negotiations with the local rating authorities which reduced the payments to them by around £10,000 a year from 1911.

This cautious progress was now to be overshadowed by darker times. Whilst the Metropolitan's own 'Dreadnoughts' were coming into service, their naval namesakes and those of Germany were multiplying ominously, a portent of the coming world war which was to provide a rude interruption to Selbie's work in building up the health of his charge.

THROUGH WAR INTO METRO-LAND

No sooner were Selbie's plans for developing outer suburban traffic coming together than the whole of Europe was seething with war fever. Although the Metropolitan was to be much less involved in the war than most other railways, managing to maintain a near-normal service over most of the period, its priorities were inevitably distorted for almost five years. Together with 129 other railway companies, including all the major ones and many tiddlers, the Metropolitan was 'taken over' by the government and made subject to the Railway Executive Committee from midnight 4/5 August 1914 under the Regulation of the Forces Act, 1871. This control was not to be finally relinquished until midnight on 15 August 1921.

The staff were told that the change was designed solely to facilitate movements of troops and war materials. The existing management remained in being, operating as in peacetime and the normal terms of employment were unaltered. Priority was to be given to the instructions of Railway Transport Officers where these clashed with those of the company's officials, and to naval and military traffic. Within a few weeks, 276 staff had left to fulfil commitments as reservists or as volunteers for the army and navy. As the appetite of war grew, many more were to go, over ten per cent never to return home. To plug this drain in staff resources, women were recruited from early 1915 onwards, although these were not the first of their sex to work for the Metropolitan (girl ticket sorters had replaced boys in an economy move of December 1913). By July 1915 there were 23 women booking clerks and 28 ticket collectors, an 'experiment' judged as 'on the whole quite satisfactory'. From the end of 1916 smartly-uniformed women were seen working as guards and as conductors on electric trains; they were also to be found as travelling ticket inspectors, porters, bill posters, carriage cleaners and as office clerks. There were 522 women on the strength by the end of 1917.

Initially there was a great fear of enemy sabotage, which prompted deployment of 250 staff to protect 'vulnerable points', but this force was quickly run down, leaving only some men to guard Neasden

Works and bored Territorial soldiers patrolling Kilburn Viaduct, which the War Office considered a prime target. From June 1915 a special 'watching staff' against air raids manned each station after traffic hours. All employees were invited to participate in some kind of war work after duty and lathes were installed at Neasden for the manufacture of parts of shells from late 1915.

There was no air raid damage to the line or stations until 11.40 am on 13 June 1917, when bombs fell on the City Lines, severing traction current cables and halting Inner Circle and the through ELR services; the latter reversed at Aldgate until normal operations were restored at 8.15 pm. An unexploded bomb in Moorgate Yard disrupted services between 10.30 am and 1.25 pm on 7 July 1917. Finally, on the night of 28/29 January 1918, debris from a bombed meat warehouse alongside the line west of Aldersgate (Barbican) station blocked both Circle and Widened Lines. Circle working was restored from the start of traffic on 29 January but although freight operation was possible on the Up Widened Lines from 6.10 am that day, normal traffic in both directions could not be handled until the afternoon of 31 January. On the same occasion glass in the Liverpool Street arcade was shattered by an unexploded anti-aircraft shell.

The onset of the 1917 air raids prompted a substantial movement of frightened Londoners into the suburbs and country around, including those areas served by the Metropolitan from the beginning of October. In response, and to reserve accommodation on trains for the longer-distance passengers, the Harrow stop was eliminated from some workings, with the changeover from electric to steam haulage made at Wembley Park. Some additional non-stop trains were run to Harrow to compensate. These arrangements proved so successful they were adopted on a more permanent basis, the requisite signal and track alterations being made at Wembley Park in the middle of 1918. Such was the eventual strength of the wartime population movement and military traffic to and from Wendover and other camps that 1918 steam train carryings showed a 250 per cent increase over 1913.

To save coal, the government required train service reductions in 1918. Pleading special circumstances, the Metropolitan made only a 12 per cent cut in mileage, which was somewhat below the suggested minimum. This was achieved by extending slack hour headways to Neasden from five to ten minutes and those to Harrow from 20 to 30 minutes; there were also late night cuts on the Hammersmith & City service. On the excuse that wartime restrictions obliged it to make better use of its staff, the SECR withdrew its passenger workings into Moorgate from Monday 3 April 1916. Late in 1918 the Metropolitan realised this had made its Smithfield signal box redundant and working was transferred to Aldersgate (Barbican). After the cessation of the SECR trains the Smithfield Curve had no further regular use, although it was not officially declared abandoned until 1927. The SECR had good reason to withdraw from Moorgate; loadings had been very light for many years, a count in 1911 showing that from the 52 trains arriving at Moorgate between 7.03 am and 11.04 pm only 78 passengers alighted, with a maximum of eight on any one train. In 1923, to release itself from the obligation in the 1870 agreement between the Metropolitan and the LCDR, the Southern Railway paid the Metropolitan £25,000.

When attacks on British merchant shipping brought food shortages of increasing severity all vacant land along the Metropolitan was offered to staff for vegetable growing. On the Uxbridge branch, the six acres taken for a second pair of tracks, together with six more at Eastcote and Ickenham, were ploughed up in 1917 and turned over to food production. Much of the produce went to the wounded in war hospitals.

But by far the most significant contribution made by the Metropolitan to the war effort was one that had little effect either on its staff or its train services. Offering as they did a short and direct link between the main lines north of the Thames and those to the south which were feeding the Western Front with men and munitions via the Channel Ports, the City Widened Lines assumed major strategic importance. At the beginning of the war they were swamped by north to south troop train movements, no less than 2,738 such trains passing this way between the outbreak of war on 4 August 1914 and the following 25 February, the total reaching 58 daily when the British Expeditionary Force was being moved to France, all this on top of the normal services. Freight traffic was also heavy. During the first two weeks of February 1915, 2,935 relief freight trains used the route in addition to military specials and the ordinary services, an increase of 120 per cent over the normal movements. Four years of war saw a total of almost 250,000 tons of freight carried over the Widened Lines, together with 26,047 military special trains for personnel and materials. The peak year was 1918, when there were 6,269 military specials and 58,902 tons of freight carried. All passed over a double track with severe limitations of loading gauge, curves and gradients. (Steam locomotives faced a quarter mile climb at 1 in 39 from Snow Hill to Ludgate Hill in the southbound direction, 1 in 48 up northwards in a single line tunnel at King's Cross and a 1 in 40 gradient up to Farringdon Street from the Ray Street Grid Iron[1].)

Whilst the route was physically incapable of taking all the traffic offering, steps were taken to maximise its capacity. From early 1915 normal GNR, Midland and SECR passenger services were restricted to rush hours (8–10 am and 5–7 pm). A second banking engine layby was provided at Farringdon and the crossover there modified in the latter part of 1915, changes which enabled all freight trains north to south to be lengthened from 20 to 30 wagons. Those moving in the opposite direction had their length restricted by the existence of the steep single line tunnel at King's Cross which precluded the use of double heading (banking engines were also excluded as they would have disrupted operations at the main line station when they returned across its approach tracks to the east side and southbound tunnel). The sharp curves prevented the use of the Widened Lines by ambulance trains carrying wounded soldiers from the Channel Ports to hospitals north of the Thames. It was fortunate that in 1914–15, following a freight train breakaway and collision of February 1913, the Metropolitan had taken notice of the recommendation of the Board of Trade and equipped the Widened Lines between Farringdon and King's Cross with track circuits. Manual signalling had been retained but the position of the signal arms was controlled by the track circuit state. At the same time, continuous lock-and-block working was introduced between these two points, allowing Granville box to be closed on 18 October 1914. At War Office instigation and the public expense, additional track circuiting was provided between Farringdon and Snow Hill in 1918, combined with repositioning of some signals, further increasing the freight train capacity of the line.

The only other significant piece of work related to wartime traffic was the construction by the War Office of a one mile light railway between Wendover station and Halton Park Camp in 1918. Connected to no 1 road of the Metropolitan & GC Joint Committee goods yard, this branch remained in use by the Air Ministry after the war. Another siding made in 1919 connected Wendover yard to a Timber Supply Depot on the south east side.

The inflationary effect of the war was marked. Between 1913 and the end of 1919 the salary and wages bill of the Metropolitan rose 200 per cent; coal prices 150 per cent; and materials, repairs and maintenance costs over 90 per cent. A 50 per cent fare increase was made to all ordinary fares outside the London area (beyond Kilburn) on 1 January 1917 but other fares were only three per cent up on 1914 at the end of the war. By 1922 ordinary fares had reached 75 per cent over 1913 (they were reduced to 67 per cent over in 1922), whilst season tickets were 50 per cent above the pre war rates. During the period of government control the railways were guaranteed their 1913 net revenue, but were obliged to carry all government traffics free of charge. With the increased loadings of wartime this worked in favour of the government but some assistance was given with payment of salary and wage increases and allowance made for interest on the cost of new works completed in the control period. As the government took all receipts and bore all costs, the traffic carried had no bearing on the dividends paid, a fact which many shareholders found difficult to accept.

By 1918 the only men left working for the railway in the age range 18–51 were those certified as essential to its operation, a qualification not investigated too closely in some cases. Each year the number of staff on active service, to whom Christmas cards and parcels were assiduously sent, steadily increased. Altogether 1,181 Metropolitan men served with the armed forces, a figure which represented 29 per cent of the total employed on 4 August 1914[2]. The 137 killed or missing were commemorated on a white Carrara marble memorial still to be seen at Baker Street. This was designed by C. W. Clark and unveiled by Lord Aberconway on Armistice Day, 1920. The chairman lost his own son, The Hon Francis McLaren MP, who had resigned his Metropolitan directorship in 1914 to join the Royal Flying Corps.

RECOVERY AND ORGANISATIONAL CHANGE

Wartime experience of operation of the railways as an integrated system engendered the formation of a permanent Ministry of Transport and filled the air with proposals for railway nationalisation, or at least some grouping of the many separate companies into large and hopefully more efficient units. Eventually the latter alternative prevailed. As usual, no-one knew what to do about London. When in the late summer of 1920 Sir Eric Geddes, the first Minister of Transport, finally produced his proposals for railway company grouping in a White Paper, he included a 'London Group (Local Lines)' implying an amalgamation of the Metropolitan and the Underground Group companies. Discussions ensued in February and March 1921. Selbie showed himself ready to consider a complete fusion of interest and amalgamation between the Metropolitan and the MDR, but his terms for this were rejected by the MDR, as were the latter's counter-proposals by the Metropolitan. The difficulty lay in desire of the MDR to remain within the Underground Group whilst the Metropolitan could not bring itself to fall into an organisation which, apart from the MDR, it considered totally incompatible with its own role and operational style. In the event both the Metropolitan and the Underground Group were quietly dropped from the grouping arrangements enshrined in the Railways Act of 1921.

Some further inconclusive 'conversations' were held between the Metropolitan and the Underground Group in 1927, apparently on the latter's initiative. Again the Metropolitan insisted that its status and role were quite different from those of the deep level tube lines, engaged as it was in all the business of a main line railway company, stressing the difficulties of amalgamating concerns of such disparate character. It was stated that the Metropolitan saw no prospect of any pooling arrangement guaranteeing the sort of returns on its ordinary stock that it believed it could achieve if it remained independent and developed longer-distance traffic. Although absorption of the MDR by the Metropolitan had been made much more difficult by the former's inclusion in the Underground Company's Common Fund pooling scheme, the Metropolitan declared itself ready to negotiate for purchase of the MDR. But as the Underground was not interested in decreasing its size and power, the matter was left until the events of 1929–33, which will be described in Chapter 15.

Two other organisational changes did mature. After the retirement, at age 73, of W. H. Parsons, the secretary and manager of the East London Railway Joint Committee, the ELR chairman proposed the Metropolitan should take over management and control on behalf of the Committee. This was accepted by the other lessee companies, the Metropolitan assuming management of the ELR from 1 July 1921. From 1 January 1924 it also undertook maintenance of the signals, buildings and permanent way in place of the Southern Railway engineer. Stores and uniforms also became a Metropolitan responsibility. In 1922 the Metropolitan considered purchasing the freehold of the line, an act which would have strengthened its position *vis-à-vis* the Underground Group, but its terms proved unacceptable to the ELR board. The freehold was then vested in the Southern Railway, as the largest holder, from 1 January 1925, but as this was subject to perpetual lease to the Joint Committee there was no practical change in the day-to-day running of the line.

At the time the SR started to electrify its suburban lines its general manager, Sir Herbert Walker, suggested to Selbie the Metropolitan should run off the ELR at New Cross on to the newly-electrified Southern. This idea, put forward late in 1925, appealed to Selbie because the ELR was by then losing local traffic to bus competition and he considered the line's only salvation lay in the development of longer-distance through services. Very careful studies were then made

Plate 24 Shaper of the modern Metropolitan: Robert H. Selbie, general manager 1908 to 1930, in the 1920s (*London Transport Museum*)
Plate 25 Woman guard, c1916, probably at Neasden (*A. Reavil*)

Plate 26 Summer evening at Aldersgate, c1922. MDR Circle train at left, Midland Railway suburban train on Down City Widened Lines at right. Note Metropolitan signal of 1880s pattern with the standard finial which lasted until 1933 (*photographer unknown*)

Plate 27 Rayners Lane Halt in August 1922 looking to Harrow. The booking hut on the road bridge, added about 1914, was a standard pattern, designed by C.W. Clark. The only platform building is a corrugated iron waiting hut on the Up side. (*photographer unknown, courtesy H.J. Patterson-Rutherford*)

Plate 28 Willesden Green as rebuilt to C.W. Clark's design in 1925. Note his bar and diamond-shaped clock, also used at other stations rebuilt in this period (*Alan A. Jackson, May 1963*)

by the Metropolitan into the possibility of operating four six-car trains an hour at peaks and three at other times (Mondays to Saturdays only) between Hammersmith and Addiscombe. It was proposed to use existing rolling stock adapted to operate over the SR's third-rail system and some trial runs appear to have been made. But the Metropolitan's terms were thought too onerous by the Southern, which closed the discussion in the latter part of 1926. Nor was any change in the SR attitude apparent in 1929 when the proposal was raised again by the Metropolitan after such a service had been recommended by the London & Home Counties Traffic Advisory Committee. The SR steadfastly maintained that it would lose revenue if it paid the Metropolitan's proposed minimum charges, but although there is no indication of the reasoning in the SR minutes, the truth may have been that the Southern now feared operating difficulties as its new electric lines engendered more and more traffic.

At the other side of London, new arrangements were agreed with the GWR in March 1923, to operate from 1 January that year, which brought the Hammersmith & City Railway closer into the Metropolitan fold. These provided that the GWR-owned half of the 20 H&CR motor cars and 40 trailers should be sold to the Metropolitan for £125,000 and the Hammersmith car sheds be leased to that company by the Joint Committee. The Metropolitan was also to charge the Joint Committee for working the H&CR at the general cost per mile (a maximum of 5½d excluding cost of current), a sum covering amongst other things good interest on the capital payment made for the GWR trains. An important part of the new regime was that the Metropolitan would supply current, with Park Royal sub-station fed from Neasden. These arrangements gave the Metropolitan greater freedom in working traffic to and from the H&CR but the GWR continued to resist the complete take-over which the Metropolitan wanted. Anticipating full integration, the Metropolitan had succeeded in arranging for the installation of automatic signalling between Westbourne Park and Hammersmith and this was operative from 17 December 1922. The remaining section between Westbourne Park and Bishop's Road, much more part of the GWR's signalling system, had to wait until 1929 for this improvement. Fog repeaters were fitted to the Hammersmith & City line in 1923.

Dividends on ordinary Metropolitan stock rose steadily from 1½ per cent in 1920, to 2¼ in 1921, 3½ in 1922, and four in 1923, results reflecting an encouraging growth in net receipts arising from increases in passenger journeys after the immediate drop from the inflated wartime traffic of 1918. Short distance traffic continued to fall away to buses whilst longer-distance journeys grew with resumption of suburban housebuilding in the early 1920s. Steps were taken to improve suburban services in anticipation of this new business; from early summer 1919 off peak intervals between Baker Street and Willesden Green were enhanced to 5 minutes, 15 to Wembley Park and Harrow and 30 to Uxbridge.

THE BIRTH OF METRO-LAND

Although the term *Metro-land* was unheard of until 1915, the beginnings of an active policy of residential development of lands along the railway date back, as we have seen, to the Willesden Park Estate of 1879. We have also noticed how Selbie had seized the importance of this source of traffic, making it a prime objective soon after he became general manager in 1908. In the 1910s he had laid down adequate foundations, including the widening of the Extension Line, the rebuilding of Baker Street station and the reorganisation of estate management and publicity work, the parts of the administration most important for the development of suburban traffic. Lastly he had worked up the outlines of a proposal which he considered crucial to the success of his policy. With the return to more normal conditions in 1919 he was therefore well prepared to press ahead.

Until 1905 the management of the surplus lands and estate, including lettings, had been dealt with partly by the Surplus Lands Committee's own staff and partly by the general manager's office, both under the general manager's direct supervision. In March that year Ellis had brought in F. Dawson of the North Eastern Railway's Rating & Estate Office, to act as assistant rating agent, taking over the work of the rating section of the Surplus Lands office where the rating agent was seriously ill and not expected to return. Soon showing ability, Dawson was appointed estate & rating agent at £250 a year from 1 July 1906 and by 1913 his salary had doubled, a recognition by Selbie of the importance of his skilful work in managing the company's estate.

There had been no proper publicity department until 1911, when James Feiron, a former timetable clerk who had developed this aspect of the administration from about 1908, was appointed the Metropolitan's first publicity manager. When he retired in 1914 this responsibility was passed to John Wardle[3], the former goods and parcels manager, who was then given the new title of commercial manager.

In common with most other UK railway companies, the Metropolitan had paid little attention to publicity until the early years of the 20th century, when improvements in printing techniques were making it possible to use photographs and colour inexpensively[4]. About 1905 the Metropolitan began to publish a series of small penny brochures entitled *Country Walks*, guides to rambles which could be made from its outer country stations. By 1912 there were 20 different issues, all in a long narrow format designed to suit the walker's pocket, and by then all joint publications with the GCR. These brochures continued to appear through the 1920s but in a more attractive coloured cover, jointly issued with the London & North Eastern Railway. The first of what were to be a long series of general guides to the area served by the Metropolitan seems to have been inspired by Ellis, whose camera may have supplied some of the illustrations when it appeared in 1905. A year later, a similar guide was issued jointly with the GCR, each company contributing half the cost of printing 20,000 copies. Publication then became annual, producing a small net profit from the proceeds of the cover charge and advertising revenue. So far the descriptions had covered only the Extension Line, but in 1908 Ellis suggested a similar guide for the Uxbridge branch 'to advertise the attractions of the district, its suitability for residential purposes and excursions, weekend and holiday traffic'. Subsequently all the districts served were covered in one guide. At first the main emphasis was on recreational and holiday traffic, then a separate publication, *The Homestead*, issued jointly with the GCR from 1911, started to concentrate on residential opportunities on the Extension Line.

Picture postcards with sepia photographic views of the 'country districts' served in Middlesex, Hertfordshire and Buckinghamshire were sold in 2d sets of six, five sets in all, from October 1909. In that year a postcard reproduction of a poster 'Underground, Metropolitan and District Railways Inner Circle Link' appeared. This was followed in 1912 by a set of six 'Geographical Postcards', showing maps of the Extension Line and districts around it, and selling at only one penny for the whole packet. Finally in 1929 a picture postcard was issued to advertise the new flats at Chiltern Court, above Baker Street station.

A new departure in publicity for 1911, suggested by Selbie, was the commissioning of cinematograph films advertising the attractions of the line north of Harrow. Shots from a surviving copy of one of these were used 60 years later in Sir John Betjeman's television production on the Metropolitan and its territory.

Invention of the description *Metro-land* (sometimes printed *Metro-Land*) was claimed in later years by James Garland, a copywriter in the Metropolitan publicity department. He told Dennis Edwards how when away sick with influenza in 1915, he had jumped out of bed with excitement when the word came into his head[5]. Certainly it cannot be found in any published material or official papers before that year and its first public use appears to have been as the title of the annual guide which came on sale in May, 1915 as a 'comprehensive description of the country districts served by the Metropolitan Railway'[6]. *Metro-Land*, at first 1d, then 2d, came out annually thereafter, its contents directed at walkers, excursionists, party organisers and house-hunters, although the latter aspect did not receive much prominence until the early 1920s. For a definition of Metro-land one has to look no further than the first page of the 1915 booklet, which describes it as 'the beautiful unknown country . . . the rural Arcadia . . . close to London' which began at Wembley Park and extended out to Chesham, Brill, Verney Junction and Uxbridge. In the following pages we are offered brief descriptions, illustrated by photographs, of the areas around each station and an 'Historical Sketch of Metro-land'. An appealing amateur tone pervades both text and photographs of this and subsequent editions, adding to the nostalgic value for today's collectors of Metropolitan bygones.

Of course Selbie's aim was that the 'beautiful unknown country' should become not only well-known but comfortably-populated, preferably with a high percentage of First Class season ticket holders and their families. And if in making that possible the scenery should become somewhat less arcadian, as much of it did, then he would lose no sleep. How was the trick to be worked?

Although the Surplus Lands Committee had accumulated some experience in developing estates at Willesden Green and Pinner, Selbie rightly concluded that more single-mindedness and profession-alism was needed to extract the full potential of Metro-land. On the last day of 1912 he outlined to the board a scheme for the formation of a new limited liability company amongst some of the largest share-holders of the railway, its object to develop estates adjacent to the line, both from land already owned by the Metropolitan and new purchases. Approval in principle was given but further work on the scheme, which had got as far as a proposed purchase of the Chalk Hill Estate at Wembley, was postponed by the events of August 1914. In a 1915 review of the railway's affairs for the board, Selbie pressed home his theme and as the war drew to a close he returned with the pro-posal, suggesting in November 1918 that:

> in view of the large demand there will be for houses as soon as Peace is declared and the Forces are demobilised, and also in view of the advertisement the districts served have received during the War, I am of the opinion that the scheme should be taken in hand forthwith.

The comment about the wartime advertisement no doubt related to the influx of air raid refugees and servicemen mentioned earlier. One wonders whether Selbie and the board gave a moment's thought to the efficient female labour working at low rates of pay which had allowed the Metropolitan to maintain a near-normal service all through the war, thus upholding the Metro-land image. Action was agreed and in January 1919 Selbie's detailed proposals emerged. A Metropolitan Railway Country Estates Ltd (share capital £150,000, later increased to £200,000), was to be formed in which the railway company was to take a controlling financial interest. No time was wasted, with arrangements made for purchase of the 123-acre Chalk Hill Estate at Wembley Park (for £22,500) and the 454-acre Cedars Estate at Rickmansworth (for £40,000)[7] through a syndicate[8] even before the new organisation had been set up. Some 40 acres of railway land at Neasden for a third estate and an additional 10¾ acres of railway land between Neasden Works and Wembley Park station to enlarge Chalk Hill were sold to the new organisation for £11,683.

Then, as the final touches were put to the scheme, it was suddenly realised that parliament might consider the Metropolitan was pushing its luck in making a proposal which openly allowed a railway company to buy and use land for purposes other than those of the railway undertaking, in a very positive fashion, and without statutory authority, in a manner that was contrary to parliament's historic attitude on this point, whatever special circumstances earlier Metropolitan Railway legislation might have created. When the prospectus of the new company was submitted to the Hon Frank Russell KC with a specific request for an opinion on this point, he remarked that although the railway company would not be holding any land in the technical sense under the proposed arrangements, the scheme effectively allowed a railway undertaking to buy and hold land without acquiring any statutory authority, thus evading the policy of the legislature that a railway company should not acquire or hold land without specific statutory authority. Should the arrangement be criticised, Russell thought the court might hold it to be invalid on the grounds that it was contrary to public policy. Of course the Metropolitan might have tried to seek parliament's blessing in special legislation, but for a railway company to seek blanket authority to acquire land for non railway purposes (as distinct from retaining land already acquired) was to risk stirring up a hornet's nest, perhaps even putting the Metropolitan's existing rather dubious powers into question. It was therefore thought prudent that the railway company as such should have no *direct* financial interest in the new Estates company, entering instead into an agreement allowing the use of its name in the Estate company's title and providing for all possible assistance from the railway's organisation in the development of the new company's estates. In return, the Metropolitan was to have the right to nominate the chairman and two other directors from its own board for an initial period of ten years[9]. Following this change of plan, the deposit monies to be advanced to the syndicate for the initial estate purchases mentioned above were now to be provided not by the railway company but by the underwriting firm of Belisha, Shaw & Co, whose Albert L. Belisha was a Metropolitan director.

Given preferential consideration, Metropolitan Railway and Surplus Lands Committee shareholders took up the shares of the new limited company formed on 7 June 1919. Selbie became a director and all but one of the rest of the new board were Metropolitan directors[10]. In these circumstances the railway company's control was virtually total. Offices were provided at Metropolitan Railway headquarters, the MRCE receiving the part time services of Henry Gibson, the surveyor and valuer to the Surplus Lands Committee and those of other Metropolitan Railway officials, in particular from the publicity, commercial and estate departments. It was a cosy arrangement which enabled the railway to direct all investment and development to where it would best serve the railway's interests, whilst the new company benefited from the close association with the railway's respectable image. 'Railway companies,' wrote Selbie in 1921, 'are trusted and not open to the suspicion that often attaches to the speculative builder and estate developer'[11].

During the remaining years of the Metropolitan Railway the MRCE was to open up nine estates in Metro-land, most of them aimed at the upper end of the housing market. Only a small number of specimen houses were erected directly by the new company; the usual arrangement was to arrange for the laying out of the estate either on surplus land owned by the railway or on new sites, then to sell-off sections, either to builders, or on the superior developments, in plots to individual purchasers who could then arrange, through the MRCE or otherwise, for erection of a house to their chosen design. Mortgages and an architect design service (enter C. W. Clark), even building, would be arranged by the MRCE. Potential clients were given free travel tickets to view, courtesy the parent railway company. Wheels worked within wheels. Someone even seems to have exercised influence in London's 'Tin Pan Alley'. To set the whole thing off with a swing, a pop song celebrating and advertising the Metropolitan's sunrise industry, *My Little Metro-land Home*, was published in 1920[12].

It did not sell very well; I was still able to purchase a new copy from the publishers 48 years later.

One of the earliest of the estates was at Neasden, where 40 acres of former railway land became the Kingsbury Garden Village. As this was close to the staff housing it was not destined to be a prestige development. About 40 houses here were available in the early part of 1921 (eight were in fact bought as railway staff houses) and Village Way, The Rise, West Way and Elm Way were all completed and occupied by the end of 1929. All the houses were semi-detached, selling at £725 and £775.

Immediately north west of this was the much superior Chalk Hill Estate, laid out along Chalk Hill and Barn Hill Roads. Plots here were at least a quarter acre in size when sales started in 1921. As it had done at Neasden, the railway company put in a temporary siding for delivery of building materials. This farmland, acquired at £183 an acre, was advertised at the equivalent of £700 upwards an acre in 1931 when there were but a few plots remaining unsold. Today the site is unrecognisable; it was redeveloped in 1966–70 as a council estate to house over 5,000.

To the west of the railway at Wembley Park station lay the domain of the separate Wembley Park Estate Company, the earlier Metropolitan estate progeny, whose beginnings immediately before 1914 have already been noticed. Building and plot purchases, which continued sporadically through much of the war period, resumed in strength in 1920 when detached houses were on offer at £1,250. Development was much stimulated by the use of the eastern section of the estate for the 1924–5 British Empire Exhibition, of which more in a moment. So successful was the Wembley Park estate that from 1919 onwards the Metropolitan Railway was compelled under the 1914 agreement to pay the Estate Company the maximum sum of £700 a year related to increases in revenue at the station. These payments continued until the agreement expired, after a three-year extension, in 1927. Independent estate developers in the area also brought business to the station, where gross passenger receipts grew from £7,735 in 1922 to £30,618 in 1929.

Moving further down the line, we find the two Surplus Lands Committee estates at Pinner, which continued under that aegis. Cecil Park was virtually filled up by 1914 and all 13 acres had been sold off by 1926. The Grange Estate on the opposite (north) side of the line was built over between 1920 and 1929.

Northwest from Rickmansworth station, where the Cedars Estate spread over both sides of the line, the MRCE used the railway to separate two classes of development. That north of the Metropolitan was the most sumptuous of all the MRCE estates, at any rate in its early years, set aside as it was for 'more pretentious' residences of the 'small country house type' standing on plots of at least one acre for gardens and paddocks. Most of the roads here had been laid out by the end of 1921, when 30 houses had been erected. To the south, the land was developed at higher density, with both houses and bungalows. Progress at Cedars was steady rather than spectacular, but by 1931 'only a few' plots remained at the equivalent of £600–650 an acre (against the £88 an acre paid by the MRCE before putting in roads and services). On the south side in that year there were still some 150ft by 50ft plots available at £200 each.

WONDERFUL WEMBLEY

An unexpected shot in the arm for the Metropolitan in the 1920s followed a decision to hold Britain's largest exhibition since 1851 in Wembley Park. This not only gave a transitory boost of extra business to the exhibition grounds, but a lasting legacy in the form of the special traffics generated by the permanent sports stadium built for the event. It also provided a general stimulus for the residential and industrial development of the whole district, from which the Metropolitan was to gain substantial benefit.

A British Empire Exhibition, promoting trade and cementing links between the 'motherland, the dominions and colonies', had first been mooted in 1902 and revived in 1910 and 1913, but could not be officially launched until June 1920 when the government agreed to contribute to a fund guaranteeing the organisers against loss[13]. Wembley Park was chosen largely because of its ready accessibility by rail from central London via three separate routes, two of them electrified. It has not proved possible to discover any Metropolitan involvement in this decision but it seems likely that Metropolitan directors in a position to influence the right quarters would not have been slow to put forward Wembley's attractions.

In January 1922 the Wembley Park Estate Company sold 216 acres, the greater part of its remaining open land, to the British Empire Exhibition Assets Co Ltd for £67,323, of which £35,000 at once went on to the Metropolitan in discharge of the 1898 mortgage. This was another uncovenanted benefit for the railway company, which would otherwise have had to wait many years for the repayment of this loan.

Construction started early in 1922 with hundreds of tons of clinker coming by rail from Neasden power station to cover the sticky and heavy clay. There were also large shipments of gravel by train from the Rickmansworth pits. Priority was given to the erection of the sports stadium on the site of the ill-fated Watkin Tower. With accommodation for some 120,000 spectators, this building was to be the largest of its kind in the world at that time. Earmarked by the Football Association as the permanent home for its cup finals, it was ready for cup final day, 28 April 1923.

That proved to be a memorable occasion, attracting a crowd of over 200,000 anxious to see Bolton Wanderers v West Ham United. When the available space in the stadium was filled, men and boys continued to invade the interior, many without paying, until the pitch itself was swamped by a seething but good-humoured mass of humanity. Eventually some order was restored by the police, whilst the railways found themselves organising return trains for the disappointed even before the outward pressure had ceased. On that day the Metropolitan alone carried between 140,000 and 150,000 additional passengers in and out of Wembley Park station without mishap or significant delay, thanks to excellent staff work and the availability of some improved facilities[14].

These new works, costing about £50,000 at the station alone, had been planned to ensure the smooth handling of large crowds and they came well out of the severe test imposed on that first Wembley cup final day. A long time beforehand Selbie had warned the board that the stadium crowds would be large, much bigger than those attending the Exhibition on any one day. He argued that expenditure at the station was fully justified as this would be a continuing feature, long after the Exhibition had closed. Rebuilding of the station by the Unit Construction Co began at the end of 1922. An additional 440ft platform (faces 5 and 6) was inserted on the London side of the road overbridge, on the north side of the railway, linked by a 20ft wide stair way to a separate booking office and entrance on that side of the bridge. Nameboards read WEMBLEY PARK EXHIBITION STATION. The four existing platforms were also lengthened at the country end, with new 15ft wide stairs provided to an entrance hall on the bridge. Here C. W. Clark built the first of his pleasant domestic styled suburban stations with tiled roof and red and blue bricks. This structure housed a large booking hall with oak and tile wall finishings. Altogether there were 19 ticket windows in the two booking halls.

Most of this new work was ready for the 1923 cup final crowds, but later that year a covered footbridge and walkway were added between the new platform on the London side and the north entrance to the exhibition grounds. Track modifications included an alleviation of the curvature of the Down Through line and additional layby sidings. Freight traffic at Wembley Park, expanded from 2,166 tons (2,200.66 tonnes) in 1914 to 8,145 (8,275.3) in 1922 and 16,026 (16,282.4) in the first ten months of 1923, required doubling of the yard size by the addition of two roads, work completed in the early part of 1924. By February that year the builders and engineers had finished at Wembley Park and all was ready for the exhibition. The rebuilt station had electric light throughout and train indicators worked from the signal box were installed at the covered way by the north entrance to the exhibition, in the main booking hall and on the centre platform. Although unconnected with the exhibition, it may be mentioned that during 1925 government war surplus sheds were brought from Hereford to the layby sidings at the north end of the station where they gave shelter to nine seven-car trains from early in 1926.

At Baker Street in April 1923 a Circle Line entrance and ticket office was opened on the south side of Marylebone Road to relieve pressure on the other entrances during the exhibition and stadium events afterwards. Soon after this a further booking office was added in the main station whilst a temporary street level ticket office for Wembley traffic was opened in vacant shop premises adjoining the main entrances. In the East station a new engine siding was laid near the signal box. Between Baker Street and St John's Wood Road, six signal sections replaced the former three, whilst additional signals were inserted between the latter station and Neasden, providing in all 17 new sections between Baker Street and Wembley Park at a cost of £9,767. This enabled all four roads to handle a uniform frequency of service.

Although most of the improvements mentioned were ready for the opening of the exhibition on 23 April 1924, one important item was not in use until 6 July. This was the new signal box at Baker Street, with its all-electric Westinghouse Brake & Saxby Signal Co power locking frame. There were 39 working levers to operate 21 sets of points, 35 lamp signals and 12 route indicators, plus seven spare levers. Signals and points were moved by 120 V dc but ac current was used for the points indicators. Simultaneous point operation replaced the previous sequential working, providing a time saving which enabled 40 more trains to be fitted into the day's workings. Room for extension of the Baker Street East platforms was made at the same time by moving points and crossings 100ft towards the tunnel mouth.

Within the exhibition itself, the image of the Metropolitan was not neglected. Demonstrating his continuing attitude of proud independence, Selbie had refused an invitation from Frank Pick to share a stand with the Underground Group in the Palace of Engineering. Instead the Metropolitan had one of its own, with a First Class driving trailer as its principal feature. This vehicle, which had dummy control equipment, had been supplied for £3,900 by Metropolitan Carriage, Wagon & Finance Co Ltd who met some of the cost of the stand. When the exhibition reopened for its second season in 1925, the Metropolitan stand was larger and in a more prominent position, showing additionally one of the company's new 1,200 hp electric locos. This was no 15, later to be named posthumously WEMBLEY 1924. Its side panels were removed to show its equipment.

During the exhibition Metropolitan guards were provided with white cap covers, whilst train crews enjoyed a flow of free tea at Wembley Park station. All staff received fortnightly payments of a bonus equivalent to ten per cent of their standard weekly wage in recognition of the additional work involved. Senior officers were awarded a total of £4,000 of which Selbie received a quarter. The total thus distributed whilst the exhibition was open was £22,000.

Advertised as 'Under Cover All The Way', the Metropolitan's exhibition train services were commendably frequent and well-operated. From 1 July 1924 there were no less than 740 trains daily serving Wembley Park station, 242 of them covering the 6½ miles from Baker Street non stop in ten minutes.

Although the spring of 1924 was cold and the summer wet and low on sun, 17.5 million people had paid to enter the grounds when the exhibition closed on 1 November. There was less interest for the second season, when only 9.7m tickets were sold between May and October despite a reduction in the price of the combined rail and entrance tickets. These great crowds were of course not solely the Metropolitan's meat; they were shared with the London Midland & Scottish Railway and the Bakerloo tube at Wembley station and with the London & North Eastern Railway at Wembley Hill station on the southern edge of the exhibition grounds and at that company's station on the new loop line through the grounds[15]. Some were also moved by the General buses and the Metropolitan Electric Tramways. But the Metropolitan Railway was the major beneficiary, handling as it did some 12.5 million passengers through Wembley Park station during the 1924 season. On the busiest day it was estimated that approximately 230,000 moved in and out. Wardle calculated that of the total visiting the exhibition, the Metropolitan carried an average of around 35 per cent or between 60 and 62 per cent of the total railborne traffic between London and the exhibition. On cup final day 1925, the LNER was rather peeved to find Metropolitan agents distributing pamphlets at Marylebone station advocating the Baker Street route as the best way to reach the Wembley stadium. Mixing his metaphors somewhat, Alex Wilson, the LNER's Southern Area divisional general manager, protested to Selbie:

> after all is said and done, your Company get the lion's share of the Wembley traffic and you must not begrudge us any few odd crumbs that may fall from the rich man's table . . .

But when the exhibition finally closed in the autumn of 1925 the LNER did receive some pickings. With sidings into the grounds, including some right into the large buildings, it got the traffic from the dismantling of the exhibits and the subsequent conversion of the buildings into industrial units and warehouses. Its loop station was also more convenient for the stadium, sold at a fraction of its original cost to be converted to accommodate greyhound racing in addition to other sports. Apart from the chaos of 1923, cured in subsequent years by issuing tickets for all admissions, the highest cup final attendance was 1924's 118,000. After that, the figure settled at 90–95,000 with the Metropolitan carrying up to one-third of the total each way.

Greyhound racing, which started both here and at the White City in 1927, at first provided excellent trade for the Metropolitan; in 1928 it attracted 1½ million additional passengers to the two stations. Business declined as interest faded and more courses were opened in other parts of London.

With the added bonus of a tram and bus strike, Wembley gave the Metropolitan ordinary shareholders a five per cent dividend in 1924, the best result for 40 years. Passenger carryings (excluding season ticket journeys) reached almost 118 million, exceeding those of 1923 by 13 million. From the early 1920s the returns continued to show a steady fall in short-distance passengers against a rising level of longer-distance and season ticket receipts. A decline in First Class revenue was first noticed in 1925. For that year, although the Wembley exhibition traffic dropped considerably over 1924, business was generally buoyant and another 5 per cent dividend was just managed on ordinary stock. After that it fell back to three per cent in 1926 and 1927, the former an ostensibly commendable result in the year of the General Strike and coal supply problems, but in fact only made possible by raiding the reserve fund, something not done for 20 years. In 1928 and 1929, with passenger traffic totals still growing and freight traffic also increasing (mainly from suburban house building) ordinary dividends reached 3½ and 4 per cent. Season ticket issues grew from 32,884 in 1922 to 35,208 in 1929, reflecting suburban development.

ENLARGING THE ESTATE

Another enterprise returning a useful five per cent in 1925 was the MRCE. After publication of its annual report for that year Selbie invited the board to agree that it was 'fulfilling one of the main objects for which it was formed in developing estates adjacent to the line and so creating traffic for the railway'. What he did not mention was the knock-on effect of its activities in stimulating independent housing developments along the Metropolitan. Satisfaction with the new off-spring increased in 1926 when there was a 6 per cent dividend for its ordinary shareholders. By the end of 1929, of a total of 952½ acres owned on eight separate estates then in development, some 322 had been sold. The increase in acreage was accounted for by additional purchases which had been made to enlarge the Rickmansworth estates together with the opening of four small developments along the Uxbridge branch in 1927: Hillingdon Mount (7¼ acres); Eastcote Hill (10¾ acres); Manor Farm, Eastcote Road, Ruislip (19½ acres); and Elm Grove, Ruislip (21½ acres).

In its final burst of activity before the trauma of 1933, MRCE opened two more large estates. The most immediately successful of all its developments, because its opening up coincided with the early 1930s housing boom in the London suburban area and because it offered the ubiquitous 2½ bedroom semi sought by the mass market, was the 213-acre Harrow Garden Village. This was sited either side of Rayners Lane station, mostly to the north of the line. Made possible by a loan from the railway company, activity here started in 1929 when five miles of roads and sewers were laid and E. S. Reid, one of the first housebuilders to purchase sections of the estate, paid the Metropolitan £1,000 for a private siding to bring in his building materials after finding the local roads could not cope with the traffic. MRCE enterprise at Rayners Lane soon attracted large scale builders to the area, notably T. F. Nash on the Tithe Farm Estate south of the line, who also bought a private siding. Within two or three years, the whole district was transformed from elm-bordered grasslands to repetitious red-roofed suburban semis and shopping parades.

At Amersham, the Weller Estate of 78 acres was purchased by MRCE in 1930 for £18,000 soon to be covered with 535 semi-detached houses (priced at £875 upwards) and 51 shops. Somewhat nervous about the success of a development so far out of London, the MRCE asked if the Metropolitan Railway would provide a subsidy of £10–15 for each house or shop built. They were disappointed. The railway board not only foresaw problems with the co-owner of the line, the

LNER, but had doubts about the validity of the precedent established by the subsidy given to the Wembley Park Estate Co in 1914–27. In July 1930 the proposal was firmly rejected.

MRCE ordinary dividends rose very satisfactorily from six per cent in the years 1926–29 to a peak of 8 per cent in 1930 and 1931 before the economic depression knocked the figure back to 4 per cent in 1932 and 1933.

A Surplus Lands Committee estate of 41½ acres on the north side of the line between Dollis Hill and Willesden Green stations was directly developed in 1927–30. Sherrick Green, acquired from the Ecclesiastical Commissioners in 1878 at £336 an acre, was let on building leases in the traditional 19th century style, yielding an income of £2,721 a year or 15 per cent on the original outlay after allowing for construction of roads and sewers and the sale of 12½ acres. (This is the figure quoted to the board; it does of course disregard inflation over the period.)

The net results of all this activity, aided by the railway improvements which are dealt with in the next chapter, encouraged a substantial population and traffic growth in Metro-land, very much as Selbie had hoped. Around the stations Wembley Park, Preston Road and Northwick Park for example, the catchment areas of the railway saw a population expansion of 116 per cent between 1921 and 1928. The number of ordinary First, Third and workmen's tickets issued in March 1928 at stations Wembley Park to Rickmansworth/Watford/Uxbridge inclusive was 164,834 (59 per cent) higher than the same figure for March 1923. Monthly season tickets issued at these stations increased from 59,232 in March 1923 to 104,826 in March 1928, the heaviest increments occurring at stations Wembley Park to Pinner inclusive (up 33,984). Between West Harrow and Uxbridge in this period the March issues grew only by 7,140. Gross passenger receipts at stations Wembley Park to Rickmansworth, Watford and Uxbridge inclusive were £203,000 in 1922 and £339,000 in 1929. In 1925 passenger earnings per Third Class seat on the Metropolitan were almost £67 against £64 on the Underground, £37 on the SR, £31 on the GWR, £26 on the LMSR and £25 on the LNER.

Such was the measure of Selbie's achievement. At a time when short-distance traffic in London was continuously falling away to the motor bus[16] he had more than maintained the earning capacity of the railway. All this heralded further traffic increases beyond Harrow, notably on the Uxbridge branch, in the 1930s. As we shall see in the next chapter, some substantial capital investment, not all of it wise, was made in the hope of sustaining these results.

14

AN INFRASTRUCTURE FOR METRO-LAND

ELECTRICS TO THE HEART OF METRO-LAND

We have already noted Selbie's 1911 comment that the seven miles between Harrow and Rickmansworth would soon justify electrification on their own merits apart from providing access to the new Watford branch. With a decision to get on with the Watford line already taken, in June 1923 the board readily agreed Selbie's scheme for electrification north of Harrow. At first the LNER hesitated, declaring that an increased service would congest the double track beyond Harrow but this objection was withdrawn when the Metropolitan proposed to build a £77,000 concrete and steel burrowing junction at Harrow for the Uxbridge branch, offering to meet three quarters of the cost, also promising to equip the double line to Rickmansworth with automatic signalling. These two measures effectively deferred the larger expenditure of quadrupling between Harrow and Rickmansworth, for which much land had already been bought. The LNER did however insist that it would have a right to use the Metropolitan installation for its own electric trains should these be introduced at some future date.

Selbie's scheme was for the equipment of 23 track miles, with new substations at Rickmansworth and Northwood and that at Harrow re-fitted to give an output of just under 4,000 kW. Final cost was to be £216,261. The works were planned and supervised by the Metropolitan's new resident engineer, Edward A. Wilson[1], who had joined the company from the GER on 1 July 1921 at a salary of £1,500.

Westinghouse Brake & Saxby Signal Co supplied the automatic track-circuited ac signalling, with its three-position searchlight signals, sanctioned early in 1924 for the section between Harrow South Junction and Watford/Rickmansworth at a cost of £46,722, to be shared with the LNER (the Metropolitan paid 55 per cent for the Harrow South Junction-Harrow North Junction section and 50 per cent for the remainder). The Ministry of Transport Inspecting Officer spoke admiringly of the finished installation, describing it in December 1924 as 'the most considerable' of its type on British [main line] railways. Pinner and Northwood boxes were closed except for

251

working in and out of the goods yards, where signals remained manually operated. At the other boxes the old manual frames were retained, supplemented by illuminated track circuit diagrams. Harrow North Junction box, with its 27 levers (ten spare) was moved to the west side of the new main line, whilst Rickmansworth box was lengthened to take a new 50-lever mechanical frame with six spare levers. The three junctions of the Watford branch and access to the Croxley Hall gravel sidings, now re-arranged, were controlled by a new 28-lever Watford Road Junction box, south of Rickmansworth.

Advertised as *Into the Heart of Metro-Land by Electric Train*, the new facility came into use on Monday 5 January 1925 with a much-improved timetable which concentrated all engine-changing at Rickmansworth, where sidings had been added for this purpose. Non-stop trains covered the 17½ miles between Baker Street and Rickmansworth in 24–25 minutes. Although in use from 14 September 1925, all the work on the new burrowing junction at Harrow was not finished until October.

METROPOLITAN AT WATFORD

Perhaps wisely in view of events, the GCR and its successor the LNER evinced little enthusiasm about finding a half share of the capital for the Watford branch. Penny-pinching as always, the LNER sought the abandonment of the Rickmansworth North Curve, but finally gave in to the Metropolitan's pressure for a start on the complete scheme of 2 miles 37 chains double track, including double line junctions towards Rickmansworth as well as those towards London.

J. M. Clark was the resident engineer for the project and the contractors were Logan & Hemingway of Doncaster, who began operations at the end of 1922. Construction proved difficult and laborious involving as many as ten bridges and a deep cutting through chalk followed by a high embankment between Croxley and the terminus to maintain a maximum gradient of 1 in 100 (designed to accommodate main line steam trains). Finishing work was carried on through the almost continuous wet weather of 1924. Final cost was £388,000 against the estimate of £300,000.

Signalling was similar to that installed on the electrified Harrow to Rickmansworth line, apart from a little meanness at Watford to be mentioned in a moment, and in addition to the Watford Road Junction cabin already mentioned there were boxes at Croxley Green (20 levers, seven spare, with king lever to enable the box to be switched out when the goods yard was inactive) and at Watford (42 levers and one spare). The Inspecting Officer commented adversely on the use of two-position semaphores as the Watford outer and inner homes, an economy measure he considered confusing, especially at night when their lamps had to be distinguished amid the stronger glow of two and three-position colour lights. His plea for standardisation was ignored; the LNER misers triumphed over the Metropolitan, which would probably have preferred power frames at Watford and at the junction in view of the constant movements necessary.

At Croxley Green (now Croxley) the station and goods yard were more centrally situated for the community than the terminus of the LNWR branch from Watford. From the gaslit station building on the road overbridge, 10ft wide stairs led down to 420ft side platforms lit from the traction supply.

Watford had a double-sided 615ft platform, 30ft wide, capable of handling a full length main line steam train and sheltered by a 280ft wood and glass canopy supported on steel girders. Locomotive escape roads were positioned each side of the platform roads. The platforms were lit from the traction current, the rest of the station from the local supply. A well-equipped seven-road goods yard contained a large shed, five-ton crane, horse and carriage dock and cattle pens, all reached by a new 40ft wide approach from the main road. Watford Council had insisted on this, not wanting vehicular traffic along Cassiobury Park Avenue, which the passenger station fronted, as this was designated a residential road.

Both station buildings were very pleasing designs in C. W. Clark's well-mannered, domestic style. With walls of red brick under steeply-pitched, multi-chimneyed roofs with dormer windows they made a telling contrast to the buildings around them, then and later. Internally, much of the woodwork was in oak and the painting was in green.

An impressed Inspecting Officer commented:

> the Companies are to be congratulated on the arrangements at these stations. They appear to have ample accommodation and are well laid-out; the buildings have character and are well-designed and executed.

A proposed halt about half a mile short of the terminus to serve the West Herts Golf Club was never built, but immediately north of the intended site, facing the canal, 16 cottages were erected in 1926 for the traffic and engineering staff, officials having observed that new housing in the area was 'of a much better class than our men require'. Four cottages were also built at Croxley Green to replace some demolished to make room for the station. All these houses were the work of C. W. Clark.

Management of the new branch was in the hands of the Watford Joint Railway Committee, reconstituted by the Metropolitan and the LNER in November 1925. Both companies provided a train service when the line opened to the public on Monday 2 November 1925. On weekdays there were 43 Up and 40 Down trains to and from Baker Street (Liverpool Street/Aldgate in rush hours) and 30 Up and 29 Down on the Marylebone route, the combination offering a half-hourly interval in the slack periods. The fastest Metropolitan electrics covered the 18½ miles to Baker Street in 35 minutes, but some LMSR steam trains from the more conveniently-sited Watford Junction station were then reaching Euston in 25. By mutual consent, the weekday service was reduced to 33 Up and 32 Down Metropolitan and 18 Up and 12 Down LNER from 1 March 1926, this reflecting the very thin patronage of the LNER trains (only one weekly season ticket was issued at Watford for Marylebone in the week ending 10 January 1926). With the outbreak of the General Strike on 4 May 1926 all LNER trains ceased, never to return on a regular basis, though some excursions were worked occasionally. In compensation, from 31 January 1927, Metropolitan electric services were augmented to provide 43 Up and 41 Down daily.

Attempting to maximise revenue from this costly speculation, the Metropolitan also provided from the opening day a shuttle service of 30 trains a day each way between Watford and Rickmansworth via the disputed North Curve, using a new bay platform at Rickmansworth. These trains always ran at a loss because they could not compete with the cheaper and very frequent motor bus services between the two towns, but the Metropolitan kept them going until the formation of the London Passenger Transport Board in July 1933[2].

Business on the main branch service was almost equally discouraging, especially in the early years. In January 1926 Watford's booking clerks were only issuing some 1,400 tickets a week and those at Croxley Green 890 or so. Season tickets to and from both stations at this time were sold at the low rate of about 70 a week. So far as the Metropolitan was concerned, the net increase from traffic induced was a trifling £4,562 in the first full year from all services (including six months' freight receipts), equivalent to just over two per cent on the company's capital outlay of £194,000. But receipts at the two stations did grow slowly, from £10,587 in 1926 to £17,142 in 1929. In the same period passengers carried expanded from 671,000 to 1,196,000 a year.

Commercial success was frustrated by three factors: Watford, with its 50,000 population, had a good deal of local industry; it was lavishly provided with electric and steam railway and motor bus and coach services; and the new branch terminus was sited in a quite hopeless position at the western extremity of the town's built-up area, a mile from the centre, flanked by large public open spaces on its north side. There were two roads serving the new terminus, partly made up, where new houses were being built in 1925, but little other sign of development[3].

Some consideration was given to moving the terminus closer to the heart of the town. Early in May 1927, J. M. Clark, who had been resident engineer for the branch construction and was now in the Metropolitan Railway Engineer's office at Edgware Road, noticed that premises at 44, High Street, with 2¼ acres of backland extending to Cassio Road, were on the market. He sent a memorandum to Selbie in which he suggested that this property would provide adequate space for a small passenger terminus and outlined two possible approach routes, one in tunnel for part of the way to avoid property demolition. Selbie took his usual positive attitude, getting the board to agree to purchase of the property 'in view of possible future eventualities'. The transaction was made through a third party in October 1927, the LNER not being told until after the event. Although parliamentary sanction for the acquisition to pass openly to the Metropolitan Railway was given in the Metropolitan Railway Act, 1929, there had been new developments by that time. In 1928 the property was sold at a profit to the Metropolitan puppet company, N. W. Land & Transport Co Ltd, who leased it to a furniture retailer, ensuring it could be re-possessed without difficulty should it ever be needed. But that it would be a railway station had now become much more unlikely.

Since the opening day of the branch a bus service had been operated between the new terminus and the town centre by the National Omnibus & Transport Co. These buses had become less frequent with the passing of time, eroding their value as a feeder to the branch. The Metropolitan accordingly decided to enter the motor bus business on its own account, purchasing four 28-seater Albion chassis with Vickers bodies duly adorned in the railway's grained teak livery, the coat of arms, and METROPOLITAN RAILWAY in prominent letters along the body sides. On 2 November 1927 a service was started on a circular route between the town centre and the station, passing close to the LMSR station at Watford West, and meeting virtually every Metropolitan train. Whilst this operation was in itself a loss-maker, its smartly-uniformed, courteous drivers and efficient operation soon brought it great popularity, loadings reaching around 500 passengers a day, twice that number on Saturdays. Bookings at

Watford station showed a marked improvement[4]. With house building on the nearby Cassiobury Park Estate proceeding apace and attracting London commuters, by the early 1930s the Metropolitan was getting the best possible results from its unwise venture into Watford.

Whilst the Uxbridge branch was seen to have great potential, there was little need for new facilities to meet traffic growth in the 1920s. Something in the nature of a population explosion was to come, but not until the early 1930s. House building on a fairly small scale had started at Ruislip Manor Estate just before 1914, stimulating the provision of a halt, as already noticed. A start had also been made with estate road construction near the railway at Eastcote, encouraging the Metropolitan to instal a ten-wagon siding and small signal box in 1913. For the first decade after the end of World War 1, pleasure traffic remained the staple diet at both places. At the end of 1922 an approach was made for a sixth halt by Halden Estates, who were proposing to develop the Hercies Farm and Hillingdon Court Estates south of the line between the river Pinn and Long Lane. A site on Long Lane, south of Ickenham village, was agreed, subject to the gift of land for a goods yard and a guarantee of £600 a year net receipts, this sum representing a 10 per cent return on the building and staff wages costs. Clark produced a simple structure with elegant 40×10ft wood and tile-roofed shelters placed in the centres of its 370ft side platforms. An iron footbridge at the Harrow end led up to a neat tiled and half-timbered booking hut at road level. Hillingdon was opened on 10 December 1923, but its name soon caused protests which were to continue over eight years, the basis of complaint being that the old village was well over a mile to the south and more conveniently reached via Uxbridge station. Selbie was unmoved. A 555ft goods siding, included in the final cost of £4,918, was put into use from December 1923 when building materials were first transhipped to the builder's light railway system. Trailing from the Down line, this siding was entered through a three-lever ground frame, the arrangements being such that shunting had to be carried out on the running line between passenger trains. Gross receipts at Hillingdon barely exceeded £2,000 in the first year, but by 1930 with about 1,000 houses erected on both sides of the line, the takings had grown to £12,220. This encouraged the Metropolitan to make some modest improvements to the station, including some much-needed lavatories, all completed by 30 April 1931.

Reference was made in Chapter 11 to the opening on 17 November 1913 of a halt called West Harrow at the point where Vaughan Road passed under the branch, 58 chains from Harrow. This had followed pressure from landowners and residents of the New Bessborough Estate south of the railway, where house building had started around 1906. Facilities here were crude, devoid of any sign of the civilising hand of Clark: two 350ft timber platforms with rough shelters and separate approaches to the roadway below, where there was a small booking hut on the Up side of the bridge. Great masses of creosoted wood created a dark and depressing image, causing an estate agent wishing to promote a new estate north of the line to seek planting of trees and shrubs on the embankment to soften the impact, a request agreed by Selbie in 1915. By the following year, some 43,000 passengers a month were using the halt, numbers thought sufficient to justify provision of lavatories and improvement to the shelters on the platforms. Despite GCR complaints that the halt was competitive with Joint Line traffic, there was no perceptible drop in business at Harrow after it had been opened (most fares were the same amount). Services here were improved in 1925 when some trains which had terminated at Harrow were extended to Rayners Lane. In 1928–9 platforms at West Harrow were lengthened to take eight cars, the canopies were extended, the stairs to the road roofed over, a waiting room provided on the Up side and a fully enclosed shelter on the Down side.

Rayners Lane had its platforms extended to take six cars in 1918, by which time it was staffed and a small booking hut of the Ickenham pattern had appeared at road level on the Up side. For the 1925 service improvement just mentioned, the crossover was moved further east. Two years later, additional waiting shelters were provided in the form of corrugated iron sheds and the platforms were lengthened to take the 8-car trains. As a response to the start of building development in the area by MRCE and others (described in Chapter 13) a public goods yard was laid on the south side of the station in 1929. Its traffic grew at a fierce pace: from 230 tons (233.7 tonnes) in July that year to 1,157 (1,175.5) in November, leading to the opening of improved facilities on 16 June 1930. A scheme was drawn up to enlarge greatly the passenger station but negotiations with the Middlesex County Council regarding reconstruction of the road overbridge and a fresh outbreak of argument with the Underground Group about its services via South Harrow[5] delayed action until after 1933.

Throughout the 1920s, business at Eastcote continued to be dominated by the summer pleasure traffic, much of it parties of children destined for The Pavilion and its grounds in Field End Road. These movements could be quite heavy, with up to 3,000 arriving on busy days. Exits and entrances had been widened to 12ft in 1914 and the platforms lengthened to take seven cars, eliminating drawing-up, a particularly dangerous manoeuvre when children were on trains in large numbers. Extension to 420ft to accommodate eight car trains was undertaken in 1927 together with the addition of a 120ft shelter. Although some modest building development had started here around 1923–4 when the siding was enlarged for the purpose, activity did not really take off until 1930, when freight facilities were further improved.

Reached only by a fieldpath, Ruislip Manor was so quiet it succumbed to wartime manpower shortages, closing from 12 February 1917. Weekday opening resumed on 1 April 1919 but Sunday closure persisted until 6 May 1928. Traffic was still light in 1926 when there was a threat of closure for the second time unless the only building developer in sight would provide a subsidy. He did so, managing a start on his houses by the end of that year.

An increase in the pace of housebuilding at Ruislip caused the goods yard there to be enlarged in 1928–9. At the same time the footbridge between the platforms was roofed and the platform shelters extended.

A 15-acre aircraft stores depot, rail-served from the GWR&GCR Joint Line, which appeared at Ickenham in 1918, was to become a permanent establishment employing about 1,000 and bringing extra business to Ickenham halt. After a re-siting of the halt nearer the depot had been considered and rejected, the platforms were extended at the Uxbridge end in 1922.

The additional signal box mentioned earlier as opening at Eastcote in 1913 was used when necessary as an intermediate block post. Another small box had been installed for the same purpose at Ickenham at the same time. These two boxes were manned when pleasure traffic was at its peak and also, latterly, as suburban development advanced, during the rush hours. With the branch re-signalling of 1930, the Ickenham box was completely closed.

We must now consider response to suburban development on the main Extension line, most noticeable in the immediate pre-1914 period in the westward growth of Harrow along the north side of the Pinner Road, much of this by the Imperial Property Investment Co Ltd and Westcott Bros on the New Headstone, Roxborough Close, Glebe and Belmont Park Estates. As the ability to let and sell these newly-erected houses slowed down noticeably the further the building advanced from Harrow, agitation for a new station near Hooking

Bridge began in 1909. The usual delays ensued whilst the two partners in the Joint Line argued first over what should be done, and then about the details. There was further difficulty about the approach to the railway from the Pinner Road; landowners were prepared to give space for a road but not to provide one. Eventually the Metropolitan and the GCR compromised by agreeing to pay for a 183 yd, 9 ft wide footpath. Construction of a halt on the embankment at 1 mile 19½ chains from Harrow was begun by a Metropolitan Railway labour force late in 1914. Selbie concurred in Fay's opinion that the name NORTH HARROW was 'more descriptive of the neighbourhood' than any alternative despite the site being in Pinner parish. When the halt opened on 22 March 1915 it had two 400ft wooden platforms with timber and corrugated iron pitched-roof shelters. Below were a booking hut and lavatories. Architectural design was conspicuously absent (Clark was away at the war). Signalling in the area was modified, with track circuits provided between Harrow and Pinner (exclusive) in 1916.

When house construction north of the railway here was resumed in 1923, it proceeded apace, bringing the number of passengers handled by the halt from 140,400 in 1922 to 723,000 in 1927. Growth in the latter year accelerated so strongly that by the end of 1928 there were some 20,000 passengers a month, excluding season ticket journeys, compared to 14,000 a year earlier. In the evenings, with 200 or more commuters alighting from successive rush hour trains, the facilities were shown to be inadequate for the traffic and as some of the users came from the Headstone direction, the Metropolitan was concerned that discontent might tempt them to sample the LMSR/Bakerloo tube services at Headstone Lane station. In 1927 a 60ft road, soon lined with shops, was built from Pinner Road up to the station and a short distance beyond, although the 40ft wide bridge under the railway remained unaltered. The road authority planned to widen it to 70ft throughout, eventually extending it through to Rayners Lane station. Responding to this and the clear implication of large scale development south of the railway, the Joint Committee agreed to reconstruction of the station at a cost of £25,000, to be synchronised with the work on the road under the line. Included in the station plan were shops and garages to provide a five per cent return on the outlay. The new street building, with its canopied entrances each side of the wider road bridge and its booking hall on the north side, was begun after the new bridge was rolled into position in November 1929. Platforms were extended to 420ft, rebuilt in concrete and widened out to 18ft under about half the new 150ft timber awning at the London end. All work was completed early in 1931. Somewhat surprisingly, Clark's white faience elevations for the single storey street frontage were in the style he had adopted for the inner area rather than suburban sites and the result was distinctly dreary. Over the main entrance there appeared the seemingly anachronistic but statutorily correct legend METROPOLITAN & GREAT CENTRAL RLYS.

Some consideration was given in 1913 to requests for a halt east of Harrow to serve the Churchill[6] Estate, between Kenton Road and the railway, immediately west of the LNWR, but building work here had not proceeded beyond laying out the estate roads, coming to a stop with the war. House construction began in 1920, soon followed by the start of another building estate, Northwick Park, in about 50 acres on the opposite side of Kenton Road. The newly-established Hill Golf Club on the south side of the railway at this point also sought station accommodation. Noting that about 200 new houses had been erected and anxious about the competition of Kenton station, where the LNWR had improved train services in July and October 1922, the Metropolitan board approved provision of a new station in February 1923, accepting a gift of land for the 27ft wide approach from Northwick Avenue. By this time work had started on a third building scheme, the extensive Northwick Estate on the opposite side of the Euston line to the Churchill Estate. Designed by the engineer's office, with some refinements by Clark, the new facility had a 420ft island platform occupying a space made by slewing the Up line. A 22ft wide, 155ft long umbrella awning covered a general waiting room, ladies' room, porters' room and men's lavatories. Reached through a subway, the booking office and entrance faced the approach from Northwick Avenue. Lighting was from the traction current. Northwick Park & Kenton was opened on 28 June 1923 in incomplete state to gain the traffic from the Harrow Pageant, held on the open land on the south side, which was reached by the subway. There were 56 Up and 58 Down trains on weekdays (Sundays 51/53). Despite the large amount of open land to the south, this station proved a very satisfactory investment at a final cost of £7,690. Steadily expanding housebuilding between Harrow and Kenton brought passenger receipts here from £3,309 in 1924 to £18,307 in 1929, when additional waiting room accommodation was provided.

Although unconnected with suburban traffic expansion, the complete reconstruction of Aylesbury Joint station can be conveniently dealt with here. At busy times, its antiquated structures and platforms, which had seen little or no change for 50 years, were said to be dangerous, calling out for replanning and renewal. Improvement had been delayed by the war and difficulties in reaching agreement with the co-owners, the GCR (later the LNER) and the GWR, but was finally decided upon after much effort by the Metropolitan and agitation from the town. Completed in 1926, it was handsomely done, to the designs of Charles J. Brown, the LNER southern area engineer. John Wilmott & Sons (Hitchin) Ltd were the contractors and the total outlay, including some freight yard improvements, was £61,114, the Metropolitan meeting one quarter[7].

The new station had main Up and Down platforms of 665ft with a general width of 27–28ft plus a 545ft bay for trains to and from London at the opposite face to the London end of the main Up platform. After all the old structures had been demolished, an L-shaped building surmounted by a lantern was erected on the Up side to contain the booking hall and other offices. This had a 144ft frontage to the road approach and 175ft to the platform. A separate building housed the general and ladies' waiting rooms. On the Down side, there was a smaller building, the two main platforms being linked by a covered footbridge in the centre of the station. The freight yard was enlarged and given additional cattle pens, a goods warehouse and offices. East of the passenger station, a new coal yard was made.

METRO-LAND'S BOTTLENECK UNBROKEN

Substantial efforts were made in the second half of the 1920s to realise Selbie's ideal of 'four tracks from the City to Metro-land'. By 1925 the two lines between Baker Street East and Finchley Road, with their up-to-date signalling, were handling 30 eight-car trains in the 8.30–9.30 morning peak hour, of which 17 went through to the City, then the destination of 80 per cent of the Metropolitan's commuters. With the new Watford services coming along in the November timetable, it was considered the section's limit of capacity would be reached, and then only by sacrificing some calls at the stations between Finchley Road and Baker Street[8]. Rightly expecting a large traffic increase on the Uxbridge branch and a continuing accretion of business from stations north of Harrow, Selbie saw the double track tunnel as a severe obstacle to the development of the outer suburban traffic which had shown such satisfyingly consistent growth up to this point.

Means of breaking open this bottleneck had been tentatively examined in 1921 and again in 1924 but by 1925 Selbie was thoroughly determined something should be done. Early that year, he asked Wilson to explore all options for a second pair of tracks outwards from the centre. When these were presented to him, he selected a deep level

line from Edgware Road to Kilburn. In his eyes this had two important advantages: all traffic would still be funnelled through Baker
Street station without any rebuilding there, preserving its position as a
focal point, a matter to which he attached much importance; and, with
intermediate stations between Edgware Road and Kilburn, the new
line would attract traffic on its own account[9]. A side benefit was the
possibility of extending southwards at some future date to Victoria,
which Selbie saw as 'a natural objective' for the Metropolitan.

But the scheme was not well thought-out and Selbie's acceptance of
it must be reckoned as one of his few costly mistakes. It envisaged a
flat junction at Edgware Road with the existing double line, thus
limiting the number of trains which could pass over the new line to a
maximum of ten an hour. Holt, the traffic manager, subsequently
questioned the operational feasibility of injecting extra trains on to the
Inner Circle at Edgware Road, where after the rebuilding there would
be 544 trains each way daily as well as those for the new line. His
protestations, which may well have been made earlier, seem to have
been ignored by Selbie.

As was customary, Selbie's proposal was not challenged by the
directors, who approved the scheme in July 1925. After some £10,000
had been spent in promotion costs, powers for the new line were duly
obtained in the Metropolitan Railway Act of 4 August 1926. This
envisaged a £2.25m railway of 3 miles 7.9 chains, mostly in deep level
15ft 6in diameter tubes which would leave the Extension Line on the
London side of Willesden Green, burrowing under the existing tracks
just west of Kilburn & Brondesbury station then descending to twin
tunnels below Kilburn High Road, Maida Vale and Edgware Road
before joining the Inner Circle by a 1,200yd cut-and-cover ramp just
west of Edgware Road station. That station was to be rebuilt with four
platforms of eight-car length at which some of the trains using the new
line would terminate. Intermediate stations would be provided at
Quex Road/Kilburn High Road; at Kilburn Park Road/Maida Vale;
and at Clifton Road/Maida Vale, the last two competitive with
Kilburn Park, Maida Vale and Warwick Avenue stations on the
Bakerloo tube line[10]. When two bore holes were sunk it was confirmed
that the subsoil was entirely London blue clay, ideal for tube railway
construction.

Not surprisingly, the Underground Group was less than enthusiastic about the proposal. At a meeting at Baker Street on 16 March
1926, Pick told Selbie the new line and its stations 'would disturb
some two million of tube passengers' and the Underground did not
like it. Particular objection was voiced (on deaf ears) to the proposed

262

station at Kilburn Park Road, and Pick told Selbie of an alleged Underground plan for a tube which would pass under the Metropolitan's tube 'through Cricklewood and on to Dollis Hill'. Selbie said the Metropolitan would strenuously oppose any such scheme. In the end, a deal was done and the Metropolitan's tube bill was not opposed by 55 Broadway; amicable arrangements were reached about revising the Inner Circle and Putney Bridge services following the rebuilding of Edgware Road and we shall return to these later.

After the financial damage suffered in 1926, the year of the General Strike and prolonged coal strike, Lord Aberconway told Metropolitan shareholders that no start could be made with the new scheme in 1927, but with a slight upturn in business in 1928, active steps were taken as that year came to a close.

Harley Hugh Dalrymple Hay[11] was engaged as consultant engineer in view of his considerable experience in construction of tube railways at deep level. His estimate of the cost, produced in June 1929, was £2.05m or £1.62m without the intermediate stations. In the following month, an application was made for Treasury assistance under the Development (Loan Guarantees and Grants) Act, 1929. This new legislation, designed to assist public utility undertakings with works calculated to relieve unemployment, changed the financial assessment, making it possible to sacrifice the intermediate stations as the government grant would compensate for loss of revenue from them. Selbie was sufficiently confident at this point to begin looking at plans to build a new suburban branch line (to Stanmore, see Chapter 15).

The Treasury committee considering applications for assistance under the 1929 Development Act required a Ministry of Transport report on the scheme. It was during the preparation of material for this in September 1929 that Selbie suddenly realised a chasm had opened before him into which the whole scheme threatened to slide. In the previous year the Ministry had published revised *Requirements for Passenger Lines* which contained a provision that on deep level tube railways, means were to be provided at both ends of all trains, in combination with train doors, so that passengers could walk through and alight from either end in an emergency. But the whole purpose of Selbie's relief tube was that it should be capable of handling all types of Metropolitan trains, including the compartment stock trailers and Pullman cars which were locomotive-hauled to Harrow and beyond. To replace a major portion of the rolling stock by a design disliked by long distance passengers was unthinkable; the only hope now was that some means might be found at low engineering cost of satisfying the Ministry's concern about tube tunnel safety. Suspending the application for Treasury assistance, Selbie instructed Hay to mark time with his detailed planning.

He then asked the board to consider an alternative, involving shorter tubes below the Finchley Road to Baker Street tunnel, to be of larger diameter than those proposed on the Edgware Road-Kilburn line as they would be fitted out with emergency platforms on to which the Metropolitan's compartment stock doors could be opened. Passengers would then move along the emergency platforms through cross passages between the tubes and emergency exits to street level. As this design, suggested by Hay, was based on a precedent established in the LNWR tube tunnels between Primrose Hill and Loudoun Road which were used by ordinary railway stock, it was confidently expected the Ministry would raise no objection to it. But in October 1929 the Metropolitan board, finding it all too difficult, deferred a decision.

Nothing more happened until shortly after Selbie's death in May 1930, when Holt gave his blessing to this second scheme which took the form of two deep level tubes from Finchley Road beneath the existing tunnels to Baker Street where there would be a deep level interchange station before climbing to join the Inner Circle near Great Portland Street. This proposal, costed at £2.1m, was a modification of a shallow tunnel scheme first investigated for steam traction in 1878. It had operational attractions, but its economics were rightly questioned and the board, now obliged to do some thinking of its own, asked whether there were cheaper alternatives.

By the end of July 1930, a makeshift plan had been concocted. This involved partial closure (and possibly at a later stage, complete closure) of the three tunnel stations on the St John's Wood line[12] combined with construction of a flyunder on the country side of Swiss Cottage station to carry Down fast trains beneath the Up Local, thus eliminating the fouling movement at the Finchley Road junction. Some improvements were also planned for Baker Street and it was calculated that the capacity of the 'throat' section would be increased to 45 trains an hour in one direction at the peak, deferring further heavy expenditure for at least ten years. Hay prepared plans for the flyunder, which it was hoped would pass the Ministry's scrutiny as there would be only 936yd of 17ft 6in internal diameter tube, all fitted out with the emergency platforms. It was also thought the works could be undertaken without parliamentary sanction as they were all on Metropolitan property but the Treasury blocked this, saying it could not consider Development Act assistance without the scheme having parliamentary authority. With that, the work on the proposal seems to have stopped; there are no references to it in the papers after January 1931, although the powers for the Edgware Road-Kilburn scheme were allowed to lapse after 31 October 1932. There is some evidence (eg a note 'may not now be required' on the capital account of November 1931 against the projected £422,000 expenditure on the Finchley Road flyunder scheme) that the Metropolitan may have had intimation of an Underground proposal to extend the Bakerloo tube to Finchley Road to connect with the Metropolitan. This, or the increasing possibility of some sort of London transport common management regime, or both, caused Baker Street to put its papers on one side.

THREE AND A HALF TRACKS TO THE CITY

Another aspect of 'four tracks from the City to Metro-land' was agreed by the board in March 1923. This put the Metropolitan's own trains on to its City Widened Lines for the first time by electrifying them and making use of the 1,200ft tunnel built in 1868 parallel to the Circle Line along the front of St Pancras station. For £50,730 Walter Scott & Middleton made a 700ft connection into the western end of this empty tunnel at Chalton Street west of King's Cross in a cut and cover operation that involved diversion of a sewer. An electrified single line was then laid, making a trailing junction at its eastern end with the Up Widened Lines at a point between the tunnels up to the St Pancras and King's Cross main lines. From here, the Up Widened Lines track was electrified as far as two new eight-car platforms at Moorgate next to the Inner Circle platforms. These new platforms were on the site of the old Midland bay, from which the LMSR steam suburban trains were ejected (they used the abandoned SECR bay on the south side from 7 September 1925). The Down track of the Widened Lines was electrified only between Moorgate and Farringdon Street, the connections enabling the Down electrics to join the Circle either there or at Moorgate wherever there was a gap between trains. These changes enabled up to eight trains an hour to be diverted from the busy Circle Lines in the morning peak as well as providing more flexibility at the City end in the evening rush hours, altogether a useful contribution to more regular running on the Circle east of King's Cross. As pressure on the Down Circle line was not so great in the evening rush hours as that on the Up in the more concentrated morning peak, Selbie considered the cost of electrifying the Down Widened Lines track west of Farringdon not justified, given the nuisance of operating a flat double line junction at Chalton Street.

Services over the electrified Widened Lines began on 15 March 1926.

To secure greater safety and efficiency both tracks of the Widened Lines were resignalled using Westinghouse Brake & Saxby Signal Co automatic two-aspect colour lights with fog repeaters at a cost of £18,889. A new Moorgate signal box, on the north east side of the Milton Street overbridge, opened on 14 October 1926, had a 44-lever mechanical frame which electrically operated the junction signals and points through circuit breakers. Barbican signal box on the Widened Lines had been closed in 1924 after track circuiting of the Widened Lines between Aldersgate Street box and Barbican Junction, the cost of which was shared with the LMSR. At Chalton Street, the new junction into the second tunnel was operated electrically from King's Cross 'C' box, which also now controlled the junction to the former Midland lines, permitting the closure of Midland Junction box from midnight 6/7 March 1926. As all stop lights on the Widened Lines were now fitted with electrically-operated train stops, the Metropolitan required the LMSR and LNER to fit all locomotives using these lines with trip-cock apparatus, an unforeseen expenditure particularly resented by the accountant-riddled LMSR. In the hope that LNER and LMSR locomotive drivers might be persuaded out of their lazy habit of filling the Widened Lines' tunnels with steam which would now form a hazard for their brothers driving Metropolitan electric trains, enamel signs with reflected lights reading ENGINES MUST CONDENSE were erected at tunnel entrances at King's Cross, Farringdon and Aldersgate (Barbican).

The final cost of the new Widened Lines connection and electrification was £118,518. Some further signalling modernisation took place in 1931, when all signals on the Inner Circle between Baker Street and Farringdon were converted to two-aspect colour lights with 6in lenses.

REBUILDING IN THE CENTRE

During and just after World War 1, Selbie had compiled a detailed plan for new works and other expenditure to meet the requirements of the Metropolitan for the 1920s and beyond. Much of this has already been covered but we have not yet mentioned the continuation of the central area station rebuilding programme. Initially the cost of this work was to be met partly from the additional commercial lettings invariably incorporated in each proposal and partly from a 'Special Fund' of £79,000 allocated in March 1922 from payments received from the government at the termination of wartime control. From time to time this fund was topped up from the Arrears of Maintenance and Depreciation Funds. Then, in 1926, the board laid down the criterion that station reconstruction expenditure must return an assured additional revenue or saving in operating expenditure of at least six per cent on the outlay.

Before turning to the specific content of the postwar station programme, it is convenient to note here that in 1920 it was decided that all platforms on the electrified lines should be of at least seven-car length. Eight years later, with the growth of suburban traffic dictating an increase of train length to eight cars, it was agreed that all platforms between Aldgate and Uxbridge should be lengthened to 420ft. Statutory authority for this work at tunnel stations was obtained in the Metropolitan Railway Act of 1929 and Treasury assistance with the interest on the £326,000 expenditure was arranged under the Development (Loan Guarantees and Grants) Act of the same year. Following the repeal of Government Passenger Duty, also in 1929, the capitalised value of the estimated relief to the Metropolitan (£46,060) was tipped into this project. Subsequently the Inner Circle platforms at Baker Street were omitted from the list of extensions and very much cheaper alternative arrangements were devised for Marlborough Road and Swiss Cottage. All the work was completed between 1930 and the end of 1932. Platform lengthening made it necessary to rebuild signal boxes at Farringdon (new box in service from 24 July 1932) and Aldersgate (Barbican) (27 November 1932). The associated resignalling for these two locations was undertaken by the British Power Railway Signalling Co.

Another general station change, on a smaller scale, was the introduction of 'Passimeter' one-man ticket issue and collection offices, controlling entry and egress to stations from an island site in the booking hall thus saving two or more ticket collectors. After an experimental installation at the Marylebone Road entrance to Baker Street station in 1927, another appeared at Drayton Park on 15 October 1928. Further units were opened at King's Cross (5 November 1928), Edgware Road (12 November 1928), and Marlborough Road (29 November 1928).

The first of the major central area station rebuildings after the end of World War 1 was at Farringdon & High Holborn (so renamed in May 1922), a scheme which had reached the stage of submission of tenders before wartime deferment in 1915. This was one of the busiest stations on the Metropolitan, with some 1,200 trains and 60,000 passengers daily in and out at the time the proposal to start was agreed by the board (July 1922). Clark designed a sober but brightly attractive street building in white faience with a 28ft wide canopied entrance leading to a circulating area, booking office, cloakrooms and parcels office erected over the line. Its first floor contained a 3,700 sq ft restaurant for Spiers & Pond. Electric light was fitted throughout. Income from rents was estimated at about ten per cent of the outlay but to increase the return, a separate two-storey building of shops and offices was erected on the opposite side of the road using space over the railway formed by bracketing out from the bridge. All the works were completed by November 1923 at a cost of £19,235.

At St John's Wood Road, the station entrance had been half hidden behind an enclosed ventilator and the parapet of the GCR bridge, but removal of the wall and girdering over the ventilator provided an opportunity to bring the entrance forward in front of the general building line, giving it greater prominence to attract passengers, including patrons of the nearby Lord's Cricket Ground. Rebuilding was authorised in July 1923, the letting of two small flats on the first floor and shops calculated to provide 5½ per cent on the outlay. Garages built over the platforms produced a ten per cent return on their cost from January 1925[13].

Clark provided the new St John's Wood Road with his now standard white faience frontage containing an entrance hall widened from 11–15ft, a booking office with five windows, a remodelled buffet and shops either side. At rail level the station was renovated, its staircases lined with tiles. The scheme was completed by October 1925, but after the MCC had refused to allow the Metropolitan to enlarge the ticket office it had maintained at Lord's Cricket Ground since June 1892, a further two ticket windows were added in 1926.

Simultaneously with St John's Wood Road, Willesden Green was extensively rebuilt, including electric lighting throughout, renovation of platforms and tiling of the concrete building on the island platform as well as a completely new structure at street level. In June 1923 Selbie had told the board that although this station occupied a commanding site, it was of 'very mean appearance' and he promised an eight per cent return on the cost. With a frontage of over 100ft, Clark was able to make the most of his white faience style in elevations which included two wide entrances with extensive canopies. This building was given seven shops, a kiosk and a bookstall, ladies' room, booking and parcels offices with lift to the platforms for the latter, and cloakroom. Beyond the ticket barriers, there was a circulating area occupying much of the bridge across the tracks, from which three staircases led down to the four platforms. Clark considered a first floor essential to 'give the station prominence' and this was used for three residential flats. His clock, set in a diamond frame echoing the station

Plate 29 Partners in the improved services of 1925 to Rickmansworth and beyond: H class 4–4–4T and electric loco No 19 posed at Neasden, 1925 (*photographer unknown*)

Plate 30 G class loco No 95 *Robert H. Selbie*, at Neasden about 1928 (*photographer unknown, courtesy London Underground Railway Society*)

Plate 31 The ultimate in Metropolitan steam: the handsome K class 2–6–4T design of 1925, No 114 at Neasden c1927 (*photographer unknown, courtesy J.H. Price*)

Plate 32 K class loco No 116 on an Up train well loaded with bricks for suburban housebuilding, south of Wendover c1928 (*H. Gordon Tidey*)

nameboard motif, projected at right angles from the frontage and was the first of a series on rebuilt stations. Completed at a cost of £31,000 (excluding platform lengthening carried out at the same time) the works were finished in September 1925.

Aldgate was described by Selbie as 'certainly at the present time the most unattractive of our City stations', a statement which shamed the board into agreeing to reconstruction in two stories in the white faience design. The frontage was given a 20ft wide central entrance under an illuminated canopy, two shops, a Lyons' tea shop and a buffet for Spiers & Pond. Inside there was a 20×55ft booking hall, parcels and left luggage offices and a ladies' room, with mosaic tiling and teak interior finish in the main areas. Here, as at the other new stations, the lettering on the frontage and canopy was of standard pattern specially designed by Clark. A large circulating area was provided at the half level between street and platforms, served by two staircases to each platform and a 20ft wide staircase up to the booking hall. Electric lighting, of which about 80 per cent was fed from the traction supply, was fitted throughout the station and sidings. All work, including renovating at rail level, was completed by the middle of 1926 at a total cost of £27,438. The signal box here was rebuilt at the same time, using the old Baker Street power frame.

A comprehensive reconstruction of Edgware Road station was related in part to the scheme for a deep level relief tube line to Kilburn mentioned earlier. A complete new layout and resignalling was undertaken in addition to reprovision of the passenger building. Earlier proposals had envisaged construction of an arcade to a new entrance on Edgware Road itself, supplementing the existing entrances in Chapel Street and Marylebone Road, but this feature was now dropped as unnecessary because it was expected that the new line would pick up much of the local traffic along the Edgware Road.

Work at rail level was started first. The old 50ft-span glazed overall roof was taken down, the Lisson Street bridge was then rebuilt in steel and retaining walls constructed to provide the space for the new layout. This was to consist of two island platforms and four through roads (main lines on the outside) instead of the former Up and Down running lines with a terminal siding between at the west end and a bay on the Down side. Two sidings south of the Down Main were also included in the new layout. An overbridge was set in the centre of the new platforms to connect them to the Marylebone Road entrance.

Resignalling, with provision for the proposed junction with the relief tubes just west of the station, was undertaken by Westinghouse Brake & Saxby Signalling Co, who also supplied train destination indicators to be worked from the signalbox, one on the concourse and one on each set of platforms. These indicators included stations to Verney Junction and Uxbridge in expectation of the opening of the relief line, but the panels for these destinations were removed to stores in 1927. The all-electric power locking frame, with 35 levers (four spare and two for the relief line junction) controlled Praed Street Junction 300yd west of the station, allowing closure of the box and with it London's first all electric power frame. Signalling current was at the new standard of 440 V ac and track circuits from Bishop's Road and Praed Street to a point east of Edgware Road were converted from dc to 33⅓ cycles ac. The Ministry of Transport Inspecting Officer was once again impressed:

> The improvement effected by the Company at this station is very creditable to all concerned and the facilities to meet the dense traffic, which I understand now amounts to 1,088 trains in 20 hours, and will be increased when the Willesden Green relief line is open, are worthy of commendation.

Although the rail level works were not entirely completed until the end of 1926, operation of the new signal box and a train service based on the new facilities began on 1 November. This gave a 7½ minute interval on the Inner Circle (now once again entirely operated on weekdays by the Metropolitan, with 14 five-car trains) and an all-round timing of 52½ minutes. The new service, operated from 7 am to 11 pm, was designed to obviate the delays at Gloucester Road and South Kensington which had been experienced with the previous six minute interval and 48-minute all-round timing. On Sundays, four-car trains ran every ten minutes round the Circle, taking 50 minutes. From the same date, the MDR projected its six Putney Bridge trains from High Street Kensington to Edgware Road at 7½ minute intervals, giving that section a 3½ minute service instead of six minutes. On Sundays, the Putney trains worked every 15 minutes. Following these changes, the MDR signal box at High Street was shared by both companies, allowing closure of the old Metropolitan box. East of Edgware Road, the six minute Hammersmith & City service continued to supplement the Circle trains, whilst Edgware Road remained the eastern terminus of the 20/29 minute service from Kensington (Addison Road) (now Olympia). In the same timetable (1 November 1926) 30 trains a day were extended from Baker Street East to and from City stations and a five minute off-peak service was given to stations between Baker Street and Swiss Cottage.

Street level work at Edgware Road station was delayed by plans to extend Harrow Road into Marylebone Road, a scheme which did not in the event materialise until after World War 2. Clark provided his now familiar white faience elevations in two stories adapted to the corner site at Chapel Street/Burne Street, with a canopied entrance leading past a buffet and tea room to a small concourse at the west end of the platforms, where there was a wall booking office. In all there were four shops and three kiosks, with residential flats on the first floor. Seven garages were also built in Lisson Street, where blue brick and flettons were thought good enough for the rather sleazy neighbourhood. The new surface building was opened on 19 January 1928. It was estimated that annual rent income combined with savings in signalling wages and increases in through bookings were providing an eight per cent return on the total outlay of £118,000 by the end of 1929.

Although well-sited at the convergence of the busy Belsize and Finchley Roads, the entrance to Swiss Cottage was obscured from passing traffic in Finchley Road. To remedy this, it was decided in January 1927 to form a new entrance leading to a 16ft wide arcade with nine shops and three kiosks, using space over the line. A remodelled buffet, three flats above and electric lighting would complete the scheme. Negotiations with the local authorities delayed a start to early 1928 when it was agreed to add a further storey containing a fourth flat in a mansard roof. Clark gave the old building a new frontage in white faience to match that of the new flats and shops. All was finished on 30 September 1929.

Selbie told the board in July 1926 that Notting Hill Gate was in need of reconstruction to bring it more prominently to the attention of the public in a road 'infested with buses'. He regarded its long dark staircase from street to platforms as 'a distinct detriment'. Clark's new building had wider stairs, a booking hall at intermediate level and additional shops and flats, the faience frontage containing an entrance widened from eight to ten feet under a large canopy. The entrance hall was carried through to Uxbridge Street. Three floors were built over the line, each with ten residential flats. Electric lighting was installed. Completed in mid-1928, the new works provided a net return of around seven per cent on the £23,500 cost.

Old Street station was shared by the GN&CR and the C&SLR. Here, from 19 August 1925, passengers used two Waygood-Otis escalators for which the Metropolitan had paid 25 per cent of the £76,400 cost of the installation, this representing the approximate proportion of GN&CR user. Five liftmen were saved and a Passimeter ticket office installed at the same time gave further staff economies. Four years later, the street building was entirely reconstructed to the designs of the Underground Group's architect, Stanley Heaps, the Metropolitan again meeting a quarter of the £23,584 outlay.

Another GN&CR station receiving new facilities was Moorgate. With the completion of an office block over it for the Anglo-Persian Oil Co in 1924, a new entrance and booking office were provided, together with a large amount of retiling.

Clark's last work on central area stations was at the adjoining Great Portland Street and Euston Square, in 1929–31. At the former, his elegant building for the island site included a Marylebone Road entrance 'to help meet severe bus competition'. There were also four shops and a motor showroom and offices on the first floor for Stanley Hunt Ltd. This firm required car washing facilities which were provided on an open site built over the line to the west of the station. For an expenditure of £27,650, including electric lighting, additional income and savings in staff wages totalled £3,000 a year or 11 per cent. A further £14,934 was spent at the same time in lengthening the platforms to take eight-car trains. All was finished on 28 June 1930.

At Euston Square, the station entrance works were confined to erection of two small pavilions either side of the street, set back to the new building line. As some compensation for the loss of 'prominence' advertising the station's presence, the LCC allowed canopies over each entrance as well as a refuge in the centre of the road embellished with an illuminated sign carrying the name of the railway[14]. Beneath the road, a new bridge was built over the line. Although this had limited headroom, it enabled a single booking office to be erected replacing the separate Up and Down offices either side of the road, which saved two clerks and two ticket collectors. Together with lettings from new properties formed on the south side, this economy returned £1,800 a year on the £30,000 cost (six per cent). Platform lengthening here involved the closure of Euston Road for six months to all vehicular traffic, a measure which also facilitated work on the new station.

SELBIE'S SWANSONG AT BAKER STREET

As bullrushes, birch and willow trees, nettles, wild fuchsia and camomile flourished on the abandoned Baker Street hotel works, the Metropolitan cast around for alternative ways of developing the site. Agreement was reached in March 1921 with Sir Oswald Stoll, who undertook to erect cinemas and a restaurant on the west side and a film industry centre on the east, depositing £16,000 as surety.

Whilst waiting for Stoll, the railway company completed the remaining 200ft of the Portland stone station frontage eastwards across the parcels depot. To add importance to the whole, Clark designed a colonnaded central *porte-cochère* surmounted by three clocks in gables, which was placed on an axial line with East (now Chiltern) Street. These new works were completed on 17 March 1924.

But alas, Stoll was unable to muster the necessary finance for his project. As no start had been made by December 1924, the agreement with him lapsed, the Metropolitan pocketed his deposit and re-possessed the site.

Clark and Selbie then put their heads together and in January 1925 Selbie presented the board with what was to be the most ambitious of his many schemes for maximising the commercial value of the railway's properties. His proposal was that the railway company should retain direct control of development on the site, using the powers given in the company's 1906 act to build over its stations and lines properties which could be let for various purposes. Selbie noted that works of this type had raised the railway's income from commercial rents from £66,903 in 1908 to £171,087 in 1924. Taking a deep breath, he suggested that the difference at Baker Street would be one 'of degree only'. He saw no reason why the Metropolitan should not embark on an adequate rebuilding scheme of its own, 'worthy of the importance of the position and to mark the headquarters of a not insignificant company'. Clark had advised against another hotel scheme, suggesting this would necessarily take up a large ground floor area which would restrict future expansion of the railway station facilities. Instead, it was suggested there should be flats and shops which would not only give a continuing return on the investment but the tenants would be likely to provide more revenue by using the railway to travel to and from the City or between their flats and country houses or golf courses. Plans for a huge building containing shops, large restaurant and a dance hall on the ground floor with numerous residential flats above were prepared by Clark[15]. On the outside there was only a limited modification of the hotel elevations prepared 15 or more years earlier by Frank Sherrin in a style described at that time as 'a free treatment of Italian Renaissance'[16].

In what was to prove an over-optimistic estimate, Selbie forecast an annual return of about £45,300, just over nine per cent on an estimated cost of £500,000. To reinforce his case, he produced a statement from the friendly neighbourhood estate agent (J. G. Head, of MRCE and Baker Street) affirming that property values in Marylebone and Baker Street were moving upwards as the area evolved from residential to commercial. Impressed, the board agreed to detailed planning. By mid-1927 Higgs and Hill had been selected to construct the building, which was to be called Chiltern Court[17]. After considering funding through a separate company or by issue of Surplus Lands Committee stock, the decision was that the railway should raise its own capital by issuing debenture stock. Preliminary loans were obtained from the National Provincial Bank at 5 per cent.

Clark had included what he described as a 'general store' on three floors fronting the northern end of Baker Street, but when Harrods', Barkers' and the Army & Navy looked into the idea, they all decided it was not for them. As no other taker could be found, the number of small shops and flats was increased to absorb the allocated space.

Work started on 2 August 1927, the early tasks including clearance of the abundant plant and tree growth, erection of a huge crane and the sinking of two artesian wells to supply boiler and drinking water for the new building. An electrified six-wagon siding was laid through the five foot thick retaining wall of Thames ballast and Portland cement west of Baker Street East no 1 platform into the basement area of the new building. From 1 September 1927 this track was used for bringing in crane parts, building materials and machinery, also for outward trains removing debris. On completion of the building, the siding was retained to bring in boiler coal and remove ash and refuse. Access to it was through a two-lever ground frame released by Annett's key and a king lever in the signal box.

Many railway works were rolled up with the Chiltern Court scheme. These included: extension of the parcels yard and cloakrooms; central heating for railway premises and offices fed from the Chiltern Court boiler plant; enlargement of the station circulating area and booking hall (completed 12 October 1930); provision of a general waiting room; enlargement and extension of platforms 1 and 2 in the East station to take eight-car trains; two additional passageways from these platforms to the Up Circle platform (these platform works all completed 23 September 1929); centralisation of the telephone exchange; cleaning down and restoration of the station frontage and terrace wall along Marylebone Road; and a new Circle Line entrance at the west end of the cab approach (completed 28 June 1930). With these railway works, the total project cost came out at £720,435 (or £834,663 if the abortive expenditure on the initial hotel project were to be included).

The massive mansard-roofed building, rising seven stories above the ground floor and mezzanine, offered a 400ft frontage of Portland stone to Marylebone Road, 300ft to the northern part of Baker Street and 200ft to Allsop Place. Its distinctly Edwardian elevations, faintly echoing Mewès & Davis' Ritz Hotel and Norman Shaw's Piccadilly Hotel, earned muted commendation from the architectural press, one writer commenting:

In architectural character this immense block will strike a harmonious note in the solid symphony of Marylebone road . . . design will stand up well in this setting . . . avoids the extreme severity which has characterised many of our latest essays in flat-building and, on the other hand, it avoids the banality of the picturesque[18].

With its suggestions of Edwardian comfort, solidity and reliability, pride in commercial success and all the highest attainments of the conservative petit-bourgeois, Chiltern Court somehow symbolised the character of the railway and its management. No wonder John Betjeman was later to enthuse over it. It was made to look positively historic when only five years later, Joseph Emberton's great block of flats, Dorset House, went up nearby and no-one would now guess it to be contemporary with Charles Holden's 55 Broadway headquarters building for the Underground Group.

With much of the building work completed, some of the first tenants were in possession at the end of September 1929, but the interior was not fully ready for another year. The residential accommodation ranged from ten-room 'mansion flats' at £1,000 a year to three-room 'bachelor flats' at £250, these rents including rates, taxes, heating and water. There were 198 units in all, plus a block of 30 bedrooms for maids[19]. By November 1931, 161 flats were let, producing together with shop and business rentals an income of £42,811 a year or about six per cent on the total expenditure including the railway improvements mentioned above. Advertising was largely in the hands of the railway commercial manager's department, which issued a special postcard and descriptive booklet as well as taking two pages of *Metro-Land* to extol its virtues. Early tenants included the authors H. G. Wells and Arnold Bennett, the latter taking two large flats but living less than a year to enjoy them. Another was the artist Edward McKnight Kauffer, who designed posters for the Underground but not for the Metropolitan. Tenants were soon complaining about night noise from car parking, from rowdy parties at Chiltern Hall, from whistling locomotives, from the shouting of staff and banging of carriage doors and milk churns. There were also problems with 'red hot' water and discoloured drinking water from the wells[20]. Chimneys smoked, dog lovers clashed with dog haters; and one tenant was asked to leave because his children were too noisy.

Some 45 staff were engaged, including six lift boys soon adorned in 'buttons' and pill box hats and a head porter in full footman's livery to flatter the *nouveaux-riches* tenants. Equipped with a police whistle, a solitary porter guarded them all at night.

On the ground floor was the 250-seat, 4,000 sq ft Chiltern Court

Restaurant, formally opened by the deputy chairman, Sir Clarendon Hyde, with a celebratory luncheon on 15 November 1929. This had a fine ceiling of painted plaster mouldings picked out in gold, with cove cornices embellished with the arms of the railway and those of the counties and some of the places it served[21]. There were fluted pilasters, a musicians' gallery and a dado of light fumed oak. Lay lights with concealed electric bulbs offered a diffused glow above the table lamps. Nearby was Chiltern Hall, opened on 29 September 1930, to provide 4,500 sq ft of space for functions, equipped with stage for cabarets and bands, a foyer, crush hall, reception room and cloakrooms.

Great difficulty was experienced in finding a firm to rent and manage these facilities. In the end Selbie exercised mild blackmail with Spiers & Pond, threatening to determine their remunerative tenancies of station refreshment rooms unless they took over the restaurant and hall. They succumbed, taking a 21 year lease from 29 September 1929 at £2,500 a year (with percentages for the Metropolitan of receipts over £25,000 a year). This proved to be a disaster for the unfortunate firm, who were soon complaining of a 'continual heavy loss amounting in all to many thousands'. The Metropolitan ascribed this to the fact that flat tenants preferred to undertake their own catering (each flat had a fully-equipped kitchen), also suggesting unkindly that whilst Spiers & Pond might be skilful at the station buffet business, running a large scale restaurant and a function hall was outside its experience. The firm responded by putting the blame elsewhere. In the middle of 1932 its general manager alleged that losses since opening the restaurant totalled £10,000 and trade was still declining. He sought redecoration and a reduction in rent, criticising Clark's décor, of which he said 'whilst no doubt of great artistic merit, [it] is not what is wanted in these times when the tendency is towards considerably brighter colours and stronger light'. It was agreed to remit £300 rent and spend £1,500 in modernising Clark's backward looking decorations of 1929, which John Betjeman later mistakenly but understandably dated at 1913.

NEW ROLLING STOCK

With 1918 passenger journeys almost a third higher than the 1913 total (159m against 122m) many and constant were the complaints of overcrowding in peak hours. Much thought was given to the rolling stock question, in particular to the interior layout of the electric cars, leading to the production of several mock-ups at Neasden. The

Metropolitan Carriage, Wagon and Finance Co were then asked to produce a re-designed six car train from existing vehicles. This emerged from Saltley Works as an elliptical-roofed stock with five swing doors each side of the trailers (four each side of the motor cars) opening into draught-screened vestibules of what was in effect an open saloon. The motor cars had 41 seats and a small luggage compartment, the First Class trailers 44, Third trailers 58, making a train total of 292 compared with 268 on the older stock. Train doors were abolished but passengers could use the luggage compartment doors. 'Steadying rails' replaced the traditional arm-ache inducing straps for standing passengers. This so-called 'Hustle Train', exhibited to press and public at Baker Street on 18 December 1919, stirred some interest but was not perpetuated as in practice it proved slow to load and unload. Longer distance travellers also showed an obstinate preference for the cosiness of compartments.

With the delivery of seven more six-car 'Dreadnought' trains by Metropolitan Carriage in 1921 for steam-hauled services at £20,214 per train, 30 older steam compartment stock trailers were converted for electric working. These were delivered between December 1920 and the end of 1921. Two more followed in 1924. Instead of more of the ill-starred 'Hustle Train', 20 new motor cars and 39 trailers were manufactured by Metropolitan Carriage at their Ashbury works to a saloon design basically similar to the 1913 stock, the principal difference being in the door layout. The trailers, 50ft 10in over underframes, had three sets of equally-spaced, 4ft wide double-sliding manual doors each side whilst the motors had two sets, with a further set of slightly narrower double doors next to the luggage compartment. A 'steadying rail' was again fitted instead of what one newspaper called the 'barbarous straps'. Delivered from December 1920, this partly steel-bodied stock was to spend most of its time on the Circle, where it enabled trains to be lengthened from four to five cars. The motor cars seated 37, First control trailers 45, and Third trailers 50. The First driving trailer exhibited at the Wembley Exhibition of 1924–5 was of similar design and was to be the last open saloon type trailer built for the Metropolitan.

More compartment stock was needed for the Watford and Rickmansworth electric services, but initially there was not enough for all trains and the continued use of saloon stock brought strong complaints from Watford, Northwood and Pinner. This new compartment stock, delivered between June 1927 and early 1933 and collectively known as 'MV' (built by Metropolitan Carriage & Wagon and fitted with Metropolitan Vickers equipment) or 'MW' (built by

Birmingham Railway Carriage & Wagon with GEC electrical equipment), eventually totalled 131 units[22]. After the formation of London Transport, it became known as 'T' stock. The Birmingham-built cars were supplied from 1930 onwards.

Completion of the first deliveries made it possible to withdraw most of the open saloons north of Harrow from 1 July 1927 but they were not eliminated altogether until 1930. In making a case for further cars in January 1929 Selbie referred to the 'exceedingly unpopular' use of open saloons for longer journeys, adding that their continuing use in slack hour trains 'militates against us, particularly during the middle hours of the day, when ladies are travelling to and from town.'

With the later additions, this stock was eventually marshalled into eight-car trains. The early driving motor cars had four 275 hp motors but when P. de Broeck & Polimont were asked to report on the railway's electrical equipment in 1931 they criticised these 1927–30 compartment motor cars as overpowered and unnecessarily costly in current consumption. In explanation it was said that they were ordered with extension of electrification to Amersham in mind, and had to be beefy enough to take a loaded eight-car train up the six miles of 1 in 100/110 into Amersham. It had also been noticed that the existing 200 hp cars had been running very heavily overloaded, in some cases up to one third. Some notice was however taken of the criticism; the 1932 batch had 235 hp, and the last (1933) batch 210 hp motors, thanks to a feature we shall mention later. All motor cars had five Third Class compartments each, seating five aside in addition to luggage and guard's compartments next to the control compartment and driver's cab. Trailers used with these 'MV' and 'MW' cars were partly newly-built, partly converted from steam stock. Driving trailers had eight Third Class compartments, First trailers seven, very comfortably upholstered, and Third trailers nine. Some cars were fitted with buckeye couplers and Westinghouse air brakes. All control gear was of the electro-pneumatic unit switch type, arranged for automatic acceleration.

The Birmingham-built stock of 1930–33 had steel-sheeted sides and steel roofing with mouldings painted on. Train lighting with improved brilliance was at 600V dc.

For the first time in a production order, ten motor cars of the 1930 batch, with the associated trailers, were experimentally fitted with roller bearings to all axles. Increased reliability (elimination of hot boxes), reduced current consumption and lower maintenance costs were promised. As the experience with these cars was generally successful, all 18 motor cars and 47 trailers of the 1933 delivery were equipped with Timken bearings, the reduction in frictional losses enabling GEC WT 545 motors with the reduced rating of 210 hp to be fitted. There was one problem: should a driver absent-mindedly release his brakes at a station stop where the gradient was close to the permitted maximum of 1 in 264, he was apt to find himself half a car length on his way and accelerating rapidly.

In addition to the new electric stock, Neasden resumed fitting of centre doors to the earlier saloon stock in 1919. This stock was the subject of a quaint feature in 1931–32, when its interiors were fitted out with penny-in-the-slot chocolate machines.

As the longer distance trains became heavier with the growth of traffic, more power was needed to haul them over the electrified section to Rickmansworth. It was therefore proposed in 1919 to rebuild all 20 electric locomotives, uprating their 800 hp motors to provide 1,200 hp per locomotive. The contract was given to Metro-politan-Vickers but in 1921–3 the Metropolitan received virtually new machines, with 35ft bodies built in the Vickers gun works at Barrow in Furness. The reason for this was that when the first of the 1904/1906 locomotives arrived at Vickers for rebuilding it was found that they required so much alteration to the underframes that the balance of 15 which followed were constructed from scratch. Vickers was allowed to take the old locomotives or their equivalent as scrap, this being the most economical way of completing the job.

All-electric automatic multiple-unit control was fitted and the new electrical equipment was arranged centrally down the middle of the body to allow ease of access. With their rounded-end 'wind-cutter' cabs, these handsome machines came to epitomise the modern Metro-politan of the 1920s and early 1930s, receiving added prestige and romance when given names in 1927[23]. Whilst mainly employed on the Extension Line hauling trains for Amersham and Chesham and beyond, they were also to be seen at the head of GWR suburban stock between Bishop's Road and the City, on freight trains to and from the Metropolitan goods depot at Farringdon, and humiliatingly, on the Chiltern Court coal and rubbish trains[24].

To cope with the increased numbers of electric cars handled at Neasden, an overhead conductor was installed in 1916 to move cars within a large car shed which had been completed two years earlier. The steam shunting engine formerly employed on this task was then sold. After the end of 1914, almost all the electric stock could be kept under cover at night, ensuring a proper examination in all weathers with consequent reduction in service failures. Further electric stock accommodation was built at Neasden in 1932–3 after the board had been informed that '1.65 miles' of new cars had been acquired since 1924.

As steam locomotive power had not been kept up-to-date, the engines were too small for the increased size and weight of trains north of Harrow, where they were being worked uneconomically at too high a pressure. This situation was corrected by the acquisition of three final classes of steam locomotive between 1915 and 1925. The first were the 'G' class inside cylinder 0-6-4T delivered between November 1915 and March 1916 by the Yorkshire Engine Co and numbered 94–7. The first two cost £3,621 each, the others £3,956. Weight in working order was 73 tons and the driving wheels were 5ft 9in in diameter. For the first time, superheating apparatus (Robinson's 18-element pattern) was fitted. As they were to be used for the best longer-distance Pullman trains they bore names on their leading driving wheel splashers: *Lord Aberconway, Robert H. Selbie, Charles Jones* and *Brill*.

After a brief hour of glory, these engines were ousted from the faster passenger trains by eight outside cylinder 4-4-4T ('H' class) obtained from Kerr, Stuart & Co of Stoke on Trent for £11,575 each. Designed by the Metropolitan's Charles Jones, these rather attractive machines arrived at Quainton Road from the makers between 4 October 1920 and 10 June 1921. Numbered 103–110, each weighed 77 tons in working order and their driving wheels, on a rigid wheelbase of 7ft 9in, were 5ft 9in diameter. They were designed to haul trains weighing up to 250 tons, negotiating curves down to 4.5 chains radius. When they came into service, eight 'C' class 0-4-4T and 'D' Class 2-4-0T were disposed of.

From 1 January 1922 following the introduction of the 'H' class, an accelerated timetable was introduced showing reductions in running time between the changeover point at Wembley Park and Aylesbury of up to six minutes. The best trains now reached Northwood in 27 minutes, Rickmansworth in 30 minutes and Amersham in 43 minutes from Baker Street.

By 1924 the limitations of existing steam loco power were restricting freight train length to 20 wagons. After electrification to Rickmansworth, the plan was to run fewer but longer freights. More powerful machines were therefore sought. George Hally, appointed chief mechanical engineer and works manager in July 1923[25], discovered that bargain basement items were available from the George Cohen & Armstrong Disposal Co. As a means of providing continuing employment at Woolwich Arsenal after the end of World War 1 the workers there had been given in 1920 the task of building 50 locomotives and additional components to a 2-6-0 design of 1916 by the SECR's chief mechanical engineer, R. E. L. Maunsell. Using the surplus components, Sir W. G. Armstrong Whitworth's works at Scotswood (Newcastle) built for the Metropolitan six powerful and elegant outside cylinder 2-6-4T at a cost of £5,000 each. Designated 'K', these were delivered in January and February 1925, replacing six 'A' class. Their weight in working order was 87.4 tons and their driving wheels were 5ft 6in diameter. For the operation of a revised freight service using these engines from 6 April 1925, the Metropolitan purchased three more 20ft brake vans, making a total stock of nine 20-ton vans (all secondhand) and 20 10-ton vans.

Two miscellaneous acquisitions in the 1920s were related to safety and accidents. A 20-ton Cowans-Sheldon steam breakdown crane was delivered in September 1925 to replace the existing ten ton hand crane. In 1930 this new crane was adapted to lift 30 tons at 16ft to make it capable of handling the latest electric stock.

In 1924 the Metropolitan bought 26 short ladders, two for each steam train, to facilitate detraining of passengers in tunnel emergencies. Emergency tools had been carried in guards' vans of steam stock since 1914, a belated conformance with practice on main lines and a Board of Trade recommendation of 1911.

SIGNALLING ADVANCES

Some signalling improvements have already been noticed when discussing new works. Others can now be mentioned. After some ten years of service, the first (1906) section of automatic signalling between Praed Street (Paddington) and South Kensington, with its depression bars and treadles, was not operating satisfactorily, producing several alarming instances of two or more trains on one section. From 22 June 1919 standard track circuiting was introduced throughout this part of the Circle.

As wartime labour shortages made it increasingly difficult to supply fogmen, experiments were undertaken from December 1915 between Willesden Green and Neasden using fog repeater lamps, switched on in fog at the approaches to the normal signals. This was found to improve working, reducing the delays of 15–18 minutes experienced in fog between Finchley Road and Wembley Park. Fog repeaters were installed throughout from Baker Street to Harrow by 31 March 1921. They subsequently became a standard feature on open-air sections of the Underground.

To eliminate delays caused by the growing suburban traffic, the double line between Wembley Park and Harrow was re-equipped with automatic signalling by the Westinghouse Brake & Saxby Signal Co at a cost of £1,529. The new installation, with its upper quadrant semaphores, came into operation on Sunday 31 January 1926.

Using the Development (Loan Guarantees & Grants) Act, 1929, the Metropolitan obtained a Treasury grant of interest for a £9,700 scheme of resignalling on the Uxbridge branch, the only electrified section which remained signalled on the manual lock-and-block system. Westinghouse Brake & Saxby completed this task in 1930 just as housing development along the line was beginning to take off. The new signals between Rayners Lane and Uxbridge, coming into operation on 20 July and 24 August 1930, were of the long range three-aspect searchlight type controlled by track circuits and they increased the line capacity to 30 trains an hour each way. Signal boxes at Rayners Lane, Eastcote and Ruislip and Uxbridge were retained for junction and freight yard movements.

A rather unusual signalling device was designed by William Willox, the Metropolitan's chief engineer, for installation in the City Widened Lines Clerkenwell tunnel in 1918. This smoky section was a dangerous place for men working on the track, and a particularly unpleasant incident in 1916 had caused the Board of Trade to suggest that warning devices of some kind should be installed. Willox's solution was a galvanised iron tube knocked by small hammers attached to electro-magnets when an oncoming train operated a depression bar. The noise produced was said to resemble the whistling of birds, whilst the vibration of the tube could be clearly felt with the hand. Another depression bar operated a klaxon horn should a freight train split, causing its wagons or vans to run back down the steep gradients either side of the Ray Street Grid Iron.

In 1921, A. F. Bound, the GCR signal engineer, installed Britain's first remotely-operated points at Quainton Road. This electrical system, in combination with track circuiting, allowed the closure of Quainton Road Junction box, with control from Quainton Road Station box, from 27 November that year.

MATTERS OF POWER

Neasden power station was not solely devoted to feeding Metropolitan needs. Since 1904 it had supplied electricity to the Northwood Electric Light & Power Co via Eastcote, Ruislip and Ickenham, and since 1921 to the Wembley Park Estate Company and golf club. Much more important, because it was eventually to influence the level of plant installed at Neasden, was the sale of current to the Underground Group. This began modestly with an agreement of 14 December 1916 which provided for supply to the London Electric Railway, the C&SLR and the MDR in the event of temporary failure of lifts, escalators and other plant. The approach had been made by these companies and the necessary connections were made at South Kensington, Baker Street, Euston Square, King's Cross and Moorgate at their expense. This arrangement led to a 1926 agreement for interchange of traction current through the adjacent substations at Baker Street[26] under which the commitment was limited to a maximum 5,000 kW, the minimum annual purchase of the London Electric Railway to be 10m units. A report to the Metropolitan board of July 1927 noted that the LER was 'practically dependent on us for current for the Bakerloo Line' for which they were paying £4,500 a month.

By 1919 the heavy traffic which had followed the end of the war brought the existing power plant to a continuous 25 per cent overload for three to four hours each day, momentarily rising to 50 per cent. This situation was corrected by the installation in January 1923 of a Metropolitan-Vickers high pressure turbo-alternator set with jet condenser, providing an output of 12,000 kW. Six John Thomson water tube boilers came with the new plant, each fitted with two Bennis forced-draught chain grate stokers, all sited in a new section of the building. A Kennicott water-softening plant of 40,000 gallons an hour capacity was also provided. This new equipment, costing £247,873 with the building work, was able on its own to handle the slack hours load from 10.30 am to 4.30 pm, in itself a considerable economy. As the original switch gear had been renewed by the General Electric Co and a new switch house opened in April 1923, the Neasden power station was now fairly up to date but its total capacity of 35,000 kW was still not enough to take the full peak hour load once the Rickmansworth and Watford electrification was completed.

For this, one of the original generators was replaced with a 15,000 kW unit, operative from 8 April 1926. As more cooling was then required, spray equipment was installed over the storage lake, this giving, with the existing eight duplex towers, a total capacity of 2.65m gallons an hour. Traffic continued to grow and with a peak hour demand for 32,000 kW in 1927 it was considered there was insufficient margin of safety should one of the larger units have to be taken out of service. Furthermore, the remaining 5,000 kW generators were now old and uneconomic. A Metropolitan-Vickers 20,000 kW turbo generator and condensing plant were ordered to replace another of the original machines at a cost of £89,340, and this new plant came into service on 22 May 1928. There followed in 1929–30 a set of six International Combustion Co high pressure boilers compatible with the new generators but able to run in parallel with the Thomson boilers of 1923.

When the agreement for supplying the Underground came to an end in September 1929, an arrangement was reached under which an emergency supply up to 25,000 kW was guaranteed, provided a minimum of 20m units a year were purchased. But the expanding Underground was hungry for external sources of power to back up its Lots Road plant, and a continuous high tension supply was afforded to its Hendon substation from 20 June 1930. A further agreement of January 1932 provided for Neasden to supply additional power for the Piccadilly Line western extensions and two substations on the Golders Green-Edgware line for 25 years from 1 September 1932, an arrangement which guaranteed an additional purchase of 30m units a year. Capital for the necessary plant was to be supplied by the Underground, on which the Metropolitan would pay 5 per cent interest. Needless to say, the Metropolitan always ensured this outside supply was priced to secure a useful profit.

In connection with the post-1929 requirements of the Underground Co, the penultimate 5,000 kW generator was replaced from 26 February 1931 by a 20,000 kW Metropolitan-Vickers unit capable of producing 25,000 kW under overload. Seven more high pressure boilers, four more cooling towers and coal and ash handling plant were purchased and an additional artesian well sunk between 1930 and 1932. The 1932 plan for new plant to meet the total requirement of 50m units a year guaranteed by the Underground was of course soon overtaken by the formation of the London Passenger Transport Board and was by no means complete at the time the Metropolitan Railway lost its individual identity in July 1933.

Over the years, mainly by improvements to the plant, coal consumption at Neasden had been reduced from an extravagant 5.73 and 4.31 pounds (2.6kg and 1.95kg) per kilowatt/hour in 1905 and 1906 to 2.25 (1.02kg) in 1927.

Substation equipment had been further enhanced in 1917–21. At Moorgate a fifth machine, of 1,500 kW six-phase capacity, had been installed in 1917, partly for the requirements of the GN&CR, but after a fire at this substation on 25 June 1922, in which the original three 1,200 kW three phase sets were destroyed, together with switchgear, three more 1,500 kW six phase units were installed in 1924. Finchley Road gave up one of its original 800 kW machines to Ickenham in

January 1921, receiving instead a 1,500 kW six phase set. One of the Ickenham 800 kW three phase transformers was moved to Neasden substation in July 1921.

Voltage drop between the widely-spaced Finchley Road and Neasden substations was creating peak hour problems by 1922, when it reached 200 V, slowing the trains and eroding the carrying capacity of the line. In an attempt to avoid the cost of a further substation, the conductor rails were crossbonded to equalise the supply of current especially on gradients, and this had been carried through as far as Harrow by 1927. Meanwhile more drastic remedies had been judged unavoidable. A new £35,000 substation was opened at Willesden Green on 23 May 1924, equipped with three 1,200 kW rotaries. Harrow substation was extended by the addition of a 1,500 kW machine, which came into use on 24 October 1924. From this time Harrow was a distribution station, receiving a bulk supply from the Neasden power house and controlling its distribution to the new substations for the Watford and Rickmansworth electrification.

On the Uxbridge branch, in anticipation of additional traffic from building development, the 4½ mile gap between Ickenham and Harrow substations was closed by providing an automatic substation at Eastcote fitted with two 1,200 kW rotaries obtained secondhand from the LMSR. This came into use on 3 March 1930 as housebuilding along the line was beginning to accelerate. Another ex-LMSR 1,200 kW machine went to Gloucester Road, Neasden substation then receiving the latter's 800 kW unit to boost its output. By 1931, substation overloading had become a matter of concern and the problem was to be dealt with in relation to the requirements for the new Stanmore branch, as we shall see in the next chapter.

15

SUNSET OVER METRO-LAND

Enough has been said to establish that during the 1910s and 1920s Selbie's drive and ability had dominated the board, his initiative overshadowing all others. It is hardly an exaggeration to state that he personified the Metropolitan Railway during this period, the final and most important stage of its development. His sudden death on 17 May 1930 after almost 22 years as general manager therefore came as a brutal loss, the more so as doubts were beginning to emerge as to whether independent existence of the company could be sustained in the face of the government's determination to bring about the coordination of London passenger transport. Yet, it must be said that whilst Selbie almost certainly would have fought doggedly to the end for autonomy, it is unlikely that even he would have been able to prevail, given the strength of the tide.

At first the board was uncertain what to do, and whilst it cogitated, decided two days after Selbie's death to set up a 'general management committee'. This consisted of John Sloane Anderson (chief legal adviser)[1], W. H. Holt (traffic superintendent) and John Wardle (commercial manager), their remit being to 'temporarily carry on the duties of general manager'. From the first meeting on 20 May, Anderson was in the chair. It proved a most unsatisfactory device[2] and in March 1931, with the company's future still very much in doubt, Anderson was made general manager in addition to his existing responsibilities. One feels some sympathy for this modest lawyer, almost smothered by Selbie's mantle, obliged to steer the railway through its final unsettling phase, with little or no help from anyone and perhaps some barely-concealed jealousy and hostility from the professional railwaymen around him.

METROPOLITAN; OR LONDON TRANSPORT?

In choosing Anderson, first as chairman of the management committee then as general manager, the board no doubt considered a legal mind best suited to deal with the major issue the company was facing: the proposed statutory imposition of some form of London passenger transport coordination. Selbie had lived to see the announcement in

December 1929 by a weak Labour government of its intention to proceed with this policy, but nothing much more had happened before he died, apart from the appointment of the chartered accountant Sir William McLintock to investigate the financial position of the potential constituents of a coordinated undertaking and make recommendations about compensation for the owners. McLintock's report on the Metropolitan was not ready until February 1931, by which time the government's detailed proposals were available. At a meeting that month with Lord Aberconway, Sir William declared he had given the Metropolitan more favourable treatment than any other undertaking as he had capitalised its profits on a 5 per cent basis at 20 years' purchase.

In the face of all earlier proposals for London transport coordination or amalgamation with the Underground the Metropolitan had always expressed its desire to remain independent, seeing itself as incompatible with almost all the rest of the London undertakings. Although Selbie was no longer there to put his steel and skill into the deliberations of the directors, it will come as no surprise to the reader to learn that the board decided flatly to resist the suggestion that the Metropolitan should be part of the new body. The company's attitude, made clear both to ministers and shareholders towards the end of 1930, and subsequently, was that it considered itself to have the same status as the four grouped main line railway companies and like them, should be allowed to continue independently. Amongst other dubious claims, exaggerated figures of freight tonnage carried by the Metropolitan were quoted in support of this contention.

But the argument did not wash with the Ministry of Transport and its advisers: in London itself, particularly in its equal partnership with the MDR in the operation and ownership of the Inner Circle, the Metropolitan appeared not greatly different from that company; and parliament's attitude to the 'main line in miniature' had been clearly shown by its rejection of the Metropolitan's application for road transport powers in 1928 at a time when such powers had been given to the four grouped companies. Finally, but by no means least, Lord Ashfield, a powerful influence in favour of coordination, was anxious to see the Metropolitan part of the single undertaking.

When the London Passenger Transport Bill was published on 13 March 1931 a Metropolitan petition was one of 80 entered against it. Four eminent counsel were engaged to provide the company's opposition. During the year 1931 the Metropolitan, with its Surplus Lands Committee, was to spend some £11,000 fighting what Lord Aberconway was later to describe as 'the predatory proposals of the late Socialist Government'. Anderson seems mainly to have been occupied in briefing counsel and when a correspondent compared the Metropolitan to David and the government and the Underground Group to Goliath, he replied, 'in my capacity as "sling carrier" against "Goliath" I have been completely immersed in searching for suitable pebbles'[3]. Behind the scenes, negotiation was pragmatically handled by Lord Aberconway, aided by fellow director Frank Dudley Docker. By May 1931 they had accepted that the extreme position initially taken was not tenable. The argument turned to compensation. Lord Aberconway told Herbert Morrison, the Labour Minister of Transport and principal architect of the Bill, that whilst the Metropolitan did not wish to sell the undertaking:

> . . . if Parliament decides that it is in the nation's interests that they should do so, they would not wish to stand in the way if the compensation receivable by them is arrived at on a basis which is fair and equitable and the compensation is payable in a form which secures to them the value of their undertaking.

He went on to say what compensation was thought suitable, making it clear that the Metropolitan would not be satisfied if this were solely in the form of the new undertaking's Transport Stock as the security offered by such stock did not commend itself; there must be a cash option. It was also considered the Surplus Lands undertaking should be excluded from the operation. As no concession was forthcoming regarding compensation, Metropolitan opposition to the bill was maintained until the dissolution of the Labour Government on 23 August 1931.

There now followed a brief period of euphoria at Baker Street. Both the interim and the elected 'National' Governments were perceptibly more right-wing, encouraging the hope that the Bill would be killed off, despite the substantial progress it had made through parliament, at considerable cost. The Metropolitan thought it could breathe again. Directors and shareholders were enjoined to use what influence they had with the new holders of power and the Conservative party generally. To no avail. Much to many people's surprise (and at Baker Street, at any rate, disappointment) the new administration of November 1931 decided to pick up the Bill at the point where it had been left in the previous parliament. Negotiations towards an agreed bill were pursued in the first part of 1932.

Once again the Metropolitan pressed for the alternative option of cash compensation; or to be allowed to continue independently, participating in the proposed London Traffic Pool on the same basis as that agreed for the four grouped companies, with the latter as the preferred course. Subsequently the new Minister of Transport, the Liberal, P. J. Pybus, was informed that if allowed the same treatment as the four grouped companies, the Metropolitan would relinquish its sections of the Inner Circle to the new undertaking, together with its running powers over the rest of the Circle. This generous offer invoked no response. Gradually the Metropolitan directors realised they had been pushed into a corner, with no alternative but to make the best of it. To this end, the company sought some kind of external guarantee of compensation and interest for its ordinary shareholders as a second best to cash. The four grouped companies now showed themselves willing to provide such a guarantee[4]. Through the good offices of Viscount Churchill, chairman of the GWR, and Sir Herbert Walker, general manager of the SR, Aberconway and Docker were given suitable assurances in June 1932 regarding a guarantee which would last for 25 years after the formation of the new undertaking. Aberconway also tried without success to obtain an improvement of the compensation terms offered by the government for ordinary stock above the proposed level of £67.10s of London Transport 'C' Stock[5] for each £100 Metropolitan Ordinary. The idea was that £67.10s should be regarded as a minimum, enhancement to be subject to arbitration, but in order to calculate the size of their guarantee, the four grouped companies needed a firm figure. Thus the board was under severe pressure, political and financial, finding itself driven to accept what the directors (in particular Sir Clarendon Hyde) regarded as an inadequate proportion of London Transport 'C' Stock.

On 28 June 1932 the board brought the proposed terms to the shareholders. Debenture and Preference Stocks would respectively be converted to London Transport 'A' and 'B' stocks, these having full trustee status, to produce the same income; holders of 3½ per cent Convertible Preference Stock also had the option of conversion to Metropolitan Consolidated Ordinary of equivalent nominal value. Holders of Ordinary Stock could elect to receive London Transport 'C' Stock at £67.10s for each £100 or they could take 'Metropolitan Assented Stock' at £100 for each £100 of Ordinary. This latter new stock would be entitled to a dividend of 3¼ per cent a year for the first 15 years from the appointed day (1 July 1933) and three per cent for a further ten years, these dividends being a first charge on the share of pooled receipts to which the four grouped main line companies would be entitled under the pooling scheme in the legislation. Assented Stock could be exchanged for 'C' Stock at £67.10s for each £100 Assented at any time until the end of the 25 year period, after which exchange would be obligatory. This option was subsequently described by Lord Aberconway at the February 1933 meeting as taking the stock of the Ordinary shareholders for 25 years out of any risk of insufficient earnings which might threaten the 'C' Stock of the new Transport Board in its early stages, an assertion which proved itself valid in the event. Those who took the option had the best of the deal.

An Extraordinary Meeting of the shareholders to seek endorsement of these terms was arranged for 14 July 1932. Aberconway's speech for this, which omitted all comment on the board's dilemma outlined above, but described the arrangements as the only alternative to postponing or even jeopardising coordination and leaving railborne traffic at the mercy of bus and coach competition, was privately described by Hyde as 'pap'. Nevertheless, the general view of the proprietors was that a reasonable bargain had been struck and all but two shareholders assented to the terms, thus sealing the Metropolitan's fate and causing the board to withdraw all opposition to the Bill. A voice from the past, in the form of a letter from Sir Robert Perks to Lord Aberconway, gave its blessing to the settlement.

The final provisions left the Surplus Lands Committee and Metropolitan Railway Country Estates Ltd to continue independently, the former becoming a separate limited company on 29 June 1933. The Chiltern Court property, which would have been difficult (but not impossible) to disentangle from the railway, went into the new London Passenger Transport Board. With all the major issues resolved, the Bill came before parliament again in the 1932–33 session, experiencing a somewhat difficult but ultimately successful passage. Royal Assent was given on 13 April 1933 and the London Passenger Transport Board came into being on the following 1 July.

But this is to anticipate. Before closing our chronological review, we must first look at some important works carried out by the Metropolitan Railway Company in 1930–33.

A NEW LINE FOR METRO-LAND

We have already noted in the preceding chapter how in July 1929 Selbie felt sufficiently confident of achieving a satisfactory solution to the Finchley Road-Baker Street bottleneck problem to take up another scheme which appeared eligible for Treasury assistance under the 1929 Development (Loan Guarantees & Grants) Act.

As early as 1892, and again in 1895 and 1901–03, attempts had been made to persuade the Metropolitan to enter the Stanmore/Bushey district, described in 1902 as:

about the only one in London still without railway accommodation and is rich in facilities for future development and building probabilities, occupying as it does a beautiful and picturesque and undulating stretch of grass country, a large part of which is within a few miles and easy reach of the Metropolis[6].

These approaches had come mostly from the independent promoters of the Watford & Edgware Railway, authorised by parliament in 1897, whose surveyor, R. T. Wreathall, suggested a line from theirs through Stanmore and Kingsbury to join the Metropolitan at Wembley Park. With hindsight, we can see that although this would have cost a little more to build, and done some damage to what became the London Green Belt, its rather more convenient terminus in Watford and much larger catchment area suitable for good middle class housing develop-ment (producing a fair crop of First Class commuters), might well have given a better financial return than the two short branches eventually built to Watford and Stanmore. Certainly the Metropolitan took some interest in the Wembley-Stanmore-Bushey-Watford con-cept, anxious as it was that no 'hostile company' (ie in the 1900s, the Underground) should invade this sector. The suggested route was inspected by Ellis, the Metropolitan's general manager, and some expenses were paid, but finally it was decided not to take it up. After some further legislation designed to link a Watford & Edgware Railway with the Underground at Golders Green, the promoters got into difficulties, eventually losing Underground patronage. Twice more, in 1908 and 1911, the Metropolitan was asked to consider a Stanmore–Watford proposal, but cooperation was again refused by Baker Street, now committed to the shorter branch from Rickmans-worth to Watford. Eventually the Watford & Edgware scheme was taken over by the Underground Group, and from the early 1920s, part of the route was firmly earmarked for extension of the tube railway beyond Edgware[7].

Interest in the southern part of the Watford-Stanmore-Wembley axis was reactivated early in 1929 when the large landowners between Wembley and Stanmore, waking up to what was taking place around them at Edgware, Hendon and Harrow, and wishing to realise to the full the potential value of their property, sought Metropolitan entry into the area. But Selbie was reluctant to recommend new suburban lines in the absence of a firm promise of an ending to the Baker Street-Finchley Road bottleneck (he was still uncertain whether the Kilburn relief tube would be built). His first mention of the Stanmore proposal to the board in May 1929 was therefore somewhat tentative. Then, as it became clear that the government was bringing in legislation to enable the Treasury to give financial assistance to railway works designed to relieve unemployment, Selbie was encouraged to go ahead both with the relief tube scheme and the branch 'towards Stanmore', both of them likely to be eligible for the subsidy.

As was so often the case, early estimates proved optimistic; in September 1929 it was suggested that a four mile branch to a point near Stanmore, with three intermediate stations, could be built for £293,780 and 'within a few years' would be returning £60,000 a year gross or £20,000 net (6.8 per cent) after deducting working expenses at 66 per cent. Selbie suggested that some land would be donated, whilst the bulk of the remainder was likely to be offered at nominal prices. Only ten houses (in Whitchurch Lane, Edgware) would need to be demolished if building were started without delay. When the bill was deposited, the proposed route between Wembley and Stanmore was seen to be very much that suggested by Wreathall 26 years earlier.

Early in 1930, an astute shareholder asked how the extra Stanmore traffic would be handled through the bottleneck south of Finchley Road. He was told that improved coaches were being built and trains would be lengthened, to add to the carrying capacity of the line. This by itself would have been inadequate, but as we have seen in the previous chapter, new works between Finchley Road and Swiss Cottage were under active consideration at this time. So the board went ahead, hoping somehow to fudge it, in true British fashion.

Opposition from the LMSR, who already had a station in Stanmore, was easily overcome by demonstrating that almost all the new line would serve an entirely different area to that of the former LNWR branch from Harrow & Wealdstone, a line that was in any case inconvenient for London commuters, with its obligatory change at the junction. The Metropolitan Railway Act of 4 June 1930 authorised a 4 mile 3.7 chain double track from a junction north of Wembley Park, together with 440yd of ancillary new track at Wembley Park station. Treasury assistance under the 1929 Development Act was agreed a month later, taking the form of a five per cent subsidy of the total works cost for five years and a 2½ per cent subsidy for a further five years, figures which were shortly afterwards confirmed against a revised estimate of £399,233 plus £110,000 for land. The Metropolitan told the Treasury committee that as it would be 'many years' before the line would yield the £55,200 a year necessary to cover its working costs and pay a 5 per cent return on the outlay, there was no question of the scheme going ahead without the subsidy.

Walter Scott & Middleton received a 21-month construction contract in November 1930 costed at £168,629. Fencing work started in that month, construction on 29 December. It was to be E. A. Wilson's last major task as Metropolitan Railway chief civil engineer[8]. Substantial earthworks were involved through the heavy Middlesex clay, work made the more onerous by exceptional and prolonged wet weather in the late summer and autumn of 1931. Two slips occurred which had to be made good with ash filling and the Ministry of Transport Inspector later found some subsidence in the platforms at Canons Park station. Completion was thus delayed, increasing the contractor's expenses. When a claim was made for an excess of £5,000 over the contract price only £2,000 was conceded. Contracts for stations at Stanmore and Kingsbury as well as the electrical sub-stations at Whitchurch Lane, Canons Park and at Preston Road were given to Pitcher Construction Company and for Canons Park station to F. R. Hipperson & Son.

Leaving the main line at a junction half a mile north of Wembley Park station, the branch curved at 15 chains radius to take a north-easterly direction after twice crossing the Wealdstone Brook, which had been disciplined into a new course for 24 chains. A deep cutting, set wide at a two to one slope on the treacherous clay, was then entered, this carrying the line beneath the main road between Harrow and Kenton and The Hyde, Hendon. Here, at 1 mile 22 chains, was Kingsbury, the first station. Its name was slightly misleading since it was closer to the then small communities of Kingsbury Green and Roe Green than to its namesake, which was much better served by the older Neasden station[9]. A 100ft wide 26ft span bridge carried the road over the line and on its south side supported Clark's station building, a long two-storey structure in red brick under a tiled, dormered roof with gable and canopied entrance. Not all completed for the opening of the line, it was eventually to contain 16 shops at ground level with residential flats on the first floor. Its entrance hall, with its Passimeter ticket office, lit by a dormer, gave on to a glazed covered way and stairs to the 440ft × 12ft wide side platforms below, each with a short red brick building containing waiting and staff rooms. There were glass and steel canopies, valanced with metal, running for 60ft on each side from the bottom of the stairs.

By the time the line was opened, building development was well-advanced around this station; indeed, the railway company had been involved in unforeseen expenditure when laying out the formation, finding it had to cross planned estate roads and sewer construction north of the main road. The developers, who of course knew the railway was coming, tempered their actions accordingly. Within a year or so of the line opening, the whole area around Kingsbury station had been transformed to new suburb with its own shopping centre and a 1,000-seat cinema.

From Kingsbury, the tracks turned north, then north-west, crossing open country on embankments formed from the spoil of the cuttings that had come before. Very soon the steepest gradient on the branch, 1 in 70 up towards Stanmore, was reached, and the Stag Lane airfield was skirted on its western boundary. At Whitchurch Lane, the line was carried over the road, through a small building development started in the 1910s. On the far side of this bridge, at 3 miles 13 chains, was Canons Park Edgware station. Angular and plain, it was one of Clark's less happy exercises, failing as it did to meet the difficult challenge of designing a station building around the abutments of a bridge over a road (Charles Holden was to show how it should be done at South Harrow in 1935). A canopied entrance each side of the bridge gave on to a booking hall placed beneath the first of six segmented blue brick arches supporting the line and platforms. Each side of these entrances were small two-storey blocks containing shops with flats above. These had Georgian sash windows, looking very out of place under the flat roofs. Clark tried unconvincingly to emphasise the horizontal motif of the bridge and flat roofs in the patterning of the brickwork and by providing a granite plinth. At platform level, the accommodation and dimensions were similar to those at Kingsbury, with a 75ft canopy each side. Except for the parts beneath these canopies, the platforms were cheaply built in timber.

Beyond this second station, the branch crossed the western edge of the ancient Canons Park, coming within half a mile of the LMSR line to the west. As the tracks approached the lower slopes of the Elstree Ridge, some cutting out was necessary and the terminus itself was scooped from the side of the rising ground, its platforms 125ft above the level at the start of the branch. Dispositions here were such that future extension northwards would have been possible, if costly, by tunnelling through the hill without disturbing the station structures.

Clark's terminal building was similar to that at Watford. Set back 77ft from the London Road, approached by a carriage drive, it was about half a mile east of the old village centre. With its multi-coloured red bricks, mock plinth of darker brindled bricks, Georgian sash windows and red-tiled, hipped and dormered roof, this 116ft by 33ft three-storey structure, set on the side of the hill, might be mistaken at a distance for the residence of a prosperous middle class family. Its upper floors contained three residential flats whilst on the street frontage, where the first floor was at ground level owing to the slope of the land, there were three shops. A khaki-tiled ticket hall with hardwood trim round the booking office window and lit by a dormer window, opened on to a 12ft 6in wide covered staircase. Below was a 440ft×30ft wide island platform protected by a 100ft canopy of the standard type which covered the lower landing of the stairs as well as a building containing waiting and staff rooms and lavatories.

At the south end of the platform, the running lines were connected by a power-operated crossover. To the east was a small freight yard with three roads, one electrified, the only such facility on the branch. As the LMSR and LNER were well-established in the district, this yard attracted little traffic and was to survive only 3¼ years after its opening.

Landowners had stipulated a fourth station at 2 miles 8 chains, between Kingsbury and Canons Park Edgware, but its construction was left to await development of the catchment area, which did not seriously begin until after the sale of Stag Lane airfield in 1933. Queensbury Station therefore did not appear in the remaining short life of the Metropolitan Railway.

Set in a formation 30ft wide (32ft on banks), the tracks were made up with 45ft long bullhead rails weighing 95lb per yard. Conductor rails were 120lb flat-bottomed, the positive placed 1ft 4in outside the inner running rail and three inches above it, the negative centrally set between the running rails and 1½ inches above. Traction current at 600 V dc was carried from substations at Preston Road and at Whitchurch Lane (Canons Park), fed from the Neasden 11,000 V three phase output. Opportunity was taken to rearrange substation equipment at this time as some of the existing substations were becoming dangerously overloaded and eight-car trains were to be introduced. On 26 November 1931, the board had approved an important programme of transfers and new purchases of GEC rotary transformers and associated equipment as follows:

New:

Preston Road (new substation)	3×1,500 kW
Canons Park (new substation)	2×1,500 kW
Chalton Street (Euston Road)	2×1,500 kW
Baker Street	2×1,500 kW

Transfers:

Chalton Street to Finchley Road	2×1,200 kW
Baker Street to Bouverie Street (Paddington)	1×1,200 kW
Baker Street to Ickenham	1×1,200 kW
Bouverie Street to store	1× 800 kW
Finchley Road to store	2× 800 kW
Ickenham to store	1× 800 kW

All these changes were made in 1932–33.

Signalling of the new branch was undertaken by the Westinghouse Brake & Saxby Signal Co for £6,945. An all-electric system, operating at 440 V ac was installed, with three-aspect colour lights working on ac track circuits fitted with train stops and fog repeaters 100ft in the rear. There were short range colour lights or electrically-worked discs for shunting movements. It was arranged for the controlled signals at Stanmore terminus to be worked on a circuit-code, three-wire centralised traffic control system from a panel in the Wembley Park signal box. This was the first application of ctc outside North America and the first anywhere for suburban working. Choice of such an advanced system was influenced by the Metropolitan's signalling superintendent, R. Falshaw-Morkill, who had come to the company in February 1925 after a wide experience of automatic signalling in the UK and North America as manager for Tyer & Co, the Carlisle signal engineers.

Once more, the Ministry of Transport Inspecting Officer found little fault and much to praise. He declared the works throughout as 'of heavy construction and in good order', the stations 'commodious, practical and attractive [in] design'. Both the railway company and Westinghouse Brake & Saxby Signal were congratulated on their enterprise in adopting the ctc system and on the perfection of the equipment.

Two 'K' class 2-6-4T were brought on to the line on the first Sunday of December 1932 to consolidate the tracks and test the bridges for deflection under load. This was followed by an official opening ceremony on Friday 9 December at which the guest of honour was the Minister of Transport, P. J. Pybus (asked to attend as this was the last development by the Metropolitan Railway as a separate entity and 'in the nature of a historic event'). Lord Aberconway and other Metropolitan notables were present to entertain the 162 guests, who were carried to and from Stanmore in an interesting special train[10]. After the minister had switched-in the signals at Wembley Park before the cameras of Movietone News, the new stations were inspected. Clutching their commemorative brochures, free whiskies and cigars, the party were then returned to Chiltern Court restaurant for luncheon, at which they were addressed by former GWR engine driver J. H. Thomas, Dominions Secretary in the National Government. Public service started on the following day, Saturday 10 December 1932. Except at peak hours, trains shuttled between Wembley Park and Stanmore. On weekdays there were 72 trains each way, the best covering the 11.09 miles between Stanmore and Baker Street in 22 minutes.

As the Metropolitan Railway Company survived barely seven months after the opening of the branch, an assessment of its performance and traffic development is out of place here and has in any case been dealt with by the author elsewhere[11]. But we can note that the Metropolitan started by creating something of a hurdle for itself by setting fares at its full standard mileage rate and season ticket scale, both of them above the level of the Underground at its Edgware and Burnt Oak stations. These two points were directly competitive, thanks to the existence of fully coordinated feeder bus services. And the LMSR had reduced all fares on its Stanmore branch to Harrow & Wealdstone station rates after the opening of a halt on that branch on 12 September 1932 to serve new housing development at Belmont. Furthermore the Metropolitan was mean with its cheap day return tickets, providing them on only three days a week including Saturdays and Sundays. And whilst the area served by the branch was soon covered with thousands of small houses, there was a certain amount of local industry, a factor which tended to dilute commuter traffic.

A final projected estimate of the first year's results was made by the Metropolitan in May 1933, based on actual gross costs where these were available, but ignoring the negligible freight revenue, interest charges, depreciation and junction working costs at Wembley Park. This showed the annual working expenses of the new line to be £15,941 against passenger receipts of £4,667 and rental income of £2,249. Contributive traffic was estimated at £9,000 in addition.

A FINAL FLING FOR METRO-LAND

Apart from the building of the Stanmore branch and other works mentioned earlier, the final years of the Metropolitan Railway saw the provision of additional tracks between Wembley Park and Harrow with associated station rebuilding, as well as the erection of one more station in Metro-land, although this was not actually opened until after the demise of the company.

Such was the pressure arising from the growth of middle and longer-distance suburban traffic by the end of the 1920s that it became essential to complete four wholly Metropolitan tracks between Finchley Road and Harrow. Powers for the work on the remaining 2¾ miles between Wembley Park and Harrow South Junction were obtained in the Metropolitan Railway Act, 1929, and some expenditure at Wembley Park station was included in the Treasury grant as it was associated with the Stanmore Extension scheme. A 15-month, £84,346 bridge reconstruction and earthworks contract was awarded

to John Bills in February 1930[12], but with the necessary station reconstruction and resignalling, total expenditure on the quadrupling of
this section was estimated at £172,000. Although Northwick Park
station was almost new, it had to be demolished as it stood on what
were to be the Through or fast lines. Despite the cost, it was decided to
rebuild it on the new Local Lines to retain traffic that would otherwise
be diverted to the Bakerloo tube and LMSR at nearby Kenton station.
The wooden halt at Preston Road was in any case due for reconstruction as it had become totally inadequate for the traffic from a catchment area being covered every week with more and more houses.

The two new tracks, laid on the north side, were to become the
Local Lines, the existing pair between them and the LNER the
Through Lines. All four were fully available for normal working from
Sunday 10 January 1932 but the new connections at Wembley Park
station and new signalling were not finally ready until 3 April. All the
old upper quadrant signals between Wembley Park and Harrow were
replaced with British Power Railway Signal Co three-aspect colour
lights at a cost of £6,089. Train describers were installed between
Neasden and Harrow and public train indicators at Wembley Park
station.

Station rebuilding was in the hands of Pitcher Construction Co.
Both new stations were to have island platforms between the Local
Lines, with no access to the Through Lines. At Northwick Park,
where alterations were confined to rail level and virtually reproduced
what had been provided in 1923 with later additions, the contract
figure was £8,740. The Up side of the new island platform came into
use on 19 April 1931, the remainder on 21 June, and the rebuilding
was finished on 31 July. At Preston Road, where £23,675 was spent,
Clark designed a large three-storey block to sit on a widened bridge
over the line. In his favoured red brick and tiled roof domestic style,
this had the usual dormer windows and a gable over the station
entrance, where the large canopy was still carrying the message
METROPOLITAN RAILWAY in the 1960s. This building, which
extended over the LNER as well as the Metropolitan tracks, included
ticket hall, shops and flats above. Covered stairs led down from the
first to an island platform on the north west side of the bridge (the halt
platforms had been on the opposite side). The Up face of the new
platform was in use from 22 November 1931, the Down on the
following 3 January. All reconstruction was completed on 1 February
1932.

To meet the demands of the widening and the Stanmore branch, a
complete resignalling of Wembley Park station area was undertaken

by Westinghouse Brake & Saxby Signal Co. All new equipment except ground signals was of the two and three-aspect colour light type, equipped with Westinghouse electrically-operated train stops and side lights which showed the signal aspect to motormen alongside a signal but out of sight of the main beam. Points were power-operated from an all-electric locking frame in a rebuilt signal box at the Harrow end of the station. This had 93 levers (of which 73 were in use initially) under an illuminated diagram showing the state of the 69 track circuits in the area. The Metropolitan's standard train-starting device was installed on all platforms. First tried at Baker Street and King's Cross in 1926 and subsequently extended to all busy stations following the withdrawal of front guards, this was operated when the guard put up the copper or brass ferrule of his flag stick to connect two bare wires strung 8ft above the platform. An electric bell then rang near the starting signal (provided that was in the 'off' position) and a gong sounded at the rear end of the platform. A three-inch high letter 'S' was then illuminated on the starting signal post. Wembley Park's new signalling came into service from Sunday 3 January 1932[13].

Other works at Wembley Park at this time included the construction of an additional through road at the back of no 4 platform to facilitate turn round of Stanmore shuttle trains and the operation of trains from the newly widened section through the station, where the Local Lines crossed from the north to the south side of the Through. This work, carried out by John Bills, had been authorised with the Stanmore branch in the 1930 act. Platforms 1, 2 and 3 were extended by T. Hedges, who also built the new signal box. Expenditure at Wembley Park on the scheme just described totalled £61,401.

From 1922 onwards there had been some agitation for a station to be provided at or near Joel Street in the 2½ mile gap between Northwood and Pinner, but whilst the area remained primarily rural, all such requests were refused. Operating staff were in any case not enthusiastic about a stop at this point, which would require a timing addition of three or four minutes for each call by a Down steam train on the 1 in 145 gradient. Commercial staff suspected that much of the traffic would simply be diversions from the adjoining stations. At the beginning of 1931, with about 390 acres near the railway becoming available for housing development and some 3,000 houses in firm prospect, the pressure was renewed. By the autumn of 1931 there were already 215 houses completed north of the line. Negotiations with the estate developers and builders concluded with an agreement in which they undertook to find half the £12,000 cost of the station which they needed to ensure the success of their enterprise. As it was estimated that a station would increase the value of the land in the district by some £80 acre, it was by no means a bad bargain for them. They also undertook to guarantee a minimum annual passenger revenue of £947 but such was the level of traffic they were never to be called upon to meet this liability. Some land was also to be transferred to the Metropolitan and GCR Joint Committee free of charge to provide a frontage opposite the station which the railways could exploit for commercial development.

The Joint Committee sanctioned a station in December 1932 but there was to be no freight siding as there was spare capacity at the adjoining yards. Some embarrassment was caused all round when the lowest tender, from one of the local building firms (included at the insistence of the guarantors) came in at £13,100, but by modifying the station design the difference was saved (the Up side canopy was shortened from 150ft to 70ft and the Down side one from 140ft to 60ft and there were other minor economies). A £5 prize competition was organised by the guarantors and a local newspaper to find a suitable name, the choice finally falling on Northwood Hills. This was suggested to the prizewinner by Pinner Hill, Hog's Back and Haste Hill, but cynics pointed out nastily that only the last, a very modest eminence only about 100ft above the surrounding land, was anywhere near the new station.

Opened on 13 November 1933, the new facility had a somewhat sparse initial service (on weekdays 25 trains to Baker Street, 22 back, 15 to Marylebone, eight back). As his last contribution, Clark produced a very simple overline structure, paying lip service to his domestic style with its token red-tiled pitched roof and red bricks, somewhat unbalanced by a disproportionately large metal canopy bearing the station name. This building was set back to allow future widening of the bridge carrying the narrow country lane over the line. Behind, covered staircases of very plain design led to side platforms equipped with a minimal range of offices.

THE DEATH OF THE METROPOLITAN RAILWAY

Reflecting the economic depression of the period and the onset of road coach competition (first becoming a real threat in 1930) the Metropolitan's closing results showed a decline in traffic and financial health. Bus and coach competition eroded cheap day and ordinary fare receipts, causing the numbers of ordinary passengers originating on the system to decline from 1930. In that year, season ticket issues, inflated by the new home owners of Metro-land, reached 64,037, but

Plate 33 Final years on the Brill branch. Metropolitan A class loco No 23 in final rebuilt form and one coach train waiting to leave Quainton Road bay platform for Brill c1930 (*photographer unknown*)

Plate 34 The ultimate in Metropolitan electric stock: motor car 254 of 1932 hauling earlier and rebuilt cars on Baker Street train at Neasden, 1932 (*Photomatic*)

Plate 35 Metropolitan apotheosis: Chiltern Court and Baker Street station as completed, 1931. Entrance to the Circle Line platforms is on Baker Street corner. The main entrance is under the triple-clocked portico which was destroyed by a World War II bomb (*London Transport Museum*)

Plate 36 Good taste for the Stanmore extension: Clark's country mansion style terminus of 1932 almost ready for opening (*photographer unknown*)

the financial depression, which affected both the builders and the house buyers to some extent, caused this figure to decline to 61,678 in 1932. Freight tonnage peaked at 4.3 million tons in 1930, dropping thereafter as building and other activity was checked by the depression. Parcels and mails receipts also fell significantly after 1930. Overall, net receipts from all sources (including the Metropolitan's portion of Joint Lines' revenue) dropped from £844,515 in 1929 to £827,998 in 1930, £796,131 in 1931 and £712,041 in 1932, producing dividends for the ordinary shareholders of 3½ per cent in 1930, 2½ in 1931 and only one and five eighths per cent in 1932. The ratio of working expenses to traffic receipts, proudly shaved by Selbie to a commendable 47.9 per cent in 1913, rose to 67.9 in 1931 and 73.3 in 1932.

At midnight on 30 June 1933 the old Metropolitan Railway died, in its 79th year. On the day before, the board had gathered for its last regular meeting, although it came together for the final time on 21 February 1934 to receive accounts for the first six months of 1933. These caused the declaration of the lowest half yearly dividend in the company's history on the ordinary shares, a mere 0.43 per cent. Lord Aberconway, chairman for 29 years, died in the previous month, escaping this final humiliation.

The transfer to the London Passenger Transport Board was effected by the issue to Metropolitan proprietors of £7,288,676 in 4½ per cent London Transport 'A' stock, £2m in LT five per cent 'A' stock, £5,259,108 in five per cent LT 'B' stock and £5,140,813 in LT 'C' stock.

Handed over to the new undertaking were 36 steam locomotives[14], 21 electric locomotives (including the ex GN&CR departmental locomotive), 104 locomotive-hauled passenger coaches, 211 electric motor cars, 422 electric train trailers (including driving trailers), 100 service/departmental vehicles, 544 freight wagons, vans and trucks, 42 goods and parcels road horse vans and 29 road motor vehicles.

Had Selbie lived, it seems probable that he would have been offered high office in the LPTB, although his relations with Ashfield and Pick had been coldly formal and at 65 he might well have preferred to retire gracefully rather than accept a post which he would have regarded as offering some loss in prestige. As it was, the new body was dominated by the old Underground top layer, which did not even have to move from its 55 Broadway headquarters in Westminster. The Metropolitan provided only two senior officers: Anderson became its secretary, treasurer and solicitor, and Hally its operating manager (railways) beneath the Underground's J. P. Thomas. Both posts were largely executive in nature allowing little or no influence on policy or direction. A temporary Metropolitan import was John Wardle, who was given a fill-in job as chairman of a committee on ticket problems. When this had concluded its deliberations at the end of 1934, he was pensioned-off.

As the effective power base in the new body, Lord Ashfield and Frank Pick set about with a will to integrate the Metropolitan into the rest of the Underground rail system. A major step in this direction was the completion in 1939 of a tube tunnel between Baker Street and Finchley Road which enabled Bakerloo trains to be projected to Stanmore, taking over all local service from Wembley Park inwards and providing all Metropolitan Extension Line stations (by cross platform interchange at Finchley Road) with the direct connection to the heart of the West End they had always lacked. Neither Ashfield or Pick had any sympathy for the 'main line in miniature' concept and after the Board had been in existence for less than seven years, most of the features which had distinguished the once proudly independent Metropolitan from the other London underground railways had gone[15]. The outer rural sections beyond Aylesbury to Brill and Verney Junction were closed, the former completely, the latter to passengers, whilst services from Aylesbury to Quainton Road were handed over to the tender mercies of the impoverished LNER. Freight and parcels operations were discarded. From 1 November 1937, 18 of the fastest and most powerful steam locomotives, 252 freight wagons and 13 brake vans were passed to the LNER for maintenance of the timetabled freight services and the passenger train working north of Rickmansworth. The Pullman cars disappeared in 1939. Although some aspects of Metro-land survived long enough to be mulled over on television and printed page by Sir John Betjeman, after 1937–39 things were never really the same again.

The careful reader will have observed that no reference has been made to any consultation with the staff over the fate of the Metropolitan Railway they had served, some for 50 years or more. This was a grievance strongly felt, as will be seen in the next chapter, where we take a belated look at the men and women who kept the railway going.

16

METROPOLITAN LABOUR

Throughout the life of the undertaking, employee pay and conditions tended to follow those of the main line companies, which in later years sometimes made them less favourable than those of the tube companies and subsequently, the Underground Group. On the Metropolitan, as much as on other railways, men looked upon the railway job as a lifetime career, with the prospect of steady, and in certain cases, spectacular advancement. As elsewhere, hours were long in the 19th and early 20th centuries, but given good health and behaviour, employment was secure and prospects and pay compared well with similar work, especially when it is remembered that uniforms were provided and also free travel to and from the workplace, a feature which allowed many to enjoy a higher standard of living by taking low rent property in the suburbs. And after the works and locomotive depot were moved to Neasden in the early 1880s, Metropolitan employees were provided with a reservoir of company housing accommodation at low rents, an amenity much sought after.

Right through to the 1930s, management attitudes towards the traffic and works staff were generally paternalistic, often patronising, but there is no evidence to show that the men were unfairly or harshly treated by the standards of the time. That this was so is demonstrated by the almost complete absence of labour troubles related to the Metropolitan Railway as distinct from national issues, a situation which applied during the whole existence of the company. Such exceptions as there were will be touched upon later.

INJURY, SICKNESS AND OLD AGE

Until 1898 there was no statutory compulsion on employers to pay compensation when an employee was killed or injured in an accident at work. The early minute books of the Metropolitan frequently record payments of £10 to the widows and families of men killed on duty, a figure sometimes increased to £25 or so if the victim was senior or long serving. Such sums would leave little if anything once funeral bills had been met.

At first there was no provision for superannuation and men were left to survive on what they had been able to save whilst earning. Not surprisingly those whose health endured worked on until very late in life. In 1903 for example we read of a chief inspector retiring in his 76th year. A Railway Clearing House Superannuation Fund based on contributions from employee and employer was established in 1873. Soon afterwards Metropolitan staff were asking to be allowed to join it, but it was not for 20 years (1 January 1893) that membership of the Fund was opened to Metropolitan employees and then only to salaried staff. Those too old to benefit from this fared badly, especially as clerks' salaries often remained static for many years and promotion was slow. An audit office clerk retiring in 1903 at age 62 had drawn the same £130 salary for 20 years; when offered a year's salary as retirement pay, he appealed and was given ten shillings a week for life. No doubt he tried hard to survive longer than five years.

In a pioneering move, initiated by A. C. Ellis, the Metropolitan obtained parliamentary powers in a special act of 1907 to set up a contributory pension fund covering all its uniformed and workshop employees from the beginning of 1908. Some difficulty was encountered in persuading the men of the benefits of participating, but by the end of 1908 there were 1,500 members. This scheme was supplemented by an Auxiliary Fund in January 1921.

Sickness was another contingency for which at first there was little or no provision, apart from any savings a man may have managed to accumulate in the railway's own savings bank[1] or any grant he could obtain from its Provident (sickness) Fund[2]. When Col J. J. Mellor retired from the chairmanship of the board in 1904, the shareholders, without any prompting from the other directors, voted him a lump sum of £500 in gratitude for his handling of the company's affairs. From this he generously donated £350 to establish a Metropolitan Railway Convalescent Fund for which subscriptions and donations were to be held in trust and payments made to staff and their families when they were incapacitated or in poor health. In 1912 clerical and supervisory staff with over six years' service were awarded sick benefit at their full rate of pay for the first six weeks of absence and half pay for a further seven weeks. At the end of 1924 this was improved to provide three months' full pay, followed by three months' half pay, after only one year of service.

MEMORIALS AND CHRISTMAS BOXES

No mention is made in the records of any kind of labour trouble until 1871 when a memorial (petition) was sent to the board by the workmen in the locomotive, carriage and building department at Edgware Road. This made the quite reasonable request that their hours be reduced from 57½ to 54 a week; it also suggested they be paid weekly instead of fortnightly. These changes, which were comparable with those being sought nationally by other railway workshop staff and railwaymen at this time (the 'Nine Hours Movement') were approved from 1 January 1872. Soon afterwards, some other unspecified 'officers' requested a reduction in hours, higher wages and weekly instead of fortnightly payment. Only the last was granted, but in November 1872 the board agreed to alter the timings of first and last trains in a move that shortened the operating staff working day by about one hour. Locomotive crews then pressed for modification of hours and increase in pay. The last was conceded at the beginning of 1874 in the form of a new scale for drivers of 6s for a ten hour day, rising to 8s after the thirteenth month of service (instead of 7s 6d after nine months) and for firemen 3s 6d a day rising to 4s 6d after seven months (instead of 3s to 4s 6d after nine months). These scales and hours continued unchanged until the early years of the 20th century[3].

A curious form of bonus was instituted in 1878, apparently by Watkin himself. At a cost of around £100, clerks in charge (senior booking clerks), booking clerks and inspectors were given as Christmas gifts turkeys, geese, or legs of mutton on a downward scale, according to grade. Later such seasonal balm was converted to cash bonuses but all such payments were withdrawn in 1911. The railway was of course working and fully manned throughout the Christmas holiday at this time and the thought may have been that the officers so rewarded were those least likely to be at the receiving end of gratuities from passengers. Or perhaps Watkin had been influenced by reading Charles Dickens.

Another custom that suggests Sir Edward Watkin's personal touch was the tendency of the workmen's annual outing to favour seaside resorts on the SER, such as Ramsgate. Contributions were made by the Metropolitan to the SER's costs on such occasions insofar as the payments made by the employees themselves were insufficient.

Bonuses as rewards for special efforts were for many years confined to senior officers and clerical staff but to commemorate Queen Victoria's Golden Jubilee (June 1887) all weekly paid staff were given an extra day's pay. Since many were required to work very long hours handling the London crowds, this was only just. The normal day service on the Inner Circle, Hammersmith & City and St John's Wood lines was extended to 3 am on 22 June 1887 and the ten minute interval Circle service was worked until midnight for the remainder of that week. John Bell, the general manager, and J. M. Eyles, the secretary, were given gold medals for masterminding the operation. On the wedding day of George (later King George V) and Victoria Mary (6 July 1893) 514,274 passengers were carried by the Metropolitan, 87,846 more than on the Golden Jubilee day. The additional work was recognised by payment of an extra day's pay. For the Queen's Diamond Jubilee, all employees except the works staff were given one week's extra pay. Neasden Works closed for the celebration on 22 June 1897 and the men there received two days' extra pay.

Other incentives encouraged good management and smart appearance of stations. Stationmasters, station foremen and station inspectors of the three best-managed stations each quarter received prizes of £5, £3 and £2 for division amongst themselves as they thought fit. Following the practice of some other companies, a best-kept station competition was inaugurated in 1927 with money dispensed for purchase of seeds and plants and prizes of £1 to £5 shared equally between the stationmaster and the rest of the station staff.

TROUBLE AT THE WORKS

Soon after his appointment as resident engineer & locomotive superintendent in July 1885, J. J. Hanbury began to create something of a stir at Neasden Works where the staff first objected to his proposal to introduce piece work. Unmoved, he quickly dismissed 36 fitters and turners, whereupon the men's craft unions withdrew fitters at Edgware Road, Hammersmith and New Cross loco sheds. The resulting vacancies were quickly filled from a bountiful pool of unemployed labour. Hanbury next tried to abolish 'shed days' when the engine drivers washed out the boilers of their charges, apparently none too efficiently. So upset where the enginemen when Hanbury appointed a separate staff to undertake this job they sought and obtained audience with the board. A restoration of the traditional procedure was ordered, but designated 'temporary' probably as a gesture to save Hanbury's face. The engineer's heavy hand again brought his activities before the board in April 1890 when the Metropolitan was subjected to what seems to have been its first taste of 'industrial action'. On the grounds that the carriages were in better condition and better maintained than formerly, Hanbury had reduced the payments for carriage lifting at Neasden from 28s per lift to 23s then to 21s, thus reducing the men's profit above their guaranteed wage. When dissatisfaction was expressed, Hanbury dismissed three men for laziness and another, a leader of the labour federation, for gross negligence. The latter's departure prompted nine more men to resign. New labour was recruited but was prevented from entering the works until police 'protection' was obtained for their passage through the picket lines. From motives closer to increased efficiency than philanthropy, Hanbury also installed the first mess room at Neasden Works. His object was to eliminate the practice of preparing food in working hours for consumption in the workshops during closing times. Further mess accommodation was added in 1896.

Neasden became the location for the Metropolitan's first attempts at staff education. On the initiative of A. C. Ellis, a general training school was opened there at the time of the electrification. Courses covered not only practical electrical matters and electric traction, but passenger and goods accounts, shorthand, signalling and train operation, and were open to all employees.

SUNDAY PAY

For many years railwaymen were regarded as available for duty over the whole seven days, so that Sunday work was seen as included in their weekly wage. Train crews were however paid on a daily basis and received seven or six days' pay according to whether they had worked on the Sunday or not. Agitation by weekly paid traffic staff for pay for Sunday working began in 1889 when the 102 signalmen applied for it, pleading that their work had increased, especially on the section between Bishop's Road and Aldgate. They considered their week's pay should reward six days' work instead of seven, the existing weekly rate (with an addition of two shillings for the overtaxed Inner Circle men) to continue, with Sundays paid as overtime at a proportion of the weekly rate. They also suggested, with some daring, that eight hours should constitute a day's work. There was some sympathy with the signalmen's demands, tempered by fear of the repercussive effects of any concession, and in the end they got nothing.

Between 1890 and 1892 the uniformed staff grew increasingly restive about Sunday pay as they watched other railway companies in London beginning to recognise the principle of six days as a week's work. Mass meetings of Metropolitan staff were held, sending a deputation to Bell, the general manager. As a concession on Sunday pay would cost up to £6,000 a year, he hesitated. When the men pointed out that in order to get a Sunday free, they had to work 16 hours every alternate Sunday, eating during the Church Interval, Bell suggested that Sunday hours could be shortened if one shift came on from 8 am until the Church Interval and a second shift followed from the end of that break to the close of traffic, which had been the practice in the early years of the Metropolitan. But the men said the system had been changed at their own request and they did not wish to revert to the double shift system on Sundays. Eventually, in the middle of 1892, a compromise was reached; another two shillings would be paid all round each week, at a total cost of £2,000 a year. Loadings of Sunday trains were then monitored to see whether any could be cut out to recoup some of the extra wages cost.

The question came up again in 1907, by which time all the other London companies had conceded Sunday pay except the GNR, LNWR, Midland and GCR. Metropolitan and Hammersmith & City traffic staff were given weekly pay for six days with an extra full day's pay for Sunday work at an annual cost of £1,772 from 1 January 1908. Booking clerks had no Sunday pay until January 1910 when they were awarded 1s 6d, 2s or 2s 6d according to annual salary. A full day's rate was paid to them and to station clerks from 1912. Stationmasters were the last to get Sunday pay, at the beginning of 1913. To reduce the impact on the revenue account, the quarterly 10s punctuality bonus for station and booking clerks was withdrawn with the introduction of Sunday pay. Some minor improvements to pay scales of booking clerks were also conceded at this time, bringing the top rate for a booking clerk to £100 a year.

CONCILIATION & ARBITRATION BOARDS

From 1905, with the introduction of electric working, the wages and leave allowances of train staff were revised[4]. Electric train motormen with seven years' service received £118.13s a year before overtime whilst head guards with three years' service got £78, including Sunday pay. This was at a time when the national average for adult males was £71 a year. From January 1907 steam locomotive drivers were divided into four classes, of which only the top grade received more than electric train motormen. Many of these men suffered reductions in pay[5].

When a national railway strike was threatened in 1908, Lloyd George, then President of the Board of Trade, skilfully avoided it by conceding a national scheme suggested to him by Fay of the GCR. This provided for the setting up of conciliation and arbitration boards by each company; the Metropolitan established two, one covering the traffic and locomotive departments, the other the permanent way, telegraph and electrical men. These boards, with the company bearing the meeting costs, discussed wages and working conditions but not disciplinary matters, and were able to refer disputes to Sectional and, later, Central Conciliation Boards. Arbitration would then follow if all else had failed.

Discontented with their pay and conditions at a period when railway traffic generally was expanding, railwaymen across the nation were now becoming more militant, campaigning hard for improvements, particularly an eight hour day in place of the standard ten hours. In April 1909 the Metropolitan men put their case but the management refused either shortening of hours or an advance in pay scales, no doubt because the Metropolitan at any rate was not particularly prosperous at this time.

During the 1909 negotiations the men had sought abolition of 'split' turns (booking-on more than once for a day's work) but the management, whilst agreeing to study possible reductions in these turns, maintained the system was indispensable for the economic operation of a continuous train service over 20 hours each day. They also accepted that split shifts should be restricted to eight and a half hours per day active work with a nine hour rest between duties. In response to a whole clutch of demands from drivers and firemen during 1909, only two significant concessions were made: motormen were awarded a time and a quarter rate for overtime (this rate to apply also on Sundays, Christmas Days and Good Fridays); and a heater in their cabs, stolen from the passenger section of the car. It was also confirmed that motormen and assistants would work a nine hour day straight shift (including a 54 minute meal break) on the Inner Circle. Elsewhere, the shift was generally nine and a half hours (including a 40 minute meal break). Time and a quarter for overtime was agreed for other grades, along with the improved terms for Sunday, Christmas Day and Good Friday working. Guards on the Inner Circle were given a nine hour day including meal break.

All this led to increased staff costs, resulting in turn in a search for staff economies. Installation of self-acting locks on the electric gate-stock trains on the Inner Circle, Hammersmith and St John's Wood line trains in 1910 produced a very substantial saving, allowing the company to dispense with two conductors (or gatemen) on each six-car train. Late in 1913 the conductors placed in the middle of the six car trains were also withdrawn. Finally a further large saving was sought in 1925 by withdrawing the 65 front guards, in common with the MDR. This went slightly wrong. It was thought that it might be manageable with a few more platform staff at stations, but experience revealed delays as motormen crossed their cabs to watch for the

313

guard's signal, or the platform configuration impeded their observation of the guard. Some not insignificant sums were then expended on installing the train starting devices mentioned in the previous chapter.

Refusal of railway directors across the country to negotiate any amendment of the 1907 conciliation machinery, which had not worked well, led to the calling of the first national railway strike by the four main railway trades unions on Friday 18 August 1911. On the Metropolitan, 924 of the 3,300 staff withdrew their labour, mainly drivers, motormen and guards. All those on strike were paid off on the Saturday and told to hand back their uniforms and other Metropolitan Railway property on the following Monday, an action smugly described in the minute book as having 'a steadying effect on the remainder of the men'.

So-called 'loyalty' bonuses of five shillings a day for steam locomotive drivers and electric train motormen and 3s 6d for guards, at a cost of £1,745, also kept men at work. Feeding and sleeping arrangements were organised at Neasden power station, Edgware Road depot and Baker Street station to enable those working to avoid passing through picket lines. Some of the officers received bonuses for the extra work they had to tackle. Altogether the management gained valuable experience which was to be put to good effect in subsequent strikes. When the excitable Winston Churchill, as Home Secretary mobilised 58,000 troops to 'protect' non-striking railwaymen and installations across the nation, some 150–200 of these, flashing their fixed bayonets, were deployed at Neasden and other 'vulnerable points' on the Metropolitan from early Friday until midday on the following Sunday.

On the Friday, what was described as a 'fair' train service was provided but the Inner Circle was worked only by the MDR and confined to that company's portion of the route (South Kensington to Aldgate). Steam trains were reversed at Harrow, where passengers changed into and out of a 'good' electric service to and from Baker Street East. The Saturday saw a ten minute interval on the Inner Circle, Hammersmith, and Harrow lines, with a limited steam service beyond Harrow. That night the strike ended, large numbers of men applying on the Sunday morning for reinstatement, only to be told that arrangements had been made for that day and they should return on Monday, 21 August 1911. On that day, all came back and normal services were resumed.

The outcome of the strike was a positive one for the unions in that a revised conciliation scheme was negotiated nationally. This dispensed with the Central Conciliation Board and admitted paid union officials as secretaries to the employees' side of the Sectional Boards for the first time. The arrangements were further revised in 1922 when the Metropolitan established local departmental committees, sectional railway councils and a Metropolitan Railway Council in response to the requirements of the Railways Act, 1921.

To the disgust of some shareholders, vigorously expressed at the 1912 meeting, the Metropolitan had bowed to the inevitable soon after the end of the strike by giving recognition to the Amalgamated Society of Railway Servants (renamed the National Union of Railwaymen in March 1913). What particularly stuck in the throat of some was that this had been done before other much larger railway companies had got around to it.

Metropolitan men continued to work normally during the coal miners' national strike from 1 March to 6 April 1912 but the train services were reduced from 6 March to 21 May by shortage of coal. Steam trains reappeared at Baker Street East from 20 March in a move to save coal at the power station and men were laid off at Neasden and Hammersmith depots.

By national agreement, the long-sought eight hour day was conceded to all railwaymen by the government from 1 February 1919. Neasden shops staff worked a 47-hour week from 1 January 1919 (in peacetime they had formerly worked 52 hours (7.15 am to 5.45 pm (5.30 on Fridays) on Mondays to Fridays with one hour for lunch and 7.15-noon on Saturdays). The 1919 hours award was followed by simplification of the grades system and national standardisation of conditions by all the main line railway companies (amongst which the Metropolitan was included).

But an attempt by the government effectively to reduce wages of non-footplate staff with the consolidation of war bonuses triggered a second national railway strike, which lasted from 27 September to 5 October 1919 inclusive. on this occasion, 3,349 Metropolitan and Joint Committees' staff withdrew labour, almost 85 per cent of the total. With the aid of 284 volunteers and much shirt-sleeve work by managers and supervisors, electric trains were worked to and from Harrow (with a shuttle to West Harrow) and from 30 September, 12 motor lorries borrowed from the Royal Air Force served stations between Chorley Wood and Harrow, supplementing three steam trains daily. A regular service was thus maintained at a time when there was a virtually complete stoppage on all other railways including the Underground. After the staff had threatened not to feed the 30 horses in the City stables, clerks led the animals through the streets to grass at Wembley Park. Once again, Winston Churchill, now Secretary of State for War and Air, ordered the army to 'protect' stations, signal boxes and bridges. On the Metropolitan, loss of traffic and special strike expenditure totalled £31,210, or a net cost of £20,553 after deducting the saving in wages payments. Selbie received £100 and some others were given payments of £20 to £50 in recognition of 'special services'. The strike gained improved pay and negotiating conditions for all railwaymen.

By a last minute decision, railwaymen did not join the miners' strike of 1 April to 30 June 1921, but coal shortages once again forced the Metropolitan to reduce train services, particularly electric mileage. Neasden boilers and one locomotive were temporarily converted to oil fuel.

When steam locomotive drivers and firemen were called out on strike nationally by the Association of Locomotive Engineers and Firemen from 21 to 29 January 1924, the Metropolitan's services suffered only minimal disruption.

APATHY MET BY SPORT AND EDUCATION

A passenger traffic commission, chaired by John Wardle, was appointed in 1921 to investigate the reasons for a decline in Metropolitan traffic and make recommendations. Its interesting report was mainly concerned with the state and prospects of particular stations, but it concluded with the observation that there was

> general apathy amongst the staff, doubtless brought about during the period of Government Control: their calibre leaves much to be desired and if they can be awakened to an intelligent interest in their work, the Company's interest would be better served.

It may have been an awareness of low morale and apathy that led the management after 1919 to encourage sports and athletics, and staff initiatives, and make another modest attempt at staff educational improvement. A war memorial fund raised amongst the staff in 1919 was used to provide recreational and sports facilities on a 13-acre site at Wembley Park. This plot, in Forty Lane, was given by the company to the trustees of the newly-formed Metropolitan Railway Athletic Association and £1,000 was lent on easy terms towards the purchase and erection on the site of a £1,500 army recreational hut which was to be used for staff meetings, lectures, ambulance training, education classes and entertainments from 29 July 1922. Annual sports meetings held at Forty Lane were attended by the chairman, vice chairman and Selbie, to present prizes and show themselves to the staff and their families in slightly relaxed conditions. Sadly the 'Remembrance Hall' at Wembley was burned down in September 1929, a portent of the coming doom of the Metropolitan.

A staff suggestions scheme was started in 1922, but subsequently the arrangements were altered so that suggestions were submitted via the sectional councils and the Neasden Works committee. This scheme was to be subsumed in a campaign introduced by Selbie in October 1927 under the spur of declining traffic returns, in which he called for staff cooperation with the management in extending the company's business; in ensuring economy of working; in eliminating waste; and in generally fostering the interests of the undertaking. On the education side, a technical lending library covering all aspects of railway work was opened in 1924 for clerical and supervisory staff use.

Another privilege at first restricted to the white collar employees was the issue from 1925 of holiday free passes over other railway companies' lines. At the same time, all permanent staff were given four free passes a year over their own system (six a year after ten years' service), these also being available for wives and children under 14. Passes were supplemented by the usual privilege tickets at reduced rates which had been first introduced, for Neasden staff only, in 1882–3. From January 1928 all permanent staff enjoyed a 'Third Class Annual Standard' pass, giving complete freedom of travel over the whole system south of Wembley Park, including the GN&CR. It was hoped they would use this to explore the railway and then advertise its facilities to their friends and acquaintances. All permanent staff were naturally encouraged to live on the MRCE estates and to assist in this, from June 1927, under a provision of the Metropolitan Railway Act, 1926, the company began to offer employees 90 per cent house purchase mortgages at a fixed rate of five per cent. They would have been fortunate at this period to have obtained such terms outside.

Morale was also boosted by the payment of bonuses during the 1924–5 Wembley Exhibition, following the tradition established in the 19th century (Chapter 13), and by the end of the 1920s it is probably fair to say that staff morale and staff relationships with management were as good as they had ever been. But there was one rude interruption to this steady improvement.

Railwaymen across the nation strongly supported the TUC call for a general strike from 4 May 1926 to back the coal miners' resistance to wage reductions. Selbie, hoping that his men at least might opt out, told them:

> This is of course an entirely irregular and unconstitutional proceeding and I hope you will think twice before acting on the instruction. It is breaking contract with the employers, dealing a blow at the prosperity of the Company and causing untold trouble and inconvenience to the thousands of people who rely on the Metropolitan to get to their places of business every day.

Some 80 per cent of the staff ignored this appeal, including for the first time many clerks, but Selbie was pleased to find some of the substation charge engineers and assistants at their posts. With the latter group, 12 naval stokers and other volunteers to keep Neasden power house going, he was able to operate an electric service from the first day of the strike. Four days later, he addressed a missive to the absent men, telling them they were not in dispute with the Metropolitan but were being exploited for ends in which they had no direct concern; the trades unions were being 'prostituted to political aims'. The railway, he added, was working in their absence, improving its services every day; no one returning to duty would be prejudiced. The message concluded with the headmasterly sentiment: 'Think it over and act like men.' Only 128 of the 3,374 on strike were thus persuaded to return.

Such was the amount of (fairly) skilled labour available in one form or another that 235 train trips were run on the first day of the strike, providing a 15-minute interval to and from Harrow and a 20-minute one on the Inner Circle. By the end of the first week (10 May) there were 565 trips a day[6].

All 'loyal men who had placed themselves unreservedly at the disposal of the Company for any duties required' received double pay, whilst outside volunteers got the normal going rate plus an extra two days' pay. Selbie earned himself a £200 gratuity from the board; other senior officers and operating staff were granted £75, £50 or £10. These sums represent an interesting assessment by the board of their assumed relative values to the company.

After the strikers returned on 14 May 1926 disorganisation of operations and arrears of maintenance prevented resumption of near-normal services until 18 May. For some time after that passenger and freight workings continued to be reduced by 20 and 40 per cent respectively to conserve coal as the miners were still on strike. Silesian coal was purchased for the power station and the locomotives. Neasden workshops were put on short time from 7 June 1926, not returning to the guaranteed week until 11 April 1927. At the annual meeting on 17 February 1927, Lord Aberconway told the shareholders that the calculable loss to the Metropolitan from the general and coal strikes was £140,000. Railwaymen, both on the Metropolitan and nationally, gained nothing from their part in the general strike, which seriously weakened the finances of their unions.

Within two years the railway unions were forced to give in to pressure from the managements for a national reduction of 2½ per cent in all gross earnings, including salaries. This cut, which for Metropolitan staff operated from 1 October 1928, was a recognition of the railways' falling revenue in the face of road competition (more freight had been lost to road during and after the 1926 strike) and the depression in trade. At first the unions resisted the inclusion of the Metropolitan in the pay reduction, asserting that it was not suffering so much as the four grouped companies. Whilst the Metropolitan management admitted its problems were not so great as those of the LMSR, LNER, GWR and SR, it could point to a significant drop in passenger earnings in 1927 over those of 1923, the last normal full year, adding that the railway was not earning the interest on the capital expenditure necessary to keep its plant and facilities up to date. Reluctantly the unions agreed and the Metropolitan staff, up to the highest levels, together with the directors, suffered a 2½ per cent reduction in their remuneration until May 1930, when the arrangement was ended by national agreement. It is interesting to note in relation to this incident and the muted plea of distress that the dividend on Metropolitan Railway ordinary stock, which had been four per cent in 1923, was inflated by the Wembley bonanza to five per cent in 1924 and 1925, and had dropped to three per cent in the year of the general strike, rose to 3½ per cent in 1928 and four in 1929. Some of this recovery was of course due to a steady growth in outer suburban traffic, which brought a substantial increase in passenger carryings between 1927 and 1929.

But the economic collapse of the early 1930s was around the corner, biting deeper into the receipts of the four grouped companies and bringing a restoration of the national 2½ per cent pay cut in March 1931. This time there was a further reduction of 2½ per cent on wages of £2 a week and more and reductions in overtime, night and Sunday pay[7]. On this occasion there was more conviction in the Metropolitan's case for inclusion; passenger carryings had fallen to below the level of the early 1920s and the ordinary dividend was down to 2½ per cent.

In their anxiety to achieve the best possible terms for the shareholders in the pending reorganisation of London transport, the Metropolitan board and management of 1931–33 seem to have entirely overlooked any consultation with the employees, who were not even given adequate information about their future. Possibly the staff representatives were not sufficiently alert and active in seeking participation or facts, or they complacently trusted their interests were in safe hands. Whatever the truth, nothing much appears to have been done before an all but post-mortem meeting between Anderson, Hally, Grainger (assistant solicitor) and staff representatives at Baker Street on 28 June 1933.

At this gathering the staff side argued that the shareholders had been given guaranteed equality of share values but nothing at all had been said about discrepancies in conditions between Metropolitan and Underground staff, most of which were pointing to improvements for the former[8]. The Metropolitan's employees had been 'treated more simply than children should be treated' and had not been fully informed as to who would be their new managers and owners after the coming Friday midnight. One staff representative commented wryly:

> To me it is a sad thought that the Transport Board, before having actually taken over, during the transitional period, are actually considering paint, uniforms, and all that class of thing, before they have even considered the lives and welfare of the people who have got to operate that paint.

Some apposite remarks were made about wage cuts at a time when productivity was being forced up (a reference to the reduction in guards and introduction of eight-car trains). These were described as

> hardships we have suffered for the Metropolitan Railway – an employer to whom we have much affection; and it is hardly to be expected that we should so readily suffer hardship for an employer to whom we have not yet had time to be affectionate – to the London Transport Board.

There was a nostalgic reference to Selbie, who, it was said, had laid down the principle that questions of management should not preclude or debar discussion on any question the staff might wish to bring forward. The fact that staff could criticise their own superior officers had become 'a condition of service on the Metropolitan'; they could even comment on the directors' report to the shareholders, which had been shown to them in advance. There was no sign that this would be sustained under the London Passenger Transport Board, although they would want it to be.

To all this Anderson and the other officers listened without making substantive comment, merely pointing out with unblushing accuracy that at this stage in the proceedings they could do nothing; they were in the position of trustees about to hand over the undertaking to the new body.

It is sad that the history of this proudly independent railway, which had in general enjoyed happy management–staff relationships, should have ended on this rather sour note. For all his pomposity and paternalism (qualities not at all unusual in the finest railway managers of the day) Selbie would certainly have handled this aspect of the transition rather more wisely.

17

AN AWKWARD SORT OF RAILWAY

An attempt is made in this concluding chapter to review the Metropolitan Railway's character, image and commercial success. Opportunity will be taken to underline an aspect which many readers will already have appreciated; that over the years there were several significant changes in direction, each closely associated with strong personalities at the top.

As a railway system, the Metropolitan was developed into an awkward but interesting combination of a small main line type operation with an intensively-worked urban transit system attached to its inner end. For many years the company was handling freight and passenger services over distances up to 51 miles whilst simultaneously coping with concentrated short-trip movements between the great London main line termini or between inner London stations generally and the City. Whilst this mixture made it a difficult and challenging railway to work economically and efficiently, it was on the whole fortunate in its managers, a circumstance which brought it modest commercial success and, at any rate in retrospect, a good deal of lasting public affection which in more recent years has been converted into nostalgia.

TRANSMUTATION AND PERSONALITIES

As its creators, Pearson, Malins and John Fowler had set out to make an urban railway of a novel kind, capable of handling local traffic within London whilst also affording access to the heart of the City and new central markets for passengers and freight from the main lines serving the north and the west. This dual function, never discarded, was further strengthened by the Metropolitan's participation in the completion of the Inner Circle and its junctions to the East London Railway, both executed at immense cost.

After his arrival in 1872 Sir Edward Watkin fostered these inner London extensions and links but also began to use the Metropolitan to further his personal and wider ambition to build a new trunk line connecting the north and the midlands to London and the Channel ports. As he set about steadily extending the little St John's Wood branch northwestwards in pursuit of this last objective, steering the Metropolitan into new waters, he was to a large extent successful in deceiving both the Metropolitan shareholders and rival main line managements as to exactly what he was about.

His objectives largely obtained, his spirit and strength weakening, Watkin chose Bell as his successor, unthinkingly setting off a further transmutation for the Metropolitan. Bell's prickly attitude and in particular his sour personal feud with Pollitt, general manager of the MSLR (later the Great Central), coloured the interface between the Metropolitan and that company, which was bringing its new main line to London, in conformance with Watkin's plan. Bell's handling of business was partly responsible for things not working out as the old master had proposed. But in one sense he did continue Watkin's expansionist policy by securing for the Metropolitan the Harrow & Uxbridge Railway, a potentially powerful generator of suburban traffic (though this was to be long in maturing). Bell's successor, Ellis, presided over the important electrification scheme whilst nurturing the development of outer suburban traffic, whose significance he fully recognised. Selbie, the last of the Metropolitan's great captains, followed, inheriting a sound foundation on which he was to develop the company's ultimate principal role, that of carrier of remunerative middle class suburban traffic beyond the area of motor bus competition. This he combined with establishment of the railway as an urban and suburban property developer on a new scale, pursuing both objectives with conviction and drive to the point where the urban rapid transit operation, with its high costs and low returns, became very much a second order priority.

Almost all the company's publicity in the 1920s and early 1930s reflected the importance attached to the outer suburban sector. The directors of the period saw themselves as helping the suburban middle class dream towards realisation. At the opening of the Watford branch in 1925, Sir Clarendon Hyde, the deputy chairman, voiced this, remarking that the Metropolitan had 'a definite policy. It was that whenever the jaded Londoner went northward in pursuit of his ideals – open air and a garden – there the Metropolitan tried to follow him.' It is not irrelevant that housing and town planning were among the many interests of the company's last chairman, Lord Aberconway.

A MINIATURE MAIN LINE

A concept of the Metropolitan as a self-sufficient undertaking possessing all the features of a main line railway as regards services, rolling stock, and functions had begun to coalesce in the 1910s. Sedulously fostered by Selbie, who no doubt saw it as a means of boosting his own importance, it had the strong support of Lord Aberconway, who once described the Metropolitan as 'a trunk line in miniature'[1]. In 1915 Selbie had drawn comparisons between the Metropolitan and the LBSCR[2], though in some respects the LTSR was a closer analogy, with little more than a 45 mile main line carrying heavy suburban and holiday traffic and an electrified connection to the Inner Circle.

This idea of the Metropolitan as a small main line company which had somehow escaped the 1921 grouping was fervently deployed as a useful defence against attempts to bring it into any form of coordinated London passenger transport body when this proposal came forward in the 1920s. Thus, in September 1925, Selbie wrote of 'the policy of building up the Company's lines into an individual and self-contained system, which for other reasons is an extremely important factor'[3]. And when the real attack came, Lord Aberconway is found asserting 'We are, although a comparatively small undertaking, a Main Line Railway Company in all essentials, and there can be no practical difficulties in our joining the Main Line Pool'[4].

We can also discern a practical embodiment of the same philosophy in the creation and careful preservation from the 1900s onwards of Baker Street as a main traffic centre with an impressive building over the station and another nearby housing the company's headquarters.

So strongly did the concept become rooted that in 1932 the company seemed ready to sacrifice its purely urban operations if by so doing it could be allowed to continue as 'a main line company' outside the new London Transport. The change in the way the railway saw itself was epitomised in the accepted nomenclature of its constituent parts. For many years the line between South Kensington and Aldgate was known and referred to as 'the Main Line' and that northwest from Baker Street as 'the Branch' or 'the Extension Line'. But in the company's closing decades, the latter was always the 'Main Line', the remainder merely the 'Inner Circle Line'.

AN OBJECT OF AFFECTION

Within this fondly-nurtured image also lies the explanation of the powerful attraction the Metropolitan has long exercised over railway amateurs. With its longer-distance passenger services hauled by elegant steam tank locomotives and handsome named electric engines, its romantic Pullman cars, its freight and parcels services, its interworking with other railway companies and its 51-mile main route (albeit ending in rural emptiness), the Metropolitan had something of everything, nectars for all tastes, yet was small enough to be thoroughly explored and understood. Its rolling stock in particular had great variety and charm, even if much was somewhat outdated. There was a satisfying diversity of station architecture and design and in signalling. It was that contradiction in terms, a model railway to full scale. One addict has even suggested, tongue in cheek, that it was created for the enjoyment of railway devotees.

And then of course there was *Metro-land*, the territory, almost a way of life, that the Railway claimed as its own. In shaping his personal Metropolitan Railway, Selbie was ably assisted by his commercial manager, John Wardle, a loyal image-maker who, after 1920, sought to see it labelled as the *Metro* rather than the *Met*, a contraction given some official usage from about 1914. Indeed Wardle was so obsessed by *Metro* that he personally altered by hand every single reference to the railway's name when material was submitted for his approval before publication. No doubt he considered it a logical step from *Metro-land*, the happy invention of his office, born like many other idealistic notions in the midst of the horrors of world war. Most of the Metropolitan's territory beyond Neasden, which constituted Metro-land, was indeed then wonderfully beautiful and unspoiled, but thanks to the enterprise of the railway company, of its associated estates arm, the MRCE, and of many independent developers and builders, it was becoming something very different by the late 1920s and early 1930s. In those ten or so short years, its appearance, notably along the Uxbridge branch and between Neasden and Northwood, changed almost beyond recognition. In the sense that Metro-land had signified a rural arcadia, it was driven further and further down the main line, becoming more constrained every year. This suburbanisation of Metro-land, which was of course exactly what Selbie had foreseen and earnestly desired, continued without check between 1933 and 1939 and to some extent was resumed from the 1950s and still goes on[5].

At Chorleywood and one or two other favoured locations there was a delightful but all too brief interlude in the 1910s and early 1920s when Metro-land simultaneously embraced both rural delights and middle class comforts and convenience. This was a time when the privileged few could enjoy an excellent train service to and from town, whilst living with the full loveliness of Metro-land at their doorsteps, or on view from their windows. At the same time, others, less fortunate, were able to use Metropolitan trains to explore Metro-land on foot at weekends, revelling in a countryside as yet unsullied by the worst environmental ravages of the motor car age.

So potent was the contemporary propaganda from Wardle's office, its amateurishness only adding to its charm, so sweet the blurred and confused recollections and folk-memory of it all, that Metro-land became capable, many years later, in the atomic, car-obsessed age, the benighted second half of the 20th century, of fostering its own minor nostalgia industry. Sir John Betjeman, who had written several poems in the 1950s which included references to the Metropolitan Railway[6], conducted in 1973 a most entertaining BBC television excursion into Metro-land[7]. This was so well-received, it was repeated several times by popular demand and translated to video tape. It was followed several years later by the publication of a series of three volumes in which a vast selection of illustrations of early and developing Metro-land were judiciously mixed with others of the railway which exploited it, each picture lovingly and nostalgically captioned[8].

So much for the image and the intangibles. But what of the railway's performance as a commercial proposition? It was, after all, a capitalist enterprise, in business to make money for its shareholders, only receiving very limited assistance from public funds, and that very late in its career. Much has already been said on this, but we should now look at it as a whole.

A FRIEND TO SHAREHOLDERS

In examining the Metropolitan's financial history in the round it is best to ignore the extraordinary distortions and accounting acrobatics of the Parson era, ie up to 1872. Their importance can be over-emphasised, and it is evident that beneath the foamy tide of bloated dividends, the railway and its property assets were providing a sufficient income to justify payment, having regard to the most exemplary accounting principles, of a steady flow of modest dividends on the ordinary shares. From the time of Watkin's arrival, despite continuing heavy investment in central London construction and his bold expansionist policy, which pushed the line into areas yielding only the thinnest of traffics for many years, his tight financial control on contracts and major purchases, combined with competent management, assured an unbroken sequence of modest but by no means trivial dividends on the ordinary shares. The size of the balance available for distribution as dividend was of course swollen by the produce of the company's uniquely large holdings of non-railway property, but for most of the Metropolitan's history, the purely railway side of the business contributed sufficient income to more than balance the associated expenditure. In the 19th and early 20th century the Metropolitan's credit was sound enough to enable it to raise in the money market without difficulty all the capital it required. This applied even for the huge amounts sucked up by the electrification in the 1900s.

From the opening of the line until the end of the 19th century the number of passengers carried each year grew annually, apart from a few minor checks, increasing from just under 12 million in 1864 to 96 million in 1899. Between 1877, when Watkin got the accounts in proper order, and 1899, gross revenue expenditure and receipts on the railway and property assets were sufficiently well balanced to provide around five per cent on ordinary stock, the railway performance representing between 2¾ and 3¾ per cent on its own account. Competition from the new deep level tube railways and improved public street transport then checked the growth in passenger carryings until 1902, when it began to rise again as Londoners indulged in a growing number of rides per head per year. After 1910 this growth levelled out, although there was a temporary boost between 1913 and 1919 associated with wartime and immediate post-war conditions. During this period, dividends on the railway's ordinary shares fell; from 3⅛ per cent in 1900 to a mere ½ per cent in 1907–08, rising then to a peak of just under 2 per cent in 1911–13, fluctuating around 1 per cent until 1920 and reaching 2¼ in 1921.

Economies in expenditure, the heavy passenger traffic for the Wembley Exhibition and the success of the Metro-land development policy brought a return to prosperity between 1922 and 1929, the railway ordinary dividend rising to 3½ per cent in 1922, four per cent in 1923 and an all-time high of five per cent in 1924–5. With a hiccup in the general strike year of 1926, followed by a slow recovery in 1927, the return went down to three per cent, rising to 3½ in 1928 and four in 1929. From 1930 to 1932 as explained in Chapter 15, the overall revenue fell perceptibly in the face of road competition and severe economic depression, dividends dropping steadily to a miserable 1⅝ per cent in the latter year.

This poor closing financial performance, the sudden loss of Selbie's strength and drive, and a wavering and uncertain grip from an interim management much preoccupied with the London transport coordination proposals all combined to cloud the final years of the company.

Its fate was probably beyond the power of its board and its management to alter. As any practicable alternative to the disappearance of the Metropolitan Railway Company would have been difficult if not impossible to sustain alongside the new London Passenger

Transport Board, the course of events at this time exuded a certain inevitability. Moreover, in a little over two decades, aided by government-encouraged mass car-ownership, the social structure and workplace pattern of the population served by the railway was to change drastically. Much as some may regret it, subsequent events have shown that there would have been no lasting place for the sort of independent railway which Selbie and Lord Aberconway had so much wanted to preserve and develop in 1929–30.

CHAPTER NOTES

Chapter 1 (pp 13–21)
1   1793–1862: Pearson served on the City Common Council 1817–20 and 1820–36; he was solicitor to the City Commissioners of Sewers 1859–62 and MP for Lambeth 1847–50.
2   18??–1875: Stevens was one of the District Surveyors for the City of London appointed under 14 Geo III c 78, 1774. He became surveyor to the North Metropolitan Railway 1853, architect and engineer to that Railway 1853–4, and architect and assistant engineer to the Metropolitan Railway 1854–7.
3   The London & Greenwich Railway had been completed between London Bridge and Greenwich in 1836–8; the London & Blackwall Railway between Fenchurch Street and Blackwall Pier in 1840–1; and the East & West India Docks & Birmingham Junction Railway (renamed North London Railway 1853) between Camden Town (LNWR) and Bow Junction (London & Blackwall Railway) in 1850–1.
4   The New Road was London's first bypass. Opened in 1756, it is now Marylebone Road, Euston Road and Pentonville Road.
5   The firm of Burchells (William Burchell Jr) was to remain solicitors and legal advisers to the Metropolitan until 17 February 1882 when its place was taken by Messrs Fowler & Perks.
6   1817–98: Fowler worked under J. U. Rastrick on bridge designs for the London & Brighton Railway, 1838. Resident engineer Stockton & Hartlepool Railway 1839; engineer, general manager and locomotive superintendent of that railway 1841; in practice on his own account from 1844, taking an active part in many 'Railway Mania' schemes. He designed and completed the first London railway bridge over the Thames at Pimlico, 1860. Engineer of the Metropolitan and MDR as described in the main text. Advised on railway construction in Egypt and India. With his partner Benjamin Baker, designed the Forth Bridge, 1890, and the first London deep-level tube, the City & South London Railway, 1890. Knighted (KCMG), 1885; Baronet, 1890.
7   The powers for the Euston connection were allowed to lapse as no agreement could be reached with the LNWR. The junctions with the GNR at King's Cross were supplemented and amended by the Metropolitan Railway Acts of 1855, 1856, 1860 and 1861.
8   The Metropolitan Railway Act of 1854 had provided for the construction of a new prison at the Railway's expense, with free conveyance of prisoners to and from it. The site of the demolished prison was to have been used as a goods depot.
9   Following the successful opening of the line, the shares rose quickly to 25 per cent, whereupon the City astutely sold, realising a handsome profit. The GWR followed suit.

Chapter 2 (pp 22–40)
1   1826–74: From the start of his career until 1870 Johnson was in Fowler's office, responsible under him for several railway projects, including the Mid Kent and

Crystal Palace–Farnborough. He later worked on Manchester Town Hall, Eaton Hall, Cheshire, and Holborn Viaduct station, LCDR.

2   1830–1918: Fenton's career started at age 15 on the Kendal & Windermere Railway. He served subsequently on the East Lancashire, Eastern Counties, LSWR and other railways, becoming secretary of the East Lancashire in 1856. General manager of the Metropolitan 1863–80. General manager of the South Eastern Railway, 1880, consulting director South Eastern & Chatham Railways Joint Committee, 1896; knighted 1889.

3   This is confirmed by the list of Fowler's responsibilities as agreed by the Metropolitan board on 12 April 1860 which include 'the making of working drawings' for the stations. He was also required to make all designs and working drawings for 'the special traction power', rolling stock, plant, locomotive sheds, workshops, etc.

4   Felix Spiers and Christopher Pond went to Australia as young men in the gold rush of the 1850s, securing a contract to supply refreshments to gold diggers on the Melbourne & Ballarat Railway. Returning to Britain, they established their reputation with the Metropolitan Railway contracts, their first buffet at Farringdon Street proving very popular. Contracts with other railway companies followed, including catering and hotel management for the LCDR, the SER, the LSWR, the Midland, the Furness and the Southern Railway. By 1916 their Metropolitan establishments were situated at Aldersgate (now Barbican); Baker Street (buffet and tea room); Bayswater; Edgware Road; Farringdon Street (buffet and restaurant); King's Cross; Marlborough Road; Moorgate Street (restaurant and buffet at street level and platform buffet); Notting Hill Gate; Praed Street (now Paddington); South Kensington; Gloucester Road; St John's Wood; and Swiss Cottage. Those added after 1916 are referred to in the main text.

5   For a full account of the known facts about this unusual locomotive and some suppositions, see Baker, Sir Benjamin, Paper to the Institution of Civil Engineers, 17 February, 1885; Robbins, Michael, 'Fowler's Ghosts', *The Railway Magazine*, June 1963; Steamologist, 'Facts and Fables of Fowler's Ghost', *Railway World*, January and February 1974; and Seymour, M., 'The Ghost Walks Again', *Railway World*, October 1974.

6   For further information on these locomotives see Bennett, Alfred Rosling, 'The Early Locomotive History of The Metropolitan Railway', *The Railway Magazine*, April and June, 1908.

7   1832–1915: Spagnoletti was a prolific inventor and designer of electrical equipment, providing the disc-block telegraph instruments used on the Metropolitan, the GWR, MDR and other railways. His interlocking system for mechanical signals was widely adopted. Between 1847 and 1855 he worked for the Electric Telegraph Company, entering GWR service as electric telegraph superintendent in the latter year, and serving in that capacity until 1892. As outside contractors, his firm maintained the Metropolitan's telegraphs until 1902 when the Metropolitan formed its own signal and telegraphs department, retaining him as consultant telegraph engineer until 1905. He was appointed consulting electrical engineer to the City & South London tube railway in 1889.

8   See Appendix 8 and Lascelles, T. S., 'Underground Signalling in the Steam Days', *The Railway Magazine*, March/April 1947.

9   See Bennett, *op cit*, for further detail.

10   There was a minor collision on 27 February 1863 when during track alterations at Farringdon Street, with interlocking disconnected, a train was switched on to the wrong line.

11   See diagram p25.

12 About twelve locomotives were sent to the Metropolitan. For details see Bennett, *op cit*, and Lee, Charles E., 'Borrowed Locomotives on The Metropolitan', *The Railway Magazine*, July 1964.

13 For a detailed account of GWR services over the Metropolitan and the H&CR, see Peacock, Thomas B., *Great Western London Suburban Services*, Oakwood Press, 1970, Chapter 7. GWR services were extended from Moorgate to Aldgate from 1 July 1894 but Liverpool Street became the terminus from 1 July 1910.

14 Heating, lighting and braking equipment of carriages were usually provided by specialist firms and manufacturers' charges therefore normally excluded the cost of these items.

15 For further details of the first Metropolitan locomotives, see Bennett, *op cit*, Ahrons, E. L. 'Locomotive & Train Working in the Latter Part of the 19th Century: Metropolitan & Metropolitan District Railways', *The Railway Magazine*, December 1924, and Reed, Brian, *Loco Profile 10: The Met Tanks*, Profile Publications, 1971, from which much of this description is taken.

16 For further details of these carriages and subsequent modifications and additions, see Benest, K. R., 'The Coaching Stock of the Metropolitan Railway', *Underground*, Vol 1, No 4 (April 1962), *et seq.*

17 For details of the promotion and financing of the H&CR, see Lee, Charles E., 'Mixed Gauge to Hammersmith', *The Railway Magazine*, June 1964.

18 For details of the locomotives used on these services, see Bennett, *op cit.*

19 Platforms had been completed on the H&CR side of the junction with the West London Railway in the summer of 1864 but were never opened to the public following GWR objections. Referred to as 'Norland' in the H&CR minutes, this facility is marked on some contemporary maps.

Chapter 3 (pp 41–45)

1 Under the Metropolitan Railway Act of 17 June 1867, the company was enabled to apply this subscription to the Metropolitan & St John's Wood Railway as a whole. Subsequent Metropolitan Railway acts authorised further purchases of St John's Wood capital by the Metropolitan (see also note 10 below).

2 Nicoll was an astute speculator, laying out roads and building plots on his land west of West End Lane to enhance his compensation before the extension had been finalised. In 1874 he offered land to the Metropolitan for their proposed new locomotive and carriage depot but his price of £1,500 an acre was thought excessive.

3 The financial difficulties led to indefinite postponement of the Hampstead branch until the powers were finally abandoned in an act of 20 June 1870.

4 In practice, the Metropolitan allowed a rebate of 12½ per cent on the traffic, a figure which averaged some £2,500 a year (MET 10/39).

5 The style can be seen at Marlborough Road station, which remains today virtually unaltered externally apart from the removal of the canopy, although heavily redecorated for its present role as a restaurant.

6 The rules for the pilotmen, 1877, are reproduced in full in the *Journal of the London Underground Railway Society*, Vol 11, No 2, February 1972.

7 This brake was modified by Burnett from the version used on the North London Railway. On the Metropolitan each carriage had its own brake power in the form of a weight acting through suitable levers on its own brake blocks. Brakes were kept out of action by tightening a cord running from end to end of the train. This cord was subject to the control of the driver at the front and the guard at the rear, who could apply the brakes by releasing it. Should there be a derailment or other accident the cord would be severed, applying the brakes, which were in this sense

331

automatic. As the action of this system was jerky, there were complaints from passengers and some injuries when alighting at stations. For a full description of the brake, see *The Engineer*, 19 July 1895.

8   They were sufficient only to pay an average dividend of 2¼ per cent a year on the 5 per cent Preference Stock. Holders of Ordinary Stock received no dividend throughout the undertaking's separate existence.

9   1823–1904: After working for the GWR as an engineering draughtsman and clerk from 1840, Forbes was made district goods manager, Gloucester, then chief goods manager, Paddington. His next post was general manager of the largely British-funded Dutch Rhenish Railway which he restored to a small profit by severe financial control, emerging with both a reputation for able management and a taste for handling the affairs of ailing companies. In 1861 he was offered the general managership of both the GWR and the LCDR; he took the latter, perhaps attracted by its financial distress, although the offer was in any case slightly better. In 1869 his advice was sought by the infant Metropolitan District Railway (see Chapter 4), which appointed him a director in 1870 and chairman in 1872.

After some competent work he was given an LCDR directorship in 1871, going on to become that railway's chairman and managing director in 1873, a post he held until the end of 1898. During that period he experienced an abrasive relationship with his peer and *bête-noir*, Sir Edward Watkin, chairman of the rival South Eastern Railway. Forbes and Watkin also faced each other in similar conflict as chairmen of the MDR and the Metropolitan, of which Watkin became chairman in 1872 (see Chapter 5). This clash of personalities fuelled much futile dispute and litigation which poisoned the relationship between the two underground railway companies, blocking the logical amalgamation. Forbes remained chairman of the MDR until 1901, outlasting Watkin's reign over the Metropolitan.

His other posts included chairmanships of the Regent's Canal, City & Docks Railway, the Whitechapel & Bow Joint Railway and the Didcot, Newbury & Southampton Railway, and of electricity, insurance and telephone companies. He was also for a time deputy chairman and joint manager of the Hull & Barnsley Railway.

He possessed a suave and charming surface manner and was able to exercise astonishing powers of persuasion. This exterior concealed an iron will and determination. To quote the obituary in *The Railway Magazine*, he was a 'past master in the art of *bunkum*, and strangely enough by its use in an unadulterated state, he was generally able to persuade shareholders . . . to do as he desired'. In private life he was an art connoisseur and collector, in contrast to Watkin, who was something of a philistine.

10   Power to purchase shares was given in the Metropolitan Railway Acts of 30 June, 1874 and 12 July 1877. By 1877 the Metropolitan held £100,000 of the £183,170 5 per cent Preference Stock which had been issued, and £200,000 of the £300,000 Ordinary Stock, as well as £38,929 in debentures.

Chapter 4 (pp 46–59)

1   'Monody on The Death of Aldersgate Street Station', *John Betjeman's Collected Poems*, 1958. The 'death' refers to the removal of the war-damaged 1865 roof in 1954–5.

2   All GNR services on to the Metropolitan were suspended, and all LCDR services reversed at Farringdon Street from 1 July 1867 to allow work to proceed on the City Widened Lines.

3   These tracks were converted to standard gauge in 1869.

Chapter Notes

4 The City Corporation opened its Smithfield Meat & Poultry Market on 24 November 1868, but the basement rail depot, with its hydraulic lifts to the market floor and circular cart approach, was not served by freight trains (GWR, standard gauge) until the following 1 May. It was last used on 28 July 1962 and is now a car park. The GNR goods depot on the west side of Farringdon Street station was first used on 2 November 1874. Enlarged in 1876, it was finally closed from 15 January 1956. At the time of writing, its gaunt shell still stands.

5 The 'Middle Circle' trains ceased to run east of Earls Court after traffic on 30 June 1900 and were withdrawn entirely after traffic on 31 January 1905. From that time trains ran from the Metropolitan to Kensington (Addison Road), now Olympia, only.

6 Fowler had originally suggested additionally the construction of an outer circle to join up existing radial railways into London. His proposals for an inner circle, which envisaged extension of the Metropolitan to Westminster via Kensington and a link from there to the Farringdon Street station via the new Embankment, were consolidated by the Select Committee with those of a similar rival scheme for a Metropolitan Grand Union Railway. Unusually, owing to the late settlement of the final route, plans for the final scheme were not deposited until after the bill had been passed.

7 In November 1866 the financial problems of Peto & Betts led to their withdrawing from the consortium; their place was taken by Charles and Thomas Lucas.

8 On 21 October 1868 Fenton reported to the Metropolitan board that 'serious inconvenience was daily being experienced' by confusion of Notting Hill Gate with Notting Hill (now Ladbroke Grove). Then, as on subsequent occasions when complaints were made by the public (the Duke of Rutland was a victim of misdirection in 1875), the GWR refused to agree to any change of name for the H&CR station. But in 1880 it was renamed Notting Hill & Ladbroke Grove, and on 1 June 1919 it became Ladbroke Grove (North Kensington). The suffix was dropped by London Transport in 1938.

9 At this time only the Metropolitan platforms were available at South Kensington, the MDR gaining access to them by a double junction at the west end controlled from a signal box on the inner rail platform. The tunnel ended in a bell mouth to facilitate eventual access to the MDR platforms, which were completed on 10 July 1871. Meanwhile, a single arch barrel roof sheltered the Metropolitan side, supported by columns erected on the outer rail platform. To oppose the lateral thrust of this roof, a substantial but temporary wall was erected at the back of this platform to support struts attached to the tops of the columns. When the top of this wall was being demolished for the completion of the station, a technically minded spectator, fearing a catastrophe, informed the Board of Trade, to which the engineer was able to supply suitable assurances.

10 References to the MDR are necessarily brief. A detailed factual account of its legislation, construction, topography and works between Kensington and Mansion House and its first locomotives and rolling stock will be found in Edmonds, Alexander, *History of the Metropolitan District Railway to June 1908*, London Transport, 1973.

11 Parliament sought to secure continuous operation of a future Inner Circle by inserting appropriate provisions in legislation, for example in section 17 of the MDR Act, 1870, which stated that any future company given powers to complete the Circle should not be opposed by the MDR, but should be granted by the latter full facilities for operating a Circle traffic.

Chapter Notes

1 The board appealed against this judgement and the case was not finally concluded until 1874 when an arbitrator decided there had been no bad faith on the directors' part. The directors (by then all removed) were allowed to settle by making a total payment to the company of £2,130, a very substantial reduction on the original liability.

2 1819–1901: A merchant's son, Watkin was educated at Manchester Grammar School, then trained in his father's office. Appointed secretary of the Trent Valley Railway in 1845 he became ill through overwork, relaxing by visiting the USA and Canada in 1851. On his return he joined the LNWR but in 1854 he was offered the general managership of the MSLR. He became a director of that railway in 1863 and its chairman in 1864, positions he held until 1900 and 1894 respectively. He was chairman of the SER from 1866 to 1894 (remaining a director until 1900) and of the Metropolitan Railway from 1872 to 1894. Directorships of other railway companies were held at various times, including the GWR and the GER, and he was a member of the Cheshire Lines Committee. An enthusiastic Francophile, he supported the Channel Tunnel concept and on his initiative the SER began experimental boring from a point between Folkestone and Dover in 1881, works which were taken over by the Submarine Continental Railway Company (later the Channel Tunnel Company) of which he was a director. Knighted in 1868, he was created baronet in 1898. Liberal in politics, he was elected MP for Stockport in 1857, 1861 and 1865 and MP for Hythe and Folkestone in 1874.

   Mary Briggs, his first wife, died on 8 March 1888. He then married Ann, widow of Herbert Ingram, founder of *The Illustrated London News*, when she was 81 and he was 74. He outlived her, after placing the fortunes of the paper on a sound basis.

   In an obituary, *The Railway Magazine* remarked that whilst he possessed the diplomatic instinct, his fighting propensities always seemed to get the better of him. 'He had an autocratic way of taking his co-directors with him but the results were not always to the company's advantage'. (The same could have been said with equal truth of his rival and peer, J. S. Forbes.) His two notable failures were the GCR London Extension (not, it is fair to say, completed as he would have wished, with its through connection to the southern lines) and the bizarre Wembley Tower venture. In terms of financial achievement and benefit for shareholders, his chairmanship of the Metropolitan was probably the most successful. Under his direction the ordinary dividend rose from 1½ to 5 per cent in six years, the tangled finances and accounts were straightened out and passenger traffic more than doubled. It is, however, interesting to note that upon his retirement from the three railway chairmanships, in 1894, not only were the shares of all three marked up on the Stock Exchange, but relations between the Metropolitan and the MDR and between the SER and LCDR rapidly improved.

   He was what is now known as a 'workaholic', believing that all about him would collapse if he relaxed his grip. It was his custom to preside at all three half-yearly meetings of the railways he chaired in the same week, having stage-managed any opposition and fully briefed himself.

3 Watkin's position on the Metropolitan board was strengthened when his son, Alfred Mellor (1846–1914) was made a director in February 1876 after Shuttleworth had moved to the GNR board. Alfred's appointment, justified at age 30 'on the grounds of his special knowledge of the working of railways', infuriated several shareholders who sought a directorship, including Kitching. Another firm ally for Watkin was Edward Hugessen Knatchbull-Hugessen, MP (later Lord Brabourne), an SER director elected to the Metropolitan board in 1876 after Lingard's death.

Chapter Notes

4 Letters at RAIL 236/313/21 63324 (Public Record Office).

5 *City Press*, 22 December 1866.

6 A similar project came forward in 1877 but got nowhere.

7 Metropolitan bills for extension to Whitechapel with junctions to the East London Railway were deposited for the 1874–5 and 1875–6 sessions without success.

8 The title of this firm became Lucas & Aird when Sir John Kelk retired at the end of 1875.

9 The original intention appears to have been to run Metropolitan trains through to Walthamstow, but after initial disputes over the terms of working, the Metropolitan and the GER argued over the routes for the through service. Watkin's preference was to run Metropolitan trains through to south London via the East London Railway, but the GER quite reasonably objected to this as it would have involved crossing all the approach tracks at Liverpool Street on the level. Instead, the GER suggested a service to the Chingford branch or along the main line and on to the Loughton branch. The discussions ran into sand, but Metropolitan Railway through bookings to ELR and LBSCR stations were started on 8 May 1878, passengers walking between the two stations at Liverpool Street. After 1875 only occasional freight trains, specials or excursions used the connecting line, the last being a Metropolitan excursion from Aylesbury to Yarmouth in 1904. Three years later the junction was disconnected. The GER used its end for stock storage for a few years, later converting the tunnel under its property for use as a staff canteen and recreation space.

10 When the original offices at Duke Street, Westminster, had to be vacated in June 1866, the Metropolitan acquired 3 Old Palace Yard, Westminster. In the early years some staff were also accommodated at what is now Euston Square station in railway-owned houses, but in June 1869 these were transferred to a railway-owned house at 32 Westbourne Terrace, Paddington. Late in 1872 the Westminster property was sold and the staff moved to Westbourne Terrace and another Metropolitan house at 5–7 Craven Road, Paddington. At this time the cashier was at Bishop's Road and the ticket sorting staff occupied the unused booking office on the MDR side of Kensington High Street station. From 1878, 26 Craven Road, another Metropolitan property, was converted to offices for the estate, accounts and stationery departments and 5–7 Craven Road, which they had occupied, was given up.

11 This shuttle service was operated at the insistence of the contractor who was working to a bonus/penalty arrangement for early/late completion and wished to establish that the line was clearly ready for use on 18 November.

12 The GWR shared some of the Aldgate–Richmond workings from 1 January 1894, but as the service was run at a substantial loss after the opening of the London United electric tramways along Chiswick High Road from Hammersmith, the ten GWR and seven Metropolitan trains each way weekdays (13 GWR each way Sundays) were withdrawn after 31 December 1906. Subsequent events are related in Chapter 11.

Chapter 6 (pp 75–103)

1 Letter to Pochin, 9 July 1874 (MET 10/39).

2 Address to shareholders of the Metropolitan Railway, July 1887. On this occasion and others, Watkin referred to the Metropolitan's inner London lines as 'our great terminus' or 'grand terminus' for the services of the main line railways. At no time did he appear to envisage a single vast terminal station but rather the distribution of long-distance passengers over the Metropolitan's Inner Circle stations.

3 For proposed branches to Hendon and High Wycombe considered during the Watkin period, see Appendix 4.

4 MSLR minutes 29 November 1872 quoted by Dow, *op cit*, p67. The curious phrase 'and some of them are not one' appears to refer to the possibility of amalgamation between two or more of the companies named.

5 Fowler, J. Kersley, *Records of Old Times*, passage from Chapter XIX reproduced in *Journal of the Railway & Canal Historical Society*, Vol 6, No 1.

6 This locomotive was sold in 1886 to the contractor Maxwell when he was building the Pinner to Rickmansworth extension and No 100, a 22-ton 0-4-0 ST, was bought in its stead. This was replaced in turn in 1897–9 by two Peckett 0-6-0 ST (101–2) weighing 39 tons in working order.

7 With the growth of the Extension Line this became inadequate, with engines standing in the open where they could not be cleaned in inclement weather. A roundhouse for twenty engines was completed in 1898 together with a 50ft turntable. Until that time carriages were also cleaned in the open with same disadvantage; a carriage washing shed, and additional sidings to the north of the works were provided in 1898, a carriage shed following in 1901.

8 This line from the A&BR'S Quainton Road station to Brill, together with its short branch from Wotton Underwood to Kingswood Lane Wharf, was completed in 1871–2 by the third Duke of Buckingham & Chandos to serve his estate. As it was almost entirely on his own land, no parliamentary authority was sought, although it carried public traffic, both passenger and freight. Horses were used initially. For detailed accounts of the history of this curious line, see Gadsden, E. J. S., *Duke of Buckingham's Railways*, Bledlow Press, 1962; Jones, K., *The Wotton Tramway (Brill Branch)*, Oakwood Press, 1974; and Melton, Ian, 'From Quainton to Brill, A History of the Wotton Tramway', *Underground*, No 13, 1984. The latter contains material based on the family archives of the Duke of Buckingham.

9 An Oxford extension was first suggested by the Duke of Buckingham to John Aird Jr in September 1873 (see Melton, *op cit*, p52).

10 The sidings at Harrow were rearranged and extended in 1889 to cope with the residential growth of the district, which brought an increase in the traffic in building materials and coal.

11 The steel sleepers on the Extension Line were replaced by wooden ones in 1898 and reused in sidings (see Chapter 10).

12 Additional sidings were authorised by the board in 1891 when there was said to be a prospect of attracting the coal traffic of the Rickmansworth Gas and Water Companies from the LNWR.

13 For a full account of the Chesham branch, see Jackson, Alan A., 'Chesham's Branch', *Railway World*, September 1984.

14 The separate undertaking, which was merely a financial device, was merged into the general capital of the Metropolitan from 1 January 1893.

15 Supported by Liddell, Firbank claimed a loss on the Aylesbury contract, alleging that instead of the solid chalk he had been told to expect, he found dirty clay and gravel in pot-holes above the chalk, requiring alterations of slopes and cleaning out the bad material. At Amersham he had encountered 'the hardest leathery clay I have ever met'. He was given £4,000 against £10,900 claimed and only then on condition he transferred his gravel pit lands to the Metropolitan free of charge.

16 One paper (MET 1/20) gives this date as 4 January but another (MET 4/10) confirms the generally accepted 1 January. Sunday trains terminated at Grandborough Road until November 1900.

17 Traffic between Aylesbury and Verney Junction was very thin. In April 1904 the Metropolitan general manager proposed replacing the heavy bogie stock trains

operating between Baker Street and Verney Junction with steam or petrol railmotors (the average load north of Aylesbury was 17 passengers per train), but no change was made, apart from a brief trial of a GCR petrol railcar in March 1906 (MET 1/107).

18   The rolling stock acquired was as follows:

Manning Wardle 'K' type 0-6-0 ST *Wotton No 2* (1899), *Brill No 1* (1894), and *Huddersfield* (built 1876, obtained second-hand, 1894), (the first two owned by Earl Temple);
two Bristol Wagon & Carriage Co tramway-type bogie saloon cars (1895), each with 40 seats (both the property of Earl Temple);
two four-wheel passenger carriages;
mineral wagon No 9 (owned by Earl Temple);
eight other mineral wagons.

The O & AT had also hired a rigid eight-wheeled Third Class compartment coach from the Metropolitan in 1899.

19   In 1900, 77 second-hand wagons of which 22 were later allocated to the permanent way department; in 1902, 79 trucks and wagons; in 1903, 2 milk vans; and in 1904, 106 trucks and wagons and 3 horse-boxes.

20   For a full account of the Park and Tower projects, see Travis A. S., 'The Metropolitan Railway in Wembley (1880–1910)' in *The Early History of The Metropolitan District and Metropolitan Railways in Wembley*, Wembley Transport Society, 1963.

21   The station had been completed in April 1891 by J. T. Firbank to a conventional double track, side platform plan with entrance building on the road bridge over the line. To accommodate the expected MSLR services and the traffic to the Park it was widened to four tracks (with up and down local lines as terminal roads) and four platform faces in 1893–4. Its first use was for football traffic to the new ground in the Park on 14 and 21 October 1893 and possibly on subsequent Saturdays that winter. Continuous weekday public service started on Saturday 12 May 1894 with the opening of the Park to the public on that day. Platform roofing, a waiting-room and a shelter on the island platform were not completed until 1896.

Chapter 7 (pp 104–116)
  1   Engineered by (Sir) John Hawkshaw, the East London Railway was opened between Wapping and New Cross (LBSCR) on 7 December 1869 with a train service worked by the LBSCR. It crossed the Thames in the 1843 tunnel designed by Sir Marc Isambard Brunel. At New Cross there was a dedicated two-road station to the east of the LBSCR platforms, used from the opening day until 31 October 1876 after which ELR services terminated at the LBSCR platforms. Spurs from Deptford Road Junction (just south of the present Surrey Docks station) to New Cross LBSCR Up Junction and Old Kent Road Junction LBSCR were opened on 13 March 1871 when a service of LBSCR trains began to work between Wapping and Old Kent Road station LBSCR. On 10 April 1876 the ELR was extended northwards via Whitechapel and Shoreditch to join the GER at Bishopsgate Junction whence there were running powers to the old No 7 road (now platform 6) at Liverpool Street, restricted to one train at a time. From this date the LBSCR worked trains between Liverpool Street and New Cross (LBSCR) and between Liverpool Street and Old Kent Road. Later, some trains were extended to Peckham Rye, to New Croydon (now East Croydon) and even Brighton. As the ELR did not pay the GER adequately for the facilities that

company had provided and as it owed money to the LBSCR, neither was inclined to succour it. Its poor circumstances attracted the attention of Sir Edward Watkin, who became its chairman in May 1878. Up and Down side connections made earlier with the SER at New Cross then came into use, with an SER service from 1 April 1880 between Liverpool Street and Addiscombe Road (now Addiscombe). For a factual account of the history of the Thames Tunnel and the ELR, see Lee, Charles E., *The East London Line and the Thames Tunnel*, London Transport, 1976.

2 1811–91: Hawkshaw was chief engineer to the Manchester & Leeds Railway (which became the Lancashire & Yorkshire Railway) in 1845 and was responsible for many miles of railway building in that area. From 1850 he was in practice on his own account in Westminster, remaining consulting engineer to the L&YR until 1888. He acted as consulting engineer to the SER 1861–81, was engineer to the ELR in 1865, for the Staines–Wokingham line of the LSWR 1853–7 and acted as joint engineer with Sir James Brunlees for the Channel Tunnel scheme 1872–86. He completed the Severn railway tunnel 1879–87. Also responsible for many harbour, bridge and canal projects at home and overseas, he was knighted in 1873.

3 The new street became Byward Street, opened in July 1884, affording valuable relief to the traffic congestion between the Docks and the City.

4 Following Hawkshaw's arbitration and the Metropolitan Railway Act of 28 July 1884, the Metropolitan assumed sole ownership of this curve.

5 Some work had been done by John Aird beneath the London & Blackwall Railway viaduct in the summer of 1880 but this had been stopped by injunction pending the passage of the 1881 act mentioned.

6 1823–94: After experience with the Stockton & Darlington Railway, the LSWR, LNWR and Midland Railway, Tomlinson was appointed locomotive superintendent of the Taff Vale Railway in 1858. Between 1869 and 1872 he practised on his own account as consulting marine and civil engineer, taking up the post of resident engineer and locomotive superintendent to the Metropolitan Railway in the latter year and continuing as such until 1885 when he became consulting engineer and a director of the Taff Vale.

7 1828–89: A civil engineer as well as a railway contractor, Walker worked on a number of home railway contracts with Thomas Brassey until 1852 when he started railway construction in Canada. Before returning to settle in London he surveyed railways in Russia and the Sudan; in 1871 he set up his own railway contracting business in Great George Street, Westminster. He built the difficult section of the ELR from Wapping to Bishopsgate Junction beneath the London Docks, for which Hawkshaw was engineer. In 1879–87 his firm completed the Severn tunnel with Hawkshaw.

8 1836–1918: Son of the architect Sir Charles Barry and pupil of Hawkshaw, he set up his own practice in 1867, gaining appointments as consulting engineer to the MDR, LBSCR, Barry and Caledonian Railways. He was engineer for the Tower Bridge (1894) and the King Edward VII bridge, Kew (1903). His firm undertook much railway and dock work at home and overseas. He founded the Engineering Standards Commission (later the British Engineering Standards Association). His appointment as engineer for the Mansion House line had been suggested by Forbes and was accepted by Watkin as a gesture of co-operation; Hawkshaw consented to the move on 16 April 1878. In May 1895 Barry was appointed consulting engineer to the Metropolitan Railway, continuing nominally as such after the company had (in 1903) given its resident engineer responsibility for new works instead of relying, as heretofore, on outside engineers.

9   The Whitechapel Junction Railway was worked and maintained by, and leased to, the Metropolitan and MDR Joint Committee from 1 October 1884 (Whitechapel Junction (City Lines & Extensions and ELR) Act, 1884).

10   The original proposal, favoured by the Metropolitan, was for the temporary station of 1882 to be extended further into Trinity Square to form a permanent station. Pending application for parliamentary powers, the two companies agreed that the works at Seething Lane, 117yd west (the site chosen by Barry for the permanent station), should be of four-track width in case a station should be required there at a later date, but it was this site which was to be used (for the station called Mark Lane), (MET 1/12, 29 August 1883). The rail level structures and fittings of the 1882 temporary station remained *in situ* until electrification works required their removal in 1903. Remarkably, the wooden surface building of 1882, latterly used as a tea warehouse, remained intact until demolished by London Transport in September 1940 as part of the Tower Hill Improvement Scheme. Mark Lane station, at the junction of Seething Lane and Byward Street, renamed Tower Hill on 1 September 1946, was closed after traffic in the early morning of 5 February 1967, to be replaced a few hours later by the present station, further east, on the site of the 1882 Metropolitan temporary station.

11   See *The Railway Magazine*, February 1917, p151, where the procedure is described in more detail.

12   See Barker, T. C. and Robbins, Michael, *A History of London Transport, Vol 1 The Nineteenth Century*, Allen & Unwin, 1963, Chapter 8.

13   Royal Commission on London Traffic, *op cit*, evidence, 17 March 1904.

14   Evidence of Sir Douglas Fox, civil engineer, to the Joint Committee on Electric & Cable Railways (Metropolis), 18 May 1892, HMSO (126). Also evidence of Sir Alexander Richardson Binnie and H. L. Cripps to the Joint Committee on London Underground Railways, 1901, HMSO (279).

Chapter 8 (pp 117–133)

1   At this time the Metropolitan was using up to 500 tons a week of the 'best hand-picked coke', delivered at York for 18s a ton (MET 1/3).

2   *The Railway Gazette*, 10 January 1913, 'The Jubilee of the Metropolitan Railway'.

3   This 3ft 8½in gauge railway was opened between Euston station and Holborn post office in 1865 and extended to the GPO St Martins le Grand about 1869, although this eastern section was seldom used. Employed solely for carriage of mail and parcels, it was closed in 1874 because the problem of keeping the air locks sufficiently tight defeated the technology of the period.

4   1840–1907: Baker joined John Fowler's office in 1861, working with him on the Metropolitan, Metropolitan & St John's Wood and MDR projects, becoming a partner in 1875. He was consulting engineer, with Fowler, for the pioneer deep-level tube railway, the City & South London of 1890, and with J. H. Greathead for the Central London tube railway of 1900. His other works included docks at Avonmouth and Hull, the floating wrought-iron cylinder which carried Cleopatra's Needle from Alexandria to Westminster, and the Forth Bridge. He was knighted in 1890.

5   The working of this ingenious device is described in *The Engineer*, 29 January 1892, pp88–90.

6   A visit to this shop is described in a letter to *The Times*, 14 June 1879. The victim reported himself as instantly diagnosed: 'Oh! I see – Metropolitan Railway'. As he gratefully downed the medicine, he was told by the pharmacist that he often treated up to twenty cases a day. See also *Pharmaceutical Journal*, 28 June 1879.

7   They voted with their feet. The half-yearly reports sometimes reported

disappointing traffic returns as attributable to unduly hot weather.

8 In October 1868 Parson and Nasmyth had considered with officers whether the weight of the locomotives should be reduced, deciding against this.

9 This Duty was imposed on English railways to make up the supposed loss of revenue from the traffic the railways were abstracting from the road coaches, which had long been taxed at ¼d a mile for each four passengers. In 1842 the railway tax was commuted to 5 per cent of gross receipts from passenger traffic and two years after this, Third Class traffic carried at up to 1d a mile was exempted from the Duty.

10 See Robbins, Michael, 'Railway Passenger Duty – A Sidelight', *Journal of the Railway & Canal Historical Society*, Vol 6, No 3.

11 Watkin, Sir Edward, letter to *The Times*, 4 June 1881.

12 The trains were:

> 5.34am Tower of London to Hammersmith
> 5.53am Tower of London to Hammersmith
> 5.52am Aldgate to Mansion House
> 5.52am Moorgate to South Kensington
> 5.13am Hammersmith to Tower of London
> 5.23am Hammersmith to Tower of London
> 5.43am Hammersmith to Tower of London
> 5.55am South Kensington to Aldgate
> 6.15am Gloucester Road to Aldgate
> 6.06am Mansion House to Aldgate
> 6.19am Baker Street East to Neasden
> 6.11am Neasden to Baker Street East

All stopped at all stations and ticket holders were able to return by any train after noon. Hand luggage only was allowed and in the event of an accident, compensation was limited to £100.

Chapter 9 (pp 134–143)

1 Report of the Committee of Investigation, 5 October 1872 (MET 1/13).

2 In towns, or where lands were otherwise built over or used for building purposes, the 1845 act required the land to be first offered to the original owners or to adjoining owners, in the former's absence or refusal to purchase.

3 Sir Edward Watkin to the Metropolitan Railway board, 24 March 1886.

4 1849–1934: In 1875 Perks became a solicitor and partner in the firm of Fowler, Perks, Hopkinson & Co, specialising in railway and parliamentary practice. Used by Sir Edward Watkin for his personal SER business, and giving satisfaction, he was retained by Watkin 'in the personal interests of the Metropolitan directors' in 1880. His firm were appointed solicitors to the Metropolitan Railway in 1881, Perks acting as legal adviser to the railway company. Perks also became solicitor to the Metropolitan and MDR Joint Committee in 1884. Following election as Liberal MP for Louth in 1892 (he continued as such until 1910), Perks's role was reduced from 31 March 1893 to part-time consulting solicitor, not involved in any parliamentary work. His connection with the Metropolitan was entirely severed in 1895. He then purchased a large quantity of MDR shares hoping to profit from electrification, playing a major part in bringing the American financier Charles Tyson Yerkes to London to organise the modernisation of the MDR and the construction of deep-level tube railways. He was a director of the MDR from 1901 to 1907 and its chairman from 1901 to 1905. He was created a baronet in 1908. Perks was founder and sometime treasurer of the Liberal

League and an activist in the Liberal Imperialist Group ('Imperial Perks'). He was also a great worker for the Wesleyan Methodist cause. Beatrice Webb thought him 'uncongenial . . . hard, pushing, commonplace . . . .'

5 *The Railway Magazine*, February 1900.
6 *Id*, April 1902, reporting on the MDR half-yearly meeting.

Chapter 10 (pp 144–156)

1 A letter of 24 December 1895 from Pollitt to Bell about this subject well conveys the flavour of their relationship even at the Christmas season: 'I have received your letter dated yesterday, and so long as you maintain the attitude you now assume and adopt such discourteous language in your letters, I agree with you that it would be a waste of time to continue the present correspondence' (MET 10/658).

2 In 1892 the Metropolitan loading gauge was:

> Inner Circle and City Widened Lines 12ft 8in×9ft
> Baker Street to Finchley Road   12ft 4in×9ft
> Finchley Road to Harrow   12ft 8in×9ft

3 These were to be located at Pinner, Northwood, Rickmansworth (Down side), Chorley Wood, Amersham (restricted to 47 wagons) and Great Missenden. At Rickmansworth the Up side siding was also to be lengthened, a new siding built alongside, and the Yard box moved to Watford Road. Authorities given by the board in 1900 also included retaining walls for the diversion of the River Brent at Wembley Park; alteration and repairs to the LNWR bridge at Harrow; goods yard improvements and additional sidings at Willesden Green, Harrow, Northwood and Chesham; enlargement of signal box and extension of refuge siding at Northwood; locomotive water tank, Rickmansworth; and additional sidings, engine pit, coal stage and water column in the East Goods Yard, Aylesbury. Most of these were completed by the end of 1901. Sidings at Aylesbury East, Aylesbury Hartwell and Quainton Road were further extended in 1904–5.

4 In his evidence to the Lords Committee on the Baker Street & Waterloo Railway Bill of 1892, Sir Benjamin Baker said that in about 1890 Sir Edward Watkin had considered building a second pair of tracks for the MSLR *beneath* the Metropolitan eastwards from Baker Street.

5 1850–1934: McLaren was born in Edinburgh, his mother a sister of John Bright. MA Edinburgh, barrister Lincoln's Inn, 1874, QC 1897, he practised at the Chancery Bar until 1897. He was elected MP for Stafford in 1880 and in 1885 and represented Leicestershire, Bosworth 1892–1910. In politics a radical, he was one of the founders of the National Liberal Club. He was actively interested in ship-building, steel and colliery companies; chairman of the Tredegar Iron & Coal Co, John Brown & Co, and the Sheepbridge Iron & Coal Co and director of other colliery companies. He married Laura, only daughter of the Metropolitan Railway director Henry D. Pochin in 1877; she inherited Bodnant Hall, Denbighshire, with its famous gardens, upon her father's death in 1895.

First baronet, created 1902; Privy Councillor, 1908; created Baron Aberconway of Bodnant 10 July 1911. Chairman of the British Iron Trade Association, 1909; vice president of the National Housing & Town Planning Council, 1911.

His association with the Metropolitan Railway had begun in 1878 when he joined the board of the Metropolitan & St John's Wood Railway, on which he served until 1882. He was appointed auditor of the Metropolitan Railway Surplus

341

Lands Committee in 1889, Metropolitan Railway director 1895, deputy chairman 1902, chairman 1904. (Mostly taken from *Who Was Who* 1929–40.)

6 1857–1931: Ellis was educated at Felstead Grammar School, Essex. Articled to an Essex solicitor, after qualification he worked in Worcestershire for local agents of the GWR. He joined the LBSCR in January 1881, becoming its assistant solicitor. He became solicitor to the Metropolitan Railway in June 1898. In 1900 when the GCR wanted him as their solicitor, the Metropolitan raised his salary to £2,000 to retain his services (he had all the information constituting the Metropolitan's position in its negotiations with the GCR). He continued as the Metropolitan's solicitor until the end of 1902 when Kitcat was given the post at £650 a year. After contracting pleurisy early in 1908, Ellis resigned the general managership from 1 October that year. Much of his long retirement was spent on the French Riviera, where the climate ensured his survival long enough to congratulate his fellow solicitor, J. S. Anderson, on his appointment to general manager of the Metropolitan in March 1931. (*The Railway Magazine*, April 1905, p281, *The Railway Gazette*, 18 September 1908, MET 1/22, 1/25, 10/720).

7 It was not Edward's first brush with the Metropolitan. He had been involved in a bizarre incident at Aylesbury station when Prince of Wales. In July 1898, on one of several visits to Waddesdon Manor, he slipped on a spiral staircase on the morning he was due to return to Windsor, breaking his leg. Strapped up and placed in an invalid chair, he was taken to Aylesbury station where it was decided to carry the chair over the footbridge. His considerable weight, or the state of the chair – perhaps both – caused the chair to collapse during this operation. As efforts were made to bring him down to his train for Windsor, he was several times engulfed in the acrid smoke of (Metropolitan?) locomotives passing beneath. (Rothschild, Mrs James de, *The Rothschilds at Waddesdon Manor*, Collins, 1979.)

8 In practice, the maintenance of Joint Line stations and permanent way was undertaken by the GCR (later the London & North Eastern Railway) from milepost 28½ (situated on the London side of Great Missenden) outwards, and by the Metropolitan between there and Harrow. Maintenance of Aylesbury station passed from the GWR to the GCR (later the LNER) in 1907.

9 Detailed plans were prepared for the Willesden Green exchange station in 1906–7, brought forward again in 1913, and for the last time in 1926. No work was done as the GCR suffered a dire shortage of capital (or the power to raise more) after the completion of its London Extension in 1899, whilst the LNER never showed any enthusiasm for spending what little capital it could muster on its GCR inheritance in the London area.

10 These alterations of 1908 involved the closure of the former Metropolitan and Joint signal boxes and their replacement by new ones at Aylesbury South and North. The former had fifty-five levers and was sited almost opposite the old Metropolitan box between the Metropolitan and GWR lines as they came to the junction. Aylesbury North (30 levers) was near the goods shed at the country end of the Up platform, controlling access to the shed and the Down siding. Some alterations were also made to the sidings around the station at this time. All the resignalling was undertaken by the GCR, whose officers then took over signalling maintenance at Aylesbury from the GWR and the Metropolitan.

11 The station became the jointly leased property of the Metropolitan & GC and GW & GC Joint Committees from 1 July 1907. The staff were a joint responsibility of the three companies.

Chapter Notes

Chapter 11 (pp 157–193)

1 Perhaps the oddest of these was the Slippery Railway. Watkin seems to have been particularly susceptible to French innovations and in 1889 persuaded his fellow directors to sanction an experiment at Neasden by the *Société des Chemins de Fers Glissants Perfectionnés* of Paris. For a nominal rent of £1 a year, this company was to build a line for 1½ miles alongside the Metropolitan between Neasden and Forty Lane bridge, Wembley, to be open to the public, with through tickets at favourable rates arranged by the Metropolitan. Of dubious practicality over such a length, the system to be employed had been demonstrated on a modest scale at the Paris Exhibition of 1889 and involved the use of water to reduce friction, propulsion being achieved by jetting water at high pressure on to a horizontal turbine. A start on the Neasden project was continually postponed for 'financial reasons' despite generous extensions of time by the Metropolitan. The final reference to the matter in the Metropolitan minutes occurs on 29 July 1893.

2 1857–1934: After graduating at the US Naval Academy, Annapolis, in 1878, Sprague experimented in electrical work for the US Navy. He was secretary for the jury for gas engines, dynamos and lamps at the London Crystal Palace Exhibition of 1882. Resigning from the Navy in 1883, he worked briefly with Thomas A. Edison before setting up his Sprague Electric Railway & Motor Co. After successfully equipping the Richmond electric tramway, this firm gained many contracts before being absorbed in the Edison General Electric Co in 1890. He then formed the Sprague Electric Elevator Co, eventually to be absorbed by the Otis Co. Sprague's successful development of the multiple-unit principle for electric rail traction in 1895 led to the establishment of the Sprague Electric Co, absorbed by the General Electric Co (USA) in 1902. He then invented an automatic train control system and assisted with the electrification of New York's Grand Central station and approaches and with the design of the conductor rail used on the New York Central RR. During World War 1 he served as a member of the Naval Consulting Board and as chairman of its committees for electricity and ship construction.

3 Miller, John Anderson, *Fares Please!*, Dover Publications Inc, New York, 1941, Chapter 4.

4 *Financial Gazette*, 23 January 1888.

5 For further details of these experiments, see Benest, K. R., 'The Rolling Stock of the Metropolitan Railway–9' *Underground*, Vol 2, No 11 (November 1963).

6 For a full account of these cars and their fate, see Benest K. R., *op cit*, *Underground*, Vol 2, No 9 (September 1963).

7 This equipment was subsequently moved to the canal bank at Alperton to provide traction current for the Ealing & South Harrow Railway until the opening of the Underground Company's power station at Lots Road, Chelsea.

8 On the disadvantages of three rails and the advantages of the four-rail electrification system as seen at the time, see Ayrton, 'Remarks on Electric Railway Magnetic Disturbance', *Proceedings, Institution of Electrical Engineers*, Part 130, Vol 26.

9 Evidence to the Joint Select Committee on London Underground Railways, 10 May 1901, Q615, HMSO 1901 (279).

10 *The Railway Magazine*, June 1901, p566.

11 Evidence to Joint Select Committee, *op cit*, Q616.

12 1837–1905. Born into a Quaker banking family, Yerkes was a shrewd manipulator and organiser, at the same time something of a visionary, a quality seen in his desire to provide London with a modern rail transit system as the culmination of his life's work. His career started as a banker and stockbroker on his own account in Philadelphia where he was once imprisoned for seven months

on an embezzlement charge. Ostracised in his native city, he moved to Chicago in the early 1880s where he made very large capital gains from financial dealings in tramway companies, eventually acquiring control of a large portion of the city's tramway and elevated railway systems. His buccaneering methods were often highly dubious, involving as they did bribery, rumour-mongering and falsified accounts, but under his regime the city's street and elevated rail systems were electrified and modernised. His methods aroused popular indignation which obliged him to sell up and retire to his Fifth Avenue mansion in New York City. It was at this time that he became interested in London. His private life was often scandalous and his career formed the theme for three 'faction' works by Theodore Dreiser, *The Financier, The Titan* and *The Stoic*, dealing respectively with his Philadelphia, Chicago and London periods. For further details see *Dictionary of American Biography*, Oxford University Press, and Hendrick, Burton J., *The Age of Big Business*, Oxford University Press, 1919. In Chapter 5 of the latter there is a description of the methods used by the Chicago tramway magnates.

13   Little is known of how Yerkes was first attracted to London, or of his early contacts with Perks. On this, see Barker, T. C., and Robbins, Michael, *A History of London Transport, Vol 2, The Twentieth Century to 1970*, Allen & Unwin, 1974, and Jackson, Alan A. & Croome, D. F. C., *Rails Through The Clay*, Allen & Unwin, 1962, p65. Perks told a Lords Committee on the Charing Cross, Euston & Hampstead (No 1) Bill in May 1902 that Yerkes had first inspected the MDR (and thus the Inner Circle) in 1898.

14   Evidence to the Commons committee on the MDR bill, July 1901.

15   Evidence, *idem*.

16   For a full description of the original power plant at Neasden, see Anon, *Metropolitan Railway Electrification*, Metropolitan-Vickers Electrical Co Ltd, 1924.

17   A contribution was also made by the contractor C. J. Wills on the understanding he would get the construction contract. When this went to Bott & Stennett, Wills successfully sued the H&UR for breach of contract, receiving £19,853.

18   For a full account of the history of the Ealing & South Harrow Railway, see Jackson, Alan A., 'North-West from Ealing', *The Railway Magazine*, September and October 1959.

19   Perks invited the Metropolitan to join the MDR and LTSR in the Whitechapel & Bow project in November 1901, in return for running powers, but with its electrification and other commitments, the Metropolitan was not prepared to assist in financing a railway with an estimated cost of £600,000 a mile.

20   For a full account of the construction of the H&UR, see Edwards, Dennis, 'Walter Atkinson – builder of the Harrow & Uxbridge Railway', *Underground*, No 12 1983.

21   In May 1904 the MDR told the Metropolitan that the running powers would not be used beyond South Harrow until the trains could be worked electrically. The Metropolitan then insisted upon payment of the £2,000 minimum a year required by the H&UR Act of 1899 and the MDR accepted this commitment. Three years then passed during which the MDR appears to have decided that it was cheaper to pay this sum than run trains to Uxbridge at a substantial loss. In July 1907 the MDR told the Metropolitan it proposed to work from South Harrow to Rayners Lane only. A long argument then ensued in which the Metropolitan challenged the legality of partial use of the MDR running powers but also insisted that if Rayners Lane were to be an MDR terminus, it would have to be staffed and rebuilt, a cost to which the MDR would be expected to make a substantial contribution. Meanwhile, Harrow UDC and other local interests were pressing for the

opening of the line beyond South Harrow. Eventually, the MDR gave way, agreeing to run through to Uxbridge. Further delays were then incurred whilst the two companies argued about the payment for electric current, a matter not covered by the legislation. Eventually, agreement was reached and the MDR began a regular service to Uxbridge from 1 March 1910, 23 trains a day each way Mondays to Fridays, 24 on Saturdays, 19 on Sundays, paying 2½d a car mile for current. Ickenham substation was reopened for the extra load. Before this there had been some special workings for pleasure parties in the summer of 1909. A trial run of an MDR car to Ruislip on 23 June was followed by a school special from Ravenscourt Park to Ruislip on 6 July. Other specials, all hand-signalled between South Harrow and Rayners Lane, were operated on 7 and 8 July (the latter from West Kensington to Eastcote), 21 and 22 July and 3 August. A private siding off the Roxeth Viaduct serving South Harrow gasworks came into use from 4 October 1910, operated by Metropolitan freight trains which necessarily had to reverse at Rayners Lane. The Harrow & Stanmore Gas Co guaranteed a minimum annual traffic of 14,000 tons a year.

22 *Middlesex & Buckinghamshire Advertiser*, 2 July 1904.

23 At this time there were 225 trains each way through Mark Lane station between 5.30am and 12.30am, of which 101 Up and 99 Down were Inner Circle. The Metropolitan claimed there was already great difficulty about conflicting movements at Aldgate East and St Mary's Junctions.

24 Second Class bookings were abolished not only on electric services; they were withdrawn on all trains north of Baker Street East from 1 March 1906 and completely from the Metropolitan (except City Widened Lines and to and from the GWR) from 17 December 1906.

25 The exceptions were the 1927 batch of MV 275 cars (206–11) which had 2×24in vacuum cylinders apiece as they were intended to work trains of the later 'Dreadnought' steam stock.

26 For further details of the original Metropolitan electric stock, see Benest, K. R., *op cit, Underground*, Vol 3, No 4 (April 1964), Vol 3, No 6 (June 1964), Vol 3, No 8 (August 1964) and Vol 3, No 10 (October 1964). The electrical equipment is fully described in the Metropolitan-Vickers booklet mentioned at note 16 above.

27 Including 154 in the locomotive repair shops, 91 in the power house, 80 in the running shed, 273 in the carriage shops and 117 in the carriage shed (MET 10/146).

28 At Ruislip (Ickenham) (2×800kW three-phase rotary converters), Harrow (3×800kW); Neasden (3×800kW); Finchley Road (4×800kW); Baker Street (3×1,200kW); Gloucester Road (3×800kW); Bouverie Street, Paddington (now Bouverie Place, on the site of a disused engine shed, and with its own siding) (3×800kW); Chalton Street, Euston Road (3×1,200kW); and Moorgate Street (3×1,200kW). The substation at Baker Street included a distribution room and switchboard controlling the supply to the Metropolitan section of the Inner Circle; it adjoined the Bakerloo tube station and had to be built at two levels (rail and street) to contain all the necessary equipment.

29 For a full account of the two batches of locomotives, see Benest, K. R., *Metropolitan Electric Locomotives*, London Underground Railway Society, 1984.

30 For a full account of the conversions, see Benest, K. R., *op cit*, in *Underground*, Vol 3, No 12 (December 1964).

31 Although the Metropolitan temporary station remained open after the closure of the Franco-British Exhibition on 31 October 1908, it was missed by alternate trains between 1 November 1910 and 15 January 1911 inclusive. It closed to regular public traffic on 31 October 1914, reopening for one day on 5 November 1920 for a motor show under the new title 'Wood Lane (White City)'. After this it

was opened only for events at the White City. Renamed 'White City' on 23 November 1947 it was last used on 24 October 1959 before being damaged by fire.

32 On 13 September 1909 an excursion worked over the 134 miles between Verney Junction and Ramsgate, hauled by a Metropolitan steam locomotive as far as Metropolitan Junction, Blackfriars, and by an SECR locomotive from there (*The Railway Gazette*, 10 September 1909).

33 Baker Street *Junction* was, however, fully track-circuited by Westinghouse, who had installed a power frame in the Circle station box at the time of the reopening of the through route to the City in July 1909, but the old 50-lever mechanical frame at Baker Street East survived until the 1912–13 rearrangement of that area when track circuits were included in the new work (Chapter 12).

34 The Belgian (Vicinal) usage *halte* had been adopted some time earlier by the GWR and was copied by the Metropolitan, with much of the associated GWR building style. The French form was used for references to Ickenham in official papers and initially on the nameboards, but was not perpetuated for subsequent Metropolitan halts.

35 In the year ended 30 June 1908 (figures in the main text are for calendar years), working expenses of the branch were £10,805 whilst passenger revenue, even including rents, totalled only £5,768, to which could be added the £2,000 being paid by the MDR for unexercised running powers. With this shortfall, there was, of course, no contribution to the payment of interest on the £492,000 capital expenditure on the branch.

36 *Financial News*, 1 July 1904.

37 There may have been some co-operation behind the scenes. Sir Charles McLaren (later Lord Aberconway), chairman of the Metropolitan, was also vice president of the National Housing & Town Planning Council, whose chairman, Alderman W. Thompson, was managing director of Ruislip Manor Ltd. Information on 1912 housing and RM Ltd from brochure, Ruislip Manor Cottage Society Ltd, 1912. All the houses at Ruislip Manor, in contrast to most of those erected in the 1920s and 1930s in this district, were architect-designed, some by A. & J. Soutar, winners of the Ruislip–Northwood garden city layout competition.

Chapter 12 (pp 194–228)

1 1868–1930: Son of the Rev R. W. Selbie, a Salford Congregational minister; educated Manchester Grammar School and Owen's College, Manchester. Selbie received his railway training with the Lancashire & Yorkshire Railway, which he joined in 1883, becoming secretary to the general manager and assistant to the chief traffic manager. In World War 1, he served at the Board of Trade as Controller of Horse Transport and was also on the Road Transport Board and the Army Forage Committee, these efforts gaining him a CBE in 1919. In that year he was appointed a director of Metropolitan Railway Country Estates Ltd and, following a special provision in the Metropolitan Railway Act of 1922, he became a director of the Metropolitan Railway whilst still serving as its general manager. He collapsed and died in St Paul's Cathedral on 17 May 1930 whilst attending a confirmation service at which his younger son was a candidate.

2 Two examples of this may be quoted. In July 1925, commenting to the company's engineer on the use made of the old signal box at Willesden Green, Selbie noted: 'Platelayers have taken the opportunity of providing themselves with skulking holes by reason of the old signal boxes not being used for any other purpose. I have noticed generally that when any accommodation on the lineside becomes vacant, it is immediately seized upon by the permanent way staff, who, no doubt, have their own objects in view.' Although Wilson defended his men,

pointing out that it was usual for railway companies to provide lineside accommodation to hang up wet clothing, Selbie was unconvinced, saying, 'It is patent to the most casual observer that the multiplication of huts and cabins, whether along the line, or in yards, increases the facility for idling' (MET 10/437).

In May, 1929 Selbie instructed Holt, the Traffic Manager, to crack down on the propensity of some booking clerks to obscure the glass panelling of the new Passimeter ticket offices with paper in efforts to secure privacy: 'One never sees this sort of thing in the similar offices of the Underground system' (MET 10/608).

3 The Metropolitan had applied for parliamentary powers to link the Hammersmith & City Railway near Latimer Road with the GWR's proposed Ealing & Shepherd's Bush Railway, over which it sought running powers to Ealing Broadway. This would almost certainly have been passed by parliament, paving the way for a train service which, with the proposed Central London tube service over the Ealing & Shepherd's Bush, would have over-congested that line, also designed to carry GWR trains. The GWR therefore insisted on the withdrawal of the offending application as a condition of the new agreement with the Metropolitan.

4 As it soon became apparent that if there was to be a double-line junction with the Inner Circle there would be no space for a cab road between the platforms, this feature was omitted from the final plans.

5 Behind the stone was placed a box containing: the current working timetables; the company's last half-yearly report; a diary for 1912; a programme of the ceremony; an impression of the company's seal; and some current coin.

6 1885–1972: After a year in the office of the LBSCR architect, Clark was appointed 'assistant architect to the engineer' of the Metropolitan in 1910 at the modest salary of £175. His value very soon became apparent and was recognised by salary increases. Returning from the war, in which he had served as an AB in the RNVR, he was made company architect from 1 July 1921 at a salary of £700, a post he held until the formation of London Transport in 1933. He designed about 25 new or rebuilt stations for the Metropolitan between 1911 and 1933, also offices, minor works, lettering and fittings. His main achievement was perhaps the superstructure at Baker Street (Chiltern Court), completed in 1929–30. A useful sideline for him was the design of houses at the Grange, Estate, Pinner and elsewhere. He was elected FRIBA in 1930. Lord Aberconway affectionately referred to him as 'our clarkitect'.

7 Earlier in 1911, Selbie had suggested a £2m line from an unspecified point between Finchley Road and Baker Street direct to the Inner Circle east of Baker Street. This had been quietly shelved as too costly.

8 In 1908 loading gauges were given as:

	Width	Centre	Side
Inner Circle	9ft 00in	12ft 8in	10ft 6in
Baker St–Finchley Rd	9ft 10in	12ft 4in	10ft 6in
Finchley Rd–Verney Junc	9ft 10in	13ft 6in	11ft 0in

9 In October 1911 the Pullmans ran in the following trains:

8.26am	Aylesbury–Liverpool St (arr 9.56am)
8.55am	Chesham–Liverpool St (arr 10.06am)
1.35pm	(Sats excepted) Aylesbury–Baker St (arr 2.57pm)
4.15pm	(Sats excepted) Aylesbury–Liverpool St (arr 6.01pm)

6pm   (Sats only) Verney Jc–Baker St (arr 8.09pm)
9.15pm   (Sats excepted) Verney Jc–Baker St (arr 11.17pm)

10.10am   (Sats excepted) Liverpool St–Aylesbury (arr 11.56am)
12.05pm   (Sats excepted) Baker St–Aylesbury (arr 1.34pm)
1pm   (Sats only) Liverpool St–Aylesbury (arr 2.33pm)
1.59pm   (Sats only) Liverpool St–Verney Jc (arr 4.19pm)
5.22pm   (Sats excepted) Liverpol St–Aylesbury (arr 7pm)
6.14pm   (Sats excepted) Liverpool St–Verney Jc (arr 8.20pm)
11.35pm   Baker St–Aylesbury (arr 12.50am)

From Monday 29 January 1917 the workings were:
8.05am   Quainton Rd–Aldgate (arr 10.05am)
9.26am   Great Missenden–Liverpool St (arr 10.40am)
4.14pm   Aylesbury–Liverpool St (arr 6.01pm); (Baker St (arr 5.44pm) on
           Sats)
9.14pm   (Sats excepted) Verney Jc–Baker St (11.17pm)

10.09am   (Sats excepted) Aldgate–Aylesbury (arr 11.56am)
11.52am   (Sats only) Liverpool St–Aylesbury (arr 1.36pm)
1pm   (Sats only) Liverpool St–Aylesbury (arr 2.35pm)
5.23pm   (Sats excepted) Aldgate–Aylesbury (arr 7.01pm)
6.14pm   (Sats excepted) Liverpool St–Verney Jc (arr 8.23pm)
11.35pm   Baker St–Aylesbury (arr 12.56am)

(MET 10/127)

10 The new menu of 1 January 1915 illustrates the range of refreshment normally available in the cars (wartime restrictions were yet to come):

Breakfast, lunch, supper	3s 0d
Tea or coffee with bread and butter	9d
Tea or coffee with buttered toast, cake and jam	1s 6d
Café noir, small	6d
Appolinaris or Perrier, bottle	6d, 9d
Soda seltzer or lemonade, bottle	3d, 6d
Schweppes' ginger ale, or ginger beer, bottle	4d
Lemon squash	6d, 9d
Ale, stout or lager, bottle	6d
Whisky, portion	6d
Brandy, cognac	9d
Brandy, liqueur (20 years old)	1s 0d
Booth's Old Mature Dry Gin	6d
Gins and bitters, or vermouth, glass	6d
Liqueurs, various, glass	9d, 1s 0d
Port or sherry, glass	6d
Bovril and biscuits, cup	6d
Sandwiches in variety, to order	
Wines, to order, as list; cigars and cigarettes	

(MET 10/127)

11 Kilburn temporary junction and box had opened 23 November 1913 to provide access to Finchley Road goods yard via the new Through Lines.
12 For a full account of the origins and history of this branch, see Jackson, Alan A., 'The Metropolitan Railway at Watford', *The Railway Magazine*, December 1961.

Chapter Notes

13 The Great Northern & City Railway was authorised by an act of 28 June 1892. S. Pearson & Son Ltd, the railway contracting firm, had put up most of the capital for the line, which was opened from beneath the GNR station at Finsbury Park to Moorgate on 14 February 1904. For extended accounts see: Jackson, Alan A. and Croome, D. F., *Rails Through The Clay*, Allen & Unwin, 1964; Bruce, J. Graeme, *The Big Tube*, London Transport, 1976; *Tramway & Railway World*, July 1902, and Kirkland, R. K., 'Jubilee of The Great Northern & City Railway', *The Railway Magazine*, February 1954.

14 The terms of purchase were arranged to provide that the takeover imposed no burden on the Metropolitan until the extra earning power arising from the new connections was available. Holders of £504,216 GN&CR 4 per cent Debenture Stock received a similar amount of Metropolitan 3½ per cent 'A' Debenture Stock; those with the 8,500 GN&CR £10 4 per cent Preference Shares were given £75,000 Metropolitan 3½ per cent 'A' Preferred Stock in similar amount, on which no dividend would be payable for the first three years. Holders of the 78,000 GN&CR £10 4 per cent Preferred Ordinary Shares received 75 per cent of their holding in Metropolitan Ordinary Stock, such stock in the first seven years to participate only in any dividend paid by the Metropolitan on this stock above 2 per cent (they got nothing until 1921 and very little after that). Finally, the holders of the 78,000 GN&CR 5 per cent Deferred shares received half their holding in Metropolitan Ordinary with the same restriction as the Preferred Ordinary holders.

15 Although the bill provided for the takeover to operate from 1 July 1913, it did not receive royal assent until 13 August, hence the later takeover date of 1 September. R. P. Brousson, the GN&CR general manager, stayed on until 31 August, then returning to work for Pearsons, his original employers.

16 The old service had provided 21 trains an hour each way with a journey time end to end of 12 minutes. By 1915 the Metropolitan had managed to raise this to better than 26 an hour (every 2¼ minutes) and some non-stop workings were making the trip in 9 minutes.

17 First-class accommodation was restricted to the rush-hour trains from 8 May 1916.

18 There was also an electric locomotive, used for shunting at the Drayton Park car sheds.

19 The decision that the Metropolitan should provide the whole train service was not thought by the MDR to include special workings. It worked a Sunday School treat special from New Cross SER to South Harrow on Saturday 20 September 1913, drawing a fierce protest from Selbie.

20 For a full account of the ELR electric stock, see Benest, K. R., 'The Rolling Stock of The Metropolitan Railway', *Underground*, Vol 5, No 1, January 1966.

21 The western terminus became Hammersmith (H&CR) from 9 February 1914.

22 For further details of this stock, see Benest, K. R., *op cit*, Vol 5, No 3, March 1966.

23 Selbie, R. H., *Report of the General Manager* (privately printed for the Metropolitan Railway, 1915).

Chapter 13 (pp 229–250)

1 This paragraph is based on Pratt, *op cit*, Chapter IX and *The Railway Gazette* (report of Metropolitan Railway meeting), 26 February 1915.

2 Pratt, *op cit*, Chapter XXVIII, p371.

3 1874–1956: Born at Kearsley, Manchester, Wardle began his railway career with eleven years in the goods department of the Lancashire & Yorkshire Railway, serving as secretary to the goods manager in the last four years. In 1900 he was

made assistant to the secretary of the Grand Trunk Railway of Canada and in 1904 became manager of that railway's traffic department in London. 1905 saw him installed as partner in a general railway and steamship agency in Fenchurch Street, City. He was appointed goods and parcels manager, Metropolitan Railway, in 1908, and commercial manager of that railway in 1913, a position he held until the formation of the LPTB in 1933. He served as director of cold storage and inland transport of food at the Ministry of Food from September 1917 but resigned on 31 December after a disagreement and was then seconded to the Ministry of Information until the end of the war. He was made director of the Lewis Omnibus Co in 1930 and chairman of that company in 1932. He filled in time with the LPTB as chairman of a committee on ticket problems from July 1933 to the end of 1934 when he reached pensionable age.

4 The first publicity pamphlet issued by the Metropolitan appears to have been one written for the company by the author Henry Mayhew, founder of *Punch*, in 1864. It was rewritten and republished in 1873. In 1880 the first guide to the line was published, illustrated with woodcuts showing the scenery around each station.

5 Edwards, D. F., *Underground*, Vol 5, No 7 (July 1966), p98 and lecture to the London Underground Railway Society, 14 September 1979. But the word also appears in a piece of doggerel published in or about 1915 by the writer and journalist George R. Sims, who had some association with the Metropolitan Railway:

> I know a land where the wild flowers grow,
> Near, near at hand if by train you go,
> Metro-Land, Metro-Land.
> Meadows sweet have a golden glow,
> Hills are green as the vales below,
> In Metro-Land, Metro-Land.
> Metro-Land, Metro-Land,
> Leafy dell and woodland fair,
> Land of love and hope and peace,
> Land where all your troubles cease,
> Metro-Land, Metro-Land,
> Waft, O waft me there.
> Hearts are lighter, eyes are brighter,
> In Metro-Land, Metro-Land.

6 *The Railway Magazine*, June 1915, p499.

7 With subsequent purchases, the area of the Cedars Estate was eventually in excess of 600 acres, making it the largest of the MRCE estates.

8 N.W. Estates Syndicate Ltd was registered on 15 March 1919 to purchase the Cedars and Chalk Hill Estates and to set up the MRCE, but was given very widely drawn articles of association. Two subscribers were named, each with a £1 share, one the assistant to the Metropolitan Railway's general manager, the other a lawyer in the railway's solicitor's office (MET 10/172). Selbie and Henry Gibson (valuer and estate agent to the Metropolitan Railway Surplus Lands Committee) were the first directors.

9 The agreement was extended in February 1929 for a further ten years from 13 June 1928.

10 The first directors of the MRCE were: The Hon Evelyn Hubbard (chairman), a Metropolitan director, also chairman of the Guardian Assurance Co; Albert I. Belisha, a Metropolitan director and partner in the City underwriting and stock-

broking firm of Belisha, Shaw & Co; J. W. Wheeler Bennett, JP, a Metropolitan director; R. H. Selbie, the Metropolitan general manager; and J. Geo Head, JP, chartered surveyor, of the firm of George Head & Co, 17 Baker Street.

11 Selbie, R. H., 'Railways & Land Development', *Modern Transport*, 11 June 1921.
12 Published by Herman Darewski Music Publishing Co, words by Boyle Lawrence, music by Henry Thrale. The cover drawing was made from a photograph appearing in the *Metro-Land* guide.
13 The Metropolitan share of the guarantee was £20,000 maximum.
14 For the handling of the Cup Final crowds by all four railways, see *The Railway Magazine*, June 1923, p482.
15 In 1921 Selbie and Fay had agreed that the GCR might construct a siding into the exhibition grounds, the GCR promising that most of the exhibition freight traffic would be routed via Quainton Road. When the LNER, as successors to the GCR, began to build a station on the loop through the grounds, the Metropolitan protested this was opposed to the spirit, if not the letter, of the agreements made with the GCR about local traffic between Marylebone and Harrow. The LNER craftily insisted that as the loop was connected to its Neasden–Northolt line the agreement did not apply. Both companies then took legal advice; the Metropolitan was told it had no case.
16 In July 1923 Selbie reported a serious loss of short-distance traffic, mainly due to the competition of newly formed bus companies, whose fare-cutting activities had forced the General to increase services and reduce fares on routes parallel to the Metropolitan.

Chapter 14 (pp 251–287)
1 1876–1933: Wilson joined the GER in 1892 as pupil to his father (John) who was then engineer-in-chief. He became engineer in charge of new works and later divisional engineer at Ipswich. On war service with the railway construction troops on the Western Front, he became chief railway construction engineer and later controller of transportation maintenance. He was awarded the Military Cross and was also rewarded with an OBE. On return to the GER, he became divisional civil engineer, Stratford. His appointment as chief engineer, Metropolitan Railway, covered the period July 1921–June 1933.
2 Passenger journeys averaged only 1,200 a week in 1926. The LPTB withdrew the trains from 1 January 1934.
3 Report by John Wardle and two LNER officials to their respective general managers, January 1925 (MET 10/225).
4 The subsequent history of this bus service is given in Appendix 5.
5 Pick wrote to Selbie in June 1929 suggesting that the 'not very satisfactory' MDR half-hourly Uxbridge–Ealing Common service should be withdrawn and the whole of the Underground's South Harrow service projected to a rebuilt Rayners Lane, allowing for cross-platform interchange between the Metropolitan and the MDR. There was a positive response from the Metropolitan, whose officers produced a £39,534 scheme for a three-island platform station at Rayners Lane, with resignalling between there and South Harrow. Whilst the Underground was happy to pay a £2,500 twenty-year annual rental in return for this capital expenditure, it insisted on all Metropolitan trains calling at Rayners Lane and wanted to extend Piccadilly tube trains to the rebuilt junction station, starting with eight trains an hour and building up to a five-minute interval. The Underground also wanted to supply its own current between South Harrow and Rayners Lane and sought amelioration of the Metropolitan's terms for running powers. Haggling with the Metropolitan's newly formed general management committee over all this continued until the end of 1930 with the Metropolitan

arguing that it would need to supplement its own service west of Rayners Lane if the MDR withdrew its Uxbridge trains. By early 1931, Pick had lost patience, let the matter drop and decided to rebuild South Harrow as an intermediate terminus instead. The MDR service was altered to run between there and Uxbridge only from 4 July 1932, the day the full Piccadilly tube service was extended to run to connect with it.

6 Named after the landowner, Captain E. G. Spencer Churchill, who had inherited it from Lord Northwick.

7 A new agreement reached in 1916 provided for the working expenses of Aylesbury station to be shared: Met and GCR Joint 63 per cent; GWR and GCR Joint, 37 per cent. Maintenance and renewal costs of locomotive accommodation were to be met in proportion to the number of engines stationed there by each company. Management for five years from 2 April 1916 was to be undertaken by the two committees alternately, beginning with the Met & GCR (effectively the Metropolitan).

8 The absolute maximum capacity was given as thirty-two trains an hour each way, as operated on Cup Final days at Wembley, but this was achieved only by virtually complete closure of the three tunnel stations.

9 Wilson's other options were: new tunnels from Finchley Road to a point on the Circle near King's Cross; and tunnels directly under the existing Baker Street–Finchley Road line, terminating beneath Baker Street station.

10 Metropolitan officials had counted passengers using the tube stations on 26 June 1925 as 8,627 at Warwick Avenue, 4,324 at Maida Vale and 6,559 at Kilburn Park. Holt considered the Metropolitan's new deep-level stations would capture much of this traffic.

11 1861–1940: Trained on the South Wales section of the Midland Railway, Hay joined the LSWR engineering department in 1894, becoming resident engineer of the company's associated Waterloo & City tube railway. He developed a hooded shield and clay stopping system for deep-level tube railway construction in water-bearing strata as refinements to Galbraith's tunnelling shield system. In 1902 he was appointed consulting engineer to the Underground Electric Railways of London Ltd and was much involved in the building of the Bakerloo, Piccadilly and Hampstead tubes. From 1907, he operated as an independent consulting engineer, supervising much of the work on the Post Office tube railway and the reconstruction and enlargement of major central area tube stations in London, notably Piccadilly Circus, as well as some Underground extensions. Knighted in 1933, he was appointed consulting engineer of the LPTB in 1935, serving in that capacity until his death, at a time of great expansion of the tube railway system. (Mostly from *The Railway Gazette*, 3 January 1941.)

12 St John's Wood Road and Marlborough Road had been closed Mondays to Saturdays inclusive before 9.40am from 1 October 1929, with a modified service in the evening peak period. This allowed eight more trains an hour to be worked through to the City, a net addition of twenty in the morning peak.

13 A similar over-line garage was completed beneath the overall glass roof of Bayswater station in December 1925.

14 Wardle was anxious for this sign to read EUSTON SQUARE METRO but was overruled by Selbie, who wanted METROPOLITAN RAILWAY. Selbie probably viewed 'Metro' as vulgar, but tolerated it in official publicity and advertising.

15 Clark received an honorarium of £3,000 for his work on the project, a sum paid in instalments from the middle of 1927. At the suggestion of J. S. Anderson, Selbie's successor, his name was also inscribed on the stonework.

16 The papers (MET/110) indicate that Sherrin prepared drawings of the proposed Baker Street building between 1907 and 1911, including a set for LCC approval

in 1908. The drawing of the elevations issued to the press in the late autumn of 1911 (eg *The Railway Gazette*, 1 December 1911), showing a building similar in many respects to that erected 18 years later, seems to have been the work of Sherrin.

17 Names rejected were: Chequers Court; Hampden House; Regent House/Court; Harrow House.

18 *Building*, February 1929.

19 Typical flats were: *First floor, south facing*: £650 pa; lounge/hall, 12ft×10ft 6in; drawing-room, 20ft 6in×20ft; dining-room, 22ft 6in×16ft; kitchen, 18ft 6in×13ft 6in; cloakroom, 2 bathrooms (1 with wc), 2 separate wc's, 4 bedrooms (14ft 6in×13ft 6in, 13ft×10ft, 14ft 6in×7ft 6in, 14ft×9ft). *Third floor, east facing*: £275 pa; lounge/hall, 15ft 6in×8ft 6in; reception room, 14ft 6in×14ft; kitchen, 14ft×12ft; 2 bedrooms, each 14ft×11ft; bathroom and separate wc.

General features included double sinks (one deep, for washing clothes), nickel-plated swinging tap spouts, elevated gas cooker with thermostat, service lifts and speaking tubes in each kitchen, lavatory basins in all bedrooms, telephones, points for relayed radio service, rustless steel fireplaces, wall jewel safes and medicine chests in principal bedrooms. There was perambulator space on the ground floor and luggage storage on the top floor. Rents covered constant hot water, central heating, lift service and upkeep of communal spaces.

20 From the end of 1931, all water was taken from the Metropolitan Water Board mains supply, leaving the wells as a standby.

21 These coats of arms, beautifully restored in 1983 by London Transport's department of architecture and design, were those of Buckinghamshire, Hertfordshire, Middlesex, Paddington, Hampstead, City of London, St Marylebone, St Pancras, Finsbury, Hammersmith and Kensington. At the time of writing, the restaurant is used as a London Transport recruitment centre but is kept in very good order.

22 For a full description of this stock covering both the Metropolitan and London Transport eras, see *The Railway Magazine*, November 1962.

23 The names were: 1 *John Lyon*; 2 *Oliver Cromwell*; 3 *Sir Ralph Verney*; 4 *Lord Byron*; 5 *John Hampden*; 6 *William Penn*; 7 *Edmund Burke*; 8 *Sherlock Holmes*; 9 *John Milton*; 10 *William Ewart Gladstone*; 11 *George Romney*; 12 *Sarah Siddons*; 13 *Dick Whittington*; 14 *Benjamin Disraeli*; 15 *Wembley 1924*; 16 *Oliver Goldsmith*; 17 *Florence Nightingale*; 18 *Michael Faraday*; 19 *John Wycliffe*; 20 *Sir Christopher Wren*.

24 For a full description of these locomotives and their history, see Benest, K.R., (note 29, p345); for dimensions and electrical equipment details, Anon, *Metropolitan Railway Electrification*, Metropolitan-Vickers Electrical Co Ltd, 1924.

25 Following the death of Willis Holt on 20 March 1931, Hally was given the additional responsibility of traffic manager (from 15 April 1931) whilst retaining all his duties as chief mechanical engineer.

26 The Metropolitan had helped the LER with traction current since a Lots Road power failure in May 1925 when a temporary connection was lashed up at Baker Street to supply up to 60,000 units daily.

Chapter 15 (pp 288–306)

1 1888–1937: Anderson qualified as a solicitor in 1911 and was appointed an assistant solicitor to the Metropolitan Railway in 1914. His war service was with the army and the Royal Flying Corps and he was seriously wounded on operations for the latter in 1916. Following I. B. Pritchard's departure (to become legal adviser to the LNER), he was appointed chief legal adviser and solicitor, Metropolitan Railway, on 1 January 1929. When made general manager in 1931, his

salary was fixed at £4,500 but was increased to £5,500 on 15 December 1932; the staff of the solicitor's office was strengthened to give him the necessary support in the dual role. He was secretary, treasurer and solicitor to the LPTB from July 1933 until his death at age 48 on 12 March 1937.

2 'I think that everybody has felt that the interests of the Railway suffered from there being no successor to Mr Selbie. However competent and energetic a committee may be, it cannot give services equal to the value of those given by an individual.' (Sir Albert W. Wyon, one of the Metropolitan's auditors, in a letter to Anderson on his appointment as general manager.)

3 Anderson, in a letter to H. N. St V. Norman, Heston Air Park, 20 November 1931 (MET 10/681). (Anderson used his former Royal Flying Corps contacts to obtain advice on the damages claimed by the de Havilland Aircraft Co for interference with Stag Lane Aerodrome when the Stanmore branch was built.)

4 Just why the main line companies agreed to this is not easily established from contemporary evidence. Most probably it was because they wanted the government's London co-ordination proposals to succeed, with their promise of rationalisation of the competing rail and road passenger operations in the area, seeing in them the only hope of securing Treasury assistance with long-postponed improvements and modernisation of the London suburban railway infrastructure.

5 The proposed 'C' stock was to have a 'standard', but not firmly guaranteed, rate of interest of 5 per cent for the first two years, rising to a maximum of 6 per cent. In practice, it never exceeded 4¼ per cent, reached for one year only (1937).

6 R. T. Wreathall, surveyor to the Watford & Edgware Railway (1897) in a letter to A. C. Ellis, Metropolitan general manager, 6 December 1902 (MET 10/86).

7 For a full account of proposed railways between Edgware and Watford, see Jackson, Alan A., 'Beyond Edgware', *The Railway Magazine*, February 1967.

8 For an account of the construction of the line and the contractor's railways, see Bradley, Philip, W., 'Construction of the Metropolitan Stanmore Branch', *Underground*, Vol 1, No 12 (December 1962).

9 In anticipation of the opening of the new station, Neasden & Kingsbury was renamed Neasden on 1 January 1932.

10 This train was composed of newly delivered Birmingham Railway Carriage & Wagon multiple-unit electric compartment stock and two special vehicles, in the following formation: motor car 236/First class trailer 579/no 1 saloon (the rebuilt Rothschild saloon)/Pullman car *Mayflower*/First class trailer 580/First class trailer 578/motor car 237. The saloon and the Pullman were revarnished and the latter received a new carpet and 'fresh' chairs for the occasion. A train telephone was fitted.

11 See Jackson, Alan A., *London's Local Railways*, David & Charles, 1978, pp308–11.

12 For an account of the construction work, see Travis, A. S., 'The Quadrupling of the Metropolitan Railway between Wembley Park and Harrow', *Underground*, Vol 2, No 8 (August 1963).

13 For a detailed account of the resignalling, see 'The Re-signalling of Wembley Park Station, Metropolitan Railway', *The Railway Gazette*, 7 October 1932.

14 8×4-4-4T ('H' Class); 5×4-4-0T ('A'); 6×2-6-4T ('K'); 4×0-6-4T ('G'); 4×0-6-2T ('F'); 2×0-6-0T ('S'); and 7×0-4-4T ('E').

15 Giving evidence before a parliamentary committee in May 1935, Frank Pick stated that it was 'a mere accident' (that the Metropolitan went out to Aylesbury and the LPTB could not be expected to run suburban services there. *The Railway Gazette* of 17 May 1935 commented '. . . it would seem evident that the Board has deserted the old Metropolitan tenet that it should be considered a main line railway'.

Chapter Notes

Chapter 16 (pp 307–21)

1 The Metropolitan Railway Savings Bank was established on 20 March 1874 under powers given in the Metropolitan Railway Act, 21 July 1873. Its first secretary (Tapson) absconded after extracting £9,273. He was arrested in Philadelphia, USA, in 1880, virtually penniless.

2 From September 1863 the Metropolitan Railway had paid an annual sum to enable its employees to participate in the benefits of the GWR Provident Society. The Metropolitan Railway Mutual Provident Society Benevolent Fund was set up on 1 February 1877, funded by subscriptions from pay of 3d or 6d a week and £200 a year from the company (£300 from 1883). Payments from the fund provided for medical aid to the employee, his wife and children under 14 and also a small death grant. Annual fêtes to build up the fund were held at Neasden from August 1881 and concerts were arranged from December 1883.

3 A similar series of settlements were made at the same time on other railways, eg the LBSCR, see Cruttenden, M. J., 'Changing Times on the Brighton Railway', *The Railway World*, December 1984.

4 The new provisions were:

Motormen: on appointment 6s per 10-hour day, from the third year, 6s 6d, from the seventh year 7s. Overtime at daily wage rate. Annual holiday with pay after 7 years, 6 days; after 12 years, 7 days; after 15 years, 8 days, after 20 or more years, 10 days. New appointees to wait 7 years before getting a paid holiday.

Head guards (electric trains): First year 27s for 7-day week; second year 28s; third year 29s. Additional pay for Sunday duty, 2s. Average, including Sunday pay, 28s, 29s, 30s.

Assistant guards (electric trains): 23s 7-day wages and 2s Sunday pay, average 24s.

Conductors (electric trains): 19–22s (third year) as 7-day wages, plus 2s Sunday pay. Average including Sundays 20–23s.

Head guards (steam trains): First 5 years 30s; second 5 years 32s; after 10 years, 34s. No Sunday pay.

Under guards (steam trains): 23–29s (after 10 years). No Sunday pay.

Porter guards (steam trains): 23s plus 2s Sunday duty. Average 24s.

Steam train guards, new recruits: Head guards 29–33s (after 10 years) and 2s for Sunday duty, average including Sundays 30–34s. Under guards: 23–28s (after 10 years) plus 2s for Sunday duty.

Annual leave, guards, etc: After 1 year, 3 days; after 3 years, 4 days; after 5 years, 5 days; after 7 years, 6 days; after 12 years, 7 days; after 15 years, 8 days; after 20 years, 10 days.

5 The daily rates were (former rate in brackets):

> *First class (passenger trains)*: Drivers 7s 6d (8s), firemen 4s 6d (4s 6d).
> *Second class (goods trains, Chesham shuttle and relief duties)*: Drivers 7s (8s), firemen 4s (4s 6d).
> *Third class (ballast trains and shunting at Harrow)*: Drivers 6s 6d (8s), firemen 3s 6d (4s 6d).
> *Fourth class (shunting at Neasden)*: Drivers 6s (new rate), firemen 3s 6d (new rate).

6 For a detailed account of the services operated in the general strike of 1926, see Benest, K. R., 'Forty Years on – Striking Days on the Metropolitan', *Underground*, Vol 5, No 5 (May 1966).
7 These cuts were not fully restored until August 1937.
8 For a general account of labour, pay and conditions, comparisons between the Metropolitan and the Underground Group immediately before 1933 and after the formation of the LPTB, see Barker, T. C., and Robbins, Michael, *A History of London Transport, Vol 2*, Allen & Unwin, 1974, Chapter XVII.

Chapter 17 (pp 322–328)
1 Lord Aberconway to Metropolitan Railway Annual Meeting, 20 February 1930.
2 In *Report of the General Manager*, privately printed by the Metropolitan Railway, April 1915.
3 *Notes illustrating the need for a Relief Line between Finchley Road and Baker Street*, 14 September 1925 (MET 10/238).
4 Lord Aberconway to Sir Donald MacLean, 3 September 1931 (MET 10/758).
5 The relationship between the Metropolitan Railway's facilities and suburban growth in its catchment area between 1900 and 1939 is by no means straightforward and needs to be assessed against the general economic climate and other factors influencing the expansion of outer London at this time. See Jackson, Alan A., *Semi-Detached London; Suburban Development, Life and Transport, 1900–39*, Allen & Unwin, 1973; Tottman, David, *Ruislip–Northwood: An Early Example of Town Planning and its Consequences*, Ruislip, Northwood & Eastcote Local History Society, 1983; Robbins, Michael, *Middlesex*, Collins, 1953; Robbins, Michael, 'Transport and Suburban Development in Middlesex Down to 1914', *Transactions*, London & Middlesex Archaeological Society, 29, 1978, pp129–36.
6 In *A Few Late Chrysanthemums*, John Murray, 1953 ('The Metropolitan Railway' and 'Harrow-on-the-Hill'); in *John Betjeman's Collected Poems*, John Murray, 1958 ('Monody on the Death of Aldersgate Street Station'); and in *Summoned By Bells*, John Murray, 1960, pp56–7.
7 *Metro-Land: A Celebration of Suburbia*, text prepared and narrated by Sir John Betjeman; film cameraman John McGlashan; film editor, Edward Roberts; producer, Edward Mirzoeff.
8 Edwards, Dennis, and Pigram, Ron, *Metro Memories*, 1977; *The Romance of Metro-Land*, 1979; and *The Golden Years of the Metropolitan Railway*, 1983; all published by Midas Books.

APPENDICES

1

PRINCIPAL DATES:
DEVELOPMENT OF THE SYSTEM

The last current station names are used, but initials of pre-1923 companies are given where this clarifies locations. For a detailed chronology of stations, including name changes, see Borley, H. V., *Chronology of London Railways*, Railway & Canal Historical Society, 1982.

10.1.1863	Paddington (GWR, Bishop's Road)–Farringdon
1.10.1863	Junctions with GNR, King's Cross in use
13.6.1864	Hammersmith (H&CR)–Paddington (GWR, Bishop's Road) (GWR service to Farringdon)
1.7.1864	Latimer Road (H&CR)–Uxbridge Road Junction (WLR)
1.4.1865	Metropolitan trains to Hammersmith (H&CR)
23.12.1865	Farringdon–Moorgate
1.1.1866	Junction with LCDR Farringdon (West Street Junction) in use
20.2.1866	GNR freight trains over the Metropolitan to the LCDR via West Street Junction, Farringdon
1.3.1866	*City Widened Lines*: Farringdon–Barbican
1.7.1866	*City Widened Lines*: Barbican–Moorgate
17.2.1868	*City Widened Lines*: King's Cross–Farringdon (passenger service; freight from 27.1.1868)
13.4.1868	Baker Street Junction–Swiss Cottage (Metropolitan & St John's Wood Railway)
13.7.1868	Junction with Midland Railway, King's Cross, in use
1.10.1868	Praed Street Junction (Paddington)–Gloucester Road
24.12.1868	Gloucester Road–South Kensington
1.5.1869	GWR freight trains over Metropolitan to Smithfield depot
1.6.1870	Junction with LSWR, Hammersmith (Grove Road) in use (GWR service from Paddington to Richmond)
1.9.1871	Junction with LCDR (Snow Hill Junction)–Smithfield, in use (LCDR service into Moorgate)
2.11.1874	GNR freight trains to Farringdon Street (GNR) depot
1.2.1875	Moorgate–Liverpool Street (GER)
12.7.1875	Liverpool Street (Metropolitan)
18.11.1876	Liverpool Street–Aldgate
1.10.1877	Metropolitan service to Richmond via Hammersmith (LSWR)
1.1.1878	Midland Railway freight trains over the Metropolitan to Midland Railway depot, Whitecross Street (east of Barbican)
30.6.1879	Swiss Cottage–West Hampstead
24.11.1879	West Hampstead–Willesden Green
2.8.1880	Willesden Green–Harrow-on-the-Hill
1.10.1880	Junction with Midland Railway at Finchley Road

Appendices

13.10.1880	Freight trains Finchley Road–Harrow-on-the-Hill
25.9.1882	Aldgate–Tower Hill (temporary Tower of London station)
1.10.1884	Metropolitan and MDR local service on the East London Railway between St Mary's (Whitechapel) and New Cross
6.10.1884	*Inner Circle completed*: Tower Hill–Mansion House (Joint with MDR from Aldgate to Mansion House): curve Aldgate to Aldgate East: Minories Junction Aldgate to Vallance Road Junction, Whitechapel; and junction with East London Railway, Whitechapel in use (Joint with MDR). Metropolitan service over the ELR to New Cross (SER) from Hammersmith (H&CR). (MDR trains ran to New Cross (ELR) adjacent to LBSCR station)
25.5.1885	Harrow-on-the-Hill–Pinner
1.9.1887	Pinner–Rickmansworth
8.7.1889	Rickmansworth–Chesham
1.7.1891	Aylesbury & Buckingham Railway (Aylesbury to Verney Junction (LNWR)) taken over by the Metropolitan
1.9.1892	Chalfont & Latimer (junction with Chesham line)–Aylesbury (temporary Metropolitan station)
1.1.1894	Aylesbury Joint Station, junction with GWR
1.12.1896	Double line Aylesbury–Granborough Road
1.1.1897	Double line Granborough Road–Verney Junction (LNWR). First through trains Baker Street–Verney Junction
26.7.1898	First use (by coal trains) of junction with GCR at Quainton Road. Two tracks for the exclusive use of the GCR from Finchley Road (Canfield Place) to south side of Preston Road bridge
15.3.1899	GCR passenger trains to London (Marylebone) via the Metropolitan south of Quainton Road
1.12.1899	Metropolitan takes a lease of Quainton Road to Brill branch
4.7.1904	Harrow-on-the-Hill–Uxbridge (station in Belmont Road)
1.1.1905	*Electric working*: Baker Street to Uxbridge (full service 20.3.1905)
1.7.1905	*Electric working*: Aldgate to South Kensington (partial)
24.7.1905	*Electric working*: Aldgate to South Kensington (full)
24.9.1905	*Electric working*: Inner Circle service
1.3.1906	GCR take over two Metropolitan tracks, Finchley Road (Canfield Place)–Harrow South Junction for all trains
2.4.1906	Metropolitan & GC Joint Committee take over operation of Harrow South Junction–Verney Junction and Chesham and Brill branches
5.11.1906	*Electric working*: Hammersmith (H&CR)–Aldgate; Latimer Road–Uxbridge Road (WLR) (service to Kensington (Olympia)). Partial service (full service 3.12.1906)
2.12.1906	Last Metropolitan steam trains over the ELR
3.12.1906	Joint Metropolitan/GWR electric service Hammersmith (H&CR)–Whitechapel (MDR) (some steam trains ran for a further ten days or so)

31.12.1906	Last Metropolitan/GWR trains Aldgate–Richmond (LSWR) but GWR worked from Ladbroke Grove to Richmond until 31.12.1910
1.11.1909	Metropolitan freight trains from Willesden Green to new Metropolitan freight depot at Farringdon (Vine Street)
1.3.1910	MDR electric trains over Metropolitan from South Harrow to Uxbridge (first regular use of Metropolitan between Rayners Lane and South Harrow)
1.6.1910	Pullman cars in certain trains between Metropolitan & GC Joint stations and City stations
31.3.1913	*Electric working*: Metropolitan service over the ELR to New Cross (SER) and New Cross Gate (LBSCR)
1.7.1913	Metropolitan acquires the GN&CR (Moorgate to Finsbury Park) (officially worked by Metropolitan from 1.9.1913)
31.5.1915	Four Metropolitan tracks: Finchley Road–Wembley Park (in addition to the two tracks leased to the GCR)
1.7.1921	Metropolitan takes over management of the ELR
1.1.1923	Metropolitan takes over working of H&CR and purchases its rolling stock
5.1.1925	*Electric working*: Harrow-on-the-Hill to Rickmansworth
14.9.1925	Burrowing junction at Harrow North Junction for Uxbridge line and additional lines between Harrow-on-the-Hill station and Harrow North Junction
2.11.1925	Rickmansworth/Moor Park–Watford (Metropolitan & LNER Joint)
15.3.1926	New junction west of King's Cross to east-bound City Widened Lines. *Electric working* of east-bound track City Widened Lines between this junction and Moorgate by Metropolitan trains
10.1.1932	Four Metropolitan tracks, Wembley Park–Harrow South Junction (in addition to the two tracks leased to LNER)
10.12.1932	Wembley Park–Stanmore (Metropolitan)

2

DIRECTORS AND CHIEF OFFICERS

Chairmen

1853–6	William Malins
1856–7	John Lewis Ricardo, MP (chairman, North Staffordshire Railway)
1858–65	William Arthur Wilkinson
1865–72	John I. Parson
1872–94	Sir Edward W. Watkin
1894–1901	John Bell (also 'Managing Director')
1901–4	Col John J. Mellor
1904–33	Sir Charles B. B. McLaren (became Lord Aberconway, 1911)

Deputy Chairmen

1853–7	Acton S. Ayrton
1860–5	John I. Parson ('Managing Director', 1859–63)
1865–72	Charles Gilpin
1872–95	Henry Davis Pochin
1895–1901	Col John J. Mellor
1901–2	Francis Pavy
1902–4	Sir Charles B. B. McLaren
1904–11	Sir William Birt (former general manager GER; GER director)
1911–12	Lord Furness
1912–14	Paul Speak
1914–33	Sir Clarendon G. Hyde (former director, GN&CR; director, Metropolitan Carriage, Wagon & Finance Co Ltd)

Ordinary Directors

1853–60	Bonamy Price
1853	Acton S. Ayrton
1853–60	Thomas E. Dicey (director, North Staffordshire Railway)
1853–6	Samuel Baker (director, GWR)
1853–64	Thomas Bulkeley (director, GWR)
1854–9	Lightly Simpson (director, Eastern Counties Railway)
1854–6	Charles W. Faber (director, GNR)
1855–72	William Lee, MP (director, MDR from 1863)
1855–9	Henry Simmonds (director, GWR)
1855	A. K. Baker (director, GWR)
1855–64	Thomas Williams (director, GWR)
1856–64	Dr Richard Prichard-Smith, MD (director, GWR)
1856	Sampson Copestake
1856–64	David Ogilvy (director, GWR)
1857	B. J. Armstrong

1857	William Arthur Wilkinson
1857–60	Dr John Challice, MD
1858–70	William Austin (director, MDR, 1863–7)
1858	Thomas Luce (director, GWR)
1858–65	Charles Gilpin
1858–60	John I. Parson ('Managing Director', 1859–63)
1860–70	Alderman Warren S. Hale (City of London Corporation)
1860–4	Benjamin Bower (City of London Corporation)
1860–4	Thomas H. Fry (City of London Corporation)
1863–4	Edward Wanklyn (director, GWR)
1863–72	Alderman Dakin (City of London Corporation)
1864–72	Russell Scott
1864–78	Alexander Clunes Sherriff (deputy chairman, MDR, 1865–8)
1866–90	James Nasmyth (director, MDR, 1868–9)
1870–1	James Caird
1870–2	Graham Menzies
1872–6	Joseph Shuttleworth
1872–6	John R. Lingard
1872–85	Andrew Cassels
1872–93	George Morphett
1872–85	Benjamin Whitworth
1876–93	Rt Hon Edward Hugessen Knatchbull-Hugessen, MP (Lord Brabourne, 1880; director, SER)
1876–99	Alfred Mellor Watkin (son of Sir Edward; director, MSLR/ GCR)
1885–1901	Henry John Barratt
1885–6	Abraham Laverton, MP
1887–95	Col John J. Mellor
1893–1901	Francis Pavy
1894–1901	Sir Edward W. Watkin
1895–1902	Charles B. B. McLaren (Baronet 1902; Lord Aberconway, 1911)
1899–1913	Jabez Light (formerly goods manager, SER)
1899–1918	Lt Col Clifford Probyn
1901–11	Sir Christopher Furness (Lord Furness, 1908)
1901–2	John Bell
1902–4	Sir William Birt (formerly general manager, GER; director, GER)
1902–19	Albert George Kitching
1904–7	Col John J. Mellor
1907–13	Thomas Parker
1911–15	The Hon Francis McLaren (son of Lord Aberconway)
1912–14	Sir Clarendon G. Hyde (former director, GN&CR; director, Metropolitan Carriage, Wagon & Finance Co Ltd)
1912	Paul Speak
1913–33	The Hon Evelyn Hubbard
1913–22	The Earl of Lauderdale (former chairman, GN&CR)
1914–33	Albert I. Belisha

Appendices

1915–33	Frank Dudley Docker
1918–26	J. W. Wheeler-Bennett
1920–9	Lt Col Sir Harry C. W. Verney, Bt, DSO
1922–30	Robert Hope Selbie (also general manager)
1927–33	Sir Edward Manville
1929–33	Sir Edmund Wyldbore-Smith
1930–3	The Rt Hon Earl of Cromer
1933	Bernard D. F. Docker (later Sir Bernard; son of Frank Dudley Docker)

General Managers
1862–79	Myles Fenton (later Sir Myles)
1880–1901	John Bell
1901–8	Abraham Charles Ellis
1908–30	Robert Hope Selbie
1930–1	(general management committee)
1931–3	John Sloane Anderson (also chief legal adviser and solicitor)

Assistant General Manager
1901–13	Alfred B. Garside

Assistant to General Manager
1913–28	Herbert Somerville Stewart

Secretaries
1853–72	John Henchman
1872–9	John Bell
1880–9	John Meredith Eyles
1889–1902	G. H. Whissell
1903–8	Robert Hope Selbie
1908–24	William Henry Brown
1925–8	Herbert Somerville Stewart (also assistant to general manager)
1929–33	H. S. Chapman

Engineers (full time)
1864–72	Robert H. Burnett ('resident engineer and locomotive superintendent')
1872–85	Joseph Tomlinson Jr ('resident engineer and locomotive superintendent')
1885–91	J. J. Hanbury ('resident engineer and locomotive superintendent'); from 1.12.1891 Hanbury was designated 'locomotive and carriage superintendent' and permanent way and works tasks were allocated to W. H. Gates (see below))
1891–1903	William Hayden Gates ('resident engineer' for way and works)
1903–5	E. P. Seaton ('resident engineer', including (for the first time) responsibility for new works)
1906–21	William Willox ('engineer')
1921–33	Edward Arthur Wilson ('chief civil engineer')

Appendices

Locomotive Engineers/Superintendents/Chief Mechanical Engineers

1864–72	Robert H. Burnett ('resident engineer and locomotive superintendent')
1872–85	Joseph Tomlinson Jr ('resident engineer and locomotive superintendent')
1885–93	J. J. Hanbury ('resident engineer and locomotive superintendent' to 1891, then 'locomotive and carriage superintendent')
1893	T. S. Raney ('temporarily in charge locomotive running department')
1896–1905	T. F. Clark ('locomotive superintendent')
1906–23	Charles Jones ('locomotive and chief electrical engineer'; from 1920 'chief electrical and mechanical engineer')
1923–33	George Hally ('chief mechanical engineer and works manager'; also traffic manager from 1930)

Chief Electrical Engineers (full time)

1903–24	Charles Jones ('chief electrical engineer' 1903–6; 'locomotive and chief electrical engineer' 1906–20; 'chief electrical and mechanical engineer' 1920–3; 'chief electrical engineer' 1923)
1924–33	P. R. Boulton ('chief electrical engineer')

Carriage and Wagon Superintendents

Before 1893 carriages and wagons were the responsibility of the resident engineer.

1893–1903	T. S. Raney
1903–6	A. Ingram ('carriage and wagon superintendent and rolling stock constructor')
	After 1906 carriages and wagons responsibility of the chief mechanical engineer.

Signal and Telegraph Engineers

Until 31.12.1901 signals and telegraphs were the responsibility of C. E. P. D. D. Spagnoletti and his firm (latterly Spagnoletti & Crook).

1902–8	E. G. Phillips
1908–21	(responsibility of chief engineer)
1922–5	W. Challis
1925–33	R. Falshaw-Morkill

Superintendents of The Line/Traffic Managers

1863–1900	Edmond Crapp ('outdoor superintendent', 'traffic superintendent', then 'superintendent of the line')
1900–8	H. B. Palmer ('superintendent of the line')
1909–31	Willis H. Holt ('traffic superintendent' including duties of former goods manager)
1931–3	George Hally ('traffic manager'; also chief mechanical engineer)

Goods Managers
Before 1902 goods were the responsibility of the superintendent of the line.

1902–8	William Henry Brown
1908–9	John Wardle ('goods and parcels manager')

After 1909 goods were the responsibility of the traffic superintendent/traffic manager.

Publicity Managers/Commercial Managers

1911–13	James Feiron
1913–33	John Wardle ('commercial manager')

Solicitors/Legal Advisers
Until 1892 all legal work and advice was undertaken by outside firms, Messrs Burchell from 1853 to 1882 and Messrs Fowler & Perks (later Fowler, Perks, Hopkinson & Co) from 1882 to 1893. From 31.3.1893, after Robert William Perks had become an MP, he acted as 'consulting solicitor' until 1895.

1892–3	J. Barrington Matthews ('law clerk to the Metropolitan Railway')
1893–8	C. A. Mason ('law clerk to the Metropolitan Railway')
1898–1902	Abraham Charles Ellis ('solicitor to the Metropolitan Railway')
1903–18	C. de Winton Kitcat ('solicitor to the Metropolitan Railway')
1918–28	I. Buchanan Pritchard ('solicitor to the Metropolitan Railway')
1929–33	John Sloane Anderson ('chief legal adviser and solicitor'; also general manager from 1931)

Surveyors/Architects

1853–7	John Hargrave Stevens ('surveyor' then 'architect and assistant engineer')
1858–73	Messrs Fuller & Withall (R. A. Withall from 1865) ('surveyors and valuers')
1873–81	Messrs Hunt, Stephenson, Jones & Ritchie (later Messrs Hunt & Ritchie; 'surveyors and valuers')
1898–1906	Matthew Garbutt ('architect and surveyor')

(All the above appear to have been employed on a part-time basis.)

1910–33	Charles Walter Clark ('architectural assistant to the engineer' 1910–21, then 'architect to the Metropolitan Railway')

Land/Estate Agents (Metropolitan Railway)

1863–72	(undertaken by the secretary)
1872–87	William Marsh
1887–1906	(undertaken by Surplus Lands Committee agent (see below))
1906–33	Frederick Dawson ('estate and rating agent'; took over Metropolitan Railway work from Surplus Lands Committee)

Estate Agents (Metropolitan Railway Surplus Lands Committee)

1887–1913	William Marsh
1913–33	Henry Gibson ('valuer and estate agent'; also valuer and surveyor, MRCE, and director, NW Estates Syndicate Ltd)

3

FREIGHT AND PARCELS SERVICES

General

Freight first began to pass over the Metropolitan from 20 February 1866 on trains moving between the GNR and points on the LCDR south of the Thames via Farringdon Street. Midland freight trains followed the same route from July 1868. The GNR worked goods trains this way to Clapham Junction, LSWR, from 15 April 1867 and to Battersea, LBSCR, from 1 May. The last destination was also served by some of the Midland trains. GWR freight services to Smithfield depot, where siding accommodation was leased from the Metropolitan, started in May 1869, mostly carrying meat. City goods depots on the Metropolitan at Farringdon and Whitecross Street were opened respectively by the GNR and the Midland in November 1874 and January 1878. The Midland and GNR trains all used the City Widened Lines from St Pancras and King's Cross eastwards and it is doubtful whether anything but a small proportion of this freight load could have been handled had not those extra tracks been provided in 1868. All this produced a healthy tolls revenue, but the Metropolitan handled no freight traffic on its own account until the early 1880s.

When promoting extensions of the St John's Wood line for reasons of his own in the 1870s, Watkin had to find public arguments for them which would not upset the Metropolitan's shareholders, whose main interest was in building up the dividend from the existing operation rather than in expanding the mileage. One such justification was the alleged need to increase the company's percentage of revenue from freight business, which was running at 4¼ per cent of receipts compared with the 50 per cent or so average of most other railways. And as the extensions were opened, Metropolitan Railway freight trains began to appear. When the railway arrived at Harrow in the summer of 1880, the coal traffic of the Harrow District Gas Co was secured, together with that of Harrow School laundry and local coal merchants. A coal yard was provided, served from 13 October 1880 by trains working over a connection with the Midland Railway at Finchley Road. In the evidence given for the Aylesbury & Rickmansworth Railway Bill in the 1880–1 session, much was made of the potential such a line would offer to the Metropolitan as a freight carrier, something that would change the whole character of the railway. There were suggestions of a London goods depot being built in the Willesden area or at Finchley Road, supplemented possibly by another at Farringdon Street or Edgware Road, once the locomotive depot at the latter had been moved to Neasden.

We have seen in the main text how goods yards were provided at almost all stations on the Extension Line as they were opened, their traffic increasing steadily until it required additional expenditure on layout improvements and rolling stock in the late 1890s and early 1900s. By 1904 there were freight facilities at all stations from Northwood to Verney Junction inclusive except Winslow Road, also at Pinner, Harrow, Ruislip, Uxbridge, Wembley Park, Neasden, Willesden Green and Finchley Road. At Hammersmith H&CR, the GWR handled freight traffic, the business here being supplemented by that for the Ford Motors warehouse, erected at Brook Green in 1916–17 with its own siding. Livestock could be handled at Finchley Road, Willesden Green, Neasden, Wembley Park, Harrow, Pinner, Northwood, Rickmansworth, Chesham, Amersham, Great Missenden, Wendover, Aylesbury, Waddesdon Manor, Quainton Road, Uxbridge and Ruislip. As late as 1912, the Metropolitan had only twelve cattle wagons of its own, considerable reliance being placed on the ability of the GCR to find such vehicles. Some embarrrassment occurred when the GCR failed, and six more were obtained at this time by converting redundant rail and timber wagons.

By 1913 the Metropolitan owned 387 low-sided wagons, 84 high-sided and 24 box wagons. In a week at this period some 400 loaded wagons would be forwarded to Metropolitan, Joint and other companies' stations whilst about 40 were under repair and some 20 in use by the engineer's staff. That year, to cope with heavy coke traffic from the gasworks at South Harrow, Pinner, Rickmansworth and Aylesbury, 24 low-sided wagons were converted to high-side vehicles. Box wagons were also in demand for food and other vulnerable traffics handled at the City depot and six more were obtained by converting rail wagons.

Traffic between stations Willesden Green and points north and places south of the Thames was generally transferred to and from the Midland at Finchley Road sidings, but after the formation of the Metropolitan & GCR Joint Committee, some went via Neasden GCR, worked by LSWR locomotives via Acton Wells and Kew. Willesden Green was a key point, dealing with the London traffic until 1909 as well as with heavy loads of milk, coal and building materials for its burgeoning suburban hinterland. London freight not passed over to the Midland or the GCR was moved by horse-drawn carts to and from the central area from 20 April 1903. Mostly this traffic was inwards, from Harrow and beyond, the business originating in the centre being sparse and irregular owing to the Metropolitan's lack of collection facilities at this time.

In 1903 the Metropolitan was paying the Midland some £4,300 a year for moving freight into central London. To eliminate this cost and develop new business, the Metropolitan board decided the company should have its own goods depot in the City. It was hoped this would attract traffic carted from the docks which could then be distributed over the Metropolitan system.

The City Goods Depot, Vine Street, 1909

The final choice of site for the new depot fell on Vine Street sidings, east of the Circle line and just north of Farringdon Street station. Here a warehouse was built out over the tracks, a £2,192 contract, given to Henry Lovatt Ltd. There were three van docks, a manually operated traverser and a 20cwt (1.02 tonne) electric hoist from rail level, the machinery being supplied by Pickerings for £127.5s including erection. At rail level, two seven-wagon sidings were separated by a loading platform. To supplement the hoist there was a spiral staircase to the road level but it soon became necessary to close this off with galvanised iron when not in use as it gave the ravenous railway rats access to the groceries and other delights stored above. Initially, the staff at Vine Street consisted of a goods agent/canvasser, clerk, boy clerk, two shunter/loaders and a 'strong youth assistant'. Some of these were drawn from Willesden Green, where the establishment had previously consisted of a goods agent/canvasser, four clerks, two loaders, two shunters, two van guards and a carman.

Vine Street depot, which dealt with all classes of traffic except minerals and livestock, was opened on 1 November 1909. Trains were hauled to and from West Hampstead yard by electric locomotives, making it the second wholly electrically served freight facility in the United Kingdom. The 14 wagon trains, restricted to 250 tons (254 tonnes) inwards and 225 (228.6) in the Down direction, were operated in the off-peak periods. Within a short time the new depot was handling up to 300 tons (305 tonnes) or slightly more a week, nearly all 'collected and delivered' traffic, about half entirely new, the rest diverted from Willesden Green. During 1910, 11,400 tons (11,582.4 tonnes) were dealt with, a figure which rose to 25,100 (25,501.6) in 1915.

A second electric hoist of 2 tons (2.032 tonnes) capacity was installed in March 1910 and a small second floor was added below the existing warehouse staging in the same year. A parcels chute, installed in 1917, saved labour at a crucial time.

From 1 January 1910 cartage to and from the depot was contracted out to Pickfords, but there was much chagrin when that firm began a motor cartage service between London and Harrow in 1912, causing a perceptible fall in the Metropolitan's traffic. The cartage work was transferred to the (unrelated) Metropolitan Cartage Co in 1915, but from 1 January 1919 the railway company began to undertake its own cartage, using Metropolitan staff, vans and horses, the latter stabled in a new depot at Warwick Yard, Whitecross Street.

By 1913 it was reported that traffic at Vine Street depot had 'completely outgrown the capacity'; a load of some 430 tons (436.9 tonnes) a week was being handled with increasing difficulty. Wagons were frequently left behind at Willesden Green owing to the lack of siding capacity whilst in the streets above vans waited for hours to be loaded and unloaded. Schemes were prepared for additional sidings near Farringdon Street station, even for a second goods depot between the running lines south-east of the station, but action was postponed apart from some minor improvements at Vine Street.

When traffic rose to about 600 tons (609.6 tonnes) a week this proved to be the peak. As soon as peace returned, motor road transport started to make serious encroachments into the freight business of all railway companies, particularly the short-distance work. As a result, traffic at Vine Street had fallen to around 300 tons (304.8 tonnes) a week by the late 1920s, a level that could be comfortably handled with the existing facilities.

Working with the GCR and the LNER
With the arrival of the GCR on the Extension Line, freight traffic began to

pass into and out of the Metropolitan at its northern as well as its southern extremity. Both companies' locomotives participated in the freight work at stations beyond Harrow, a circumstance which at first led to a great deal of difficulty and friction. An attempt was then made to allocate part of the work on alternate weeks to each company, but this was found to be wasteful. Eventually, the Metropolitan consented to undertake all the local haulage and shunting at Joint Committee stations for three years from 1 January 1910, an arrangement the GCR accepted once the Metropolitan had offered to reduce its locomotive charges from $33\frac{1}{3}$ per cent to $27\frac{1}{2}$ per cent of receipts. Each company continued to receive one-third of receipts for working its own traffic.

This arrangement continued, at increasing loss to the Metropolitan, until 1927. Growth in the intensity of passenger trains on the double-track main line, the severe gradients, the existence of block sections unhelpfully long for the clearance of freight trains, and inadequately laid out yards all contributed to delays, adding to overtime and other working costs. Another problem was that many of the sidings had to be shunted uphill; Amersham was especially bad, with loose shunting achieved only with difficulty and every wagon placed having to have its brakes pinned down. In 1927 it was found that the five principal daily freight trains absorbed forty-eight men, achieving little more than one round trip between Harrow and Quainton Road/Verney Junction. Finding the case convincing, the LNER agreed to pay locomotive charges at one-third from 1 February 1927 and to pay its share of improvements at the points of greatest pressure.

An additional siding was then put in at Pinner. At Amersham, where total tonnage had increased from 14,704 (14,939.3 tonnes) in 1915 to 34,331 (34,880.3) in 1925, two of the existing sidings and a cart road were extended, together with rearrangement of the shunting neck, to provide accommodation for 28 more wagons. And at Quainton Road, where traffic was exchanged with the LNER at some 2,000–2,500 wagons a week, an existing siding was extended to take 80 wagons and a new siding added for 40, increasing total capacity by 211 per cent.

Later in 1927 further work was agreed. At Northwood, where the 356 wagons forwarded and received in October 1917 had grown to 755 in October 1926, a new shunting neck was built. As construction of the burrowing junction at Harrow had erased standing for 33 wagons, two additional sidings were installed. Rickmansworth received a new trailing connection to the Up line for its Up Sidings. All this work was finished by September 1929.

From 1 November 1927, beginning at Pinner and Northwood, the Joint Committee used its own motor vehicles for goods and parcels cartage instead of employing agents. A similar change was made at Amersham and Chalfont & Latimer from 29 April 1929; at Aylesbury from 23 September 1929; and at Great Missenden and Wendover from 5 September 1931.

Types of Traffic

The staple freight business was, of course, coal inwards to gasworks and for domestic use, normally through the suburban yards from Finchley Road outwards. These yards also imported road and house-building materials, food and miscellaneous goods of all kinds, the first two in great quantities during the period of suburban expansion 1910–14 and from about 1923 onwards. All this traffic moved in via Quainton Road and Finchley Road or the London City depots. Milk from the Vale of Aylesbury to the suburban stations, mainly through Willesden Green, was also important for many years, and eventually six special vans were provided for the large churns used. At West Hampstead, incredibly, traders manhandled over thirty of these heavy churns daily up and down the passenger staircases. Chesham was a source of traffic in manufactured goods outwards, principally woodware and footwear. A good deal of timber in the form of felled trees was moved out from the country stations.

The suburban building boom of the late 1920s and early 1930s demanded additional siding accommodation at Neasden (completed in October 1929); at Eastcote (4 March 1930); and at Hillingdon (1 August 1930). As already mentioned in Chapter 13, an entirely new goods yard and private sidings for builders were provided for the new suburb at Rayners Lane in 1929–30.

Among the special traffics of the Metropolitan were foodstuffs in bulk between the docks and Alfred Button & Sons, the Uxbridge wholesale grocers, mostly passing through the Vine Street depot. That depot also handled hams for Adamsons of Harrow and paper in special 'kennels' for the Aylesbury printers, Hazell, Watson & Viney, a traffic which had been attracted away from the GWR in 1910. Aylesbury was also the source of substantial business for the Dominion Dairy Co.

A warehouse built in Uxbridge goods yard by the Metropolitan in 1912 was handed over to Buttons after they had guaranteed a minimum traffic of £1,200 a year. The Metropolitan also provided a bacon-curing plant in the yard for the same firm in 1916, by which time their account was worth £2,000 a year to the railway. When the Metropolitan agreed to further extend Buttons' premises in the yard at a cost of £8,000 in 1926, the firm paid additional rent which produced a 6 per cent return and withdrew their road vehicles between London and Uxbridge, consigning via the Metropolitan two-thirds of all their traffic from London. This was an astute bargain on Selbie's part, securing a minimum income of £2,000 a year for the railway at a time when road transport was threatening to steal much of the short-haul freight business. The usefulness of road motor vehicles in a feeder role was not overlooked by the Metropolitan; goods and parcels cartage at Uxbridge was undertaken by the railway's own lorries and vans from 1 January 1929.

A curiosity was the fish traffic passing through the joint station at Monument, the nearest point to the Billingsgate Market. This freight had to be brought through the passenger booking hall and down the public staircase to the platforms. Clearing away the fishy liquids trickling from the boxes and laying sawdust to soak up the slime and effluvia provided a regular chore for the station staff. On Fridays, especially during Lent, the movements intensified, causing Sir Charles McLaren, later Lord Aberconway, some distress when he observed it in 1902. He complained that the station and its approaches were in an 'indescribably filthy condition' with caked mud, fish offal and 'other unpleasant-looking substances' littering the upper landings and staircases. About this time, the MDR, which shared the traffic and the station, suggested a separate entrance for the fish boxes in Fish Street Hill, to a second bridge over the line. This was agreed, but nothing was done, as after electrification of its line, the MDR refused to carry the fish. With this and the introduction of GCR cartage to Marylebone, the quantities handled dropped substantially. Fishy business on the Inner Circle, however, did survive to outlast the Metropolitan Railway, not finally disappearing until 1 January 1936, when the LPTB abolished parcels accommodation on Inner Circle trains, partly because complaints were still being received about the condition of Monument station.

Another unusual feature of the passenger train business was carriage of chairs in small quantities from GWR stations to the furniture wholesalers and retailers through Gower Street (Euston Square) and Moorgate stations. Palmer, superintendent of the line, reported in 1907 that this traffic was delaying the train service every weekday morning. Some at least of the Gower Street traffic would have been for Maple's store, where Blundell Maple had wanted a siding (and passenger subway) at basement level in 1889. He promised ten wagonloads of outwards traffic every night, but when the work had been costed had second thoughts.

To end on a bizarre note, it is interesting to find in the 1913 minutes (not on 1 April) a report from the general manager that borings for coal were in progress near Great Missenden with 'satisfactory results so far'. Nothing more is recorded on this topic, which could have changed dramatically the balance between the Metropolitan's passenger and freight traffics.

Parcels

Schemes administered by concessionaires, in conjunction with the MDR, for carrying parcels on the Metropolitan passenger trains were considered in 1870–3 and again in 1878, but came to nothing as Forbes was characteristically awkward. From 1 February 1882 until March 1883 the Metropolitan experimented with a parcels service organised by F. Flack, one of its employees, who took half the gross receipts. Parcels were delivered within ¾ mile of stations in the inner London area, making use of the passenger booking offices, the booking clerks and the Metropolitan's horse-bus conductors to receive and carry them. Much to Flack's disappointment, the board concluded that the railway company was spending more than it was getting back.

No doubt making use of this experience, on 8 July 1889 the Metropolitan started its own parcels and local delivery service on the Extension line, extending it to the City stations in the following March. Post Office parcels were carried on the railway from the beginning of 1892. Except in central London, stations collected and delivered parcels in their own area, or they would be handed in by the consignor or received by the consignee at the station. London parcels were processed at a central depot at Baker Street station, completed in 1893, an establishment employing by 1907 a chief clerk and canvasser, 7 clerks, 2 foremen and 58 messengers. Collection and delivery was undertaken by 8 hired single-horse vans and the messengers. On the Inner Circle, messengers and vans delivered once the parcel had been taken off the first train available from the handing-in station. Parcels were also collected at regular intervals from the 67 'receiving offices' in central London operated by the various railway companies and by private firms.

In the 1900s there was intensive competition for parcels business: the larger shops and stores employed their own fleets of vans, and independent parcels firms, notably Carter Paterson and Pickfords, charged much lower rates than the Metropolitan; other railway companies competed for parcels traffic in the London area; and last but by no means least, there was, of course, the Post Office service. Despite this, the Metropolitan operation earned a modest profit (in the six months ended 30 June 1908, for example, a net revenue of almost £1,700). Whilst parcels handling delayed working of passenger trains, it was considered that such delays were in any case inevitable for the handling of passengers' luggage, a service which could not be avoided (the Metropolitan attached considerable importance to the luggage facility, particularly between its stations and Victoria, and succeeded in retaining luggage accommodation on the Inner Circle, after the MDR had abandoned it generally at the end of 1912).

Under Selbie, the parcels work was fostered and modernised. The number of parcels handled in 1913 was 778,906 against 402,971 in 1907, an increase of over 93 per cent. A fine new depot provided within the rebuilt Baker Street station in 1913 was extended in 1928–9. Trials were made at an early date with motor and electrically powered vans, and cycle carriers were introduced for the short-distance deliveries and collections. In 1915 around 26 horse vans were in service, almost all owned by the Metropolitan, and in April the following year, parcels cartage became wholly in-house, with the purchase of 39 horses and construction of stables on Metropolitan property at Loveridge Road, Kilburn. Here the horses enjoyed 100 tons (101.6 tonnes) of good quality hay cut every year from the railway slopes and stored at Rickmansworth, Eastcote and Wembley Park. They were put out to grass, as necessary, on a 5 acre paddock at Wembley Park.

Parcels business was still turning a reasonable profit (about £18,000 a year) in 1923–4 when around 860,000 items were handled in a twelve-month period. By 1925 the fleet consisted of 31 horse-drawn vans, 2 electric vans, 10 motor vans and 4 cycle carriers. The last were given up in 1929 in favour of 2 30cwt (1.524 tonne) Morris vans.

When economies were being sought in 1931, Lord Aberconway suggested the abandonment of the parcels business, but it survived to be handed over to the LPTB in July 1933.

SELECTED FREIGHT AND PARCELS STATISTICS

Gross Receipts £[1]

	Freight	Parcels
1895	55,184	7,980
1900	117,844	28,042
1905	147,101	35,053
1910	66,695[2]	not available
1922	138,715	29,239
1925	145,864	not available
1930	157,643	not available

Freight Tonnage Handled

	Including Other Companies' Traffic Over the Metropolitan	Originating on the Metropolitan
	Tons (tonnes in brackets)	
1912	3,320,328 (3,373,453)	not available
1913	3,256,129 (3,308,227)	32,538 (33,059)
1918	5,800,000 (5,892,800)[3]	not available
1919	not available	49,897 (50,695)
1920	not available	35,281 (35,845)
1921	not available	24,719 (25,114)[4]
1922	3,931,926 (3,994,837)	32,607 (36,063)
1923	4,193,580 (4,260,677)	34,762 (35,227)
1924	4,887,504 (4,965,704)	37,275 (37,871)
1925	4,519,520 (4,591,832)	37,262 (37,858)
1926	3,057,242 (3,106,158)[5]	48,653 (49,431)
1927	4,655,115 (4,729,597)	38,003 (38,611)
1928	3,931,535 (3,994,439)	28,476 (28,932)
1929	4,219,287 (4,286,795)	31,388 (31,890)
1930	4,324,115 (4,393,301)	26,682 (27,109)
1931	4,156,477 (4,222,981)	33,749 (34,289)
1932	3,727,141 (3,786,775)	

1 When making comparisons, especially between the pre-1914 and post-1920 figures, allowance must be made for inflation.
2 Reflects diversion of traffic to GWR & GCR Joint line.
3 Estimated; includes government traffic.
4 Depleted by coal strike.
5 Depleted by general and coal strikes.

Station Traffics

An analysis of traffic at each station in August 1927 and in the same month a year later shows Harrow-on-the-Hill as the busiest, handling 7,543 tons (7,663.7 tonnes) including 4,785 tons (4,861.6 tonnes) solid fuels, in August 1927 and 7,131 tons (7,245.1 tonnes), including 4,820 tons (4,897.1 tonnes) solid fuels, a year later. Other busy yards were:

		Total		Solid Fuels	
		Tons	Tonnes	Tons	Tonnes
Willesden Green	August 1927	2,659	2,701	1,292	1,313
	August 1928	3,943	4,006	1,961	1,992
Neasden	August 1927	2,873	2,919	7	7
	August 1928	4,284	4,352	11	11
Pinner	August 1927	3,611	3,669	1,203	1,222
	August 1928	3,499	3,555	1,407	1,429
Croxley Green	August 1927	3,065	3,114	368	374
	August 1928	2,382	2,420	276	280
Chesham	August 1927	4,059	4,124	1,794	1,823
	August 1928	5,102	5,184	1,617	1,643
Amersham	August 1927	2,502	2,542	817	830
	August 1928	1,707	1,734	887	901

In contrast, Granborough Road handled only 39 tons (39.6 tonnes) in August 1928, 22 (22.4) of them coal and coke.

Aylesbury did most business in livestock, with 134 wagons in August 1927 and 118 in August 1928.

Altogether, in August 1928 Metropolitan stations dealt with 15,062 tons (15,303 tonnes) of freight, including 3,649 (3,707.4) of coal and coke and 18 wagons of livestock, the corresponding figures for Metropolitan and GC Joint stations being 33,811 (34,352), 14,385 (14,615.2) and 305 wagons.

4
UNFULFILLED SCHEMES

Proposals for lines north of Aylesbury are dealt with in Chapter 6 and the proposal for a service to Addiscombe is mentioned in Chapter 13.

Hammersmith (H&CR)– Richmond	A Hammersmith & City Railway bill, 1863–4 session, rejected by Parliament in favour of LSWR proposal for Kensington–Hammersmith–Richmond with H&CR running powers.
Swiss Cottage–Hampstead	Metropolitan & St John's Wood Railway Act, 1865. Climbing at 1 in 27 almost the whole length, with terminus at Flask Walk/Willow Road, Hampstead. Short length of tunnel built at Swiss Cottage, but lack of capital stopped further progress. Abandoned by 1870 act (see 1875 below).
South Kensington–Royal Albert Hall	Pneumatic tube from Metropolitan and MDR station; act, 1872. Metropolitan and MDR made an agreement with the promoter and patentee (Rammell) guaranteeing interest on cost of construction, but he was unable to raise the capital (see also 1883–4 below).
South Kensington– Holborn–Farringdon Street (I)	'City & West End Railway'. Supported by Watkin. Bill 1872–3 session withdrawn after GNR, GWR and Midland refused support (see second scheme below).
Aldgate–Bow	Bill 1875–6 session; failed.
Hammersmith (H&CR)– Fulham	Supported by Metropolitan and GWR 1875, bill in 1875–6 session; withdrawn. Bill in 1877–8 session; withdrawn after fare arrangements made with MDR, which obtained powers for same route.
Farringdon Street–Oxford Circus and branch to Charing Cross	Proposed by Sir E. Watkin 1876 to make use of new streets planned by the Metropolitan Board of Works. Discarded 1877

374

owing to high cost and difficulty of making a junction at Farringdon Street.

Swiss Cottage–Hampstead–Alexandra Palace

'North Metropolitan High Level Railway', bill 1875–6 session. Myles Fenton, Metropolitan Railway general manager, initially in support, but GNR refused to take any interest and the bill was withdrawn after difficulties over the parliamentary deposit. Bill revived 1877 but withdrawn for lack of Metropolitan and GNR support.

South Kensington–Oxford Circus–Holborn–Farringdon Street (II)

Proposed by Watkin in 1877 to run under planned new streets, variously known as 'City & West End Railway', 'Parks Railway', 'Mid-Central Railway', 'Mid-London Railway'. After the Commissioners of Works had refused to allow railway construction beneath the Royal Parks, the route was cut back to Oxford Circus–Farringdon Street only. A 'Metropolitan & Regent Circus' bill was produced for the 1877–8 session but was withdrawn after the MBW refused co-operation.

Latimer Road and Acton

Branch from the H&CR; authorised by act of 1882 to a nominally independent company. At first the H&CR insisted on a separate exchange platform at Wood Lane with no through running. Some construction started at the Acton end in 1883. Further legislation 1885–95, including in the latter year confirmation of an agreement with the Metropolitan and the GWR who consented to work the line jointly. As capital could still not be raised the scheme was abandoned by an act of 1900 (see 'West Metropolitan Railway', 1899, below).

Brill–Oxford

Act, 1883 (see Chapter 6).

Whitechapel–Bow (LTSR)

Proposed 1883 (see end of Chapter 7).

Edgware Road–Wesminster

To run beneath the Royal Parks to Parliament Street. Bill 1883–4 session; rejected (preamble not proved).

South Kensington–Royal Albert Hall	Clauses in Metropolitan bill 1883–4 session; to be worked by electric or cable power. Clauses struck out by Parliament.
West Hampstead–Hendon	Following pressure from local interests in 1882, powers were obtained in an act of 7 August 1884 for a 3½ mile branch to Hendon (Blind Lane/Finchley Lane) where some residential development in progress was hampered by the remoteness of the poorly-served Midland station. An intermediate station was proposed at Golders Green, which would no doubt have become a suburb much sooner than it did had this line been built. Lack of financial support from local interests, or from the GNR (with which a connection at Finchley was tentatively suggested) caused the scheme to wither, but 34½ acres of land at Hendon were bought on behalf of the Metropolitan Railway in 1883 (the Shire Hall and Bridge House estates). The powers were allowed to lapse in 1889 but the land was not sold until 1905–22.
Whitechapel– Walthamstow– Chingford Green	Proposed by local interests in 1884 and again in 1889. Metropolitan rejected the scheme in the latter year.
Chesham–Tring	Contemplated by Sir E. Watkin in 1884, possibly in conjunction with the LNWR, who would be given running powers from Rickmansworth to Chesham. Land at Chesham end purchased 1889–90. No bill prepared.
New Cross (ELR/SER)– Crystal Palace	Promoted by the Metropolitan and SER at Sir E. Watkin's prompting but strongly opposed by the LBSCR. Metropolitan, South Eastern & Crystal Palace Railway Bill 1884–5 session; failed.
Great Missenden–High Wycombe *or* Harrow– Rickmansworth– Beaconsfield–High Wycombe	Agitation by High Wycombe interests for a connection to the Metropolitan started in 1887; a line via Chalfont or via Beaconsfield was suggested. Metropolitan investigated possible routes 1889–91, choosing Great Missenden–High Wycombe as the

Appendices

least costly, but this was not popular with the local interests. The high prices asked for some of the land caused interest to fade. Alternative routes from Harrow or Rickmansworth via the Chalfonts and Beaconsfield considered in 1896, but resolved not to proceed (see 1924 below).

Wembley Park–Stanmore–Watford *or* Northwood–Watford	Proposed from 1892 onwards (see Chapter 15).
Wood Lane (H&CR)–Acton	'West Metropolitan Railway', Act, 1899. Shuttle service by H&CR proposed. Supported by the Metropolitan and GWR which agreed to work. Abandoned by act of 1904 after failure to raise capital.
Wendover–Oxford	Considered by the Metropolitan 1899. No bill prepared.
Hillingdon–Harefield	In 1922 a light railway was independently proposed from Uxbridge (GW&GC Joint) to Harefield. The Metropolitan then suggested a connection into it from Hillingdon. A Light Railway Order (without the Metropolitan connection) was granted on 10 February 1923 but the powers were allowed to lapse in February 1928 before any construction had started. No Metropolitan bill or application for Light Railway Order.
Eastcote–Harefield–Chalfont St Giles	Proposed by the Metropolitan, 1924; application for Light Railway Order considered, but opposition from LNER, GWR and LMSR expected and no further action taken. Local authorities pressed for construction as far as Harefield in 1928; bill considered but none prepared.
Edgware Road–Kilburn *or* Finchley Road–Great Portland Street	Proposed 1925–31 (see Chapter 14).
Watford (Met/LNER)–Watford High Street	Considered 1927–8 (see Chapter 14).

377

METROPOLITAN RAILWAY BUS SERVICES

From 1866 until 1901 it was the Metropolitan's policy to promote, and in almost every case subsidise losses on, horse-bus feeder services to its inner London stations, principally to provide a connection to the West End, but also from the late 1880s, as a competitive irritant for the London General Omnibus Co (LGOC) and the London Road Car Co, whose buses were tapping off the railway's local traffic. All these Metropolitan bus services were operated without any statutory authority.

In most cases the railway provided the buses and the conductors, relying on a contractor to supply the horses and drivers (known as 'horsing'). Initially, the buses provided separate accommodation for first-class passengers; through bookings to and from Metropolitan stations were available, issued at stations and at the bus offices mentioned below. In the chaotic London street traffic, the buses were easily distinguished by the presence of a large red umbrella adorned with the message METROPOLITAN RAILWAY around its edge, always kept open over the driver's head.

A few routes were established to feed suburban stations or to build up traffic on routes where a railway extension was to be opened; there was also an isolated attempt to drain off North London Railway traffic at Camden Town. Steady losses, exacerbated by frantic competition from other operators and the arrival of electric tube railways, brought all these services to an end, the last on 29 September, 1901.

Finally, just before the sun set on the Metropolitan, there was an interesting intervention into motor-bus operation in Watford, briefly associated with wider but abortive plans to operate feeder motor-bus services in the Metropolitan's suburban catchment areas.

Basic details of each service are given below, with a concluding note on the consideration given to operating motor-bus services on a moderate scale from 1928 onwards. Those seeking further details on the horse-bus services are referred to Keen, P. A., 'Metropolitan Railway Road Services', *Journal of Transport History*, Vol 1, 1954, p216.

Portland Road (Great Portland Street) station–Regent Circus (Oxford Circus)–Piccadilly Circus–Charing Cross (SER)
Started 6 August 1866 between Portland Road station and Regent Circus, running every ten minutes (soon increased to every five minutes). Operated by Samuel Crews with five three-horse double-deck buses. First-class front compartment (abolished 28 August 1882). Extended to Piccadilly Circus February 1874 and to Charing Cross (SER) station 11 June 1883. Some morning and evening journeys extended to Camden Road 30 July 1883. Converted to two-horse buses (lit by Pintsch's shale oil gas) October 1888. Late journeys 8.30pm to midnight operated between September 1891 and 26

September 1892. Cut back from Charing Cross to Piccadilly Circus from 24 October 1892. Operated entirely by S. Crews on Metropolitan Railway's behalf from 13 February 1893. Ceased 1 December 1894 after losses from LGOC and LRCC competition.

The Metropolitan Railway operated a booking office at 288 Regent Street (Oxford Circus) from 6 August 1866 to 5 March 1887, another at Piccadilly Circus from 2 March 1874 to 31 March 1900 and another at Charing Cross (SER) from 1 July 1883 to 21 July 1890.

South Kensington station–International Exhibition
Started 1 May 1871 jointly with the MDR, subsidy shared with the Exhibition Commissioners. Operated by S. Crews. Through bookings from Metropolitan and MDR stations, including admission to the Exhibition, from 8 May 1871. Ceased when Exhibition closed, 30 September 1871.

Gower Street station (Euston Square)–Camden Town
Started 2 August 1872 with hired buses worked by S. Crews, running every ten minutes. Operated with five Metropolitan-owned buses from 26 September 1873. Service reduced 31 January 1874. Taken over by LGOC and Camden Town Association (with Metropolitan Railway subsidy) 16 May 1874. Metropolitan through bookings ceased 30 April 1880, service discontinued 2 May 1880. Metropolitan Railway booking office open at Camden Town 2 August 1872–31 January 1874.

Baker Street station–Wigmore Street–Charing Cross
Started after 1880 (no date given in Metropolitan papers). Worked by S. Crews with six buses. Discontinued from 31 March 1900 owing to heavy losses and competition. Purchased and taken over by Perry of the Star Omnibus Co.

Baker Street station–Oxford Street–Bond Street–Piccadilly Circus
Started 15 October 1888 with four one-horse buses, horsed by E. J. Wragg. Aim was to remove business from the LGOC in retaliation for its competition for Metropolitan Railway traffic between King's Cross and Baker Street. Carrying 9,300 a week by December 1888, 21,600 by May 1889 and earning a profit for the Metropolitan. Worked with six new oil gas-lit two-horse buses from June 1889. Late journeys 8.30pm to midnight November 1891 to September 1892. Working wholly taken over by Wragg 6 June 1892 under Metropolitan guarantee, using six buses. Worked as a 'horseshoe' from 3 December 1894 (Baker Street station–Oxford Street–Bond Street–Piccadilly Circus–Regent Street–Wigmore Street–Marylebone High Street–Nottingham Place–Baker Street station). Wragg withdrew, the Metropolitan purchasing his stables and horses and taking over the whole operation, 22 July 1895. Metropolitan connection ceased 31 July 1900 when, suffering heavy losses and growing competition, the service was transferred to the Star Omnibus Co (Perry) with an undertaking that Metropolitan season tickets to Piccadilly Circus would be honoured for at least a year. (Metropolitan booking office, Piccadilly Circus, see above.)

Appendices

Edgware Road station–Marble Arch–Orchard Street–Baker Street station
Started 5 April 1875 with four one-horse buses. Ceased 10 June 1876 under heavy LGOC competition. Service diverted to Kilburn, see below.

Shepherd's Bush (H&CR)/Hammersmith (H&CR)–Hammersmith Road–Turnham Green ('Robin Hood')
Started 1 May 1875 Shepherd's Bush station (H&CR) to Hammersmith Road, extended to Turnham Green 5 July 1875. GWR bore half the cost. Four one-horse buses horsed by S. Crews. Ceased 10 June 1876. Diverted to run from Hammersmith (H&CR) station from 12 June 1876, ceased 16 February 1878 (Metropolitan and MDR trains west of Hammersmith absorbed the traffic).

Hammersmith (H&CR)–Barnes ('Bull's Head'/'White Hart')
Started 18 February 1878 by the H&C Joint Committee with three one-horse buses and MDR sharing the subsidy. Horsed by S. Crews. Two-horse buses introduced 2 April 1888. Ceased 30 April 1899.

Bishopsgate station (Met) (Liverpool Street)–Cannon Street (SER)
Started 3 January 1876 jointly with SER, using six one-horse buses running every five minutes. Horsed by S. Crews. Horsing taken over by E. J. Wragg 25 March 1878. Diverted to Moorgate (see below) 22 February 1892.

Moorgate Street (Met) station–Cannon Street (SER)
Started 22 February 1892 jointly with SER, horsed by E. J. Wragg. Ceased 4 June 1892, diverted to London Bridge station (see below).

Moorgate Street (Met)–London Bridge (SER)
Started 6 June 1892 jointly with SER. Wholly worked by E. J. Wragg. Calls made at King William Street station (C&SLR). SER withdrew, Metropolitan paying whole subsidy from 6 June 1896. Subsidy ceased 29 September 1901. (Rendered superfluous by extension of the C&SLR tube railway.)

Edgware Road station (Met)–Kilburn ('Queen's Arms')
Started 12 June 1876 with four one-horse buses. Ceased 24 April 1878 after heavy losses.

Neasden station (Met)–Harlesden
Started 1 October 1880 to Harlesden police station, operated by W. Memory, using two-horse buses owned by the Metropolitan. Extended to 'Royal Oak', Harlesden, 20 October 1880. Operated by John Cakebread, 4 April 1881. Ceased 24 October 1885 (heavy losses).

Rickmansworth (Met)–Chorley Wood–Chenies–Latimer–Chesham ('Crown')
Started 19 September 1887; operated by William Large with a Metropolitan two-horse bus. Ceased 7 July 1889, rendered superfluous by railway extension.

380

Edgware Road station (Met)–Chapel Street–Edgware Road–Oxford Street–Tottenham Court Road–Gower Street (Met) – (Euston Square)
Started 1 February 1892. Operated by Solomon Andrews, Star Omnibus Co, under Metropolitan guarantee with fourteen two-horse buses, 8am to midnight at five-minute intervals. Object was to remove business from the LGOC and LRCC in retaliation for their competition with the Metropolitan Railway. Losses increased and Andrews took over the service from the railway company after 31 October 1900.

Watford (Met/LNER)–Cassiobury Park Avenue–Rickmansworth Road–Merton Road–High Street (St Mary's church)–Church Street–Vicarage Road–Hagden Lane–Queen's Avenue–Watford (Met/LNER) (and vice versa)
Started 2 November 1927 with four twenty-eight seat Albion motorbuses owned and crewed by the Metropolitan Railway (see Chapter 14). Taken over 1 May 1929 by the Metropolitan Railway puppet company NW Land & Transport Co Ltd. Taken over 22 November 1929 by the Lewis Omnibus Co Ltd in which the NW Land & Transport Co had taken a 50 per cent share. Absorbed into the LPTB, 1 October 1933.

Note on Metropolitan Railway road transport policies and arrangements 1928–33
From about the middle of 1928, the Metropolitan management became much exercised by the inroads being made into the railway's suburban traffic by coach services to and from central London being started at that time by independent operators. In common with the four grouped railway companies, the Metropolitan had applied late in 1927 for statutory powers to operate road transport services; the 'big four' (LMSR, LNER, GWR, SR) acquired these powers on 3 August 1928 but the Metropolitan Railway (Road Transport) Bill was rejected by the Joint Select Committee in June 1928. Thus frustrated, the Metropolitan formed a wholly-owned Companies Act company, the NW Land & Transport Co Ltd, whose purpose was *inter alia* to take over the technically illegal Watford operation (see above) and also operate other feeder bus services on the railway's behalf. Incorporated on 5 November 1928, the new company had an initial capital of £50,000 in £1 shares, entirely drawn from Metropolitan Railway funds. All its directors were Metropolitan Railway officials (Selbie, Anderson, Dawson, Gibson, Stewart, Wardle). The registered office was on MRCE property at the estate office, Shepherd's Way, Rickmansworth.

Wardle was given the task of drawing up proposals for suitable feeder bus routes to be operated by the new company in Harrow, Wealdstone, Pinner, Kenton and Neasden, which he did in 1929. None were established as the policy was changed to seeking arrangements with existing operators. Several firms were approached, but no satisfactory terms could be reached. Meanwhile, a saloon coach was purchased by NWL&T in August 1929 and employed on tour operations and for party traffic.

The next step was to merge the existing operation with that of Frederick Lewis, an independent bus operator working the Watford and Rickmansworth area. This was done on a fifty-fifty basis from 22 November 1929, as noted above. On Sundays 17 and 24 November 1929 the NWL&T buses and

Appendices

coach, together with some of Lewis's buses, worked railway replacement services between Pinner and Harrow-on-the-Hill whilst Metropolitan trains were interrupted for reconstruction of the underline bridge at North Harrow station.

With the aid of Metropolitan Railway finance, the partly owned Lewis Omnibus Co Ltd formed in 1929 started a thirty-minute interval double-deck motor-bus service between Rickmansworth, Watford and St Albans on 11 March 1930. When it passed to the LPTB on 1 October 1933, Lewis was operating twenty-five buses with a fully uniformed staff on six stage services (St Albans–Watford–Windsor; Watford–Rickmansworth–Windsor; St Albans–Watford–Rickmansworth; Watford (Met)–Watford High Street; Watford–Berkhamsted; and Watford–The Swilletts–Chorley Wood).

6

SELECTED STATISTICS

Passengers Carried During Year[1]

1863	9,455,175
1865	15,763,907
1870	39,160,849
1875	48,302,324
1880	63,759,573
1885	77,170,601
1890	84,289,282
1895	88,271,486
1900	93,333,025
1905	95,694,616
1910	102,849,458
1915	not available
1920	123,441,851[2]
1925	142,000,000[2,3]
1930	134,657,733[2]
1931	128,116,042[2]

1 Includes passengers originating on other companies' lines (eg all those on GNR/LNER and Midland/LMSR trains over the City Widened Lines and on GWR trains passing on and off the Metropolitan. Also includes journeys made by season ticket holders, estimated at 300/312 each way for the equivalent number of annual seasons.
2 Includes GN&CR (20 million in 1920).
3 Swollen by Wembley Exhibition second-year traffic.

Number of Staff

1871	1,196
1884	1,685
1898	2,605
1907	3,140
1913	3,519
1918	3,345 (including 543 women)
1920	4,220 (including 207 women)
1928	3,979 (including 148 women)
1932	4,091

Figures from 1913 onwards include GN&CR staff.

Hammersmith & City Railway (Joint with GWR): Financial Performance (50 per cent to the Metropolitan)

1880	£10,344 profit
1890	£13,204 profit
1907	£ 9,000 *loss*
1913	£ 9,478 *loss*

DEVELOPMENT OF SUBURBAN AREA AND TRAFFIC 1901–39

Population

The population of the administrative areas served, Finchley Road to Chesham inclusive, increased between 1901 and 1905 from 228,488 to 267,270 (plus 17 per cent). Within this the largest increases were seen at Pinner (38.5 per cent), at Harrow (34 per cent) and at Chorley Wood (31.4 per cent).

The population of the administrative areas served, Willesden to Aylesbury inclusive, also Watford and Uxbridge, increased between 1901 and 1921 as follows:

1901   260,133
1911   355,458 (36.6 per cent; largest increases at Wembley (136.7 per cent), at Wealdstone (102.1 per cent), at Ruislip–Northwood (74.3 per cent) and at Harrow (67 per cent)).
1921   403,946 (13.6 per cent); largest increases at Kingsbury (126.1 per cent (village for war factory workers)), at Wembley (51.3 per cent), and at Ruislip–Northwood (46.6 per cent)).

The population growth of the major suburban administrative areas served 1921–38 was as follows:

	1921	1931	Mid-1938 Estimate
Willesden UDC	165,742	185,025	187,600
Wembley UDC	18,239	65,799	118,800
Harrow UDC	49,020	96,656	183,500
Ruislip–Northwood UDC	9,112	16,035	40,820
Rickmansworth UDC	8,634	11,529	18,700
Watford Borough	48,222	58,533	65,690
Uxbridge UDC	20,626	31,887	42,800

The commercial manager's staff calculated in 1928–9 that between 1919 and 1928 some 12,000 houses had been erected on land within half a mile of stations between Willesden Green and Rickmansworth/Uxbridge/Watford and that a further 17,000 were planned.

Traffic Growth 1921–8

Season Tickets issued at:	1921 Equivalent Monthly Tickets	Value £	1928 Equivalent Monthly Tickets	Value £
Preston Road, Northwick Park, Wembley Park	3,359	2,687	26,326	24,905
Harrow, West Harrow	37,498	36,248	39,626	44,579
Eastcote	591	697	2,023	2,765
Ruislip, Ruislip Manor	2,353	2,814	3,955	5,454
Ickenham	59	73	1,497	2,114
Hillingdon	not yet open	–	1,889	2,896
Uxbridge	2,381	3,542	2,916	4,994
North Harrow, Pinner	7,513	8,421	19,146	23,853
Northwood	5,377	6,991	6,853	10,079
Moor Park	11	16	404	633
Croxley Green	not yet open	–	795	1,276
Watford	not yet open	–	1,643	2,635
Rickmansworth	2,217	3,648	4,179	7,557
Chorley Wood	2,132	3,696	2,192	4,056
Chalfont & Latimer, Amersham	2,471	4,736	5,120	11,116
Chesham	2,313	4,683	2,187	4,994
Great Missenden	874	1,831	1,289	3,073
Wendover	280	678	324	885
Stoke Mandeville	32	86	62	183
Aylesbury	423	1,200	420	1,292

Appendices

Numbers of Tickets Sold

	First, Third, Workmen's		Metropolitan Monthly Seasons	
	March 1923	March 1928	March 1923	March 1928
Wembley Park	19,138	46,401	3,000	13,548
Preston Road	4,281	10,217	468	3,288
Northwick Park	not open	16,243	330[1]	7,908
West Harrow	15,229	18,176	8,784	10,476
Rayners Lane	1,384	837	nil	24
Eastcote	8,560	15,000	1,272	2,196
Ruislip Manor	892	2,498	48	480
Ruislip	18,181	24,375	2,988	3,132
Ickenham	5,443	11,325	192	1,428
Hillingdon	not open	11,215	10[2]	2,208
Uxbridge	58,867	63,361	3,000	3,480
Harrow-on-the-Hill	87,515	91,751	26,604	29,748
North Harrow	3,151	15,133	876	8,412
Pinner	20,208	26,323	5,112	7,320
Northwood	21,343	36,701	4,152	5,340
Moor Park	652	3,674	12	228
Rickmansworth	14,564	26,229	2,724	3,420
Croxley Green	not open	9,264	not open	780
Watford	not open	15,519	not open	1,680
Total	279,408	444,242	59,572	104,826

1 Figure for November 1923.
2 Figure for December 1923.

The Immediate Post-Metropolitan Years (see also *Population* above)
In the thirteen administrative areas through which the Metropolitan line passed, the population increased from 727,000 in mid-1931 to 958,700 in 1938 (plus 32 per cent). Between Finchley Road and Wembley Park inclusive, the figures were 140,500 to 149,000 (these areas were almost built up by 1931); between West Harrow and Uxbridge the growth was from 48,300 to 95,000; between Harrow-on-the-Hill and Preston Road from 26,500 to 49,800; between Kingsbury and Stanmore from 17,800 to 33,100; and between North Harrow, Watford, Chesham and Amersham 66,800 to 100,600.

During the five years 1933–8 tickets purchased at former Metropolitan stations increased from 25.348 million to 38.446 million (plus 52 per cent). Between Kingsbury and Stanmore inclusive, ticket issues in the period increased from 742,000 to 2.622 million (plus 253 per cent) and there was a 150 per cent increase in ticket issues between Harrow and Uxbridge.

(These two paragraphs are mainly based on an article in *Modern Transport*, 2 March 1940.)

Appendices

MILEAGE OF ROUTE OWNED OR WORKED OVER

Fully Owned
Inner Circle, Aldgate/Aldgate East to South Kensington (junction with MDR), including lines to Midland and GNR at King's Cross, to LCDR at Farringdon and Smithfield, to GWR at Bishop's Road, Paddington: 9 miles 4 chains

Baker Street Junction to Harrow South Junction, including junction with Midland at Finchley Road, but excluding the parallel 7 miles 5 chains Finchley Road–Harrow leased to GCR/LNER: 9 miles 30 chains

Harrow North Junction to Uxbridge and South Harrow, (junction with MDR): 7 miles 42 chains

Drayton Park to Moorgate (GN&CR): 2 miles 57 chains

Stanmore Branch: 4 miles 4 chains

Total fully owned: 32 miles 57 chains

Jointly Owned
(Except at Aylesbury, the Metropolitan Railway owned half, but worked over the whole distance shown.)
Aldgate to Mansion House (with MDR): 1 mile 7 chains

Minories Junction to St Mary's Whitechapel station (with MDR): 41 chains

St Mary's Whitechapel station to Whitechapel Junction (junction with the ELR), (with the MDR): 25 chains
Aylesbury Joint Station (with GWR and GCR), (Metropolitan owned one-third): 18 chains

Westbourne Park (Green Lane Junction) to Hammersmith, with spur to Uxbridge Road, (junction with the WLR), (with the GWR): 2 miles 74 chains

Watford branch (with the LNER): 2 miles 37 chains

Total Jointly-owned worked over: 7 miles 42 chains

Leased to Metropolitan & GCR Joint Committee
Harrow South Junction to Verney Junction, also Chesham branch, excluding Aylesbury Joint Station: 45 miles 16 chains

Other Companies' Lines Worked Over
Bishop's Road station and approaches (GWR): 12 chains

387

Bishop's Road, Paddington to Westbourne Park, (Green Lane Junction), (GWR): 73 chains

Drayton Park to Finsbury Park (GNR): 64 chains

Shoreditch station to New Cross (SER), (ELR and 12 chains of SER) and New Cross (LBSCR): 4 miles 35 chains

Quainton Road to Brill (Wotton Tramway or Oxford & Aylesbury Tramroad): 6 miles 49 chains

South Kensington to Mansion House (MDR): 4 miles 4 chains

Uxbridge Road Junction to Kensington (Addison Road), (WLR): 52 chains

Total other companies' lines worked over: 17 miles 49 chains

Grand total of lines regularly worked over: 103 miles 4 chains

(NB These figures omit 4 miles 74 chains from Hammersmith to Richmond (LSWR), LSWR track over which running powers were not continuously exercised; 5 chains from St Mary's Junction, Whitechapel to MDR boundary, Whitechapel, not regularly worked over; and 9 chains, Shoreditch station to Bishopsgate Junction, ELR track not regularly worked over.)

Sources for these tables: 'Metropolitan Railway & Connections', official map at GLRO ACC 1297 MET 10/669; *Railway Clearing House Junction Diagrams* (1915 edition); Metropolitan Railway Annual Report, 1913; Ministry of Transport Inspecting Officer's Reports on Watford and Stanmore branches; MET 10/262. As these sources occasionally conflict, a judgement has been made as to the most accurate version in compiling these tables.

7 METROPOLITAN RAILWAY STEAM LOCOMOTIVES

NB For classes 'A' to 'K' the dimensions shown are those given officially by the Metropolitan Railway in 1925 and may differ from those given when the engines were acquired, especially for classes 'A' and 'B'.

Class	*A*	*B*	*C*	*D*	*D*	*E*	*F*	*G*	*H*	*K*	*Shunting Locos, Neasden*		
Type	4-4-0T	4-4-0T	0-4-4T	2-4-0T	2-4-0T	0-4-4T	0-6-2T	0-6-4T	4-4-4T	2-6-4T	0-4-0ST	0-6-0ST	0-6-0ST
Nos/Name	1–33; 39–49	34–38; 50–66	67–70	71–72[1]	73–76	1; 77–82	90–93	94–97	103–110	111–116	100[1,5]	'Nellie'[1]	101–102[1]
Date of delivery/acquisition	1864–70	1879–85	1891[4]	1895	1895	1896–1901	1901	1915	1920–21	1924	1886	1907[3]	1897–9
Heating surface (sq ft) small tubes	841	864	1,050	1,005	1,000	1,050	1,050	765	765	1,034	?	?	644
Heating surface (sq ft) large tubes	–	–	–	–	–	–	–	281	281	356.6	?	?	–
Heating surface (sq ft) firebox	101.6	94.7	95.6	86	93	95.6	100	132	132	135	?	?	68
Heating surface (sq ft) *Total*	942.6	958.7	1,145.6	1,091	1,093	1,145.6	1,150	1,178	1,178	1,525.6	?	370	712
Heating surface (sq ft) Superheater	–	–	–	–	–	–	–	268	268	285	?	?	–
Grate area (sq ft)	19	17.2	16.7	14.4	16.74	16.7	17.9	21.2	21.2	25	?	7	13.25
Boiler pressure (lb per sq in)	160	160	160	160	160	160	160	160	160	200	?	?	140
Adhesive weight (tons)	34	36.7	31.95	31.2	33.3	33	47.5	52.6	39	54.8	?	?	39
Tractive effort at 85% working pressure (lb)	13,500	13,500	15,480	14,970	14,970	16,400	18,000	20,498	18,498	26,040	?	?	14,550
Adhesive factor	5.64	6	4.6	4.66	5	4.5	5.9	5.74	4.72	4.33	?	?	6
Cylinders (in)	17×24	17×24	17×26	17×24	17×24	17×26[2]	17½×26	20×26	19×26	19×28	13×20	12×17	16×22
Water tank (gal)	1,170	1,170	1,050	800	800	1,300	1,430	2,000	2,000	2,000	600	450	1,160
Coal capacity (tons)	1.5	1.25	1.8	1.8	1.8	2.2	2.5	4.5	4.5	4	?	?	1.25
Weight in running order (tons)	45	46.6	50.4	41.2	43.5	54.5	56	73	77	87.35	22	16.75	39
Weight empty (tons)	37	38.35	40.95	33	35.5	43	44	56.25	61	70.75	17.5	13.5	31
Width over footplate (ft/in)	8′ 4″	8′ 4″	8′ 5″	8′ 6½″	8′ 6½″	8′ 5″	8′ 5″	8′ 4½″	9′	8′ 4″	?	?	7′ 10″
Length over buffers (ft/in)	33′ 1″	31′ 10″	32′ 8″	30′ 2½″	30′ 2½″	33′	35′ 3″	41′ 4″	41′ 10½″	44′ 10¾″	?	?	24′ 10″
Diameter of driving wheels (ft/in)	5′ 10″	5′ 10″	5′ 6″	5′ 3″	5′ 3″	5′ 6″	5′	5′ 9″	5′ 9″	5′ 6″	3′ 3″	3′	3′ 10″
Diameter of bogie wheels (ft/in)	2′ 11⅞″	2′ 11⅞″	3′ 9⅛″	3′ 6″	3′ 6″	3′ 9⅛″	3′ 6″	3′ 6″	3′	3′ 1″	–	–	–

Sources: The Railway Gazette, 13 March 1925; Bennett, A. R. *The Railway Magazine*, September 1908, p204 (for the shunting locomotives).

Notes: (1) Non-condensing. (2) Nos 79–82 17½in×26in. (3) Built 1867, rebuilt 1891. (4) Rebuilt 1901–3. Dimensions are as rebuilt. (5) This loco replaced one purchased for shunting in 1883 about which no details are available.

METROPOLITAN RAILWAY SIGNALLING

by K. R. Benest

When the Metropolitan opened in 1863 railway signalling was still in its infancy, most companies relying on 'time interval' working, whereby signals were placed to danger for five minutes after the passage of a train, thereafter to caution for a further ten minutes (the exact periods varied), the 'all clear' indication then following. Where semaphores were in use, these indications were given respectively by the arm projecting horizontally to the left of the post (as seen by the driver); by the arm lowered to an angle of 45°; and by the arm hanging vertically, usually in a slot in the post, invisible to the driver. At night a red, green or white light was displayed for the three indications. Sporadic attempts had been made to establish an electric telegraph system between stations but all had failed, mainly owing to the unreliability of the materials and apparatus employed.

At first the Metropolitan directors favoured an all-mechanical system. This included a starting signal at the departure end of each platform with two arms, one mounted behind the other on a common pivot. Each arm had a number of vertical slots cut into it, partly to lighten its weight, partly perhaps to reduce wind resistance, the two sets of slots being offset one from the other so as to present a solid appearance when the positions of the two arms coincided. One of the arms was worked by the local signalman, the second being operated as the 'home' signal of the box in advance. The local signalman was forbidden to lower his own semaphore until the man in advance had cleared his and the driver was not to start until both arms had been lowered. Save that the 'home' signal has a return wire to the operating cabin, which worked a single stroke bell to indicate that the arm had been correctly restored to danger, no mention is made of communication between boxes under this system. The connecting solid iron unstranded wires were laid upon the ballast except where guide pulleys were fixed to prevent the wire pulling taut across the tracks on curves. The physical effort involved in working the signals from a distance was severe and in the case of the return wire for the gong over the distance of almost a mile between King's Cross and Farringdon Street, the frictional forces involved made the mechanism quite impossible to work.

Salvation appeared in the form of the GWR's telegraph engineer, C. E. Spagnoletti, who had devised a disc-block telegraph instrument which was immediately adopted by the Metropolitan in its initial form as a two-position instrument. When de-energised, the device displayed a flag bearing the legend 'Train on Line' seen through a slot in the panel and 'Line Clear' when current flowed through the coils via the line wire and a key which was depressed and locked to complete the electrical circuit. 'Line Clear' was to be given as soon as the previous train had departed from the station in advance, leading to the peremptory 'I am sending you a train for . . .' in place of the better-known (even today) 'Can you accept a train for . . .?'. Single stroke bells were used for signalling purposes, operated by a tapper key, one bell signifying 'Local', two 'GWR' and three 'Line Clear'. At the request of the Board of Trade, in addition to the block instruments, each signal cabin had three 'speaking instruments', each comprising a telegraph tapper key and a needle-type sounder, allowing messages to be transmitted and received in Morse code. Two sets of instruments provided direct communication with the boxes either side whilst the third was connected to an omnibus circuit eventually linking fourteen other stations. After an accident in Clerkenwell Tunnel in July 1876 the Board of Trade demanded removal of these instruments on the grounds of improper use for signalling, but officers and men asserted that the railway could not be worked without them and that if they were removed there was a danger that the block circuits would be used to call the attention of the adjacent signal cabins and thereby cause disarrangement of the block indications. So they stayed until replaced by telephones in 1888–9.

Signalmen had been under instruction for some time when Col Yolland of the Board of Trade made his first visit as chief railway inspecting officer. He drew attention to one disadvantage of the two-position block in that in the event of a failure there was nothing to indicate that a state other than 'Train on Line' existed in the absence of current flow. He suggested this might be overcome by indicating 'Train on Line' by a current flow reversal, causing the flag instrument to operate in the reverse direction to that occupied when 'Line Clear' was shown. A flag hanging vertically would then at once indicate an abnormal condition and much time would be saved. As there was no time to retrain the men, the new method was superimposed upon the old with as little alteration as possible to avoid confusion. Thus, on the inner area lines, 'Line Clear' remained the normal condition of the block until its replacement, after electrification, by train describers.

Col Yolland also indicated that with the establishment of a satisfactory 'space interval' system of working, it was no longer necessary to place home signals at the station in the rear but one-third to one-half that distance would be satisfactory. At the enclosed stations, starting signals were not on posts but took the form of a centre-pivoted arm and lamp above the tunnel headwall; in tunnels, there were low-level lamp signals in the 6ft way. Distant signals were not 'led' by the starters but were lowered only when the preceding train had left and passed out of sight. A driver finding one at danger had to stop before drawing his train ahead inside the signal's protection, remaining stationary until his rear guard indicated the distant signal had cleared. Signalmen were not to lower starting signals until the train had stopped, even if they had received 'Line Clear' on their telegraph instrument from the box in advance. Home or stop signals were installed some 40–50yd in the rear of platforms only where there were junctions or crossover connections in the rear of or close in advance of the starting signals.

All these signals displayed two aspects only as Col Yolland considered that

391

railways underground were potentially dangerous and that caution should be observed at all times. There were, however, apparent exceptions to this edict in that (for example) at the facing junction at Baker Street in 1868 a light signal in the roof of the bell-mouth displayed the customary red for STOP, green for PROCEED TO ST JOHN'S WOOD BRANCH and white for PROCEED TO MAIN LINE (ie Edgware Road). This was undesirable in that breakage of red or green glasses could lead a driver into danger.

Points and crossings in the early days were of simple design and at first the switch rails of crossovers were worked by separate levers in the signal box for each end. Complications arose with the mixed gauge tracks, sharing one of the rails in common, of necessity that nearest the platforms. Normally, when both gauges served both arms of a divergence, the connections were straight-forward, with a set of three moving switches, one to each rail. But when trains of one gauge only were to be served by one arm of the bifurcation, provision had to be made that irrespective of the 'lie' of the points, a vehicle of either gauge approaching in a facing direction was assured a safe passage through the turnout. This implied that a movable switch rail could be applied only to the individual rail for the gauge to which the bifurcation applied. In the crossover rail a small gap was left for the wheel flanges and additional check rails were located in the opposite rail of the non-diverging gauge to prevent misdirection. The tendency was further resisted by judicious super-elevation of the appropriate rail. In the case of a crossover between Up and Down lines the usual three switch rail provision was made in each main line, but it was necessary to transfer a standard gauge train from right-hand side common rail to left-hand side common rail on the other track and this was done by inserting crossing rails with no moving blades at all but with the usual additional check rails for guidance, between the two ends of the cross-over. Needless to say, a very low speed limit was strictly enforced at all such locations.

There were a few single-bladed switches to be found in use in standard gauge areas and Baker Street and Mansion House became notable as subject to inquiries after trains had been derailed by such switches.

From 1870 onwards the provision of bolts and lock bars became a require-ment for new passenger lines. Locking frames were ill-provided with spare levers at this period. As the mixed gauge tracks were now disused it became feasible to work both ends of crossovers by a single point lever, the surplus lever being appropriated for the operation of the bolt and bar. The bar, longer than the wheel spacing of any vehicle, was fixed on the inside of the running rail and linked to the bolt. When operated to unbolt the points, the bar was lifted above the surface of the running rail in a parallel motion on a series of short links before dropping down to the fully reversed position. It was prevented from doing so by the wheel flange of any vehicle standing upon the bar, thus ensuring that the points were not moved under a train.

At about the same time as the requirement for bolts and locking bars was promulgated, Yolland had let fly at the lack of standardisation in the setting out of signals at facing junctions. The prevailing practice had been to mount the semaphore arms one above the other on a single post, this being more economical than constructing a bracket or a gantry with individual posts for each route (the so-called 'geographical' arrangement). The colonel's fury was roused by finding an installation on the West London Railway where the place of honour at the top of the post was occupied not by the main line signal but by a shunt signal leading to the coal yard. He immediately required that in a single post arrangement, the topmost signal should read over the route furthest to the left and then, in downward order, the next to the left until the route furthest to the right was controlled by the lowest arm. Failing this, the geographical method was to be employed. It was unfortunate that the Metropolitan had hitherto standardised, but with the topmost arm reading to the *right*, and so on, in reverse to the desired order. With important junctions such as King's Cross and Praed Street worked over by trains from foreign lines it was too dangerous merely to reverse the connections from top to bottom as drivers would have been confused after long usage of the earlier system, so the geographical arrangement was adopted in every case where physical limitations permitted.

Yolland stoutly upheld the sanctity of the block section and the fundamental concept that, the section having been defined as that section of railway between the starting signal at one signal station to the starting signal of the signal station in advance, then on any one running line there might be only one train between these two points. This left the Metropolitan (among others) in serious difficulty insofar that when a train had left a terminal station, then the locomotive which had brought that train in and remained pinned against the buffers could not legally pass the end of the station platforms in order to shunt to the head of the next train to depart until the previous train had arrived at the next station down the line. Depending upon the distance between the two signal boxes, this imposed a maximum service of twelve trains an hour or even less, which was hardly enough for the Metropolitan. 'Could we not,' asked the superintendent of the line, 'after consultation erect an advanced starting signal beyond the crossovers at the terminus to enable the light engine to shunt so far within the station limits?' Yolland's stiff answer was that the Metropolitan was attempting to compromise him in a conspiracy to admit two trains into one block section.

But the advance starting signals were reluctantly allowed, although the colonel's end was achieved in 1885 when the working of GWR trains out of the Up side bay road at Moorgate seriously delayed 'main line' Up trains to Bishopsgate (Liverpool Street) and beyond which, of necessity, were held back at Barbican signal box, 500yd to the west, until the move had been completed. The opening of Whitecross Street signal box enabled these trains to advance an additional 330yd before being brought to a stand, thereby not only increasing line capacity but assuaging the colonel's fears of the past years. In effect, as a new block post, Whitecross Street exercised a slot control on practically every main line signal in sight of it, both Circle and City Widened Lines.

After the Abbot's Ripton accident on the GNR in 1876, which was caused by a signal being falsely held at clear by frozen snow, a new signal arm was developed with a kidney-shaped spectacle frame used in conjunction with a lamp on the left-hand side of the post. It appeared mainly on the extension from Finchley Road to Harrow and beyond. In 1885 an accident occurred at

Earls Court MDR owing to the breakage of the down rod on the signal post. Not self-balancing, the arm fell to clear, causing a collision which killed a driver. The MDR solution was a square balance weight attached to the back of the arm behind the post, but the Metropolitan produced an enormous cast-iron spectacle plate with circular glasses weighing approximately 70lb (31.75kg), one of which survived at Amersham until 1961. As an additional precaution, a 'T'-sectioned extension piece of steel plate was secured to the back edge of the spectacle plate to counterbalance the effect of falling snow congealing on the blade of the arm. This design remained the new works standard until the opening of the Harrow & Uxbridge Railway in 1904.

The next milepost was the introduction of the electrical interlocking of the outdoor signals with the Spagnoletti block telegraph. The matter had been urged upon the company by the Board of Trade after a number of minor collisions in the middle 1870s. In response to the pressure various trials were made, the most promising being that of a system designed by Spagnoletti, first installed between Praed Street and Bayswater in 1882. This applied the electric lock to the signal lever in the locking frame, but Spagnoletti experimented with fifty variations with treadle and contact before he was satisfied as to reliability. His system was generally adopted.

Following the completion of the extension to Aylesbury, there was relatively little new work in progress but the signal department took the opportunity of updating the equipment to meet the latest requirements of the Board of Trade. There was much to do in the provision of repeaters of signal positions and lights where they were beyond the signalman's view and providing all points with facing point bolts and bars. The latter was carried out beyond the Board's requirements; in the case of ordinary connections which joined the main lines in a trailing direction not only were the connections to the main line protected but also the trap points which prevented unauthorised egress to the running lines from the sidings.

With the coming of the GCR at the turn of the century, some of the archaic practices of thirty-five years' usage were reluctantly abandoned. The clean sweep to a standard bell code and operating methods which had been made by most companies after the disaster in Canonbury GNR tunnel in December 1881 had passed over the heads of the Metropolitan without effect. Understandably, the GCR insisted that working between Harrow South Junction and Quainton Road Junction be brought up to accepted main line standards, including adoption of the standard bell code and starting and advanced starting signals preceding the distant signals in the locking instead of the home signals only so doing.

In contrast to the virtually complete resignalling of the MDR for electrification, this change on the Metropolitan brought no immediate signalling alterations of significance. With all steam passenger services withdrawn on the inner London lines, the existing distant signals were converted to repeater signals of the corresponding homes, the latter being provided where not hitherto supplied. In all cases the home and its repeater were wired to the same lever-tail to ensure unison in operation. The danger aspect of the distant (always red until this time and more than once a source of confusion and tail end bumps) now became orange on the Circle lines and later, on other sections. All this was by way of makeshift as very few of the signals could have been ideally sited having regard to the accelerative and braking properties of the electric trains and the achievement of minimum headways with safety between trains.

The next move was an experimental automatic installation between Notting Hill Gate and Praed Street Junction which employed electric treadles and depression bars to operate signals of the Sykes' banner type and constituted an attempt to achieve automatic working without the expense of track circuiting. At first it functioned well enough although some wrong side failures were reported. The installation, which was eventually extended to South Kensington, lasted until after World War I. It suffered the defect of all such systems in not providing continuous proof that any given section was totally unoccupied when a train had passed over the treadle beyond the exit end. As mentioned in Chapter 11, owing to the presence of loose-coupled GWR freight trains, liable to leave the odd wagon or two behind, the Board of Trade refused to sanction its use east of Praed Street Junction, and normal track circuits were then fitted between that point and Aldgate. What have come to be regarded as conventional short-range colour light signals with dc track circuit control were used west of Farringdon Street. In the open these signals were protected against sun glare by large hoods over the lenses. East of Farringdon Street, lower quadrant semaphores worked by an electro-oleomatic system were put into operation. In this system, movement of a signal or point lever caused an electric motor to drive a pump which forced oil round a closed system in turn driving a double-acting piston which was mechanically coupled to the appropriate apparatus. Hardly had this work been completed when, owing to sediment in the oil, a signal jammed in the Off (proceed) position, causing a collision. After fitting improved valves as a temporary measure, the system was replaced by conventional direct drive by electric motor.

Difficulty had been experienced at Aldgate in sighting the Down advanced starter signals owing to the construction of an additional bridge at the north end of the station. No details survive of the signals installed but a contemporary notice describes the semaphores as operating in the right-hand upper quadrant. It is possible that ordinary semaphore arms, adequately counterbalanced, had been employed in an inverted position to enable the lamps to be placed as low as possible without fouling the structure gauge with the semaphore arms. The opinions of the motormen were favourable and the concept was adopted for the open sections between Baker Street and Neasden when this was converted to automatic operation. Normal light signals were installed in the tunnels, but between Finchley Road and Neasden low-voltage top-mast mechanisms with left-hand upper quadrant semaphores were introduced with, on single-armed posts, a down-drive rod to operate the train stop. In the case of splitting junction signals and all other locations, ground-level electrically operated train stops were installed, working in sympathy with all stop signals. The latter were conventionally painted with red arms and in the case of controlled signals the customary white square. Automatic stop signals had a narrow central horizontal white stripe to enable early differentiation to be made. This was unnecessary with repeater signals, which were all painted yellow with a black chevron on the face and the usual fish-tail notch. Signals were numbered either by enamelled iron plates for wall mountings or directly painted on the face of the square wooden posts approximately at the motorman's eye level. Automatic signals bore the prefix 'S' (signal) whilst controlled signals took the numbers of their operating levers prefixed by the code letter of the signal box. The original series ran from 'A' at Praed Street Junction to 'H' at Aldgate, although these two cabins were the only ones to be equipped with power frames. Mechanical interlocking was employed, but all outdoor apparatus was electrically operated. The intermediate signalboxes retained their mechanical frames for some years, those at Moorgate, Aldersgate and Farringdon Street being replaced by new flat-roofed structures in the 1920s in which full-sized levers were used for point operations only, retaining the mechanical connections, the signals operated by handled pull-push slides on a shelf above (inevitably dubbed 'chocolate machines' by the staff). The two frames were electrically interlocked. A considerable economy in space was thus effected, with both the Circle and the Widened Lines controlled from a space no greater than that previously required for working either side of the stations separately.

Baker Street Junction signal box, located in the bell-mouth, was replaced in 1908 by a power frame in the junction 'round-house' to permit the ultimate restoration of the double line junction for through services to the City. This in turn was rendered redundant by a new cabin with a 39-lever frame at the north end of the Extension Line platforms in 1913. (It should be explained that early Westinghouse power frames were cast in 7- and 11-lever sections, each of which had a half-lever position at each end; thus a frame made up of 2 11- and 2 7-lever sections plus the 3 intermediate joints gave a total of 39.) This frame in fact had 36 levers, some of which stood spare, with 3 blanked off spaces at the right-hand end. The 1913 installation incorporated several novel features. Instead of the customary dc track relays, there were single-element $33\frac{1}{3}$ cycle single-phase relays, transformer-fed at 240-V from the 11,000-V high-tension traction current supply. It was also the first installation in Britain to eliminate the facing point lock bar. The lock itself was, of course, retained but the integrity of the working was ensured by track locking. All the signals were track controlled with the exception of the shunt signals beneath the four platform starting signals at the north end. No interlocking existed between the starting and shunt signals and although it was possible to have a starting and shunt lever reversed simultaneously, both signals could not be clear at the same time. This facility enabled a locomotive to follow its train out for disposal with the minimum of delay.

To speed up working, inner home signals were provided at some stations on the Metropolitan Circle Line in 1912. By shortening the overlap of the original (now outer) home signal to a point two-thirds of the way down the platform, a following train held at the original home signal was enabled to make an earlier start as the preceding train left the station; by the time it reached the inner home that also had cleared as the first train cleared the overlap track of the starting signal.

In 1918 a position-light signal of the type in use on the Pennsylvania RR (USA) was installed experimentally on the new Down Fast line at Willesden

Green home signal, mounted on an offset bracket post with the starting signal repeater below the stop signal. The light signal comprised three sets of lamps with reflectors set horizontally, at 45° and vertically in the left upper quadrant pivoting about the second lamp from the right of the display. Fitted with stepped lenses, the lamps were arranged to display the three-position equivalent of the stop, caution and proceed indications of the double-arm semaphore with which the signal co-acted. The daylight visibility range of 4,500ft (1,372.5m) and the absence of moving parts were appreciated, but the cost of the precision lamp mountings and replacement lamps apparently precluded general adoption and the signal was eventually removed.

In 1925–6, for the Rickmansworth/Watford electrification, the Metropolitan adopted three-aspect long-range colour light working. Harrow station area received the full treatment but northwards a compromise was adopted. The LNER, which had inherited the GCR interest in the Metropolitan and GCR Joint Committee, was by no means averse to colour light signalling, only to paying for it; it was therefore used only for passenger lines and movements. The old signal boxes and mechanical frames remained and the only additions were illuminated track diagrams and the lever controllers for operating the electric signal circuits. Outside, the pointwork and the shunt signals remained unaltered but the main lines were, of course, track-circuited throughout. The three signal boxes for the new Watford branch had mechanical frames. Colour lights were deployed in a niggardly way which left the Down line to be completed into Watford with wire-worked lower quadrant semaphores for the inner and outer homes. The points at the remote junctions with the main line were indeed worked by electric point machines purely because this was more economical than providing separate signal boxes. The South Junction connections, to be the most used, were worked by rodding only, although it must be remembered that the Metropolitan's four busy City stations (Farringdon, Aldersgate, Moorgate and Liverpool Street) were still at this time in a like state and the treatment was to be the same when the Uxbridge branch was equipped with three-aspect signalling in 1930.

For the Stanmore branch of 1932 no signal boxes were provided at all. Preston Road Junction was directly under the control of Wembley Park box and apart from an emergency crossover at Canons Park the only other controlled signalling was at the Stanmore terminus. There were three aspect automatic signals intermediately. The centralised traffic control installation mentioned in the main text was evolved from apparatus devised for operating small automatic telephone exchanges. The principle was an interesting one whereby a unit comprising a shaft of convenient length carried upon it a number of discs of insulating material. These discs had phosphor-bronze contact pieces of suitable shape riveted through from side to side. Fixed pairs of spring contacts bore upon the opposing sides of each disc, which, according to its angular relationship to a 'normal' position, completed electric circuits which would operate points and signals whilst preventing other circuits being made which would conduce to setting up conflicting routes. The shafts were driven from common shafting electrically moved via clutch plates to set up the switch unit in the angular position required to instigate the completion of the desired route.

All this was controlled over a three-wire system from a small control desk in Wembley Park signal box by coded impulses sent down the wires when the necessary switches were set up on the panel. When the route was correctly set, a second series of impulses set up at Stanmore was transmitted to Wembley Park to indicate that the correct operation had been performed. Press handouts of the time stated that Wembley Park controlled the entire branch but insofar as communication could be established by local telephone, this was a gross exaggeration.

Sources: Metropolitan Railway Minute Books (MET 1/1–1/31); Board of Trade Inspection Reports (PRO); Tattersall, A. E., *Modern Developments in Railway Signalling*; 'The Railway Engineer', 1921 (references to Metropolitan Railway practice).

SOURCES

Original Sources
The extensive series of Metropolitan Railway papers in the Greater London Record Office (GLRO ACC 1297), together with certain MDR and Joint Committee papers noted below, have formed a major foundation for this book. The series used are as follows:

Board Minutes 10 January 1853–21 February 1934: MET 1/1–1/31
Board Reports/Appendices: MET 1/32–36
General Purposes Committee 1930–1: MET 1/65
Parliamentary, Law & Lands Committee 1901–6: MET 1/74
Engineering Committee 1902–11: MET 1/69
Traffic Committee 1902–7: MET 1/95
Electric Traction Committee 1902–4: MET 1/66
General Manager's Reports to the Board: 11 February 1903–25 March 1933: MET 1/107–1/116
General Manager's Circulars: MET 4/6, 4/19
Guard Books (Notices, etc) (1864–1932): MET 4/9–4/13
Chronology: MET 4/13
Diaries 1931–2: MET 4/21
Statistics, 1911–12: MET 4/1
Officers' Monthly Conferences (1924–33): MET 1/102–1/106
Memorials: MET 7/2–7/8
Correspondence and General Manager's papers (buses): MET 10/2–10/9
Correspondence and General Manager's papers (all subjects): MET 10/10–10/877
Board Minutes MDR: MDR/1
Board Minutes Metropolitan and MDR Joint Committee: M&DJ 1/23, 1/53

Half Yearly and Annual Reports & Accounts, Metropolitan Railway, 1864–1933
Annual Reports MRCE, 1925–33
Annual Reports & Accounts LPTB, year ended 30 June 1934
Acts of Parliament mentioned in text and related papers (House of Lords Record Office)
Annual Reports Metropolitan Board of Works, 1867–8, 1868–9
Census Returns (including Registrar-General's Estimates for mid-1938)

Secondary Sources
Use was made of certain of the books mentioned in the Select Bibliography and also the following:

Sources

Herapath's Railway Journal, 1853–72, *passim*

Bradshaw's Shareholders' Manual, 1858–73

The Times, 30 November 1861

The Railway News, 20 August 1864, 25 February 1865

Proceedings, Institution of Civil Engineers, 39, (1875)

The Railway Times, 1872, *passim*

The Railway Magazine, July 1897, May 1901, November 1902, June 1904, December 1906, September 1908, October 1908, June 1915, August 1915, January 1916, October 1917, April 1918, August 1920, April 1925, April 1926, September 1926, June 1964, January 1966

Tramway & Railway World, February 1900, June 1900

Underground, Vol 2, No 5 (Borley, H. V.); Vols 1, 2, 3 and 5 *passim* (Benest, K. R.)

Journal, Railway & Canal Historical Society, Vol 4, No 4 and 4, No 6 (Borley, H. V.); Vol 8, No 3 (Borley, H. V.)

The Railway & Travel Monthly, October and November 1913

Transport & Travel Monthly, December 1920

The Railway Gazette, 1905–33, *passim*

The Locomotive Magazine, 1906–8, *passim*

Dictionary of National Biography, (second supplement), (on Forbes)

SELECT BIBLIOGRAPHY

This bibliography brings together all the books with substantial or significant references to the Metropolitan Railway which have been mentioned in the Chapter Notes, together with others of importance or special interest. It omits the several publications by Charles Pearson advocating his schemes; for these, see Ottley, George, *A Bibliography of British Railway History*, 2nd edition, HMSO, 1983, to which the reader is also referred for works of fiction which mention the Metropolitan.

Space limitations preclude a full listing of the many articles in periodicals, but some of the more useful ones have been included in the Chapter Notes.

★Works consulted when preparing this book.

1 General Works Covering the Metropolitan in Some Detail
★Barker, T. C. and Robbins, Michael, *A History of London Transport: Vol I, The Nineteenth Century*, (Alan & Unwin, 1963); *Vol 2, The Twentieth Century to 1970* (Allen & Unwin, 1974)
★Borley, H.V., *Chronology of London Railways* (Railway & Canal Historical Society, 1982)
Day, J. R., *The Story of London's Underground* (London Transport, enlarged edition, 1964)
Douglas, H., *The Underground Story* (Robert Hale, 1963)
Passingham, W. J., *The Romance of London's Underground* (Sampson Low, 1932)
★Pratt, Edwin A., *British Railways and The Great War* (two volumes, Selwyn & Blount, 1922)
★Sekon, G. A., *Locomotion in Victorian London* (Oxford, 1938)

★*Bradshaw's Railway Manual, Shareholders' Guide and Official Directory*, (published annually, 1863–1923)

2 Metropolitan Railway, General Works
★Anon, *The Jubilee of the Metropolitan Railway* (reprinted from *The Railway Gazette*, 1913)
Baker, J. C. Y., *The Metropolitan Railway* (Oakwood Press 1951, reprinted with some amendments, 1960)
Edwards, Dennis and Pigram, Ron, *Metro Memories* (Midas Books, 1977)
——, *The Romance of Metro-Land* (Midas Books, 1979)
——, *The Golden Years of The Metropolitan Railway and The Metro-Land Dream* (Midas Books, 1983)
Lee, Charles E., *The Metropolitan Line: A Brief History* (London Transport, 1972)

Select Bibliography

Privately circulated works
★Anon, *Metropolitan Railway, Record of Events from the Opening of The Line in 1863* (printed for the Metropolitan Railway: three editions are known: 1878; 1910, and 1927, with amendments to 1929)
★Anon, *History of The Metropolitan Railway* (two bound volumes of typescript with photographic illustrations and diagrams pasted-in, prepared for the Metropolitan Railway, 1917, revised 1920, circulated on a limited basis, 1921)
★Selbie, R. H., *Metropolitan Railway Company: Report of the General Manager* (printed for the Metropolitan Railway and circulated to the board, etc, 1915)

3 State Publications
★Board of Trade, Committee on Ventilation of Tunnels on the Metropolitan Railway; *Report* (HMSO, 1898, C 8684)
★Royal Commission on London Traffic; *Vol II, Minutes of Evidence* (HMSO, 1905, Cd 2751), *Vol III, Appendices to the Evidence* (HMSO, 1905, Cd 2752)

4 Locomotives and Rolling Stock
★Ahrons, E. L., *Locomotive and Train Working in the Latter Part of the Nineteenth Century, Vol 5* (Heffer & Sons, 1953), (reprinted from articles in *The Railway Magazine*)
★Benest, K. R., *Metropolitan Electric Locomotives* (2nd Edition, London Underground Railway Society, 1984)
Bruce, J. Graeme, *Steam to Silver* (2nd Edition, Capital Transport, 1983)
Casserley, H. C., *The Later Years of Metropolitan Steam* (Bradford Barton, 1979)
Day, J. R. and Fenton, W., *The Last Drop: The Steam Age on The Underground from 1863 to 1971* (London Transport, 1971)
Densham, P., *London Transport: Its Locomotives* (author, 1947)
Gadsden, E. J. S., *Metropolitan Steam* (Roundhouse Books, 1963)
★Reed, Brian, *Loco Profile No 10: The Met Tanks* (Profile Publications, 1971)

5 Electrification
★Anon, *The Metropolitan Railway 1863–1906* (British Westinghouse Electric & Manufacturing Co, 1906)
★Anon, *The Metropolitan Railway Electrification* (Metropolitan-Vickers Electrical Co Ltd, 1924?)

6 Specific Locations and Lines (see also 7 below)
Anon, *London's Metropolitan Railway from Paddington to Finsbury Circus. Photographic Views to Illustrate the Works in Progress* (1862)
Anon, *The History of the Inner Circle Railway and The Efforts to Complete It* (1879)
★Anon, *The Building of The Inner Circle Railway: A Remarkable Series of Photographs* (reprinted from *The Railway Gazette*, 1946)
★Anon, *Baker Street Station Alterations* (reprinted from *The Railway Gazette*, 1911)

*Edwards, Dennis, *Walter Atkinson – Builder of the Harrow & Uxbridge Railway* ('Underground' No 12), (London Underground Railway Society, 1983)

*Egan, H., Graham, R. and Travis, A. S., *The Early History of the Metropolitan District and Metropolitan Railways in Wembley* (Wembley Transport Society, 1963)

Gadsden, E. J. S., *Duke of Buckingham's Railways* (Bledlow Press, 1962)

Jackson, Alan A., *London's Local Railways* (David & Charles, 1978), (Uxbridge and Stanmore branches; proposed lines to Acton, Harefield and the Chalfonts)

Jones, Ken, *The Wotton Tramway (Brill Branch)*, (Oakwood Press, 1974)

*Melton, Ian, *From Quainton to Brill: A History of The Wotton Tramway* ('Underground' No 13), (London Underground Railway Society, 1984)

Simpson, Bill, *The Brill Tramway – Including The Railway from Aylesbury to Verney Junction* (Oxford Publishing Co, 1984)

*Thompson, F. M. L., *Hampstead, Building a Borough, 1650–1954* (Routledge & Kegan Paul, 1974)

*Wolfe-Barry, John, *The City Lines and Extensions (Inner Circle Completion) of the Metropolitan and Metropolitan District Railways* (Proceedings, Institution of Civil Engineers, LXXXI 1884–5)

Privately Circulated Works

*Robbins, Michael, *Baker Street for The Midlands?* (unpublished typescript, 1961)

——, *Baker Street Station* (unpublished typescript, 1974)

7 Metropolitan Railway and MRCE Publications

*Anon, *Country Walks* (editions 1906–32)

*Anon, *Metro-Land* (editions 1915–32)

*Anon, *The Homestead* (jointly published with the GCR, 1911, 1912)

*Anon, *Where to Live* (MRCE Ltd, editions 1920–32)

*Anon, *Formal Opening of The Harrow & Uxbridge Railway . . . 30 June 1904* (1904)

Anon, *Illustrated Guide to The Metropolitan Extension* (1904)

*Anon, *Metropolitan Railway – Reconstruction and Enlargement of Baker Street Station* (1912)

*Anon, *Diamond Jubilee of The Metro: A Souvenir* (1923)

*Anon, *The Story of Chiltern Court* (1929)

*Anon, *Stanmore's New Railway* (1932)

*Ellis, Luke, *Guide to the Metropolitan Railway Extension to Harrow, Pinner, Northwood, Rickmansworth, Chenies and Chesham* (1887?)

8 Relations with Other Companies and the GN&CR

*Atkinson, J. B., *The West London Joint Railways* (Ian Allan, 1984)

*Borley, H. V. and Kidner, R. W., *The West London Railway and the West London Extension Railway* (Oakwood Press, second edition, 1975)

*Bruce, J. Graeme, *The Big Tube: A Short Illustrated History of London's Great Northern & City Railway* (London Transport, 1976)

*Dow, George, *Great Central Vol 2: Dominion of Watkin, 1864–1899* (Ian Allan, third impression, 1985)

——, *Great Central Vol 3: Fay Sets The Pace, 1900–1922* (Ian Allan, third impression, 1985)

*Edmonds, Alexander, *A History of The Metropolitan District Railway to June 1908, prepared for publication with Preface and Epilogue by Charles E. Lee* (London Transport, 1973)

*Grinling, Charles H., *The History of The Great Northern Railway 1845–1922* (with additional chapters by H. V. Borley and C. Hamilton Ellis), (Allen & Unwin, 1966)

*Jackson, Alan A. and Croome, D. F., *Rails Through The Clay: A History of London's Tube Railways* (Allen & Unwin, second impression, 1964)

*Lee, Charles E., *The East London Line & The Thames Tunnel* (London Transport, 1976)

*MacDermot, E. T., *History of The Great Western Railway, Vols 1 and 2* (revised by C. R. Clinker), (Ian Allan, 1964)

Peacock, Thomas B., *Great Western London Suburban Services* (Oakwood Press, second edition, 1970)

*Wrottesley, John, *The Great Northern Railway, Vol 1: Origins and Development* (Batsford, 1979)

——, *The Great Northern Railway, Vol 2: Expansion and Competition* (Batsford, 1979)

——, *The Great Northern Railway, Vol 3: Twentieth Century to Grouping* (Batsford, 1981)

9 Suburban Development in Metropolitan Railway Territory

Jackson, Alan A., *Semi-Detached London: Suburban Development, Life and Transport, 1900–39* (Allen & Unwin, 1973)

*Kemp, W. A. G., *The Story of Northwood and Northwood Hills, Middlesex* (author, 1955)

Massey, David, *Ruislip–Northwood: The Development of the Suburb with special reference to the period 1887–1914* (Ruislip, Northwood & Eastcote Local History Society, 1967)

Robbins, Michael, *Middlesex* (Collins, 1953)

Tottman, David, *Ruislip–Northwood: An Early Example of Town Planning & Its Consequences* (Ruislip, Northwood & Eastcote Local History Society, 1982)

INDEX

Notes
(1) Unless otherwise noted the entry (eg Offices) refers to the Metropolitan Railway.
(2) There may be more than one reference on the page indicated.
(3) Directors not mentioned in the main text are not indexed but are listed in Appendix 2.
(4) Figures in brackets after page numbers in the index show the note number and chapter number when the reference is to Chapter Notes, thus 349(13/3) means page 349, note 13 relating to Chapter 3.
(5) In the main text some references may only give abbreviated names or early titles and names for firms and individuals but the index gives full names and final titles and names.

Index

410

411

Index

414

Index

415